Selections from Virgil's *Aeneid*
Books 1–6

Selections from Virgil's *Aeneid* Books 1–6

A Student Reader

Ashley Carter

BLOOMSBURY ACADEMIC
LONDON · NEW YORK · OXFORD · NEW DELHI · SYDNEY

BLOOMSBURY ACADEMIC
Bloomsbury Publishing Plc
50 Bedford Square, London, WC1B 3DP, UK
1385 Broadway, New York, NY 10018, USA

BLOOMSBURY, BLOOMSBURY ACADEMIC and the Diana logo are trademarks of
Bloomsbury Publishing Plc

First published in Great Britain 2020

Cover design: Terry Woodley
Cover image: *Aeneas flees burning Troy with father Anchises on his shoulder.*
Azoor Photo Collection / Alamy Stock Photo.

A catalogue record for this book is available from the British Library.

Library of Congress Cataloging-in-Publication Data
Title: Selections from Virgil's Aeneid books 1–6 : a student reader / Ashley Carter.
Other titles: Aeneis. Liber 1–6. Selections
Description: New York : Continuum International Publishing Group Inc., 2020. | Summary: "This
reader of Virgil's text features passages from the first half of the Aeneid and is designed to help
students understand and appreciate Virgil's poem, as well as improve their Latin reading skills. Each
Latin passage is accompanied by running vocabulary, on-page commentary notes and targeted
questions. The book can be used as a source of one-off unseen passages or as a reader for students
working through individual books or the whole poem. The commentary notes explain references to
characters, places and events, provide linguistic and grammatical help on more challenging Latin
phrases, and point out stylistic features. The questions test students' comprehension of the
characters and storyline, and give them practice in handling literary terms. The passages are linked by
summaries of the continuing plot, so students can grasp the progression of the poem as a whole. An
in-depth introduction sets the story of the Aeneid in its mythological, literary and historical context,
and at the end of the book is a complete alphabetical vocabulary list, a glossary of literary devices,
and essays explaining the principles of Virgil's word order and metre"—Provided by publisher.
Identifiers: LCCN 2019021055 (print) | LCCN 2019981554 (ebook) | ISBN 9781472575708
(paperback) | ISBN 9781472575715 (epub) | ISBN 9781472575722 (pdf)
Subjects: LCSH: Virgil. Aeneis.
Classification: LCC PA6802.A1 C37 2020 (print) | LCC PA6802.A1 (ebook) | DDC 873/.01—dc23
LC record available at https://lccn.loc.gov/2019021055
LC ebook record available at https://lccn.loc.gov/2019981554

ISBN: PB: 978-1-4725-7570-8
        ePDF: 978-1-4725-7572-2
        eBook: 978-1-4725-7571-5

Typeset by RefineCatch Limited, Bungay, Suffolk

To find out more about our authors and books visit www.bloomsbury.com
and sign up for our newsletters.

CONTENTS

PREFACE

The purpose of this book and the subsequent volume is to provide a source of selections from all twelve books of Virgil's *Aeneid*. Each of these books has contributed around 250 lines of text, sufficient to provide comprehensive coverage of the storyline and principal characters.

Virgil's great work has inevitably been dipped into many times over the years. The intention behind this set of selections is to provide the kind of layout and help appropriate to the needs of students with only a few years of study behind them. The book is suitable as a reader for its own sake or to act as a prescribed text for examination. The characters and storyline are summarised in the Introduction; students reading a single book should read this summary first. Significant gaps between Latin passages are summarised in Italics.

The principle behind the glossing of words is that all except for the commonest words are glossed, with meanings appropriate to the context. Students wanting a reminder of the word's meaning can consult the complete alphabetical word list, which is printed at the end of the book. When a word is repeated in the same book, it is not glossed again, unless the meaning has changed. Verbs are given two principal parts if they are used with the present stem, otherwise three or four parts; following the principle used in a number of current text books, the perfect participle passive replaces the supine as the fourth principal part. Since students are likely to focus on one book, full glossing recommences at the start of each book.

The Introduction aims to set the story of the *Aeneid* into its mythological, literary and historical context. Students preparing for GCSE or similar examinations will need little of the information provided there, but those progressing beyond the boundaries of a single book may find at least some of the detail helpful. Those who wish to explore further will find the long-established editions of Williams or Page helpful.

The notes aim to help students to understand references to characters, places and events, though only at a basic level. Teachers may wish to expand these references in class. The notes also help students to cope with more challenging linguistic items, and point out some stylistic features.

The questions test students' comprehension of the characters and storyline, and give them practice in handling literary terms. The Introduction contains a list of the commonest literary devices, which are generally considered appropriate for students at this level of study.

The text is that of Williams (1972 and 1996), with the following exceptions: all accusative plural endings in *-is* have been changed to *-es*, and the lower case is used for initial letters of paragraphs.

Line numbers alongside the text are the standard line numbers from the complete books, following Williams where the manuscripts are unclear.

I am grateful to Bloomsbury for the encouragement given.

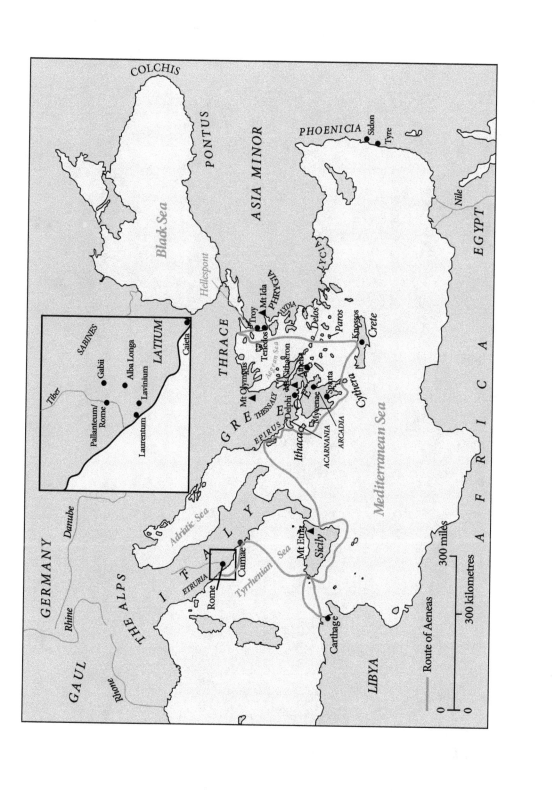

Introduction

1. Virgil and the *Aeneid*

Virgil began composing the *Aeneid* in about 30 BC, continuing to work on it until his death at the age of 50 in 19 BC. He was commissioned to write the work by Octavian, who in 31 BC had defeated Mark Antony and Cleopatra at the Battle of Actium, thereby gaining supreme power in Rome. Octavian devoted the next four years to making his power secure, with the result that, in 27 BC, he became the first emperor, with the title Augustus. Although he was popular with many sections of Roman society from the moment of his triumph over Antony, he was anxious to avoid the same fate as his adoptive father, Julius Caesar, who, in similar circumstances, had been assassinated in 44 BC by a group of senators.

One means available to Octavian of securing his position was self-publicity. Among the various methods regularly used by statesmen of the time was glorification through poetry; in fact it was entirely fashionable for successful and wealthy statesmen to pay poets within their patronage to write poems of various lengths extolling the virtues and achievements of their patron. The poets Horace, Propertius and Virgil were in turn invited to produce an epic poem with Octavian, later Augustus, as its hero. All at first refused, deterred no doubt by the conflicting demands of historical distortion and artistry. Then Virgil changed his mind, having devised a way of combining the positive presentation of Octavian and his victory with the need of all true poets for creative self-expression. And so the *Aeneid* was born.

By the time of Virgil, the tradition of epic poetry was at least 700 years old. Many poets of the classical, Hellenistic and Roman periods produced a wide range of epic poems of very varying quality. None came close to achieving the status accorded by general consent to Homer, the first of the surviving epic poets, who composed the *Iliad* and *Odyssey* probably during the late eighth century BC. Homer's works were widely known and read in Virgil's Rome, much as Shakespeare is in today's society.

Virgil took upon himself the delicate task of composing an epic similar enough to the *Iliad* and *Odyssey* for the two poets to be directly compared, but different enough for Virgil to avoid charges of plagiarism. The *Aeneid* would combine a conventional epic tale of heroic endeavour (the story of Aeneas), the ancestry of Rome and its leaders, glorification of Rome and the Augustan regime, and an example of the social and moral responsibilities that a *pius* or dutiful leader ought to be prepared to shoulder.

Doubtless Virgil's contemporaries would have been surprised by a first reading of this literary cocktail: Augustus and his victory at Actium are barely mentioned; and yet from a closer scrutiny, Augustus and his achievements shine forth with more persuasive clarity than any more overt form of flattery could have achieved. Virgil presents his contemporary Rome as the climax of twelve hundred years of history, all foretold and so sanctioned by Jupiter in Book 1; Aeneas' father, Anchises, in Book 6 repeats the prophecy, while the shield made by Vulcan for Aeneas in Book 8 shows the great moments of Roman history.

That Augustus was satisfied with Virgil's achievement is clear from his veto of the poet's will, in which, dissatisfied with its unfinished condition, he had given orders for the poem to be burned; Augustus demanded publication. He is also said to have been overcome with emotion when listening to the recitation of parts of the poem.

The conclusion may therefore be drawn that, at least as far as Virgil's patrons were concerned, the *Aeneid* was successful in terms of its glorification of Rome and its leader. But what of heroic dimension? Aeneas undergoes adventures parallel to those of Homer's Odysseus, and fights battles every bit as bloody as those of the heroes of the *Iliad*. But Homer's heroes lived and fought for the present, with responsibilities only to their own heroic status and to their fellow-heroes. Aeneas, in contrast, in addition to these still-important considerations, has a destiny to fulfil, a destiny which demands his absolute *pietas*. This destiny is nothing less than the transfer of the spirit and survivors of Troy to a new homeland, from which will spring Rome and ultimately Augustus.

Aeneas earns a place in the ranks of the great heroes of legend, having negotiated his way past all the obstacles to his success; but, unlike the Homeric stereotypes, who exist on a plane somewhere between gods and ordinary mortals, Aeneas is essentially human, with all the weaknesses and flaws of his fellow men and without the constant help and guidance of an Athena. Venus' interventions are infrequent and sometimes of questionable value to him.

2. Synopsis of the twelve books of the *Aeneid*

Book I

The fleet of Trojan ships, on their way to a new home in the West after the destruction of their city, is blown off course by the intervention of the goddess Juno, who is hostile to the Trojans and jealous of Venus, the mother of Aeneas. The scattered ships come to land on the shore of North Africa, where Aeneas is directed by his disguised mother to the new city of Carthage, still being built by its queen, Dido. Dido welcomes the Trojans and lays on a dinner for them. She is charmed by Aeneas' son, Ascanius, who is actually Cupid, the god of love, in disguise, instructed by his mother Venus to trap Dido into falling in love with Aeneas.

Book II

Dido persuades Aeneas to tell the story of his adventures. The whole book is devoted to his account of the sack of Troy, starting with the the building of the wooden horse and its induction into the city. The Trojans are persuaded to believe the horse is a gift to Minerva when they witness the killing of their priest, Laocoon, after he has tried to persuade the people not to accept the horse. A Greek captive, Sinon, also helps to persuade the Trojans to accept the horse. As the Greeks flood into the city and embark upon an orgy of killing and burning, during which Priam, the king of Troy, is killed. Aeneas, awakened by the ghost of Hector, at first tries to resist the Greeks. Then his mother appears to him and tells him to make his escape while he can. He returns to his house and with difficulty persuades his father to leave. He sets off with his son and father, while his wife Creusa follows close behind. She, however, is killed on their way out of the city, as Aeneas discovers when he turns back in search of her, only to be confronted by her ghost, which tells him of his destiny to found a new kingdon in the West and to remarry.

Book III

Aeneas completes his narration with an account of his journey from Troy to Carthage, including several attempts to settle on lands that they wrongly thought were intended for them by the prophecies. His first attempt, in Thrace, is quickly ended by the words of the spirit of a dead Trojan, who was murdered by locals. Next he sails to Delos, birthplace of Apollo; he prays to the god to give him a prophecy. Anchises interprets the prophecy as indicating a new home in Crete, and the Trojans sail there. When they start building a city there, they are struck by a pestilence. In a vision, Aeneas is told the new home must be built in a land further west, called Hesperia. They set sail again, but are blown by a storm to the island home of the Harpies, monsters with the bodies of birds but the heads of women. The Harpies attack the Trojans, and a tense battle ensues, at the end of which Celaeno, the leader of the Harpies, tells Aeneas he must sail to Italy. They set off westwards again and come to a land ruled over by Helenus, one of Priam's sons. Helenus welcomes his countrymen. Being also a prophet, he gives Aeneas many more details of his journey ahead, including an instruction to visit the Sibyl, a prophetess who lives at Cumae, on the west coast of Italy. The Trojans set sail again and reach the home of the Cyclopes, one-eyed giants. There they rescue a starving man who had been left behind by Odysseus after he had blinded Polyphemus, one of the giants. By the end of this book, the Trojans have a clearer idea of their true destination, Italy, but Aeneas' father dies while they are calling at a port in Sicily. It is immediately after this that they are blown off course to Carthage.

Book IV

Dido has fallen in love with Aeneas as she listened to his narration. She voices her doubts to her sister Anna, who persuades her that she should forget her promise to remain faithful to the memory of her recently murdered husband, Sychaeus. Dido entertains Aeneas and the other Trojan leaders with a hunting expedition. Meanwhile the goddesses Venus and Juno agree a plan to try to keep Dido and Aeneas together in Carthage. When a storm drives them to take shelter in a cave, they make love, which leads Dido to consider them married. Aeneas gives no thought to leaving, being content to stay with Dido and help her to continue building her new city, but the god Mercury brings a message to him from Jupiter, telling him he must leave Carthage and pursue his allotted destiny. Aeneas can find no way to break the news to Dido; when she discovers his plans, she attempts in vain to make him change his mind. When he refuses, her love turns to anger and hostility, and finally she commits suicide as Aeneas sails away.

Book V

The Trojans sail from Carthage to Sicily (on their route to the west coast of Italy, which is where their destiny lies). In Sicily they are welcomed by Acestes, a local king and fellow Trojan. Aeneas organises funeral games to commemorate the anniversary of his father's death there on an earlier visit. The main contests are a boat race, a running race and a boxing match. Juno, annoyed to see the Trojans enjoying themselves, sends her assistant Iris down to stir up trouble; Iris, disguised as one of the Trojan wives, persuades the other women, weary of travelling, to set fire to their ships, so that their husbands would be forced to end their journey in Sicily. Aeneas prays for rain, which the gods send, so that only four ships are destroyed. Aeneas is advised by a prophet and the vision of his father, Anchises, to leave behind the women and the infirm, taking just his warriors with him to Italy. Anchises reminds him that he must visit the underworld before proceeding to their final destination, and seek him out there. Aeneas heeds the advice and settles the women and the infirm in a new city before setting out with the rest. During the night, the helmsman Palinurus is lost overboard.

Book VI

The Trojans make landfall in Italy at Cumae (near Naples), where the Sibyl, a prophetess inspired by the god Apollo, agrees to lead Aeneas down into the underworld, as his father's spirit has twice requested. First though, he has to arrange the funeral of one of his men, Misenus, of whose death he is unaware; and also he must find and bring back the Golden Bough, which has to be offered to Proserpina, queen of the underword, as a gift. The Sibyl leads Aeneas to the shores of the underworld river, where Charon the ferryman reluctantly agrees to take them across into the main part of the underworld. After passing by Tartarus, where the souls of the wicked are punished, they proceed through the fields of Elysium until they find the spirit of Aeneas' father, Anchises. Anchises is privileged now he is dead to know the future, and he introduces to his son a parade of the yet-to-be-born souls of many of the great figures from Roman history down to Virgil's own day, climaxing in Augustus. In this way Aeneas is reinvigorated with a determination to complete his mission.

3. Virgil's metre

Every line has the same basic rhythm or metre, called the dactylic hexameter. The word 'dactylic' indicates the nature of the rhythmical unit being used; 'hexameter' tells us that there are six of these units (called 'feet') in each line.

In Latin poetry, rhythm is determined by the length of each syllable, either short or long. Scansion involves writing out a line of verse and marking the length of each syllable, by writing above the syllable ∪ if it is short, – if it is long; also the divisions between feet should be marked with a vertical line through the text.

A dactylic hexameter, therefore, consists of six feet, with each foot containing one dactyl (or equivalent). A dactyl consists of one long syllable followed by two short ones, and is marked like this: – ∪ ∪. To provide variation of rhythm, each dactyl in the line (apart usually from the fifth one) may be replaced by a spondee, which comprises two long syllables, marked – – . The sixth foot always contains two syllables only, either long + short or long + long.

The metrical scheme for a dactylic hexameter therefore looks like this:

$$
\begin{array}{cccccc}
-\,- & -\,- & -\,- & -\,- & & -\,- \\
-\cup\cup\mid & -\cup\cup\mid & -\cup\cup\mid & -\cup\cup\mid & -\cup\cup\mid & -\cup.
\end{array}
$$

There are fairly precise rules for determining whether a syllable is short or long. The following are always long:

- diphthongs (in Latin *ae* and *au* are the commonest; also *oe* and, in proper names, *eu* and sometimes *ei*;
- vowels followed by two or more consonants, whether in the same word or the next. An exception to this rule is when the second of two consonants is *l* or *r*, in which case the syllable may be short or long;
- vowels that are long by nature (such as ablative singular endings of the first and second declensions). Where the vowel appears in the stem of a word, dictionaries generally indicate its length.

The following syllables are short:

- single vowels that are followed by a single consonant, or by another vowel that does not form a diphthong, so long as they are normally pronounced as short (dictionaries here too are useful guides).

Scanning a line can be a very useful indicator of which part of a word is being used; e.g. *puellă* must be nominative or vocative, while *puellā* must be ablative.

Some further rules that need to be mastered are:

- *qu-* and *-gu* before a vowel count as a single consonant (i.e. the *u* is ignored) – e.g. *sanguis*;
- *x* and *z* always count as double consonants (and so the vowel before them is always scanned long);
- *i* when followed by another vowel sometimes becomes a consonant (e.g. *iam*, which has one syllable, not two, and *cuius*, which has two syllables); at other times it is treated as a separate vowel (e.g. *audiet, ierat*);
- a vowel at the end of a word elides before a vowel at the start of the next word; when scanning such a line, you should place brackets round the elided vowel and ignore it when scanning the rest of the line;
- there is one other type of syllable that elides in the same way: any word ending in *-am, -em, -im, -om* or *-um* before a word starting with a vowel should be bracketed and then ignored;
- *h-* at the start of a word should be ignored;
- every dactylic hexameter has a natural pause around the middle; this is known as a caesura (a Latin word with the literal meaning 'cutting'); the caesura is marked by a double vertical line through the verse; in most verses the caesura comes after the first syllable of the third foot, as long as it coincides with the end of a word; if that is not possible, the caesura may be placed in the second or fourth foot, again after the first syllable.

It should be noted that the above rules are slightly simplified, but are sufficient for the needs of anyone reading this book. For a more detailed treatment, other sources of information are available (see 7. Further Reading, p. 16).

Here are some examples:

  –   ∪ ∪| –   ∪   ∪| –|| –|–   –| – ∪   ∪| – –
arma virumque cano, Troiae qui primus ab oris (I.1)

  – ∪ ∪|–   –| – –|–|| – |– ∪   ∪| – –
litora, mult(um) ill(e) et terris iactatus et alto (I.3)

It can be seen from the above examples that each line is slightly different; in this way, variation is introduced. Poets capitalised on this by sometimes making lines strongly dactylic or strongly spondaic. Dactylic rhythm was considered fast, while spondaic rhythm was thought of as slow. This convention allowed poets to match the rhythm to the subject matter: rapid action or excitement could be emphasised by the abundant use of dactyls, while inactivity, solemnity, sadness or awe could be enhanced by the use of spondees. An example of the former is:

  –   ∪∪| –   ∪∪ |– || ∪ ∪| –   ∪∪ |– ∪ ∪| – ∪
substitit atqu(e) utero sonitum quater arma dedere (II.243)

Here the wooden horse is progressing inexorably through Troy; the rhythm is the fastest possible, to underscore the haste. An example of the latter is:

  – –|–   – |– || –|–   – |– ∪ ∪| – –
triginta magnos volvendis mensibus orbes (I.269)

Here Jupiter predicts that Ascanius will reign for thirty years; the rhythm is the slowest possible, to emphasise the length of the reign.

4. Virgil's word order

The word order in verse is very different from that in prose. The most obvious difference is that words that belong together in sense are often separated from each other. Examples can be seen under hyperbaton and synchysis in the following section, but they are so frequent that they rarely call for comment. One major determining factor for word placement is the fact that the beginning and end of a line are seen as places for emphasis, and so very often, but not always, key words are placed there; see also enjambement in the next section. Where the poet wishes to achieve sound effects with, for example, alliteration, he places words together for their sound qualities rather than because they form a discrete phrase. The requirements of rhythm are the other main reason for words being apparently jumbled; very often there is only one place in a line where a particular word will fit the metre.

Students will need to develop the habit of scanning whole sentences to see how they fit together, keeping an eye out for subjects, verbs and objects; other words can then be slotted in around these. An example is I.228–31:

> tum vero tremefacta novus per pectora cunctis
> insinuat pavor, et scelus expendisse merentem
> Laocoonta ferunt, sacrum qui cuspide robur
> laeserit et tergo sceleratam intorserit hastam.

For translation, the order is *tum vero novus pavor insinuat per tremefacta pectora cunctis, et ferunt Laocoonta merentem expendisse scelus, qui laeserit sacrum robur cuspide et intorserit sceleratam hastam tergo*. It will be seen that there are two main verbs (*insinuat* and *ferunt*), and two subordinate subjunctive verbs introduced by *qui*. This gives a basic structure: two main clauses separated by *et* and two relative clauses. To analyse further, it is necessary to link adjectives to nouns (*tremefacta* with *pectora*, and *novus* with *pavor*, for example). It will also be seen that bare dative and ablative nouns are frequent (*cunctis, cuspide* and *tergo*), and readers must familiarise themselves with their numerous uses (here dative of disadvantage, ablative of instrument and dative of goal of motion, respectively).

Some teachers may prefer a different approach, relying more on intuition to take each word as it comes and place it into its context within the sentence.

5. Stylistic features

The *Aeneid* is a rich treasure-house of stylistic features, which, just like the storyline, characters and metre, are integral to the poetry. Indeed, it can be argued that it is the liberal and intelligent use of these features that turns ordinary poetry into great poetry.

It is almost impossible to find a line of the *Aeneid* that does not contain at least one identifiable stylistic feature; many contain several. So many are there, indeed, that it would be impractical to identify them all in the commentary. Instead, only the most significant features are mentioned. Readers are encouraged to familiarise themselves with all the commonest features so that they can identify them as they meet them.

To help readers to achieve this, a list of the commonest and most important features is given below. This is not an exhaustive list; rather the most frequently met ones are listed. Although some scholars would argue that we cannot know Virgil's purpose in using any given stylistic feature, because he is not around to be asked, it is legitimate to discuss the effect it has on the reader. For a modern reader, the only way to achieve expertise in this is through frequent exposure to them through reading and regular analysis and evaluation of their usage.

Alliteration

The use of the same letter to start two or more adjacent words, usually, but not always, in the same line. Occasionally the alliterated words may be separated by another word. At its most basic level, the effect is simply to draw attention to the words alliterated or to give a pleasing sound. Some letters can have more particular effects. For example *a* and *m* are regularly used by Virgil to express high emotion, usually fear, horror or anger; *s* can represent hissing, whether of serpents, the sea, sleep or to express anger (see also Sibilance); hard consonants can represent harsh events, while *l* or *m* can suggest softness or calm. For example:

> *haec ubi dicta, cavum conversa cuspide montem*
> *impulit in latus; ac venti velut agmine facto* (I.81–2)

Anaphora

The repetition of a word to introduce two or more parallel statements. The effect is to increase the importance of that word and to emphasise the parallel nature of two objects or actions. This feature is much used in oratory. For example:

> *ter conatus ibi collo dare bracchia circum;*
> *ter frustra comprensa manus effugit imago* (VI. 700–1)

Antithesis

The inclusion of opposite or contrasting words or phrases within a sentence. The effect, to heighten the contrast, is further enhanced if the contrasting words or phrases are placed next to each other (see Juxtaposition). For example:

> *hic demum collectis omnibus una*
> *defuit, et comites natumque virumque fefellit.* (II.743–4)

Apostrophe

Literally a 'turning away' from the general audience or reader to address a person, place or abstract idea that is not present. This is used to express heightened emotion by giving a dramatic twist to a narrative or speech. For example:

> *o patria, o divum domus Ilium et incluta bello*
> *moenia Dardanidum!* (II.241–2)

Assonance

The repetition of the same sound, usually a vowel, in adjoining words. The effect is usually to project some emotion: assonance of *u* often indicates surprise or sadness, while *a* regularly (like alliteration of *m*) reflects a more visceral emotion. For example:

> *ascensu supero atque arrectis auribus asto* (II.303)

Asyndeton

The omission of conjunctions in a sequence of parallel words or phrases. The effect may be no more than to focus attention on the parallel ideas; it may also be to emphasise the rapidity of a sequence of events. For example:

monstrum horrendum, informe, ingens, cui lumen ademptum (III.658)

Chiasmus

A group of usually four words that together form a symmetry about a central point. Examples are *verb, noun / noun, verb*; *adjective, noun / noun adjective*; *nominative, accusative / accusative, nominative*. Any two parallel pairs of words, where the order of the second is reversed, is chiastic. A single word may provide a central pivot, while conjunctions may be ignored. The effect of a chiasmus is to draw attention to the words and to emphasise the parallel importance of the two pairs. Very rarely three pairs of words may form a chiasmus. NB: the sequence *adjective, noun / adjective noun* is not chiastic. For example:

immiscentque manus manibus pugnamque lacessunt (V.429)

Consonance

The repetition of a consonant within neighbouring words. This is similar to **ALLITERATION**, and is usually used in conjunction with it. For example:

his dictis incensum animum flammavit amore
spemque dedit dubiae menti solvitque pudorem (IV.54–5)

Enclosing word order

A phrase in which two or more words relating to one object, action or state enclose one or more words relating to a second object, action or state, in such a way that they reflect the sense of the phrase. For example, *in medio stat foro* has the verb enclosed within *in medio foro*, reflecting what is actually happening. For example:

paribus palmas amborum innexuit armis (V.425)

Enjambement

The carrying over of sense to the beginning of the next line. The effect is to place extra emphasis on the word that is carried over. For example:

duri magno sed amore dolores / polluto (V.5–6)

Hendiadys

The separation of an adjective-plus-noun phrase into two parallel nouns linked by a conjunction. It is used to give greater emphasis to the words. For example:

non tamen abstinuit nec voci iraeque pepercit (II.534)

Hypallage *or* Transferred Epithet

The transfer of an adjective from the noun to which it logically belongs to another noun in the same phrase. For example, *primi sub lumina solis*: 'just before the light of the first sun', i.e. 'just before the first light of the sun'. For example:

  ecce autem primi sub lumina solis et ortus (VI.255)

Hyperbaton

The separation of words that belong syntactically together by intervening words that are not part of the same phrase. This is so common in poetry that it rarely deserves special comment. For example:

  haec ubi dicta, cavum conversa cuspide montem
  impulit in latus (I.81–2)

Hyperbole

Exaggeration, used to emphasize a point. For example:

  attollitque globos flammarum et sidera lambit (III.574)

Metaphor

The use of a word with a meaning different from its literal or normal one. Whereas a simile says that one thing is *like* another (e.g. 'the world is like a stage'), a metaphor says one thing *is* another (e.g. 'the world is a stage'). For example:

  uterumque armato milite complent (II.20)

Metonymy

Calling something not by its own name but by the name of something related to it. For example:

  vela dabant laeti et spumas salis aere ruebant (I.35)

Onomatopoeia

A word that sounds like what it means. For example:

  qualis mugitus (II.223)

Polyptoton

The repetition of a noun, verb, adjective or pronoun with different endings (closely related to **Anaphora**). For example:

> *tu moenia magnis*
> *magna para longumque fugae ne linque laborem* (III.159–60)

Polysyndeton

The repeated use of conjunctions (usually 'and') in quick succession to join words or phrases; sometimes more are used than necessary. The effect may be to give a sense of rapidity to a sequence, or it may stress the number of items in the sequence. For example:

> *quem non incusavi amens hominumque deorumque* (II.745)

Prolepsis

The anticipation of a future act or state by treating it as if it already existed. For example:

> *donisque furentem*
> *incendat reginam* (I.659–60)

Rhetorical question

A question (often in a series) asked, not to elicit a reply, but as a stronger alternative to a statement. For example:

> *num fletu ingemuit nostro? num lumina flexit?* (IV.369)

Sibilance

Alliteration of the letter *s*, or the repetition of *s* within adjacent words. For effects, see **ALLITERATION**. For example:

> *Laocoon, ductus Neptuno sorte sacerdos,*
> *sollemnes taurum ingentem mactabat ad aras* (II.201–2)

Simile

A comparison of one thing, event or scene with another one. A simple simile is generally introduced by the prepositional 'like' or 'as'. Like Homer, Virgil most often uses extended or 'epic' similes, often several lines long; they are introduced by some part of *qualis* or *ut cum*, where the following *haud aliter*, meaning 'in just the same way', relates the simile to the narrative episode or *velut*, followed by *haud secus*. For example:

> *quale manus addunt ebori decus, aut ubi flavo*
> *argentum Pariusve lapis circumdatur auro* (I.592–3)

Synchysis

An interlocking of the word order of two pairs of words, so that the words that belong syntactically together are separated. For example the order may be adjective – noun – adjective – noun, where the first adjective defines the second noun; or it may be adjective – adjective – noun – noun (this variety, with the verb in the middle, is known as a 'golden line'). For example:

sic fatus validis ingentem viribus hastam (II.50)

Synecdoche

The substitution of a part of something for the whole thing. For example:

iamque fere sicco subductae litore puppes (lines 135)

Tautology

Saying the same thing twice using different words. For example:

fixum immotumque (IV.15)

Tricolon

A sequence of three parallel ideas, events or descriptions. Often the second and third ideas add little to the first. The effect is to give heavy emphasis to an argument. A common version of this is the Ascending Tricolon, or Tricolon Crescens: here each parallel expression is more extravagant than the previous one, so that a climax is reached. This is a powerful rhetorical effect, and so is found less frequently in poetry. For example:

o patria, o divum domus Ilium et incluta bello
moenia Dardanidum! (II.241–2)

Zeugma

Here a verb is given two objects, each requiring a different meaning of the verb. For example:

fugam . . . sociosque parabat (I.360)

6. List of Names of People and Places

Acarnania	A region of Greece
Acestes	A Trojan exile, now a local king in Sicily
Achates	Aeneas' arms bearer and loyal friend
Acheron	One of the five rivers of the underworld
Achilles	Most famous and powerful warrior in the Greek army that fought at Troy; he killed Hector

Acidalia	A spring in Greece where Venus was reputed to bathe
Aea	The island home of the witch Circe, near Colchis on the Black Sea
Aegean	The sea to the east of Greece
Aeneas	The leader of the Trojan survivors, son of Venus and Anchises
Aetna	Active volcano in Sicily
Agenor	An early king of Tyre and ancestor of Dido
Alba Longa	City of Latium, founded by Aeneas' son, Ascanius
Amazons	A mythical race of female warriors, noted for their archery
Amycus	A king of Bebrycia (in Asia Minor) who challenged all visitors to a boxing match
Anchises	Father of Aeneas and lover of Venus
Andromache	Widow of Hector, later married to Helenus
Anius	King of Delos, priest of Apollo and old friend of Anchises
Anna	Sister of Dido
Apollo	God of prophecy, born on the island of Delos
Arcadia	A region of Greece
Argives	Another name for the Greeks, lit. 'people of Argos' (a Greek city)
Ascanius	Son of Aeneas and Creusa, also known as Iulus
Atreidae	The sons of Atreus, Agamemnon and Menelaus, who led the Greek expedition to Troy
Augustus	The first emperor, who commissioned Virgil to write the *Aeneid*
Aurora	Dawn, often personified as a goddess
Ausonia	Southern Italy
Avernus	A volcanic lake near Cumae; the entrance to the underworld
Bacchante	A female worshipper of Bacchus
Bacchus	God of wine, called by the Greeks Dionysus
Bebrycia	A city of Asia Minor, ruled over by Amycus
Butes	A boxer, only mentioned once
Byrsa	Another name for Carthage, meaning 'ox-hide' in Greek
Caesar, Julius	Roman general and statesman; adoptive father of Octavian; assassinated in 44 BC
Caieta	A town and promontory between Cumae and the river Tiber
Carthage	City in modern Tunisia founded by Dido; later fought Punic Wars against Rome
Cassandra	Daughter of Priam and Hecuba, gifted with prophecy but cursed to be believed by no one
Caucasus	A mountainous region between the Black and Caspian Seas
Celaeno	Leader of the Harpies
Cerberus	Huge three-headed dog; guarded the entrance to the underworld
Ceres	Goddess of Corn; called by the Greeks Demeter
Charon	Ferryman who conveyed souls across the Styx or Acheron into the underworld
Circe	A witch who turned men into animals
Cithaeron	A mountain in Greece famous for the orgiastic worship of Bacchus
Cleopatra	Queen of Egypt; lover of Mark Antony; committed suicide 31 BC
Cocytus	One of the rivers of the underworld
Colchis	A country by the Black Sea; home of the Golden Fleece and Medea
Corybantes	Female worshippers of the goddess Rhea
Corythus	Founder of the town of Corythum in Italy
Crete	Greek island, noted for archers and its main city, Knossos
Creusa	Wife of Aeneas; mother of Ascanius; killed fleeing from Troy
Cumae	City of Campania in southern Italy; home of the Sibyl; close to Avernus
Cupid	God of love (in Greek Eros); son of Venus

Cybelus	A mountain near Troy
Cyclopes	One-eyed giants who worked in Vulcan's forge; one, Polyphemus, was blinded by Odysseus
Cynthus	A mountain on the island of Delos; sacred to Apollo and Diana
Cythera	An island off the south coast of Greece; Venus worshipped there
Danai	Another name for the Greeks, after Danaus, the founder of Argos
Dardania	Another name for Troy, after Dardanus
Dardanii	Another name for the Trojans
Dardanus	A founder of Troy; brother of Iasius; both came from Italy
Dares	A famous boxer
Delos	Island in the Aegean Sea; birthplace of Apollo and Diana
Diana	Goddess of hunting, named by the Greeks Artemis; sister of Apollo
Dicte	A mountain in Crete
Dido	Founder and queen of Carthage; fled from homeland of Tyre after murder of husband Sychaeus
Didymaon	An unknown craftsman
Diomedes	One of the Greek heroes of the Trojan War; now a king in Italy; also known as Tydides
Diores	A competitor in the running race in the funeral games (Book V); later killed by Turnus
Dis	The underworld or its king (i.e. Pluto or Hades)
Dolopians	A tribe of people living in Thessaly (northern Greece)
Drepanum	A town in Sicily, where Anchises died
Elissa	The original name of Dido
Elysium	Part of the underworld reserved for the souls of the blessed; also Fields of the Blessed
Enceladus	A Titan who fought in the war against the gods; when defeated he was buried under a mountain
Entellus	A Sicilian boxer
Eous	The Morning Star
Erebus	Another name for the underworld
Erymanthus	A mountain in central Greece
Eryx	Half-brother of Aeneas who lived in Sicily
Eurotas	A river flowing through Sparta in southern Greece
Euryalus	Young Trojan warrior and friend of Nisus
Fama	Personification of Rumour, perceived as a monstrous, many-mouthed goddess
Fates	Three sister-goddesses who controlled the destinies of all humans
Fortuna	Personification of fortune or luck
Furies	Three sisters who pursued murderers to punish them or drive them mad; also Erinyes, Eumenides
Gaetuli	A North African tribe, ruled by Iarbas
Gyaros	A Greek island, near Mykonos
Hades	The underworld or its king; also Dis or Pluto
Harpies	Monstrous creatures with the bodies of birds and the heads of women; they stole food from sailors
Hector	Son of Priam and Hecuba; the greatest warrior in the Trojan army; killed by Achilles
Hecuba	Wife of Priam and queen of Troy
Helen	Wife of Menelaus and so queen of Sparta; her abduction by Paris caused the Trojan War
Helenus	A son of Priam and Hecuba; became king of Buthrotum in north-western Greece; married Hector's widow

Helymus	A young Sicilian who competed in the running race (Book V)
Hercules	The strongest man who ever lived; worshipped later as a god; carried out the Twelve Labours
Hesperia	The Western Land, i.e. Italy; Aeneas' final destination
Hydra	A giant, many-headed serpent killed by Hercules
Hyrcania	A region near the Caucasus known for its tigers
Iarbas	King of the Gaetuli in North Africa and former suitor of Dido
Iasius	Brother of Dardanus; both sailed from Italy to found Troy
Ida	One of two mountains: one near Troy and one in Crete
Idalium	A centre of the worship of Venus
Ilium	The Greek name for Troy
Ilus	A cognomen of Ascanius, later changed to Iulus
Iris	Goddess of the rainbow and messenger of Juno
Iulus	Cognomen of Ascanius, the son of Aeneas; thus became the founder of the Julian *gens*
Juno	Wife of Jupiter and queen of the gods; called by the Greeks Hera; hated the Trojans
Jupiter	King of the gods; ensured that Aeneas achieved his destiny
Knossos	Main city of Crete; home of Minos and Rhadamanthus; also Cnossus
Laocoon	Trojan priest of Apollo; tried to reject the Wooden Horse; killed by sea-serpents
Laomedon	An early king of Troy, known for his dishonesty and treachery
Latinus	King of Laurentum; father of Lavinia, destined to marry Aeneas
Latium	Region of Italy in which Rome would be founded
Latona	Mother of Apollo and Diana
Laurentum	City of Latium, ruled by Latinus
Lavinia	Daughter of Latinus, destined to marry Aeneas
Lavinium	Coastal town of Latium founded by Aeneas; named after Lavinia
Lethe	One of the rivers of the underworld; it induced forgetfulness
Libya	Either a North African country or North Africa in general
Lycia	A kingdom of Asia Minor, where Apollo had an oracle
Lydia	A kingdom of Asia Minor, possibly the origin of the Etruscans
Marpesus	A mountain on the Greek island of Paros, famed for its marble
Mars	God of war; named by the Greeks Ares; sometimes the personification of war
Massylians	A North African tribe near Carthage
Mercury	The messenger god; named by the Greeks Hermes
Minerva	Goddess of wisdom and war; named by the Greeks Athena; inspired the Wooden Horse
Minos	King of Knossos on Crete; later a judge in the underworld
Misenus	Trojan musician; challenged the gods to a contest and was drowned
Mnestheus	A close companion of Aeneas
Muses	Nine sister-goddesses responsible for the arts
Myconos	A Greek island; also Mykonos
Myrmidons	A tribe of Greeks living in Thessaly and led by Achilles in the Trojan War
Neoptolemus	The son of Achilles; also known as Pyrrhus
Neptune	God of the sea; named by the Greeks Poseidon
Nereids	Sea-nymphs; daughters of Doris and Nereus
Nisus	Young Trojan warrior; friend and protector of Euryalus
Numidians	A North-African tribe
Oceanus	The Sea, thought to encircle the Earth; sometimes personified
Octavian	Adopted son of Julius Caesar; became the first emperor and took the name Augustus
Odysseus	Hero of Homer's *Odyssey*; a Greek leader in the Trojan War

Oenotrians	An ancient race of Southern Italy
Olympus	Mountain in Northern Greece; home of the gods
Oreads	Mountain nymphs
Orion	Constellation named after a legendary hunter
Ortygia	Another name for the island of Delos
Palinurus	The helmsman on Aeneas' ship; fell overboard; killed by natives
Pallas (1)	Another name for Minerva
Pallas (2)	The son of Evander and ally of the Trojans; killed by Turnus
Panopes	A young Sicilian who competed in the running race (Book V)
Parcae	Another name for the Fates
Paris	Son of Priam and Hecuba; abducted Helen; caused the Trojan War
Paros	Greek island famous for its marble
Patroclus	Young friend of Achilles; killed by Hector during the Trojan War
Patron	A Greek from Arcadia; competed in the running race (Boook V)
Peleus	Father of Achilles
Penates	Roman household gods, supposedly brought from Troy by Aeneas
Pergama	The citadel or fortified central high point of Troy
Phlegethon	One of the five rivers of the underworld
Phoenicians	Inhabitants of the east coast of the Mediterranean (modern Lebanon)
Phrygia	One of the kingdoms of Asia Minor
Pluto	God of the underworld; also Hades, Dis
Poeni	The Carthaginians
Polites	A son of Priam and Hecuba; killed in front of his father by Pyrrhus
Polyphemus	One of the giant Cyclopes; blinded by Odysseus in the *Odyssey*
Polyxena	A daughter of Priam and Hecuba; sacrificed by Pyrrhus
Priam	King of Troy
Proserpina	Wife of Pluto and queen of the underworld
Pygmalion	Brother of Dido; killed Sychaeus, Dido's husband, causing Dido to flee from Tyre
Pyrrhus	The son of Achilles; also Neoptolemus
Quirinus	Another name for Romulus
Remus	Brother of Romulus; killed by Romulus
Rhadamanthus	Brother of Minos of Knossos; one of the judges in the underworld
Rhea Silvia	Mother of Romulus and Remus
Rhoeteum	A headland near Troy
Romulus	Son of Rhea Silvia and Mars; founded Rome
Rutulians	A Latin tribe living to the south-east of Lavinium; led by Turnus
Salius	A Greek from Acarnania; competed in the running race (Book V)
Sarpedon	A son of Jupiter; a Trojan ally leader; killed by Patroclus
Saturn	Father of Jupiter and other gods.
Serestus	A close companion of Aeneas
Sergestus	A close companion of Aeneas
Sibyl	Prophetess of Apollo; lived at Cumae; conducted Aeneas through the underworld
Sicani	Native inhabitants of Sicily
Sicily	Island off the toe of Italy; the Trojans called there twice
Sidon	One of the two main cities of Phoenicia
Simois	One of the rivers that flowed past Troy
Sinon	A Greek who allowed himself to be captured by the Trojans; tricked them into accepting the horse
Sirius	The Dog Star; its rising heralded the hottest time of the year
Styx	One of the five rivers of the underworld
Sychaeus	First husband of Dido; murdered by Pygmalion for his wealth and status
Tartarus	The part of the underworld reserved for the damned; also Tartara

Tegea	A city in Arcadia, Greece
Tellus	The Earth; sometimes personified
Tenedos	An island just off the shore of Troy; the Greek fleet hid behind it before the final onslaught
Teucer	One of the founders of Troy
Teucri	One of the names of the Trojans; named after Teucer
Thrace	Part of northern Greece, including the northern shore of the Aegean Sea
Tiber	River that flows through Rome; also the god of the river
Tisiphone	One of the Furies; supervised the entrance to Tartarus
Titans	Race of giants who fought against the gods for supremacy, and lost
Trinacria	Another name for Sicily
Troy	City on the southern shore of the Hellespont; ruled by Priam
Typhoeus	One of a race of giants; killed by the thunderbolt of Jupiter
Tyre	One of the two main cities of Phoenicia; first home of Dido
Tyrrhenian Sea	The sea that lies to the west of Italy
Ulysses	The Roman name for Odysseus; also Ulixes
Venus	Goddess of love and beauty; mother of Aeneas; supported the Trojans; in Greek Aphrodite
Vesta	Goddess of the hearth, fire and home; in Greek Hestia

7. Further Reading

There have been three Penguin translations, by W.F. Jackson Knight (1963), David West (2003) and Robert Fagles (2012).

General editions consulted in the preparation of this book are those of T.E. Page (*The Aeneid of Virgil, Books I–VI*, Macmillan, 1960); R.D.Williams (*Virgil, Aeneid I–VI*, Bristol Classical Press, 1972 and 2005); and C. Pharr (*Vergil's Aeneid*, Bolchazy-Carducci, 1998).

Also of interest are K.Quinn, *Virgil's Aeneid*, Routledge & Kegan Paul, 1968; W.A. Camps, *An Introduction to Virgil*, Oxford University Press, 1969; S.E. Winbolt, *The Latin Hexameter*, Blackie and Son Ltd, 1906; D.S. Raven, *Latin Metre: An Introduction*, Faber and Faber, 1965.

Book 1

arma virumque cano, Troiae qui primus ab oris
Italiam fato profugus Lavinaque venit
litora, multum ille et terris iactatus et alto
vi superum, saevae memorem Iunonis ob iram,
multa quoque et bello passus, dum conderet urbem   5
inferretque deos Latio, genus unde Latinum
Albanique patres atque altae moenia Romae.
Musa, mihi causas memora, quo numine laeso
quidve dolens regina deum tot volvere casus
insignem pietate virum, tot adire labores   10
impulerit. tantaene animis caelestibus irae?

*There was a town called Carthage, which Juno loved more than any other. But she had
heard of a race of men descended from the Trojans, who were destined one day to destroy
Carthage. She also remembered helping the Greeks to fight the Trojans in the Trojan War,
because of the judgement of Paris.*

his accensa super iactatos aequore toto
Troas, reliquias Danaum atque inmitis Achilli,   30
arcebat longe Latio, multosque per annos
errabant acti fatis maria omnia circum.

arma, -orum n.pl.	arms	*numen, -inis* n.	divinity
cano, -ere	I sing	*laedo, -ere, laesi, laesus*	I offend
Troia, -ae f.	Troy	*-ve*	or
ora, -ae f.	shore	*doleo, -ere*	I resent
Italia, -ae f.	Italy	*tot*	so many
fatum, -i n.	fate	*volvo, -ere*	I pass through,
profugus, -a, -um	fleeing		roll
Lavinus, -a, -um	of Lavinium	*casus, -us* m.	disaster
litus, -oris n.	shore	*insignis, -e* 10	famous
iacto, -are	I toss, toss about	*pietas, -atis* f.	dutifulness
altum, -i n.	sea	*adeo, -ire*	I face
vis (no gen.) f.	power, force	*impello, -ere, -puli, -pulsus*	I drive, strike
superi, -um m.pl.	gods	*caelestis, -e*	of the gods
saevus, -a, -um	cruel	*accendo, -ere, -ndi, -nsus*	I inflame
memor, -oris	mindful	*super*	in addition
Iuno, -onis f.	Juno	*aequor, -oris* n.	sea
ob + acc.	because of	*Tros, -ois* m. 30	Trojan
ira, -ae f.	anger	*reliquiae, -arum* f.pl.	those left alive
patior, -i, passus sum 5	I suffer	*Danai, -orum* or *-um* m.pl.	Greeks
condo, -ere	I found, establish	*inmitis, -e*	pitiless
infero, -ferre	I install	*Achilles, -ei* or *-i* m.	Achilles
Latium, -i n.	Latium	*arceo, -ere*	I keep … from
genus, -eris n.	race	*longe*	a long way
Latinus, -a, -um	Latin	*erro, -are*	I wander
Albanus, -a, -um	Alban	*ago, -ere, egi, actus*	I drive, treat
moenia, -ium n.pl.	walls	*mare, -is* n.	sea
Musa, -ae f.	Muse	*circum* + acc.	around
memoro, -are	I relate		

1 **virum:** Aeneas is the man. **qui:** to be taken first.

2 **Italiam:** accusative of goal of motion. **fato:** either 'from Fate' or 'because of Fate'. **Lavina:** Lavinium was a town about 30 miles south of Rome, founded by Aeneas and named in honour of Lavinia, the daughter of king Latinus of the neighbouring city of Laurentum, whom Aeneas was destined to marry once he had settled in Italy.

3 **litora:** parallel to *Italiam*. **et alto:** parallel to *et terris*.

4 **Iunonis:** Juno, queen of the gods, was hostile to the Trojans because it was a Trojan, Paris, who declared Venus rather than her to be the most beautiful goddess. **memorem:** i.e. she never forgot her anger against the Trojans.

5 **et:** to be taken first. **conderet:** notice the subjunctive: 'until he *could* found' a city; this was the goal of all Aeneas' wanderings.

6 **Latio:** dative of destination; Latium was the region of Italy to the south of Rome, modern Lazio, and the homeland of the Latin race. **unde:** supply *sunt*.

7 **Albani:** Alba Longa was an ancient city of Latium, founded by Aeneas' son, Ascanius or Iulus. From Alba, in direct line of descent from Aeneas, would come Romulus, the legendary founder of Rome. **altae . . . Romae:** because of the seven hills.

8–9 **Musa:** there were nine Muses, responsible for the arts; Calliope looked after epic poetry. Virgil prays to her for inspiration. **numine:** the divinity is Juno's, and so *quo numine laeso* must mean 'because of what offence to her divinity'. **deum:** = *deorum*.

10 **pietate:** *pietas* was Aeneas' supreme quality, of which Virgil repeatedly reminds the reader throughout the *Aeneid*. It means that Aeneas has a strong sense of duty to the gods, his family and his country.

11 **impulerit:** the subjunctive is for the indirect question introduced by *quo* and *quid*. **tantaene . . . irae:** supply *sunt*. **animis:** local ablative.

29–31 **his:** 'by these things'. **accensa:** the subject is Juno. **aequore toto:** 'across the whole sea'. The order is *iactatos . . . Troas . . . arcebat*.

30 **reliquias:** 'the leavings of the Greeks', i.e. 'those left alive by the Greeks'. **Achilli:** Achilles was the most successful fighter in the Greek army. Notice how this name is at the opposite end of the line from *Troas*, emphasising their opposition.

Questions

1 What do the first eleven lines tell us about Aeneas' destiny?

2 What difficulties does Aeneas face before he achieves his destiny?

3 In lines 6–7, *genus . . . Romae* forms an ascending tricolon. What does this mean, and what effect does it have?

4 In line 11, *impulerit* is an example of enjambement. What effect do you think this has here?

5 Why does Juno hate the Trojans?

6 In lines 29–32, how does Virgil emphasise the extent of the Trojans' suffering?

tantae molis erat Romanam condere gentem.
vix e conspectu Siculae telluris in altum
vela dabant laeti et spumas salis aere ruebant,   35
cum Iuno aeternum servans sub pectore vulnus
haec secum: 'mene incepto desistere victam,
nec posse Italia Teucrorum avertere regem?'

Juno bade Aeolus, the Lord of the Winds, to send a storm to sink the ships. Aeolus obeyed.

haec ubi dicta, cavum conversa cuspide montem
impulit in latus; ac venti velut agmine facto,
qua data porta, ruunt et terras turbine perflant.
incubuere mari, totumque a sedibus imis
una Eurusque Notusque ruunt creberque procellis   85
Africus, et vastos volvunt ad litora fluctus.
insequitur clamorque virum stridorque rudentum.
eripiunt subito nubes caelumque diemque
Teucrorum ex oculis; ponto nox incubat atra.
intonuere poli et crebris micat ignibus aether   90
praesentemque viris intentant omnia mortem.

moles, -is f.	task, trouble		sedes, -is f.	depths, home
gens, gentis f.	race		imus, -a, -um	lowest
vix	scarcely		Eurus, -i m.	85 the East Wind
laetus, -a, -um	happy		Notus, -i m.	the South Wind
conspectus, -us m.	sight		creber, -bra, -brum	abounding
Siculus, -a, -um	Sicilian		procella, -ae f.	violent gust
tellus, -uris f.	land		Africus, -i m.	Southwest Wind
vela do, dare	35 I set sail		vastus, -a, -um	enormous
spuma, -ae f.	foam, spume		fluctus, -us m.	wave, roller
sal, salis m.	salt, i.e. the sea		insequor, -i	I follow
aes, aeris n.	bronze		clamor, -oris m.	shouting
ruo, ruere, rui	I churn, rush		stridor, -oris m.	creaking
aeternus, -a, -um	eternal		rudens, -entis m.	rope, rigging
servo, -are	I keep		eripio, -ere	I snatch away
pectus, -oris n.	heart, breast		subito	suddenly
vulnus, -eris n.	wound		nubes, -is f.	cloud
inceptum, -i n.	purpose		caelum, -i n.	sky
desisto, -ere + abl.	I give up		dies, diei m.	day
vinco, -ere, vici, victus	I defeat		oculus, -i m.	eye
Teucri, -orum m.pl.	Trojans		pontus, -i m.	sea
averto, -ere	I keep away		nox, noctis f.	night, darkness
cavus, -a, -um	81 hollow		incubo, -are + dat.	I settle upon
converto, -ere, -verti, -versus	I reverse		ater, -tra, -trum	black
cuspis, -idis f.	sceptre		intono, -are, -ui,	90 I thunder
mons, montis m.	mountain		polus, -i m.	pole
latus, -eris n.	side		creber, -bra, -brum	frequent
ventus, -i m.	wind		mico, -are	I flash
velut	just as if		ignis, -is m.	fire
qua	where		aether, -eris m.	sky
turbo, -inis m.	tornado		praesens, -entis	instant
perflo, -are	I blow across		intento, -are	I threaten
incumbo, -ere, -cubui + dat.	I settle upon		mors, mortis f.	death

33 **tantae molis:** 'so great a task' was it: the use of the genitive is unusual; it is similar to the genitive of characteristic. **condere:** it was Aeneas' destiny to found the Roman race.

34 **Siculae telluris:** the Trojans were sailing from Sicily on their way to Italy when the storm drove them off course.

35 **salis aere:** both words are examples of <u>metonymy</u>, naming the whole after a constituent part; 'bronze' refers to the cladding of the prows. **ruebant:** here used transitively.

36 **vulnus:** notice how the words *aeternum* and *vulnus* enclose Juno's *pectus*: a good example of Virgil's <u>enclosing word order</u>, emphasising the all-embracing force of her 'wound'. The *vulnus* is the insult inflicted on her by Paris.

37 **haec:** supply a verb, such as '*dixit*'. **me . . . desistere:** this use of the accusative and infinitive is used to express an indignant question: 'Am I to give up . . .?'

36–7 Note the very slow rhythm, perhaps emphasising her long-lasting indignation.

38 **Teucrorum . . . regem:** although Aeneas was not King of Troy, since the death of King Priam and the abandonment of Troy, he has automatically become the king of the survivors.

81 **dicta:** supply *sunt*. **conversa cuspide:** Aeolus used the butt of the sceptre to strike the side of the mountain.

81–3 Note the heavy use of <u>alliteration</u> in these lines.

82 **in latus:** movement towards the side of the mountain is implicit in the verb *impulit*: 'He struck it (the spear) against the side of the hollow mountain.' The winds, when not in use, were kept imprisoned inside the hollow mountain, which had a gate provided (*data*) in the side. **velut agmine facto:** 'as if in an army formation that had been set up'.

83 **data:** supply *est*. **ruunt:** this is the first of many historic presents.

84–6 **incubuere:** = *incubuerunt*; similarly *intonuere* in line 90 and many subsequent verbs. **totum:** supply *mare*. **una:** 'together'. **creberque procellis:** 'frequent with gusts', and so 'with frequent gusts'. **Africus:** the <u>enjambement</u> places extra emphasis on this wind. Roman poets often visualised the violence of storms as being caused by the clashing of several contrary winds. Note the <u>polysyndeton</u> in these lines.

87–8 **virum:** = virorum. **insequitur, eripiunt:** note the position of these two verbs at the start of their lines and preceding their subjects. Virgil focuses on the speed with which the events unfold. Lines 84 and 90 start similarly. Note again the <u>polysyndeton</u>.

91 Note the <u>assonance</u> of *em* and *en*, which enhances the solemnity of the slow, <u>spondaic rhythm</u>.

Questions

1 In line 37, Juno refers to her 'purpose' (*incepto*). What do you think her purpose was?

2 Why does Juno want to keep Aeneas away from Italy?

3 In line 81, how does Virgil use sound effects?

4 In lines 82–86, how does Virgil show the violence of the winds? You should refer to sound effects, choice and position of words, and imagery.

5 In line 90, why do you think Virgil uses the word *poli* (poles)?

6 In line 91, the two words *praesentem* and *mortem* enclose the rest of the words in the line. What effect does this have?

extemplo Aeneae solvuntur frigore membra;
ingemit et duplices tendens ad sidera palmas
talia voce refert: 'o terque quaterque beati,
quis ante ora patrum Troiae sub moenibus altis   95
contigit oppetere! o Danaum fortissime gentis
Tydide! mene Iliacis occumbere campis
non potuisse tuaque animam hanc effundere dextra,
saevus ubi Aeacidae telo iacet Hector, ubi ingens
Sarpedon, ubi tot Simois correpta sub undis   100
scuta virum galeasque et fortia corpora volvit!'

*The storm severely damaged the Trojan fleet and would have destroyed it, had not Neptune
restored calm and allowed the ships to reach the shore of Africa. Aeneas found the crews of
seven other ships and together they feasted on venison and wine, uncertain of their future.*

et iam finis erat, cum Iuppiter aethere summo
despiciens mare velivolum terrasque iacentes
litoraque et latos populos, sic vertice caeli   225
constitit et Libyae defixit lumina regnis.

extemplo	immediately	*dextra, -ae* f.	right hand
solvo, -ere	I weaken, dispel	*Aeacides, -ae* m.	Achilles
frigus, -oris n.	cold	*telum, -i* n.	weapon
membrum, -i n.	limb	*iaceo, -ere*	I lie
ingemo, -ere	I groan	*Hector, -oris* m.	Hector
duplex, -icis	both	*Sarpedon, -onis* m. 100	Sarpedon
tendo, -ere	I hold up, extend	*tot*	so many
sidus, -eris n.	star	*Simois, -entis* m.	Simois
palma, -ae f.	palm, hand	*corripio, -ere, -ripui, -reptus*	I seize
talis, -e	such	*unda, -ae* f.	water, wave
vox, vocis f.	voice	*scutum, -i* n.	shield
refero, -ferre	I speak	*galea, -ae* f.	helmet
ter	three times	*corpus, -oris* n.	body
quater	four times	*finis, -is* m.	end
beatus, -a, -um	blessed, fortunate	*Iuppiter, Iovis* m.	Jupiter
ante + acc. 95	before	*summus, -a, -um*	the top of, highest
os, oris n.	face	*despicio, -ere*	I look down upon
altus, -a, -um	high	*velivolus, -a, -um*	covered with sails
contingit, -ere, -tigit + dat.	it happens (to)	*latus, -a, -um* 225	wide-spread
oppeto, -ere	I die	*populus, -i* m.	people, nation
fortis, -e	brave	*vertex, -icis* m.	the highest point
Tydides, -ae m.	Diomedes	*consisto, -ere, -stiti*	I stand, stop
Iliacus, -a, -um	Trojan, of Troy	*Libya, -ae* f.	Libya, Africa
occumbo, -ere	I die	*defigo, -ere, -fixi, -fixus*	I fix
campus, -i m.	battlefield	*lumen, -inis* n.	light, eye
anima, -ae f.	soul, life	*regnum, -i* n.	realm, kingdom
effundo, -ere	I pour forth		

92 This is Aeneas' first appearance. Note the immediate focus upon his human frailty.

93 **palmas:** the raising of upturned hands was the normal attitude for prayer.

94 **voce refert:** the two words together mean no more than 'speaks'.

95 **quis:** the alternative form of *quibus*, dative dependent on *contigit*. Aeneas is addressing the spirits of his fellow Trojans and their allies, who were killed during the Trojan War. Aeneas would have preferred their heroic deaths to the one now facing him at sea.

97 **Tydide:** vocative; Aeneas includes a Greek hero because Diomedes had fought against and wounded Aeneas in single combat during the War. Aeneas would rather have been killed by the Greek then than face his current situation.

97–8 **me non potuisse:** the construction is similar to that in line 37, but takes the form here of an exclamation rather than a question. Translate 'Why could I not have died . . .?' **Iliacis . . . campis:** local ablative.

98 **tuā:** take with *dextrā*: '(killed) by your right hand'.

99 **Aeacidae telo:** 'Hector lies (killed) by the spear of Achilles.' The combat between the two champions was the climax of Homer's account of the Trojan War in his *Iliad*.

100 **Sarpedon:** a Trojan ally killed by Patroclus, the close friend of Achilles. **Simois:** one of the two rivers that flowed past Troy, and the scene of much bloodshed in the *Iliad*. **virum:** = *virorum*; this belongs with *scuta, galeas* and *corpora*. **volvit:** the river bowls them along.

223–6 **finis:** i.e. the end of the Trojans' meal. **cum . . . constitit:** the inverse *-cum* construction, with the indicative. The sequence is 'when Jupiter . . . while looking down upon . . . stood'. **velivolum:** this vivid adjective indicates how the sea would appear from Jupiter's standpoint high in heaven. **Libyae:** the name often refers to any central part of the North African coast, and so can, as here, include Carthage.

Questions

1 What picture of Aeneas does Virgil present here? Is this how you would expect the hero of the *Aeneid* to be portrayed? Why do you think Virgil chose to present him in this way?

2 Why do you think Aeneas describes the fallen heroes of Troy as *terque quaterque beati*?

3 What is the effect of the enjambements in lines 97 and 100?

4 In lines 99–100, *ubi* appears three times. This is an example of <u>anaphora</u>. What is anaphora, and what is its effect here?

5 In lines 223–226, how does Virgil show the extent of Jupiter's power?

atque illum tales iactantem pectore curas
tristior et lacrimis oculos suffusa nitentes
adloquitur Venus: 'o qui res hominumque deumque
aeternis regis imperiis et fulmine terres,   230
quid meus Aeneas in te committere tantum,
quid Troes potuere, quibus tot funera passis
cunctus ob Italiam terrarum clauditur orbis?
certe hinc Romanos olim volventibus annis,
hinc fore ductores, revocato a sanguine Teucri,   235
qui mare, qui terras omnes dicione tenerent,
pollicitus. quae te, genitor, sententia vertit?'

*'I was willing to accept the fall of my beloved Troy, because of this new destiny you
promised. But ill fortune still pursues the Trojans. Is this how our loyalty to you is to be
rewarded?'*

olli subridens hominum sator atque deorum
vultu, quo caelum tempestatesque serenat,   255
oscula libavit natae, dehinc talia fatur:
'parce metu, Cytherea, manent immota tuorum
fata tibi; cernes urbem et promissa Lavini
moenia sublimemque feres ad sidera caeli
magnanimum Aenean; neque me sententia vertit.   260

cura, -ae f.	care, worry	*polliceor, -eri, pollicitus sum*	I promise
tristis, -e	sad	*genitor, -oris* m.	father
lacrima, -ae f.	tear	*sententia, -ae* f.	opinion, thought
suffusus, -a, -um	brimming	*verto, -ere, verti, versus*	I turn, change
nitens, -entis	shining	*subrideo, -ere*	I smile
adloquor, -i, -locutus sum	I address	*sator, -oris* m.	creator
imperium, -i n.	230 power	*vultus, -us* m.	255 face, look
fulmen, -inis n.	thunderbolt	*sereno, -are*	I calm
terreo, -ere	I terrify	*osculum, -i* n.	lip, kiss
committo, -ere	I commit an offence	*libo, -are*	I lightly kiss
		nata, -ae f.	daughter
funus, -eris n.	death	*dehinc*	then
cunctus, -a, -um	all	*for, fari, fatus sum*	I speak
orbis, -is m.	world, cycle	*parco, -ere* + dat.	I spare
claudo, -ere	I bar, shut	*metus, -us* m.	fear
certe	yet	*Cytherea, -ae* f.	Venus
olim	one day, formerly	*maneo, -ere*	I remain
hinc	235 from them	*immotus, -a, -um*	unchanged
ductor, -oris m.	leader	*cerno, -ere*	I see
revoco, -are	I restore	*promitto, -ere, -misi, missus*	I promise
sanguis, -inis m.	blood	*Lavinium, -i* n.	Lavinium
Teucer, -ri m.	Teucer	*sublimis, -e*	raised up, exalted
dicio, -onis f.	control	*magnanimus, -a, -um*	260 great-hearted

227 tales: 'such troubles' are the ones relating to the peoples and places he observed, especially the plight of the Trojans previously described.

228 tristior: i.e. Venus was sadder than she normally was. The structure is *illum . . . adloquitur Venus.* **lacrimis oculos suffusa:** this is one of Virgil's favourite constructions for describing people, modelled on the Greek middle verb. Venus was literally 'suffused as to her eyes with tears', i.e. 'her eyes brimming with tears'.

229 o qui . . . regis: supply the antecedent *tu.* **deum:** = *deorum.*

230 fulmine: the thunderbolt was Jupiter's weapon, with which he controlled the universe.

231 quid: supply *potuit* from *potuere.* **in te:** 'against you'. **meus Aeneas:** Venus was Aeneas' mother; his father was a mortal, Anchises.

232 potuere: = *potuerunt.* **quibus:** 'to whom the whole world is barred because of Italy'. That is, Juno continally persecutes the Trojans to stop them achieving their destiny of settling in Italy.

234 The order is *certe pollicitus (es) . . .* **volventibus annis:** 'as the years roll by'.

235 Teucri: Teucer was one of the founders of Troy, for whom the Trojans are often called *Teucri.* The promise was that his bloodline would be restored after the fall of Troy, eventually being passed on to the Romans.

237 Jupiter's promise spanned a thousand years. **sententia:** 'what has changed your mind?' (lit. 'what thought has changed you?').

254–5 olli: an archaic form of *illi*, to be taken with *fatur*; Virgil is fond of using such words. **vultu quo:** 'with the look with which'.

257 metu: this is an archaic form of the dative, dependent on *parce.*

257 Cytherea: one of several commonly used titles of Venus, deriving from the island of Cythera, which was a centre of her worship. **tuorum:** 'of your people', i.e. Aeneas and the Trojans.

258 tibi: an example of the so-called ethic dative, used to indicate a person interested in the action, but not involved directly in it. **Lavini:** Lavinium will be founded by Aeneas as his first settlement in Italy (see line 2).

259 sublimem: best translated as an adverb: 'you will bear Aeneas aloft'. The idea is that Venus will make him into a god by bearing his spirit up to the stars.

260 Aenean: this is a Greek accusative ending, used regularly with names belonging to the cycle of Greek myths.

260 neque me sententia vertit: this neatly answers Venus' accusation in line 237.

Questions

1 In lines 228–229, why do you think Venus' name is left till last?

2 How does Virgil use word order to good effect in line 233?

3 Why does Venus remind Jupiter of his promise (lines 234–237)?

4 In lines 254–255, how does Virgil indicate the power and authority of Jupiter?

5 In lines 258–260, what two promises does Jupiter make?

hic tibi (fabor enim, quando haec te cura remordet,
longius, et volvens fatorum arcana movebo)
bellum ingens geret Italia populosque feroces
contundet moresque viris et moenia ponet,
tertia dum Latio regnantem viderit aestas,   265
ternaque transierint Rutulis hiberna subactis.
at puer Ascanius, cui nunc cognomen Iulo
additur (Ilus erat, dum res stetit Ilia regno),
triginta magnos volvendis mensibus orbes
imperio explebit, regnumque ab sede Lavini   270
transferet, et Longam multa vi muniet Albam.
hic iam ter centum totos regnabitur annos
gente sub Hectorea, donec regina sacerdos
Marte gravis geminam partu dabit Ilia prolem.
inde lupae fulvo nutricis tegmine laetus   275
Romulus excipiet gentem et Mavortia condet
moenia Romanosque suo de nomine dicet.
his ego nec metas rerum nec tempora pono:
imperium sine fine dedi. quin aspera Iuno,
quae mare nunc terrasque metu caelumque fatigat,   280
consilia in melius refert, mecumque fovebit
Romanos, rerum dominos gentemque togatam.

quando	since	*munio, -ire*	I fortify
remordeo, -ere	I torment	*centum*	one hundred
arcanum, -i n.	secret, mystery	*Hectoreus, -a, -um*	of Hector, Trojan
moveo, -ere	I reveal, move	*donec*	until
gero, -ere	I wage	*sacerdos, -otis* f.	priestess
ferox, -ocis	fierce	*Mars, -tis* m.	Mars
contundo, -ere	I overthrow	*gravis, -e*	pregnant
mos, moris m.	custom	*geminus, -a, -um*	twin
pono, -ere	I establish	*partu do, dare*	I give birth to
tertius, -a, -um	265 third	*Ilia, -ae* f.	Ilia (Rhea Silvia)
regno, -are	I reign	*proles, -is* f.	offspring
aestas, -atis f.	summer	*inde*	275 then
terni, -ae, -a (plural)	three	*lupa, -ae* f.	female wolf
transeo, -ire, -ii, -itus	I pass	*fulvus, -a, -um*	golden brown
Rutuli, -orum m.pl.	the Rutulians	*nutrix, -icis* f.	nurse
hiberna, -orum n.pl.	winters	*tegmen, -inis* n.	covering, hide
subigo, -ere, -egi, -actus	I conquer	*Romulus, -i* m.	Romulus
Ascanius, -i m.	Ascanius	*excipio, -ere*	I take over
cognomen, -inis n.	cognomen	*Mavortius, -a, -um*	of Mars
Iulus, -i m.	Iulus	*nomen, -inis* n.	name
addo, -ere	I add	*meta, -ae* f.	bound, boundary
Ilus, -i m.	Ilus	*res, rei* f.	thing, affair
sto, -are	I remain strong	*sine* + abl.	without
Ilius, -a, -um	Trojan	*quin*	indeed
triginta	thirty	*asper, -era, -erum*	resentful, cruel
mensis, -is m.	month	*fatigo, -are*	280 I harass
expleo, -ere	270 I complete	*consilium, -i* n.	advice, plan
transfero, -ferre	I transfer	*foveo, -ere*	I favour, fondle
Longa Alba, -ae f.	Alba Longa	*dominus, -i* m.	master
vis, vim, vi f.	force, violence	*togatus, -a, -um*	wearing the toga

261 tibi: another ethic dative, which may be translated as 'as you will see'.

262 longius: with this punctuation, *longius* belongs with *fabor* rather than *volvens*, as some editors take it. Translate 'I shall speak at greater length', i.e. he will reveal the future at greater length than he normally would. **volvens:** a <u>metaphor</u> from the unrolling of a Roman book. Translate 'unrolling them, I shall reveal'.

263–4 Italia: local ablative. **viris:** 'upon men'; dative of advantage.

265 tertia aestas: the 'third summer', together with the 'three winters' in the next line, indicate that Aeneas will reign for three years as king of Lavinium, at the end of which he will die (or at least depart from the earth). **regnantem:** supply *eum*. **Latio:** local ablative.

266 Rutulis: a Latin tribe living to the south-east of Lavinium. Their leader, Turnus, led the opposition to the settlement of the Trojans in Latium, because he loved king Latinus' daughter, Lavinia, whom Aeneas was destined to marry. **Rutulis . . . subactis:** either an ablative absolute or a dative of disadvantage.

267–8 Ascanius is the lynch-pin of Virgil's design to make Augustus a direct descendant of Aeneas. Virgil invents a *cognomen* for him, Ilus (the name belonged originally to one of the first kings of Troy, which took the name *Ilium* from him), and promptly converts it to Iulus, only one step away from Iulius or Julius, the *nomen* of Julius Caesar, the uncle and adoptive father of Octavian, who added Caesar's names to his own. **Iulo:** the name is attracted into the case of the relative pronoun, *cui*. **res:** *res Ilia* is parallel to *res publica*: 'the Trojan state'. **regno:** ablative of respect: 'in sovereignty'.

269 volvendis: 'with the months rolling by'. **magnos . . . orbes:** clearly annual cycles. The sense is that he will rule for 30 years. Note the apt slow rhythm of this line.

270 ab sede Lavini: 'from its seat at Lavinium'.

271 Longam Albam: note the heavy <u>alliteration</u> and <u>assonance</u> of *mu-* and *-am*, suggestive perhaps of solemnity. It was important for Virgil to have Iulus transfer to Alba Longa, because in existing Roman legend, Romulus came from that city.

272 regnabitur: impersonal passive; translate 'kings will reign'.

273 regina: best translated here as 'royal'; the reference is to Ilia, a descendant of Aeneas, better known as Rhea Silvia. By Mars she was the mother of Romulus and Remus. In this way Virgil connects Greek with Roman legend.

275–7 tegmine: causal ablative; the legend is that Romulus, after being saved and suckled by the wolf, later proudly wore her hide. **Mavortia moenia:** the Rome that Romulus founded is called 'Martian' because he was the son of Mars. **dicet:** 'will call (them)'.

278 metas rerum et tempora: 'bounds in space and time'; the idea is repeated in the next line. Here Virgil gives divine sanction for the boundless Roman empire.

281 in melius: 'for the better'.

282 rerum: 'of the world'. **gentem togatam:** only civilians wore the toga; in this line Virgil embraces war and peace.

Questions

1 Line 264 contains a <u>chiasmus</u>. What is this, and what effect does it have?

2 To what extent do you think Jupiter's promises in lines 263–266 will reassure Venus?

3 In lines 267–274, how does Virgil use names to make a connection between the Trojans and contemporary Romans?

4 How long will Ascanius reign as king?

5 Explain the importance of Alba Longa in linking Aeneas to Rome.

6 Lines 278–279 (*his ego . . . dedi*) are very famous. Can you explain this?

'Such is my will. There will come an age when the descendants of the Trojans will conquer Greece.'

nascetur pulchra Troianus origine Caesar,
imperium Oceano, famam qui terminet astris,
Iulius, a magno demissum nomen Iulo.
hunc tu olim caelo spoliis Orientis onustum
accipies secura; vocabitur hic quoque votis.   290
aspera tum positis mitescent saecula bellis:
cana Fides et Vesta, Remo cum fratre Quirinus
iura dabunt; dirae ferro et compagibus artis
claudentur Belli portae; Furor impius intus
saeva sedens super arma et centum vinctus aënis   295
post tergum nodis fremet horridus ore cruento.'

At dawn Aeneas went for a walk to investigate the country. He came upon a girl bearing a bow and arrows. Aeneas, surprised by her appearance, asked for information about the country, little suspecting that the girl was in fact his own mother, the goddess Venus, in disguise. Thus she spoke:

'Punica regna vides, Tyrios et Agenoris urbem;
sed fines Libyci, genus intractabile bello.
imperium Dido Tyria regit urbe profecta,   340
germanum fugiens. longa est iniuria, longae
ambages; sed summa sequar fastigia rerum.

nascor, -i, natus sum	I am born	*artus, -a, -um*	tight-fitting
pulcher, -ra, -rum	beautiful	*Furor, -oris* m.	Frenzy
origo, -inis f.	lineage	*impius, -a, -um*	wicked, impious
Iulius Caesar, -is m.	Julius Caesar	*intus*	inside
Oceanus, -i m.	Ocean	*sedeo, -ere* 295	I sit
fama, -ae f.	fame, glory	*super* + acc.	over, on
termino, -are	I bound, end	*vincio, -ire, vinxi, vinctus*	I bind
astrum ,-i n.	star	*aënus, -a, -um*	of bronze
demitto, -ere, -misi, -missus	I hand down	*post* + acc.	behind, after
spolia, -orum n.pl.	spoils	*tergum, -i* n.	back, hide
Oriens, -entis m.	the East	*nodus, -i* m.	knot
onustus, -a, -um	laden	*fremo, -ere*	I roar
accipio, -ere 290	I receive, listen to	*horridus, -a, -um*	frightful
securus, -a, -um	free from anxiety	*cruentus, -a, -um*	gory
voco, -are	I call, invoke	*Punicus, -a, -um*	Carthaginian
votum, -i n.	vow, prayer	*Tyrius, -a, -um*	of Tyre, Tyrian
mitesco, -ere	I become civilised	*Agenor, -oris* m.	Agenor
saeculum, -i n.	age, generation	*fines, -ium* m.pl.	frontiers
canus, -a, -um	ancient	*Libycus, -a, -um*	Libyan, African
Fides, -ei f.	Honour	*intractabilis, -e*	unconquerable
Vesta, -ae f.	Vesta	*Dido, -onis* f. 340	Dido
Remus, -i m.	Remus	*germanus, -i* m.	brother
Quirinus, -i m.	Quirinus, Romulus	*iniuria, -ae* f.	injustice, outrage
ius, iuris n.	law	*ambages, -um* f.pl.	a complicated story
dirus, -a, -um	dread, dreadful		
ferrum, -i n.	iron, sword	*sequor, -i secutus sum*	I follow
compago, -inis f.	fastening	*fastigium, -i* n.	point

286 **nascetur Caesar:** note the inverted word order and separation, building to a climax. The Caesar in question is probably Augustus, rather than Julius Caesar. He is 'Trojan' because of his descent from Aeneas.

287 **terminet:** the subjunctive expresses purpose. The order is *qui terminet imperium Oceano, (et) famam astris.* **Oceano:** 'at (the) Ocean'; local or instrumental ablative; similarly *astris.*

288 **Iulius:** to be taken with *Caesar.* **nomen:** in apposition to *Iulius.*

289–90 **caelo:** 'in heaven' or 'to heaven'. **spoliis Orientis:** the 'spoils of the East' were gained after Augustus' defeat of Cleopatra followed by the whole of Egypt. **secura:** agrees with *tu* (Venus): she will no longer be troubled as she is at the moment. **vocabitur:** Augustus 'will be invoked' by mortals praying to him as a god. Julius Caesar had already been deified, and the same would happen to Augustus upon his death; indeed in the East he was already worshipped as a living god.

291 **positis bellis:** 'when wars are at an end'. One of Augustus' greatest claims was his termination of the long series of civil wars that had torn Rome apart for much of the previous century. The *aspera saecula* were to be replaced by the new Golden Age.

292 **cana Fides:** this personification of one of the great Roman virtues, closely associated with *pietas*, was worshipped in Rome from the age of king Numa onwards. **Vesta:** goddess of fire and the family home, also worshipped since antiquity. **Remo . . . Quirinus:** these now-deified heroes will be reunited in support of Augustus' regime.

293–4 **dirae . . . Belli portae:** the doors of the temple of Janus were symbolic of war; they were only closed in times of peace. Augustus was only the third statesman to close them. **ferro et compagibus:** an example of <u>hendiadys</u>.

294–6 **Furor:** another personification, Frenzy was the opposite of *Fides* and *pietas*, here indicating civil strife. Note the heavy <u>alliteration,</u> particularly of *s.* **intus:** i.e. inside the temple. **vinctus:** supply *manus*: 'bound with respect to his hands behind his back', and so 'his hands bound behind his back'; the idea is that Strife is now impotent because Augustus has brought peace to the Roman world. Note how the *centum . . . nodis* <u>enclose</u> the rest of the phrase.

338 **regna:** plural for singular. **Tyrios:** Dido's people are called 'Tyrians' because they came with her from Tyre. **Agenor:** an early king of Tyre and an ancestor of Dido.

339 **fines Libyci:** the territory around Carthage belonged to the indigenous Libyans.

340 **Tyria . . . urbe:** 'from the city of Tyre'.

341 **germanum:** Pygmalion (see line 347). **longae:** supply *sunt.*

342 **summa . . . rerum:** 'I shall trace the main points of the story.'

Questions

1 In lines 286–288, how does Virgil glorify Caesar?

2 What do lines 289–290 promise will happen to Caesar?

3 How does line 292 present a positive picture of Caesar's reign?

4 In lines 294–296, how does Virgil emphasise the terrible nature and appearance of *Furor*? Why do you think he wishes to present this picture at this point?

5 What is the connection between Phoenicia and Carthage?

6 In line 342, how does Virgil use word order and sound effects to support Venus' words?

huic coniunx Sychaeus erat, ditissimus agri
Phoenicum, et magno miserae dilectus amore,
cui pater intactam dederat primisque iugarat   345
ominibus. sed regna Tyri germanus habebat
Pygmalion, scelere ante alios immanior omnes.
quos inter medius venit furor. ille Sychaeum
impius ante aras atque auri caecus amore
clam ferro incautum superat, securus amorum   350
germanae; factumque diu celavit et aegram
multa malus simulans vana spe lusit amantem.
ipsa sed in somnis inhumati venit imago
coniugis ora modis attollens pallida miris;
crudeles aras traiectaque pectora ferro   355
nudavit, caecumque domus scelus omne retexit.
tum celerare fugam patriaque excedere suadet
auxiliumque viae veteres tellure recludit
thesauros, ignotum argenti pondus et auri.
his commota fugam Dido sociosque parabat.   360

coniunx, -ugis m.	husband	*spes, spei* f.	hope
Sychaeus, -i m.	Sychaeus	*ludo, -ere, lusi, lusus*	I deceive
dives, -itis	wealthy	*amans, -ntis* f.	lover
ager, agri m.	land	*somnus,-i* m.	sleep
Phoenices, -um m.pl.	Phoenicians	*inhumatus, -a, -um*	unburied
miser, -era, -erum	unfortunate	*imago, -inis* f.	ghost, image
diligo, -ere, -lexi, -lectus	I love	*modus, -i* m.	way
intactus, -a, -um 345	as a virgin	*attollo, -ere*	I raise
iugo, -are	I unite	*pallidus, -a, -um*	pale
omen, -inis n.	marriage ceremony	*mirus, -a, -um*	amazing
		crudelis, -e 355	cruel
Tyrus, -i f.	Tyre	*traicio, -ere, -ieci, -iectus*	I stab
Pygmalion, -onis m.	Pygmalion	*nudo, -are*	I reveal
scelus, -eris n.	wickedness	*retego, -ere, -texi, -tectus*	I reveal
immanis, -e	cruel, immense	*celero, -are*	I hasten
medius, -a, -um	in the middle (of)	*fuga, -ae* f.	flight
ara, arae f.	altar	*patria, -ae* f.	homeland
aurum, -i n.	gold	*excedo, -ere, -cessi, -cessus*	I depart
caecus, -a, -um	blind, unseen	*suadeo, -ere, suasi, suasus*	I urge
clam 350	secretly	*auxilium, -i* n.	help
incautus, -a, -um	off one's guard	*vetus, -eris*	old
supero, -are	I overcome	*recludo, -ere, -clusi, -clusus*	I reveal
securus, -a, -um	heedless	*thesaurus, -i* m.	treasure
germana, -ae f.	sister	*ignotus, -a, -um*	unknown
diu	for a long time	*argentum, -i* n.	silver
celo, -are, -avi, -atus	I hide	*pondus, -eris* n. 360	weight
aeger, -gra, -grum	sick	*commoveo, -ere, -movi, -motus*	I shock
simulo, -are	I pretend	*socius, -i* m.	ally
vanus, -a, -um	false	*paro, -are*	I prepare

343–4 **huic:** i.e. Dido. Translate 'Dido had a husband, Sychaeus', or 'Sychaeus was Dido's husband'. **ditissimus agri Phoenicum:** 'richest of the Phoenicians in land'. **miserae:** dative of agent: 'loved by an unfortunate woman' (because of what her brother did).

345–6 **intactam:** supply *eam*. **iugarat:** = *iugaverat*; supply *eam ei*. **primis ominibus:** lit. 'at the first omens'; the 'omens' were the auspices taken before a wedding ceremony, which could only go ahead if the omens were favourable; translate 'on the first day sanctioned by the omens'; the idea is that she was married at the first opportunity.

346–7 **regna:** plural for singular. **scelere:** ablative of respect: 'in wickedness'.

348 **quos inter:** inversion of the normal word order; *quos* refers to Pygmalion and Sychaeus. **medius:** this adds little to *inter*. **furor** is here 'a furious quarrel'.

348–9 **ille:** Pygmalion. The order is *ille impius . . . et caecus . . . Sychaeum . . . superat*. **ante aras:** a sacrilege, hence he was *impius*. **caecus:** he was blinded by greed.

350–1 **ferro:** 'with a sword'. **securus amorum germanae:** 'heedless of his sister's love', i.e. for her husband.

351–2 **factum:** i.e. the murder. **multa simulans:** 'making up many stories'. **aegram . . . amantem:** here '(love-)sick wife' rather than 'lover'. Note the heavy <u>alliteration</u> and <u>consonance</u> of *m*, reflecting the deep emotion.

353–4 **ipsa sed . . . imago:** = *sed imago ipsa*. **somnis:** plural for singular. **modis miris:** lit. 'in strange ways', and so 'strangely', qualifying *ora pallida*.

355–6 **crudeles aras:** the altars are 'cruel' because his murder took place there. **domus:** genitive.

358–9 **veteres tellure thesauros:** 'old treasures in the ground', and so 'treasures long buried in the ground'. **auxilium viae:** 'as a help of the way', and so 'as a help for her journey'; *auxilium* is in apposition to *thesauros*. Note the slow rhythm of line 359, matching the weightiness of the buried treasure.

360 **his:** 'by these revelations'. **fugam . . . sociosque parabat:** an example of <u>zeugma</u>, in which the verb *parabat* carries two meanings: 'prepared' and 'gathered together'.

Questions

1 In line 344, how is Dido's misfortune emphasised?

2 In line 347, how does Virgil emphasise the wicked nature of Pygmalion?

3 Why did Pygmalion kill Sychaeus?

4 In line 349, why particularly is Pygmalion called *impius*?

5 In lines 349 and 352, what special sound effects are there? What effect do these have?

6 In lines 353–356, how does Virgil bring out the horror of the scene in which the ghost appeared to Dido?

7 In lines 357–360, what help did Dido receive?

8 In lines 357–360, identify one example of <u>chiasmus</u>, one of <u>alliteration</u>, and one of <u>enjambement</u>, and say how each is effective.

conveniunt quibus aut odium crudele tyranni
aut metus acer erat; naves, quae forte paratae,
corripiunt onerantque auro. portantur avari
Pygmalionis opes pelago; dux femina facti.
devenere locos ubi nunc ingentia cernes   365
moenia surgentemque novae Carthaginis arcem,
mercatique solum, facti de nomine Byrsam,
taurino quantum possent circumdare tergo.
sed vos qui tandem? quibus aut venistis ab oris?
quove tenetis iter?' quaerenti talibus ille   370
suspirans imoque trahens a pectore vocem: 371
'sum pius Aeneas, raptos qui ex hoste penates   378
classe veho mecum, fama super aethera notus;
Italiam quaero patriam, et genus ab Iove summo'.   380

Venus reassured Aeneas that all his ships and crews had survived the storm. It was only as she departed that Aeneas recognised his mother. He and his friend Achates made their way towards Carthage, concealed in a mist created by Venus.

corripuere viam interea, qua semita monstrat.
iamque ascendebant collem, qui plurimus urbi
imminet adversasque aspectat desuper arces.   420
miratur molem Aeneas, magalia quondam,
miratur portas strepitumque et strata viarum.

convenio, -ire	I come together	*iter, itineris* n.	370 journey, course
odium, -i n.	hatred	*quaero, -ere*	I ask, seek
tyrannus, -i m.	tyrant	*suspiro, -are*	I sigh
acer, acris, acre	keen, sharp	*pius, -a, -um*	378 dutiful
navis, -is f.	ship	*rapio, -ere, rapui, raptus*	I seize
forte	by chance	*hostis, -is* m.	enemy
onero, -are	I load	*penates, -ium* m.pl.	household gods
avarus, -a, -um	miserly	*classis, -is* f.	fleet
opes, -um f.pl.	wealth	*veho, -ere*	I convey
pelagus, -i n.	sea	*notus, -a, -um*	380 well-known
dux, ducis m.	leader	*interea*	418 meanwhile
femina, -ae f. 365	woman	*semita, -ae* f.	footpath
devenio, -ire, -veni, -ventus	I reach	*monstro, -are*	I show
locus, -i m.	place	*ascendo, -ere*	I climb, go up
surgo, -ere	I rise	*collis, -is* m.	hill
novus, -a, -um	new	*immineo, -ere* + dat.	420 I tower over
Carthago, -inis f.	Carthage	*adversus, -a, -um*	opposite, facing
arx, arcis f.	citadel	*aspecto, -are*	I look at
mercor, -ari, -atus sum	I buy	*desuper*	from above
solum, -i n.	ground, land	*miror, -ari, -atus sum*	I wonder at
Byrsa, -ae f.	Byrsa (bull's hide)	*moles, -is* f.	massive work
taurinus, -a, -um	of a bull	*magalia, -ium* n.pl.	huts
quantus, -a, -um	as much . . . as	*quondam*	once, formerly
circumdo, -are	I enclose	*strepitus, -us* m.	din
tandem	at last	*stratum, -i* n.	paving

361 quibus: in full this would be *ei conveniunt, quibus erat aut odium . . . aut metus*.
crudele: this may be interpreted as an example of <u>hypallage</u>, or <u>transferred epithet</u>: it is the tyrant that is cruel, not the people's hatred of him; however, some see *crudele* as a fitting description of the hatred inspired by such a tyrant.
362 paratae: supply *sunt*.
364 pelago: 'over the sea' (local ablative); notice the heavy, spitting <u>alliteration</u> of *p*,
followed by *f*. **dux femina facti:** supply *est*; it would have been most unusual for a woman to take such a leading role.
365–6 devenere: = *devenerunt*. **Carthaginis:** the city lay on the coast of North Africa, in what is now Tunisia.
367–8 mercati: supply *sunt*. **facti de nomine Byrsam:** 'called Byrsa after the deed'; *Byrsam* is in apposition to *locos*: Virgil is providing an etymological link between the Carthaginians' own name for their city and the Greek word meaning a bull's hide. According to the legend, Dido bought from the natives as much land as 'they could enclose with an oxhide'; she had the oxhide cut into very thin strips and laid end to end in a circle, thereby gaining a much larger area than the seller had intended. Note the example of <u>enclosing word order</u> in *taurino . . . tergo*.
369 qui: supply *estis*. **tandem:** almost 'pray tell me'. **aut:** to be taken first.
370 quaerenti: supply *ei respondit*. **talibus:** supply *verbis*.
378–9 qui: to be taken first. **penates:** these are the household gods of Troy; without them a new city could not be founded successfully. **fama:** 'by reputation' (ablative of respect).
notus: supply *sum*. **super aethera:** 'above the sky', and so 'in heaven'. Is Aeneas displaying arrogance in these lines, or irony?
380 patriam: 'to be my fatherland'. **genus:** supply *est*. Venus was the daughter of Jupiter.

418 corripuere viam: 'they hurried on their way'. **qua:** 'where'. **monstrat:** the footpath 'shows' them where to go.
419–20 plurimus: the hill towers 'huge' over the city. **arces:** here 'tall buildings'.
421 magalia: a Carthaginian word. Notice the heavily spondaic rhythm and <u>alliteration</u> of this line.

Questions

1 In lines 361–362, what two groups of people joined Dido?

2 How did Dido obtain the land on which to build Carthage?

3 In lines 370–371 (*quaerenti . . . vocem*), what emotion does Aeneas display, and how does Virgil emphasise this?

4 In lines 378–380, what impression does Aeneas give of himself? Give at least three examples from the Latin to support your answer.

5 In lines 421–422, how does Virgil emphasise Aeneas' admiration for the what he sees?

6 Why do you think Virgil says that the buildings were *magalia quondam* (line 421)?

instant ardentes Tyrii: pars ducere muros
molirique arcem et manibus subvolvere saxa,
pars optare locum tecto et concludere sulco;   425
hic portus alii effodiunt; hic alta theatri   427
fundamenta locant alii, immanesque columnas
rupibus excidunt, scaenis decora alta futuris.

In the centre of the city a huge temple to Juno was being built of bronze.

hoc primum in luco nova res oblata timorem   450
leniit, hic primum Aeneas sperare salutem
ausus et adflictis melius confidere rebus.
namque sub ingenti lustrat dum singula templo
reginam opperiens, dum quae fortuna sit urbi
artificumque manus inter se operumque laborem   455
miratur, videt Iliacas ex ordine pugnas
bellaque iam fama totum vulgata per orbem,
Atridas Priamumque et saevum ambobus Achillem.
constitit et lacrimans 'quis iam locus' inquit 'Achate,
quae regio in terris nostri non plena laboris?   460
en Priamus! sunt hic etiam sua praemia laudi,
sunt lacrimae rerum et mentem mortalia tangunt.
solve metus; feret haec aliquam tibi fama salutem.'

insto, -are	I press on	confido, -ere + dat.	I trust
ardens, -ntis	keen	namque	for
Tyrius, -a, -um	Carthaginian	lustro, -are	I inspect
molior, -iri	I toil at	singula, -orum n.pl.	individual details
subvolvo, -ere	I roll up	templum, -i n.	temple
saxum, -i n.	stone	opperior, -iri	I wait for
opto, -are	425 I choose	artifex, -icis m.	455 artist
tectum, -i n.	building	manus, -us f.	skill
concludo, -ere	I enclose	opus, operis n.	work
sulcus, -i m.	furrow	labor, -oris m.	work, task, toil
portus, -us m.	harbour	miror, -ari, -atus sum	I wonder at
alii . . . alii	some . . . others	ordo, -inis m.	order
theatrum, -i n.	theatre	pugna, -ae f.	fight, battle
effodio, -ere	I dig out	vulgo, -are	I make known
fundamenta, -orum n.pl.	foundations	Atridae, -arum m.pl.	the Atreidae
loco, -are	I lay out	Priamus, -i m.	Priam
columna, -ae f.	column	ambo, -ae, -o	both
rupes, -is f.	rock	lacrimo, -are	I cry
excido, -ere	I quarry	Achates, -ae m.	Achates
scaena, -ae f.	stage	regio, -onis f.	460 region
decorus, -a, -um + dat.	fitting, beautiful	plenus, -a, -um	full
lucus, -i m.	450 sacred grove	en!	see, behold!
offero, -ferre, obtuli, -latus	I present	praemium, -i n.	reward
timor, -oris m.	fear	laus, laudis f.	praise
lenio, -ire	I calm	mens, mentis f.	mind
spero, -are	I hope, hope for	mortalis, -e	mortal
salus, -utis f.	safety	tango, -ere	I touch
audeo, -ere, ausus sum	I dare	aliqui, -qua, -quod	some
adfligo, -ere, -flixi, -flictus	I crush		

423–8: **pars . . . pars . . . alii . . . alii:** an example of *variatio* (variation of parallel expressions). **ducere:** historic infinitive (like the subsequent ones); here the meaning is 'build'. **concludere sulco:** probably digging not a foundation trench but a furrow to mark the boundary, reflecting the ancient Roman ritual of marking the boundary of a new city.
429 **scaenis decora alta futuris:** 'to be lofty embellishments for the stage yet to be built'. *decora* is neuter plural, here used in effect as a noun in apposition to *columnas*. In his description of the theatre, Virgil is extrapolating from the Roman empire of his day, where such theatres were common.

450 **hoc primum in luco:** note the way *primum* is <u>enclosed</u> by *hoc luco*, emphasising that Aeneas' change of outlook happened here first. **nova res oblata:** 'a strange sight that met him'. **timorem:** he was still afraid that the Carthaginians would not welcome him.
452 **ausus:** supply *est*. **adflictis rebus:** 'his crushed fortunes', i.e. his fortunes that until now had been against him.
453 **sub:** 'in the shadow of' or 'under the roof of' the temple; notice the misplaced *dum*, a common feature of poetry.
455 **manus inter se:** a difficult phrase here: perhaps 'various skills' or 'variety of craftsmanship'. **operumque laborem:** 'the hard work involved in their achievements'.
456 **ex ordine:** 'in sequence'.
458 **Atridas:** Agamemnon and Menelaus, the two sons of Atreus, were the leaders of the Greek expedition to Troy. **Priamum:** Priam was the king of Troy at the time of the Trojan War. **ambobus:** Achilles was 'fierce towards both' because, besides opposing the Trojans, he had a quarrel with Agamemnon and refused to fight.
459–60 **Achate:** Aeneas' loyal friend. **quis locus, quae regio:** supply *est*.
461 **en Priamus:** Aeneas points to a representation of Priam on the temple wall. **sunt . . . praemia laudi:** 'there are to glory its own rewards', i.e. 'glory has its proper rewards'.
462 One of the most famous lines from the *Aeneid*; 'there are tears for events and the sufferings of mortals touch the heart'; Aeneas means that the pictures of human suffering in the war draw sympathy from other humans.
463 **haec fama:** i.e. the fame of the Trojans, having reached Carthage, will ensure a Carthaginian welcome. **tibi:** the singular (referring to Achates) stands for all the Trojans.

Questions

1 In lines 423–424, there are examples of alliteration. What do you think is their effect?

2 In lines 427–429, what picture of the Carthaginians does Virgil present?

3 In lines 450–452, what effect did the sight of the temple have on Aeneas? Why was this?

4 How does Virgil emphasise this effect on Aeneas?

5 Explain the references to the Atreidae, Priam and Achilles.

6 In lines 459–463, how does Virgil effectively bring out the emotions of Aeneas?

On the temple walls were many scenes from the Trojan War.

haec dum Dardanio Aeneae miranda videntur,
dum stupet obtutuque haeret defixus in uno,   495
regina ad templum, forma pulcherrima Dido,
incessit magna iuvenum stipante caterva.
qualis in Eurotae ripis aut per iuga Cynthi
exercet Diana choros, quam mille secutae
hinc atque hinc glomerantur Oreades; illa pharetram   500
fert umero gradiensque deas supereminet omnes
(Latonae tacitum pertemptant gaudia pectus):
talis erat Dido, talem se laeta ferebat
per medios instans operi regnisque futuris.
tum foribus divae, media testudine templi,   505
saepta armis solioque alte subnixa resedit.

As Dido began to deal with the problems of her people, Aeneas saw a number of his
fellow-Trojans, whom he had thought lost in the storm, enter the temple. One of them
explained their presence and asked for help repairing the ships.

tum breviter Dido vultum demissa profatur: 561
'solvite corde metum, Teucri, secludite curas.
res dura et regni novitas me talia cogunt
moliri et late fines custode tueri.
quis genus Aeneadum, quis Troiae nesciat urbem,   565
virtutesque virosque aut tanti incendia belli?

Dardanius, -a, -um	Trojan	*Latona, -ae* f.		Latona
stupeo, -ere	495 I am spellbound	*tacitus, -a, -um*		silent
obtutu (no nom.)	in contemplation	*pertempto, -are*		I affect deeply
haereo, -ere	I concentrate,	*gaudium, -i* n.		joy
	cling	*foris, -is* f.	505	door
forma, -ae f.	beauty	*diva, -ae* f.		goddess
incedo, -ere, -cessi, cessus	I proceed	*testudo, -inis* f.		vault
iuvenis, -is m.	young person	*saepio, -ire, saepsi, saeptus*		I surround
stipo, -are	I accompany	*solium, -i* n.		throne
caterva, -ae f.	crowd	*subnixus, -a, -um*		propped up
qualis, -e	just like (when)	*resido, -ere, -sedi*		I sit down
Eurotas, -ae m.	the river Eurotas	*brevis, -e*	561	brief
ripa, -ae f.	bank	*demissus, -a, -um*		downcast
iugum, -i n.	mountain ridge	*profor, -fari, -fatus sum*		I speak out
Cynthus, -i m.	Cynthus	*cor, cordis* n.		heart, mind
exerceo, -ere	I supervise	*Teucri, -orum* m.pl.		Trojans
Diana, -ae f.	Diana	*secludo, -ere*		I banish
chorus, -i m.	band of dancers	*novitas, -atis* f.		newness
mille	a thousand	*cogo, -ere*		I compel
hinc atque hinc	500 on each side	*late*		far and wide
glomero, -are	I gather round	*custos, -odis* m.		guard
Oreas, -adis f.	Oread	*tueor, -eri, tutus sum*		I protect, watch
pharetra, -ae f.	quiver	*Aeneades, -um* m.pl.	565	Aeneas' family
umerus, -i m.	shoulder	*nescio, -ire*		I do not know
gradior, -i, gressus sum	I walk	*virtus, -utis* f.		courage, virtue
superemineo, -ere	I tower over	*incendium, -i* n.		fire, flame

494 **Dardanius:** the name comes from Dardanus, an ancestor of the royal family of Troy. It is an appropriate description of Aeneas here as he has been observing the scenes of the Trojan War. **haec . . . Aeneae miranda videntur:** generally taken as 'these marvels were observed by Aeneas' (with *Aeneae* dative of the agent), rather than the simpler 'these things seemed worthy of admiration to Aeneas'.

495 **obtutu . . . in uno:** lit. 'in one contemplation', i.e. 'in contemplation of a single object'.

496 Note the heavily spondaic rhythm used to increase the majesty of Dido's entrance.

498 **qualis:** a word regularly used by Virgil to introduce a simile. **Eurotae:** the Eurotas flowed through Sparta in Greece. **Cynthi:** Mt Cynthus was on the island of Delos, where Latona bore Diana and her brother Apollo.

499 **choros:** the simile is borrowed from Book 6 of the *Odyssey*, where Nausicaa dances among her maidens.

500–1 **Oreades; illa:** note the antithesis contrasting the 'background' characters (the mountain nymphs) with the central focus, Diana. **umero:** local ablative.

502 **tacitum pectus:** Latona, the mother of Diana, silently watches her daughter and rejoices at her majesty.

504 **instans:** 'urging on'. **operi regnisque futuris:** hendiadys: 'the work of her future realm'.

505 **foribus:** local ablative: 'by the doors'. **divae:** they are the doors 'of the goddess' because they give access to the *cella* or inner shrine, in which (in Classical times) the statue of the deity was kept. **media testudine:** local ablative again: 'beneath the central vault'; the *cella* was in the centre of the temple. In Virgil's day the Roman senate often met in such a temple *cella*; it is fitting, therefore, for Dido to be holding court there.

506 **armis:** i.e. by armed men. Notice the heavy alliteration of s (sometimes called sibilance) in this line, perhaps intended to emphasise the cessation of movement as Dido takes her seat.

561 **vultum demissa:** 'with her eyes downcast': see note on line 228 for the construction.

563–4 **res dura:** 'harsh fortune': she fears attack from both her brother and the neighbouring tribes. **talia . . . moliri:** 'to take such serious measures', i.e. drive strangers away from her land. **custode:** collective singular, standing for the plural.

565–6 **nesciat:** 'who could be unaware of': potential subjunctive. **incendia:** metaphorical.

Questions

1 In lines 494–495, how does Virgil show the strength of Aeneas' reaction to what he has seen?

2 In lines 496–497, how does Virgil make Dido's entrance impressive?

3 From the simile in lines 498–502, pick out and explain three ways in which the comparison with Diana is appropriate for Dido.

4 In line 506, identify one sound effect and suggest what effect it has.

5 In lines 561–562, suggest three ways in which Dido tries to set the Trojans' minds at rest.

6 In lines 563–564, what two things does Dido say her circumstances compel her to do?

non obtunsa adeo gestamus pectora Poeni,
nec tam aversus equos Tyria Sol iungit ab urbe.   568
vultis et his mecum pariter considere regnis?   572
urbem quam statuo, vestra est; subducite naves;
Tros Tyriusque mihi nullo discrimine agetur.
atque utinam rex ipse Noto compulsus eodem   575
adforet Aeneas! equidem per litora certos
dimittam et Libyae lustrare extrema iubebo,
si quibus eiectus silvis aut urbibus errat.'

Achates asked Aeneas whether they should reveal themselves.

vix ea fatus erat cum circumfusa repente   586
scindit se nubes et in aethera purgat apertum.
restitit Aeneas claraque in luce refulsit
os umerosque deo similis; namque ipsa decoram
caesariem nato genetrix lumenque iuventae   590
purpureum et laetos oculis adflarat honores:
quale manus addunt ebori decus, aut ubi flavo
argentum Pariusve lapis circumdatur auro.
tum sic reginam adloquitur cunctisque repente
improvisus ait: 'coram, quem quaeritis, adsum,   595
Troius Aeneas, Libycis ereptus ab undis.

obtunsus, -a, -um	unfeeling	*nubes, -is* f.	mist
adeo	so much, such	*purgo, -are*	I disperse
gesto, -are	I have	*aperio, -ire, -ui, -rtus*	I open
Poeni, -orum m.pl.	Carthaginians	*resto, -are, -stiti*	I stand
aversus, -a, -um	distant	*clarus, -a, -um*	bright
equus, -i m.	horse	*refulgeo, -ere, -fulsi*	I shine
Sol, Solis m.	the Sun god	*similis, -e* + dat.	similar (to)
iungo, -ere	I join, yoke	*caesaries*, acc. *-em* -f.	590 hair, locks
pariter	572 equally	*natus, -i* m.	son
consido, -ere	I settle	*genetrix, -icis* f.	mother
statuo, -ere	I establish	*iuventa, -ae* f.	youth
subduco, -ere	I beach	*purpureus, -a, -um*	radiant
discrimen, -inis n.	distinction	*adflo, -are*	I breathe upon
utinam!	575 if only!	*honos, -oris* m.	grace, beauty
compello, -ere, -puli, -pulsus	I drive	*ebur, -oris* n.	ivory
adsum, -esse	I am present	*decus, -oris* n.	grace
equidem	I for my part	*flavus, -a, -um*	yellow
certus, -a, -um	certain	*Parius, -a, -um*	Parian
dimitto, -ere	I send out	*lapis, -idis* m.	stone, marble
extrema, -orum n.pl.	furthest parts	*improvisus, -a, -um*	595 unexpected
eicio, -ere, -ieci, -iectus	I cast out	*aio* (defective verb)	I say
circumfusus, -a, -um	586 enveloping	*coram*	in person
repente	suddenly	*Troius, -a, -um*	Trojan
scindo, -ere	I part		

568 **equos . . . iungit:** the Sun god was believed to convey the sun across the sky in a chariot drawn by winged horses. Dido means that her new kingdom is not remote from civilisation. **Tyria . . . ab urbe:** 'from the Tyrian city', i.e. 'from Carthage'.

569 **his . . . regnis:** local ablative: 'in this kingdom'.

572 **et:** 'also'.

573 **urbem:** this more prosaically would be *urbs*, as subject of *est*. This attraction of the antecedent into the case of the relative draws particular attention to the city, of which Dido is proud.

574 **Tros Tyriusque:** note the similarity of sound, bringing them closer together. **mihi:** 'by me', dative of the agent.

575 **Noto . . . eodem:** i.e. by the same wind that has brought the other Trojans to her.

576–8 **adforet:** = adesset; the subjunctive expresses a wish. **certos:** 'reliable men'. **eiectus:** the subject is Aeneas. **silvis, urbibus:** local ablatives.

586–7 **circumfusa:** refers to *nubes*. **scindit:** indicative because it is the 'inverse *cum*' construction.

589 **os umerosque:** accusative of respect. **ipsa:** refers to *genetrix*.

590–1 **adflarat:** = *adflaverat*; his mother 'had breathed beautiful locks and the radiant light of youth upon her son and joyful grace upon his eyes'.

592–3 **quale . . . decus:** 'like the grace that . . .'. **manus:** i.e. the craftsman's hands. **flavo:** refers to *auro*; note how these words <u>enclose</u> the *argentum Pariusve lapis*, reflecting reality. **Parius lapis:** Paros was a major source of marble in the ancient world. The simile is adapted from Homer (*Odyssey* 6.232–4), where Athena enhances the grace of Odysseus in a similar way when he appears before Nausicaa.

594 **cunctis:** to be taken with *improvisus*: 'unexpected by all'.

Questions

1 In lines 565–566, how does Virgil make Dido's praise of the Trojans particularly effective?

2 In lines 569–576, how does Dido make the Trojans feel welcome?

3 In lines 588–591, suggest five ways in which Virgil makes Aeneas stand out.

4 How appropriate is the simile in lines 592–593?

5 In lines 594–595, which two Latin words emphasise the drama of Aeneas' appearance?

o sola infandos Troiae miserata labores,
quae nos, reliquias Danaum, terraeque marisque
omnibus exhaustos iam casibus, omnium egenos,
urbe, domo socias, grates persolvere dignas   600
non opis est nostrae, Dido, nec quidquid ubique est
gentis Dardaniae, magnum quae sparsa per orbem.'

*Aeneas praised Dido and greeted his fellow-Trojans. Dido welcomed Aeneas, who sent
Achates off to fetch his son.*

at Cytherea novas artes, nova pectore versat   657
consilia, ut faciem mutatus et ora Cupido
pro dulci Ascanio veniat, donisque furentem
incendat reginam atque ossibus implicet ignem.   660
ergo his aligerum dictis adfatur Amorem: 663
'nate, meae vires, mea magna potentia, solus,
nate, patris summi qui tela Typhoea temnis,   665
ad te confugio et supplex tua numina posco.
frater ut Aeneas pelago tuus omnia circum
litora iactetur odiis Iunonis acerbae,
nota tibi, et nostro doluisti saepe dolore.
nunc Phoenissa tenet Dido blandisque moratur   670
vocibus, et vereor quo se Iunonia vertant
hospitia: haud tanto cessabit cardine rerum.

solus, -a, -um	only, alone	adfor, -fari	I address
infandus, -a, -um	unspeakable	Amor, -oris m.	Cupid
miseror, -ari, -atus sum	I pity	vires, -ium f.pl.	strength
exhaurio, -ire, -si, -stus	I wear out	potentia, -ae f.	power
casus, -us m.	misfortune	Typhoeus, -a, -um	665 of, against
egenus, -a, -um	in want (of)		Typhoeus
socio, -are	600 I unite	temno, -ere	I scorn
grates (no gen.) f.	thanks	confugio, -ere	I appeal
persolvo, -ere	I give	supplex, -icis	humble, begging
dignus, -a, -um	worthy	numen, -inis n.	divine power
(ops), opis f.	power	posco, -ere	I ask for, beg
ubique	anywhere	frater, -ris m.	brother
spargo, -ere, -rsi, -rsus	I scatter	acerbus, -a, -um	harsh, bitter
ars, artis f.	657 scheme	doleo, -ere, -ui	I grieve
facies, -ei f.	appearance	dolor, -oris m.	grief
muto, -are, -avi, -atus	I change	Phoenissus, -a, -um	670 Phoenician
verso, -are	I consider	blandus, -a, -um	flattering,
Cupido, -inis m.	Cupid		charming
pro + abl.	instead of	moror, -ari	I delay, detain
dulcis, -e	sweet	vereor, -eri	I fear
furens, -ntis	frenzied	quo	to where
incendo, -ere	660 I inflame	Iunonius, -a, -um	of Juno
os, ossis n.	bone	hospitium, -i n.	hospitality
implico, -are	I instill	haud	not
ergo	therefore	cesso, -are	I am inactive
aliger, -gera, -gerum	winged	cardo, -inis m.	crucial moment
dictum, -i n.	word		

597 **o sola . . . miserata:** 'o you who alone have pitied'. **infandos . . . labores:** these are the 'sufferings' caused by the fall of Troy.

598 **quae nos:** the verb is *socias* (line 600): '(you) who unite us in city and home'.

599 **exhaustos:** agrees with *nos*; 'exhausted by all the misfortunes of land and sea'.

601 **non opis est nostrae:** 'it is not in our power'.

601–2 **nec quidquid . . . est gentis Dardaniae:** 'nor (in the power of) whatever is (left of) the Trojan race'. **sparsa:** supply *est*. Aeneas and his followers were not the only survivors from the sack of Troy to flee to other parts of the ancient world.

657–8 **novas artes, nova consilia:** an example of <u>tautology</u>.

658–9 **faciem . . . ora:** accusatives of respect, or treating *mutatus* as a Greek middle verb (see note on line 228). **pro . . . Ascanio:** 'in place of Ascanius'. Cupid was also a son of Venus.

659–60 **furentem:** proleptic, i.e. Cupid's activities will make Dido frenzied. Note the heavy <u>alliteration</u> of *i* in line 660, with the two words signifying fire at the beginning and end of the line, <u>enclosing</u> *reginam* and her *ossa*.

663 **aligerum . . . Amorem:** Cupid was traditionally depicted in Greek and Roman art as having wings.

664 **vires . . . potentia:** both vocative, in apposition to *nate*. **solus:** to be taken with *qui . . . temnis*; note the tangled word order.

665 **patris summi:** i.e. Jupiter. **tela Typhoea:** the 'Typhoean weapons' are the thunderbolts of Jupiter, which he used to kill the giant Typhoeus. The idea is that Cupid's arrows of love are more powerful than the thunderbolts of Jupiter, because no one, not even gods, can resist them.

666 **tua numina:** i.e. Venus begs Cupid to use his divine power to make people fall in love.

667–9 The order is *nota sunt* (more commonly *notum est*) *tibi ut* ('how') *frater Aeneas iactetur*. **frater . . . tuus:** Cupid is only the half-brother of Aeneas; his father was variously said to be Jupiter, Mars or Mercury. **odiis:** instrumental ablative. **nostro dolore:** 'grieved with my grief'; the word is repeated to emphasise the empathy between them.

670 **tenet, moratur:** supply *eum*.

671–2 **Iunonia hospitia:** Venus assumes that Juno, as patron goddess of Carthage, has inspired Dido to welcome Aeneas (in fact it was Jupiter). **quo se . . . vertant:** 'how it will turn out'.

Questions

1 What impression do you think Aeneas is trying to give Dido in lines 597–602?

2 What exactly are the nature and purpose of Venus' plan?

3 Based on this passage, give as full a description of Cupid as you can. Why do you think Venus turns to him for help?

4 In lines 664–665, why do you think Venus repeats *nate*?

5 How does Venus try to make her appeal to Cupid persuasive?

quocirca capere ante dolis et cingere flamma
reginam meditor, ne quo se numine mutet,
sed magno Aeneae mecum teneatur amore.   675
qua facere id possis nostram nunc accipe mentem:
regius accitu cari genitoris ad urbem
Sidoniam puer ire parat, mea maxima cura,
dona ferens pelago et flammis restantia Troiae;
hunc ego sopitum somno super alta Cythera   680
aut super Idalium sacrata sede recondam,
ne qua scire dolos mediusve occurrere possit.
tu faciem illius noctem non amplius unam
falle dolo et notos pueri puer indue vultus,
ut, cum te gremio accipiet laetissima Dido   685
regales inter mensas laticemque Lyaeum,
cum dabit amplexus atque oscula dulcia figet,
occultum inspires ignem fallasque veneno.'

Cupid gladly obeyed his mother and took the place of Ascanius. He arrived at the palace to find a banquet just beginning. The leading citizens of Carthage were all enchanted by the Trojans and the gifts they brought from the ships.

praecipue infelix, pesti devota futurae,   712
expleri mentem nequit ardescitque tuendo
Phoenissa, et pariter puero donisque movetur.

quocirca	and therefore	amplius	more
dolus, -i m.	trickery	fallo, -ere	I imitate, cheat
cingo, -ere	I surround	induo, -ere	I assume
flamma, -ae f.	flame, fire	gremium, -i n.	685 lap, bosom
meditor, -ari	I consider, plan	regalis, -e	royal
qua	676 how, in any way	mensa, -ae f.	table, feast
regius, -a, -um	royal, of the king	latex, -icis m.	liquid
accitu (abl. only)	at the summons	Lyaeus, -a, -um	of Bacchus
carus, -a, -um	dear	amplexus, -us m.	embrace
Sidonius, -a, -um	Sidonian	figo, -ere	I fix, plant
cura, -ae f.	love	occultus, -a, -um	hidden, secret
donum, -i n.	gift	inspiro, -are	I breathe into
resto, -are	I am left over	venenum, -i n.	poison, venom
sopio, -ire	680 I put to sleep	praecipue	712 especially
Cythera, -orum n.pl.	Cythera	infelix, -icis	unfortunate
Idalium, -i n.	Idalium	pestis, -is f.	disaster
sacratus, -a, -um	sacred, holy	devotus, -a, -um	doomed
recondo, -ere	I hide	futurus, -a, -um	future
scio, -ire	I know	nequeo, -ire	I cannot
occurro, -ere	I appear	ardesco, -ere	I am inflamed

673 **ante:** i.e. before Juno can intervene to turn Dido against Aeneas. **flamma:** i.e. the flame of love, though the metaphor is more commonly associated with a military attack upon a town. It should be noted that at the end of Book 4, Dido commits suicide upon a funeral pyre, and so the word here has an ominous undertone.

674 **ne quo se numine mutet:** 'so that she may not change her mind as a result of any divine interference'; she has Juno in mind, of course.

675 **Aeneae:** objective genitive: 'love for Aeneas'. **mecum:** 'on my side'. Notice how *magno . . . amore* surround the three persons (Aeneas, Venus and Dido), binding all of them together in a single fate: an example of enclosing word order.

677–8 **regius . . . puer:** i.e. 'prince (Ascanius)'. **urbem Sidoniam:** i.e. Carthage; Sidon (along with Tyre) was in the district of Phoenicia from where Dido set out to found Carthage. **mea maxima cura:** in apposition to *puer*.

679 **pelago et flammis:** ablatives: 'from the sea and the flames'.

680–1 **sopitum somno :** 'when he has been put to sleep'. **Cythera . . . Idalium:** both places were centres of the worship of Venus. The heavy alliteration of *s* in these lines could be said either to emphasise the idea of sleep, or to give a hissing sound to show the relish with which Venus reveals her plan. **sacrata sede:** local ablative.

682 **ne qua:** 'lest in any way'. **medius occurrere:** 'to intervene'.

683 **noctem non amplius unam:** 'for one night – not more'; or *quam* could be supplied.

684 **dolo:** 'by a trick', i.e. 'using trickery'. **puer:** 'you – a boy'. **pueri puer:** the polyptoton points out that Ascanius and Cupid share characteristics.

685 **gremio:** local ablative. **laetissima:** proleptic: she will be happy once the child is in her lap.

686 **laticem Lyaeum:** i.e. 'wine'.

687 Note the chiastic word order.

688 **occultum inspires ignem:** 'you may breathe hidden fire (of love) into her'. **fallas veneno:** 'you may cheat her with the poison (of love)'; i.e. he should poison her without her knowing. *Ignem* and *veneno* are strong metaphors for the destructive power of love; *ignis* also foreshadows Dido's suicide on the pyre in Book IV.

712 **infelix:** to be taken with Phoenissa, i.e. Dido; her unhappiness (proleptic, because it refers to the unhappiness to come), contrasts with the delight of the people described in the previous lines. **pesti . . . futurae:** Virgil again anticipates the suicide of Dido at the end of Book 4, after Aeneas has left her.

713 **expleri mentem nequit:** lit. 'cannot be satisfied with respect to her heart', i.e. 'cannot satisfy her heart'; see note on line 228. **ardescit tuendo:** 'she is inflamed (with passion) from looking at him'.

714 **Phoenissa:** note the suppression of the subject until this enjambement in the third line, where it also links to *pariter puero* through alliteration.

Questions

1 Why is Virgil's use of the word *flamma* effective (line 673)?

2 How and why does Virgil use sound effects in lines 680–681?

3 In line 684, what is the effect of placing *pueri puer* together?

4 In lines 685–688, how does Venus emphasise the closeness of the relationship that she expects to see between Dido and Ascanius?

5 In lines 712–714, how does Virgil show how far Dido is ensnared in Venus' plan?

ille ubi complexu Aeneae colloque pependit   715
et magnum falsi implevit genitoris amorem,
reginam petit. haec oculis, haec pectore toto
haeret et interdum gremio fovet inscia Dido
insidat quantus miserae deus. at memor ille
matris Acidaliae paulatim abolere Sychaeum   720
incipit et vivo temptat praevertere amore
iam pridem resides animos desuetaque corda.

As the banquet continued into the middle of the night, Dido asked Aeneas to tell the story of his adventures from the beginning.

complexus, -us m.	715 embrace	*incipio, -ere*	I begin
collum, -i m.	neck	*vivus, -a, -um*	living
pendeo, -ere, pependi	I hang	*tempto, -are*	I try
falsus, -a, -um	deceived	*praeverto, -ere*	I take possession
impleo, -ere, -evi, -etus	I satisfy		of first
interdum	at times	*iam pridem*	for a long time
inscius, -a, -um	unaware		now
insido, -ere + dat.	I possess, settle on	*reses, -idis*	inactive,
Acidalius, -a, -um	720 Acidalian		slumbering
paulatim	gradually	*desuetus, -a, -um*	unaccustomed
aboleo, -ere	I remove		

715 **ille . . . pependit:** lit. 'he hung from'; and so 'he clung to his embrace and neck'.

716 **implevit . . . amorem:** 'he satisfied the love'. **falsi . . . genitoris:** 'of his deceived father' (subjective genitive).

717 **petit:** the ending of the sentence at the end of the second foot places emphasis on the verb, almost suggesting attack.

718 **haeret:** 'she clings (to him)', i.e. 'she fixes her attention upon him'. **gremio:** local ablative. **Dido:** in apposition to *haec* ('she'); her name is postponed as a climax.

719 **insidat quantus miserae deus:** 'how great a god was possessing her, poor woman'.

719–20 **ille:** Cupid. **Acidaliae:** Acidalia was apparently the name of a spring in Greece where Venus used to bathe; Virgil is displaying his erudition. **abolere Sychaeum:** i.e. 'drive Sychaeus from her mind'; see line 343.

721 **praevertere:** the idea is to 'ensnare' her mind and heart before she realises what is happening. **vivo . . . amore:** i.e. as opposed to her 'dead' love for Sychaeus.

722 **resides . . . desueta:** there is little difference between these two adjectives, which together emphasise the fact that Dido is out of the habit of being in love.

Questions

1 What is unusual about the word order in line 716? What effect does this have?

2 In line 717, why does Virgil repeat the word *haec*?

3 Explain how, in the last four lines, Cupid ensnares Dido.

Book 2

Dido and her people fell silent. Aeneas was at first reluctant to speak of the horror of the fall of Troy. 'You are asking me to live through our terrible grief again,' he said.

'sed si tantus amor casus cognoscere nostros   10
et breviter Troiae supremum audire laborem,
quamquam animus meminisse horret luctuque refugit,
incipiam. fracti bello fatisque repulsi
ductores Danaum tot iam labentibus annis
instar montis equum divina Palladis arte   15
aedificant, sectaque intexunt abiete costas;
votum pro reditu simulant; ea fama vagatur.
huc delecta virum sortiti corpora furtim
includunt caeco lateri penitusque cavernas
ingentes uterumque armato milite complent.   20

During the night the Greeks left the wooden horse outside the walls of Troy and sailed away, hiding their ships on the far side of Tenedos, an island a few miles off the shore. Next morning the Trojans, seeing the Greek camp abandoned, thought their enemies had given up the war and gone home. There were various opinions about what to do with the horse.

tantus, -a, -um	10	such great	*divinus, -a, -um*	divine
amor, -oris m.		love	*Pallas, -adis* f.	Pallas (Athena)
casus, -us m.		misfortune	*ars, -tis* f.	art, skill
cognosco, -ere		I find out	*aedifico, -are*	I build
brevis, -e		brief	*seco, -are, -cui, -ctus*	I cut, saw
Troia, -ae f.		Troy	*intexo, -ere*	I interweave
supremus, -a, -um		last	*abies, -etis* f.	pine wood
labor, -oris m.		work, suffering	*costa, -ae* f.	rib
quamquam		although	*votum, -i* n.	votive offering
animus, -i m.		mind	*pro* + abl.	in return for
memini, -isse		I remember	*reditus, -us* m.	return
horreo, -ere		I shudder	*simulo, -are*	I pretend
luctus, -us m.		grief	*fama, -ae* f.	rumour, report
refugio, -ere		I recoil, wish to avoid	*vagor, -ari*	I circulate, spread
			huc	to this place, here
incipio, -ere		I begin	*deligo, -ere, -legi, -lectus*	I choose, select
frango, -ere, fregi, fractus		I break	*sortior, -iri, -itus sum*	I choose by lot
bellum, -i n.		war	*corpus, -oris* n.	body
fatum, -i n.		fate	*furtim*	secretly
repello, -ere, -ppuli, -pulsus		I drive back	*includo, -ere, -usi, -usus*	I enclose
ductor, -oris m.		leader	*caecus, -a, -um*	blind, dark
Danai, -(or)um m.pl.		the Greeks	*latus, -eris* n.	side, flank
tot		so many	*penitus*	deep within
labor, -i, lapsus sum		I slip by, pass	*caverna, -ae* f.	hollow, cavity
annus, -i m.		year	*uterus, -i* m.	20 womb, belly
instar + gen.	15	like	*armatus, -a, -um*	armed
mons, -tis m.		mountain	*miles, -itis* m.	soldier
equus, -i m.		horse	*compleo, -ere*	I fill

10 **sed si tantus amor:** supply *est vobis*: 'if you have . . .'. Note the weak <u>chiasmus</u> of *tantus amor casus nostros* and the jarring <u>antithesis</u> of *amor casus*.

10–11 These two lines are largely <u>spondaic</u> in rhythm, to reflect the reluctance of Aeneas to begin the tale.

12 **animus:** supply *meus*. **refugit:** perfect tense: 'has recoiled'.

13 **incipiam:** the <u>enjambement</u> followed by a strong pause marks the transition from conversation to narrative. The <u>spondaic</u> rhythm of this and the following three lines mark the horror of the events. **fracti . . . repulsi:** note the neatly balanced <u>chiasmus</u>.

14 **tot . . . annis:** the siege of Troy has lasted for ten years.

15 **instar montis:** by placing these words before *equum*, Virgil focuses attention on the size of the horse, which the following descriptions all exaggerate. **Pallade:** Athena was the goddess of war and crafts; she also supported the Greeks during the war, because the Trojan prince Paris had chosen Aphrodite rather than her as the most beautiful goddess in the contest for the golden apple.

16 **aedificant:** historic present. **secta . . . costas:** 'they interwove the ribs with sawn (planks of) pine'. Virgil uses a metaphor, partly from ship-building (where the planks forming the sides of a ship are attached to the vertical 'ribs'; and partly from weaving (where the warp and weft are interwoven).

17 **votum . . . simulant:** supply *equum esse*. **pro reditu:** the idea is that the Greeks built the horse as an offering to the gods in return for a safe journey home. Note the change to a more <u>dactylic</u> rhythm in this line, perhaps reflecting the speed with which the rumour spread. Virgil does not tell us how the rumour spread.

18 **delecta . . . corpora:** 'picked bodies of men' means little more than 'picked men', though the use of *corpora* may project the image of the bodies crammed into the horse. **virum:** = *virorum*.

19 **caeco lateri:** dative of goal of motion; singular for plural, as frequently in poetry; see *milite* below.

19–20 **penitusque cavernas ingentes:** these three words, together with the <u>enjambement</u> of *ingentes*, all exaggerate the size of the horse. **cavernas uterumque:** these two words may be translated as 'hollows of the belly': an example of <u>hendiadys</u>.

20 **uterum:** a <u>metaphor</u> from a living creature and childbirth. **milite:** singular for plural.

Questions

1 In lines 10–13, how does Aeneas show his reluctance to speak of the sack of Troy?

2 In lines 13–14, why do you think Aeneas focuses on the Greek leaders?

3 In the same lines, how does Aeneas emphasise the depth of the Greek leaders' feelings?

4 In line 15, why do you think Aeneas mentions Pallas?

5 From lines 16–20, identify two Latin words that might make Aeneas' audience think of the wooden horse as alive.

primus ibi ante omnes magna comitante caterva   40
Laocoon ardens summa decurrit ab arce,
et procul "o miseri, quae tanta insania, cives?
creditis avectos hostes? aut ulla putatis
dona carere dolis Danaum? sic notus Ulixes?
aut hoc inclusi ligno occultantur Achivi,   45
aut haec in nostros fabricata est machina muros,
inspectura domos venturaque desuper urbi,
aut aliquis latet error; equo ne credite, Teucri.
quidquid id est, timeo Danaos et dona ferentes."
sic fatus validis ingentem viribus hastam   50
in latus inque feri curvam compagibus alvum
contorsit. stetit illa tremens, uteroque recusso
insonuere cavae gemitumque dedere cavernae.
et, si fata deum, si mens non laeva fuisset,
impulerat ferro Argolicas foedare latebras,   55
Troiaque nunc staret, Priamique arx alta maneres.

A Greek soldier named Sinon was captured on the shore and brought to the city. He claimed to have been abandoned by the Greeks and to want revenge on them. He persuaded the Trojans that they should accept the horse as a gift to Athena and take it into the city. Then the goddess would give Troy her protection.

comitor, -ari	I accompany	error, -oris m.	deception
caterva, -ae f.	crowd	Teucri, -orum m.pl.	the Trojans
Laocoon, -ontis m.	Laocoon	quisquis, quidquid	whoever,
ardens, -ntis	furious		whatever
summus, -a, -um	the top of	timeo, -ere	I fear
decurro, -ere, -curri, -cursus	I run down	for, fari, fatus sum 50	I speak
arx, arcis f.	citadel	validus, -a, -um	strong, mighty
procul	from far off	vires, -ium f.pl.	strength
miser, -era, -erum	unfortunate	hasta, -ae f.	spear
insania, -ae f.	madness	ferus, -i m.	wild beast
civis, -is m.	citizen	curvus, -a, -um	curved
avehor, -i, -vectus sum	I sail away	compages, -is f.	jointed timber
hostis, -is m.	enemy	alvus, -i f.	belly
aut	either, or	contorqueo, -ere, -si, -sus	I hurl
ullus, -a, -um	any	sto, -are, steti, status	I stand, stick
puto, -are	I think	tremo, -ere	I quiver
donum, -i n.	gift	recutio, -ere, -cussi, -cussus	I shake
careo, -ere + abl.	I am without	insono, -ere, -ui, -itus	I resound
dolus, -i m.	trick, deceit	cavus, -a, -um	hollow
notus, -a, -um	known	gemitus, -us m.	groan
Ulixes, -is m.	Ulysses	mens, -ntis f.	mind, intention
lignum, -i n. 45	wood(work)	laevus, -a, -um 55	left,
occulto, -are	I conceal, hide		unfavourable
Achivi, -orum m.pl.	the Greeks	impello, -ere, -puli, -pulsus	I compel
fabrico, -are, -avi, -atus	I build	ferrum, -i n.	iron, sword
machina, -ae f.	engine of war	Argolicus, -a, -um	Greek
murus, -i m.	wall	foedo, -are	I despoil, smash
inspicio, -ere, -exi, -ectus	I spy on	latebra, -ae f.	hiding place
desuper	from above	Priamus, -i m.	Priam
aliquis, -quid	some	altus, -a, -um	high
lateo, -ere	I lie hidden	maneo, -ere	I remain

40–1 **primus . . . Laocoon**: note the heavy emphasis on *primus* and the delayed name, creating drama and suspense. **magna . . . caterva**: this ablative absolute serves to enhance the status of Laocoon. In Virgil's society, important men were generally escorted by large numbers of retainers. **Laocoon**: he was a son of king Priam and a priest of Apollo. **arce**: the citadel was the highest and most strongly fortified central part of an ancient city, usually the site of the king's palace and other important buildings.

42 **et procul**: supply *clamavit*. **quae . . . insania**: supply *est haec*.

43 **avectos**: supply *esse*. The omission of so many words in lines 42–3 perhaps reflects Laocoon's haste.

44 **dona . . . dolis Danaum**: note the heavy <u>alliteration</u>, giving strong emphasis to these words. **notus**: supply *est*. **Ulixes**: Ulysses or, to give him his Greek name, Odysseus, was famous for his cunning. Laocoon could not have known that Ulysses had had a hand in the building of the horse: his reputation was enough to convince him.

45 **hoc inclusi ligno**: note the way in which the word *inclusi* ('enclosed') is itself enclosed within the two words that refer to the horse: this <u>enclosing word order</u> is commonly used by Virgil to make the word order mimic the storyline. This line has a very slow rhythm (in sharp contrast with line 44, which is mainly <u>dactylic</u>), to add weight to Laocoon's warning.

46 This line, with its adjective 1 – adjective 2 – verb – noun 1 – noun 2 word order, is sometimes referred to as a 'golden line'. It is a form of <u>synchysis</u>, here enabling the two nouns to be alliterated with *m*, a sound often associated with high emotion.

47 Laocoon is suggesting that the horse was built so big to tower over the city walls, enabling men inside to spy on the city and even attack it from above, like a siege-tower.

49 **et dona ferentes**: 'even when bearing gifts'. The gift of course is the horse. This fast-moving line is one of the most famous lines in the *Aeneid*, spawning modern proverbial expressions.

50 Note the <u>synchysis</u> again: two adjectives followed by two nouns; the effect is to emphasise the power of Laocoon's throw.

51 **in latus inque . . . alvum**: this <u>tautology</u> heightens the drama of the spear throw.

52 **contorsit**: a powerful <u>enjambement</u>. **stetit**: the *t* sounds in this word and elsewhere in the line represent the quivering of the spear as it pierced the wood.

52–3 **utero . . . gemitum**: these two words make the horse seem alive.

53 **insonuere, dedere**: *-ere* is an alternative for *-erunt*. Note the <u>assonance</u> of *cavae . . . cavernae* and *-er*, adding their own contribution to the emphasis on sound in the line.

54 **deum**: = *deorum*. **si fata deum**: supply *non laeva fuissent*. The 'fates of the gods' (subjective genitive) suggests that it is the gods that determine fate. **fata . . . mens**: some editors supply *Troianorum* with *mens*, but most supply *deum*, which gives a better balance.

55 **impulerat**: the indicative in a past unfulfilled condition suggests that it very nearly happened; supply *nos* as object.

56 **arx . . . maneres**: *arx* is vocative; the use of the vocative and second person verb is an example of <u>apostrophe</u>, which lends vividness and pathos to Aeneas' words.

Questions

1 How does Virgil show the importance of Laocoon?

2 How close were the Trojans to thwarting the Greek plans?

3 Why do you think line 49 has become so famous?

4 How and why does Virgil make the spear throw so dramatic?

hic aliud maius miseris multoque tremendum
obicitur magis atque improvida pectora turbat.   200
Laocoon, ductus Neptuno sorte sacerdos,
sollemnes taurum ingentem mactabat ad aras.
ecce autem gemini a Tenedo tranquilla per alta
(horresco referens) immensis orbibus angues
incumbunt pelago pariterque ad litora tendunt;   205
pectora quorum inter fluctus arrecta iubaeque
sanguineae superant undas, pars cetera pontum
pone legit sinuatque immensa volumine terga.
fit sonitus spumante salo; iamque arva tenebant
ardentesque oculos suffecti sanguine et igni   210
sibila lambebant linguis vibrantibus ora.
diffugimus visu exsangues. illi agmine certo
Laocoonta petunt; et primum parva duorum
corpora natorum serpens amplexus uterque
implicat et miseros morsu depascitur artus;   215

hic	at this point	*ceterus, -a, -um*	the rest of
tremendus, -a, -um	terrifying	*pontus, -i* m.	sea
obicio, -ere	200 I thrust upon	*pone*	behind
magis	more	*lego, -ere*	I pass through
improvidus, -a, -um	unprepared	*sinuo, -are*	I bend
pectus, -oris n.	heart, breast	*volumen, -inis* n.	coil
turbo, -are	I trouble, confuse	*tergum, -i* n.	back
duco, -ere, duxi, ductus	I draw, choose, emit	*fio, fieri*	I am made
		sonitus, -us m.	noise
Neptunus, -i m.	Neptune	*spumo, -are*	I foam
sors, -tis f.	lot, fate	*salum, -i* n.	sea
sacerdos, -otis m.	priest	*arvum, -i* n.	field
sollemnis, -e	customary	*teneo, -ere*	I hold, reach
taurus, -i m.	bull	*ardens, -ntis*	210 blazing, furious
macto, -are	I sacrifice	*oculus, -i* m.	eye
ara, -ae f.	altar	*suffectus, -a, -um*	tinged
ecce	see, behold	*sanguis, -inis* m.	blood
geminus, -a, -um	twin	*ignis, -is* m.	fire
tranquillus, -a, -um	calm	*sibilus, -a, -um*	hissing
alta, -orum n.pl.	the depths	*lambo, -ere*	I lick
horresco, -ere	I start to shudder	*lingua, -ae* f.	tongue
refero, -ferre	I relate	*vibro, -are*	I flicker
immensus, -a, -um	immense	*os, oris* n.	mouth, face
orbis, -is m.	coil, circle	*diffugio, -ere*	I scatter
anguis, -is m./f.	snake, serpent	*visus, -us* m.	sight
incumbo, -ere + dat.	205 I lean upon	*exsanguis, -e*	bloodless, pale
pelagus, -i n.	sea	*agmen, -inis* n.	line, course
pariter	together	*certus, -a, -um*	fixed, unwavering
litus, -oris n.	shore	*natus, -i* m.	son
tendo, -ere	I go	*serpens, -ntis* m./f.	snake, serpent
fluctus, -us m.	wave	*amplector, -i, -plexus sum*	I entwine, embrace
arrectus, -a, -um	raised up		
iuba, -ae f.	crest	*uterque, -traque, -trumque*	each
sanguineus, -a, -um	blood-coloured	*implico, -are*	215 I clasp, embrace
supero, -are	I rise above, mount	*morsus, -us* m.	bite
		depascor, -i	I devour
unda, -ae f.	wave	*artus, -us* m.	limb
pars, -tis f.	part		

199–200 hic: i.e. just as the episode with Sinon came to an end. Note the powerful
<u>alliteration</u> of *m* in this line, showing high emotion (cf. line 46). The order for translation
is *hic aliud, maius multoque magis tremendum, obicitur (nobis) miseris*. The jumbled word
order reflects Aeneas' horror at the recollection.

201 Neptuno . . . sacerdos: Laocoon was traditionally a priest of Apollo. Here he has taken on
the priesthood of Neptune, perhaps because Neptune had helped repair the walls of Troy; the
death of his priest would then foreshadow the destruction of the walls.

201–2 sorte sacerdos sollemnes: the <u>sibilance</u> foreshadows the hissing of the serpents, which
are not actually mentioned until the end of line 204. **sollemnes . . . aras:** note how these
two words bracket the whole line, emphasising that the sacrifice was following the correct
ritual. The word order is <u>chiastic</u>, with the two accusatives plural on the outside and the two
accusatives singular on the inside. The line is, apart from the fifth foot, entirely spondaic,
emphasising the solemnity of the occasion.

203–4 gemini . . . angues: note the huge separation of these two elements of the subject; the
effect is to build suspense rising to a great climax. **a Tenedo:** Tenedos was an island just off the
coast of Troy; the Greek fleet was hiding out of sight of Troy behind this island, in order to
make the Trojans think they had gone home. The appearance of the serpents from the direction
of Tenedos foreshadows the return of the Greek fleet from there.

203–5 Note the sequence: two (things), coming from Tenedos, cross the sea, and make for
the shore – serpents! The word order reflects the reality, with the certain identification only
possible once the creatures are close to the shore.

205 incumbunt pelago: the serpents 'lean upon the sea', i.e. their breasts appear to lean into
the sea as they swim.

206 pectora . . . iubaeque: again the two elements of the subject (of *superant*) bracket the line,
emphasising both words. The crests give the serpents the appearance of dragons.

205–8 Note the <u>sibilance</u> and frequent <u>alliteration</u> of *p*, adding striking sound effects to the
vivid visual images.

207 pars cetera: i.e. the rest of the bodies and tails. **volumine:** 'into a coil'.

209 fit sonitus spumante salo: the <u>sibilance</u> suggests the hissing of the sea, churned up by the
fast passage of the serpents. Note the variety of words Virgil uses for the sea in the space of
a few lines.

210 oculos suffecti: this is one of Virgil's favourite constructions for describing people and
occasionally animals, in which the participle agrees with the person rather than the part
of the body. **oculos:** accusative of respect. The serpents were literally 'suffused as to their
blazing eyes with blood and fire', i.e. 'their blazing eyes were suffused with blood and fire'.

211 lambebant linguis: the <u>alliteration</u> of *l* reflects the licking action. Note how, the closer
the serpents get, the greater the detail observed.

212 visu: ablative of separation: 'from the sight'. **agmine certo:** ablative of manner.

213–15 The sequence is *uterque serpens, amplexus parva corpora duorum natorum, implicat.*
The <u>synchysis</u> of *parva . . . natorum* suggests the intertwining of the serpents. **miseros morsu:**
alliteration of *m* again to reflect the horror. **morsu:** ablative of instrument.

Questions

1 How does Virgil make good use of sound effects in these lines?

2 How does Virgil emphasise the size of the serpents?

3 Many have described these lines as forming one of the most dramatic episodes in the
Aeneid. How far do you agree with this? How does Virgil increase the drama?

post ipsum auxilio subeuntem ac tela ferentem
corripiunt spirisque ligant ingentibus; et iam
bis medium amplexi, bis collo squamea circum
terga dati superant capite et cervicibus altis.
ille simul manibus tendit divellere nodos   220
perfusus sanie vittas atroque veneno,
clamores simul horrendos ad sidera tollit:
qualis mugitus, fugit cum saucius aram
taurus et incertam excussit cervice securim.
at gemini lapsu delubra ad summa dracones   225
effugiunt saevaeque petunt Tritonidis arcem,
sub pedibusque deae clipeique sub orbe teguntur.
tum vero tremefacta novus per pectora cunctis
insinuat pavor, et scelus expendisse merentem
Laocoonta ferunt, sacrum qui cuspide robur   230
laeserit et tergo sceleratam intorserit hastam.
ducendum ad sedes simulacrum orandaque divae
numina conclamant.

auxilium, -i n.	help	*securis, -is* f.	axe
subeo, -ire	I go up, occur	*lapsus, -us* m.	225 gliding
telum, -i n.	weapon	*delubrum, -i* n.	temple, shrine
corripio, -ere	I seize	*draco, -onis* m.	serpent
spira, -ae f.	coil	*effugio, -ere*	I escape
ligo, -are	I bind	*saevus, -a, -um*	cruel
bis	twice	*Tritonis, -idis* f.	Athena
collum, -i n.	neck	*pes, pedis* m.	foot
squameus, -a, -um	scaly	*clipeus, -i* m.	shield
circumdo, -dare, -dedi, -datus	I put . . . round	*tego, -ere*	I cover, hide
caput, -itis n.	head	*tremefacio, -ere, -feci, -factus*	I make to tremble
cervix, -icis f.	neck	*cunctus, -a, -um*	all
simul	220 at the same time	*insinuo, -are*	I steal (into)
tendo, -ere	I struggle	*pavor, -oris* m.	fear
divello, -ere	I tear apart	*scelus, -eris* n.	crime
nodus, -i m.	knot	*expendo, -ere, -pendi, -pensus*	I pay for
perfundo, -ere, -fudi, -fusus	I soak	*mereo, -ere*	I deserve
sanies, -ei f.	gore	*fero, ferre*	230 I say
vitta, -ae f.	headband	*sacer, -ra, -rum*	sacred
ater, -tra, -trum	black, dark	*cuspis, -idis* f.	spear-point
venenum, -i n.	venom	*robur, -oris* n.	oak, timber
clamor, -oris m.	shout, scream	*laedo, -ere, -si, -sus*	I damage
horrendus, -a, -um	dreadful	*sceleratus, -a, -um*	wicked, impious
sidus, -eris n.	star	*intorqueo, -ere, -si,-tus*	I hurl . . . at
tollo, -ere, sustuli, sublatus	I raise	*sedes, -is* f.	seat, sanctuary
qualis, -e	just like	*simulacrum, -i* n.	image, ghost
mugitus, -us m.	bellowing	*oro, -are*	I beg
fugio, -ere	I flee	*diva, -ae* f.	goddess
saucius, -a, -um	wounded	*numen, -inis* n.	will, good will
incertus, -a, um	badly aimed	*conclamo, -are*	I shout
excutio, -ere, -cussi, -cussus	I shake out		

216–17 **post:** adverb: 'then'. **auxilio:** dative of purpose: 'to help them'. **et iam:** the pause before the sixth foot and the two monosyllables ending the line point forward to the death of Laocoon.
218 **medium:** 'his middle' or 'his waist'. **bis . . . bis:** the <u>anaphora</u> emphasises the thoroughness of the serpents' attacks. 'Twice' refers either to the two serpents, or to each one coiling twice round Laocoon's body.
218–19 **circum . . . dati:** this is written as two words as a result of *tmesis* or 'cutting', a poetical device to allow flexibility in the use of compound verbs. This is also an example of the Greek middle construction, where the past participle is given an active meaning: 'having put their backs round'. **collo:** dative dependent on the compound verb: 'round his neck'. **capite et cervicibus:** probably ablative of instrument.
220–2 **simul . . . simul:** <u>anaphora</u> to stress the speed of the attack: 'while . . . at the same time'. **perfusus . . . vittas:** this is exactly parallel to *oculos suffecti* in line 210. *Vittas* is accusative of respect. **vittas:** used in the plural to mean one headband; the *vitta* symbolised the priesthood.
223 **qualis mugitus:** *qualis* is regularly used by Virgil to introduce a <u>simile</u>, the function of which is to imply Laocoon's death; note also the irony: Laocoon was engaged in sacrificing a bull when the serpents attacked; now he is the sacrificial victim, like the bull. *Mugitus* is an <u>onomatopeic</u> word, with the *u* sounds echoed in the later words in the line, creating an <u>assonance</u> that strongly conveys the distress of Laocoon. **fugit cum:** the metre shows that *fugit* is perfect; *cum* is relegated to second word in its clause; translate 'when . . . has fled'. This line is entirely spondaic (apart from the fifth foot), prolonging the agony.
224 Note the preponderance of hard *c* sounds in this line, perhaps representing the repeated blows of the axe.
225 **at:** a strong conjunction regularly used to mark a transition to a new episode; here it closes the description of the death of Laocoon. **lapsu:** ablative of manner: 'by gliding'. **delubra ad summa:** = *ad summa delubra*; they are *summa* because they are on the top of the citadel.
226 **saevae . . . Tritonidis arcem:** Athena is called *saevae* because of her hostility to the Trojans (only now do the Trojans realise that it must have been Athena who sent the serpents to kill Laocoon). The citadel is described as being Athena's because her shrine was prominent on it.
227 Statues of Athena in the Greco-Roman period traditionally showed her as a warrior goddess, helmeted and with a round shield resting on its edge on the ground. Sometimes serpents were added to the base of the statue.
228–9 The order is *tum vero novus pavor insinuat per tremefacta pectora cunctis.* The interlocking adjectives and nouns are an example of <u>synchysis</u>. **cunctis:** although a dative (of disadvantage), it can be translated as if genitive. **novus pavor:** the Trojans have suddenly realised that Athena could easily extend her punishment of Laocoon to include them all.
231 The order is *qui laeserit sacrum robur cuspide.* Note the subjunctive after *qui*: 'because he damaged'. **tergo:** dative of goal of motion; since we were told earlier that Laocoon hurled his spear into the belly or side of the horse, we have to imagine that *tergum* is used loosely of any part of the framework of the horse.
232–3 **simulacrum:** i.e. the horse. **ducendum . . . oranda:** supply *esse* to complete the indirect statement. **sedes:** supply *divae*. **numina:** plural for singular; usually 'divine will', here 'good will'. Note the short line, one of many in the *Aeneid*: Virgil died before revising the work.

Questions

1 In lines 216–219, how does Virgil emphasise the power of the serpents?

2 How does the simile in lines 223–224 help the reader to visualise Laocoon's suffering?

3 What are the consequences of the manner in which the serpents disappear?

dividimus muros et moenia pandimus urbis.
accingunt omnes operi pedibusque rotarum   235
subiciunt lapsus, et stuppea vincula collo
intendunt: scandit fatalis machina muros
feta armis. pueri circum innuptaeque puellae
sacra canunt funemque manu contingere gaudent;
illa subit mediaeque minans inlabitur urbi.   240
o patria, o divum domus Ilium et incluta bello
moenia Dardanidum! quater ipso in limine portae
substitit atque utero sonitum quater arma dedere;
instamus tamen immemores caecique furore
et monstrum infelix sacrata sistimus arce.   245
tunc etiam fatis aperit Cassandra futuris
ora dei iussu non umquam credita Teucris.
nos delubra deum miseri, quibus ultimus esset
ille dies, festa velamus fronde per urbem.

During the night, while the Trojans slept, the Greek fleet sailed back to Troy from the island. On receiving a signal from the flagship, Sinon released the bolt on the trapdoor in the belly of the wooden horse, and the Greek soldiers hidden inside dropped to the ground, ready to kill the guards and open the gates of the city.

divido, -ere	I break through	inlabor, -i + dat.	I glide into
moenia, -um n.pl.	walls, buildings	patria, -ae f.	fatherland
pando, -ere	I open up, expose	divus, -i m.	god
accingo, -ere	235 I make myself ready	Ilium, -i n.	Ilium, Troy
opus, -eris n.	task	inclutus, -a, -um	famous
rota, -ae f.	wheel	quater	four times
subicio, -ere	I place . . . under	limen, -inis n.	threshold
lapsus, -us m.	gliding	subsisto, -ere, -stiti	I stop
stuppeus, -a, -um	made of hemp	insto, -are	I press on
vinculum, -i n.	chain, rope	immemor, -is	regardless
intendo, -ere	I stretch taut	furor, -oris m.	frenzy, madness
scando, -ere	I climb over	monstrum, -i n.	245 monster, omen
fatalis, -e	deadly	infelix, -icis	unfortunate
fetus, -a, -um	pregnant, full	sacratus, -a, -um	holy
arma, -orum n.pl.	arms	sisto, -ere	I set, place
circum	around	tunc	then
innuptus, -a, -um	unmarried	aperio, ire	I open
sacer, -cra, -crum	sacred	Cassandra, -ae f.	Cassandra
cano, -ere	I sing	futurus, -a, -um	future
funis, -is m.	rope	iussus, -us m.	order, command
contingo, -ere	I touch	umquam	ever
gaudeo, -ere	I rejoice	ultimus, -a, -um	last, final
subeo, -ire	240 I come up	festus, -a, -um	festive, joyful
minor, -ari	I threaten	velo, -are	I cover
		frons, -ndis f.	garland, foliage

234 dividimus . . . pandimus: note the <u>chiasmus</u>. The horse was too tall to pass through the gate and so the Trojans had to enlarge the opening by demolishing the upper part of the wall where it ran above the gate. **moenia:** strictly 'city-walls', this often means the buildings enclosed within the walls. The fast rhythm reflects the speed with which the Trojans set to work.

235–6 pedibus: *subicio* takes an accusative (*lapsus*) and a dative (*pedibus*). **rotarum lapsus:** a poetic phrase meaning 'rollers'.

237 intendunt: note the <u>enjambement</u>; this verb also takes an accusative (*vincula*) and a dative (*collo*). **collo:** 'round its neck'. Note the extremely slow rhythm of this line, which reflects the struggle the Trojans had to move the horse; it perhaps also underscores the ominous nature of the activity (*fatalis*). **scandit . . . muros:** the horse does not literally 'climb over the walls', because it passes through the gap the Trojans have made; rather it 'passes beyond the walls'. **machina muros:** an echo of Laocoon's warning in line 46.

238 feta armis: 'pregnant with arms': another <u>metaphor</u> from childbirth (cf. line 20); the <u>enjambement</u> gives the image greater menace. Note the slow rhythm again. **pueri . . . puellae:** the innocence and gaiety of the children contrast harshly with the menace of the horse.

239 sacra: 'sacred hymns'. **contingunt:** they touch the rope for good luck, a poignant image. Note the <u>assonance</u> of *u*, along with repeated *n* sounds, perhaps indicative of the singing.

240 minans inlabitur: Virgil's <u>enclosing word order</u> places the gliding threat inside *mediae . . . urbi*, as it was in reality; <u>alliteration</u> of *m*, and *n* in line 239, adds emotion to the words. Note the fast rhythm of the line, emphasising the inexorable progress of the horse up the slopes of the citadel.

241–2 Aeneas uses an <u>ascending tricolon</u> of appeals to his homeland to give expression to his intense grief as he recalls the harrowing events; these appeals are examples of <u>apostrophe</u>. **divum:** an alternative form of the genitive plural.

242–3 quater . . . substitit: stumbling on the threshold was for the Romans an omen of bad luck (which is why brides were carried over the threshold); here it happened four times; each time the weapons inside the horse clattered against the sides, but the Trojans, confident of their decision, ignored the warning. Note the fast rhythm of the two lines, especially line 243; this seems at odds with the the horse stopping, but it shows the determination of the Trojans to continue.

244 Note the repeated *m* sounds again. **furore:** ablative of cause: their ecstasy made them blind.

245 The very slow rhythm marks the eventual coming to rest of the 'monster'. **sacrata sistimus arce:** Virgil's <u>enclosing word order</u> brings the horse to a stop in the middle of the sacred citadel, word order matching reality. Note the <u>antithesis</u> of *infelix sacrata*.

246 Cassandra: a daughter of King Priam, she was given the gift of prophecy by Apollo, but when she rejected his advances, he decreed that no one should ever believe her true prophecies. **fatis . . . futuris:** probably datives of purpose, lit. 'for the fates to be'.

247 dei: i.e. Apollo. **Teucris:** dative of the agent after the perfect passive.

248 deum: an alternative form of the genitive plural. **esset:** subjunctive in a relative clause to express either a concessive idea: 'although that day was'; or a causal idea: 'we, wretched because that day was'. **festa . . . fronde:** the ironic image of joyful celebration continues.

Questions

1 Describe in your own words the scene as the horse is moved inside the city.

2 Virgil begins lines 235, 236 and 237 with verbs ending in *-unt*. Why do you think he did this?

3 In lines 237–240, what contrast does Aeneas make? List the words that show this contrast.

4 How close were the Trojans to discovering the secret of the horse? What stopped them?

5 How does Virgil use sound effects in this section?

tempus erat quo prima quies mortalibus aegris
incipit et dono divum gratissima serpit.
in somnis, ecce, ante oculos maestissimus Hector   270
visus adesse mihi largosque effundere fletus,
raptatus bigis ut quondam, aterque cruento
pulvere perque pedes traiectus lora tumentes.
ei mihi, qualis erat, quantum mutatus ab illo
Hectore qui redit exuvias indutus Achilli   275
vel Danaum Phrygios iaculatus puppibus ignes!
squalentem barbam et concretos sanguine crines
vulneraque illa gerens, quae circum plurima muros
accepit patrios. ultro flens ipse videbar
compellare virum et maestas expromere voces: 280
"o lux Dardaniae, spes o fidissima Teucrum,
quae tantae tenuere morae? quibus Hector ab oris
exspectate venis? ut te post multa tuorum
funera, post varios hominumque urbisque labores
defessi aspicimus! quae causa indigna serenos   285
foedavit vultus? aut cur haec vulnera cerno?"

quies, -etis f.	rest, quiet	*Phrygius, -a, -um*	Phrygian, Trojan
mortalis, -is m.	human being	*iaculor, -ari, -atus sum*	I hurl
aeger, -gra, -grum	sick, weary	*puppis, -is* f.	stern, ship
incipio, -ere	I begin	*squaleo, -ere*	I am stiff, rough
donum, -i n.	gift	*barba, -ae* f.	beard
gratus, -a, -um	pleasing, welcome	*concretus, -a, -um*	matted together
serpo, -ere	I creep	*crinis, -is* m.	hair
somnus, -i m.	270 sleep	*gero, -ere*	I bear
ecce	see, look	*patrius, -a, -um*	of his country, of
maestus, -a, -um	sad		a father
Hector, -oris m.	Hector	*ultro*	spontaneously
adsum, -esse	I am present	*fleo, flere*	I weep
largus, -a, -um	abundant	*compello, -are*	280 I address
effundo, -ere	I pour out	*expromo, -ere*	I utter
fletus, -us m.	weeping, tears	*lux, lucis* f.	light
rapto, -are, -avi, -atus	I drag violently	*Dardania, -ae* f.	Troy
bigae, -arum f.pl.	a two-horse	*spes, spei* f.	hope
	chariot	*fidus, -a, -um*	trustworthy
quondam	once, formerly	*mora, -ae* f.	delay
cruentus, -a, -um	blood-stained	*ora, -ae* f.	shore
pulvis, -eris m.	dust	*ut!*	how!
traicio, -ere, -ieci, -iecus	I pierce	*funus, -eris* n.	death
lorum, -i n.	thong	*varius, -a, -um*	various
tumeo, -ere	I swell	*aspicio, -ere*	285 I look at, see
ei! + dat.	alas!	*causa, -ae* f.	cause, reason
muto, -are, -avi, -atus	I change	*indignus, -a, -um*	undeserved
exuviae, -arum f.pl.	275 spoils	*serenus, -a, -um*	calm
induo, -ere, -ui, -utus	I clothe	*cerno, -ere*	I see
Achilles, -i m.	Achilles		

268–9 There are many *m* and *s* sounds in these and the following lines, echoing sleep.
269 After the first foot, this is a very slow line, reflecting the drowsiness of the Trojans. **dono divum:** 'as a gift of the gods'; *dono* is probably a dative of purpose; *divum = divorum.* **serpit:** a verb often associated with serpents; here add 'over them' to complete the sense.
270 **in somnis:** either plural for singular ('in my sleep') or 'in my dreams'. This is the first time in Aeneas' account that he mentions himself. This is therefore a crucial point in the story, when he begins the momentous task of saving the gods and survivors of Troy and finding a new home for them. This first appearance is one of confusion, because he has happily gone to bed convinced that the Greeks have abandoned the war and gone home. It takes the ghost of Hector to bring him back to reality. The description of the dream is full of psychological interest, because Aeneas' questions and comments show just the sort of confusion that is associated with dreams. **Hector:** son of King Priam and, until his death at the hands of Achilles, the greatest warrior in the Trojan army. **maestissimus:** he is 'very sad' either because of the manner of his death, or (more likely) because of the terrible news he has to deliver to Aeneas.
271 **visus:** supply *est.* **mihi:** either 'seemed to me to be present' or 'seemed to be at my side'. **largos effundere fletus:** note how the 'abundant tears' <u>enclose</u> the verb, reflecting the reality.
272 **raptatus bigis:** after killing Hector in single combat, Achilles had fastened his heels with leather thongs to his chariot and dragged the body three times round the walls of Troy. **ut quondam:** 'as he once was', i.e. as did happen to him on one occasion.
273 **pulvere perque pedes:** heavy alliteration to reflect strong emotion. **perque pedes . . . tumentes:** note how the swollen feet <u>enclose</u> the thongs: the word order again matches the reality. **traiectus lora:** an unusual adverbial use of the accusative; translate 'his feet pierced with thongs'. **tumentes:** poetic licence, as feet do not swell after death.
274 **qualis erat:** 'what he was like', i.e. 'how he looked'.
275 **redit:** an unusual historic present, because this is not normal historic narrative; perhaps in his dream Aeneas imagines Hector continuing to return from battle as he had done so many times. **exuvias indutus Achilli:** *indutus* is used like a Greek middle verb, with an active sense: 'having put on'; in Homer's *Iliad* (Book 17), Achilles' best friend, Patroclus, borrowed his armour and was killed by Hector, who stripped the armour off the body and wore it himself.
276 **Danaum Phrygios:** a forceful <u>antithesis</u>. *Danaum* is genitive plural. **iaculatus:** the Trojans frequently tried to set fire to the Greek ships drawn up along the beach. Note the fast rhythm.
277 Note the very slow rhythm, reflecting the horror of the description.
278–9 **quae . . . plurima . . . accepit:** 'which he received in great number'. **ultro:** this word indicates that Aeneas took the initiative in addressing the ghost.
280 **voces:** 'words', as often in poetry.
281–2 **Teucrum:** genitive plural. **tenuere:** = *tenuerunt.* **morae:** Aeneas relates his dream as if it were not a dream at all, and that he was addressing a living Hector, who had been mysteriously absent. **quibus . . . ab oris:** his irrational mind gropes for an explanation of Hector's absence.
282–3 **Hector . . . exspectate:** both vocative. **ut:** introduces an exclamation: 'how gladly!'; take with *aspicimus.*
284 **labores:** 'troubles' rather than 'tasks'.
285–6 **quae causa . . . vulnera:** the waking Aeneas of course knows perfectly well what befell Hector. Note the slow rhythm of these two lines, drawing out the confusion.

Questions

1 In lines 268–271, how do Aeneas' words establish a peaceful setting for the dream?

2 How do Aeneas' confused words to Hector contrast with his description of the ghost?

3 How does Virgil bring out the pathos of this episode?

ille nihil, nec me quaerentem vana moratur,
sed graviter gemitus imo de pectore ducens,
"heu fuge, nate dea, teque his' ait 'eripe flammis.
hostis habet muros; ruit alto a culmine Troia.   290
sat patriae Priamoque datum: si Pergama dextra
defendi possent, etiam hac defensa fuissent.
sacra suosque tibi commendat Troia penates;
hos cape fatorum comites, his moenia quaere
magna pererrato statues quae denique ponto."   295
sic ait et manibus vittas Vestamque potentem
aeternumque adytis effert penetralibus ignem.
diverso interea miscentur moenia luctu,
et magis atque magis, quamquam secreta parentis
Anchisae domus arboribusque obtecta recessit,   300
clarescunt sonitus armorumque ingruit horror.
excutior somno et summi fastigia tecti
ascensu supero atque arrectis auribus asto:
in segetem veluti cum flamma furentibus Austris
incidit, aut rapidus montano flumine torrens   305
sternit agros, sternit sata laeta boumque labores
praecipitesque trahit silvas; stupet inscius alto
accipiens sonitum saxi de vertice pastor.

vanus, -a, -um	pointless, vain	*Anchises, -ae* m.	300 Anchises
moror, -ari	I delay, take	*arbor, -oris* f.	tree
	notice of	*obtego, -ere, -exi, -ectus*	I conceal
imus, -a, -um	the bottom of	*recedo, -ere, -ssi, -ssus*	I stand back
heu	alas	*claresco, -ere*	I become audible
ait	he says	*ingruo, -ere*	I rush towards
eripio, -ere	I snatch away	*horror, -oris* m.	horror, terror
flamma, -ae f.	flame	*excutio, -ere*	I shake out, rouse
ruo, -ere	290 I fall down, rush	*fastigium, -i* n.	roof-top
culmen, -inis n.	top, summit	*tectum, -i* n.	roof, house
sat	enough	*ascensus, -us* m.	climbing
Pergama, -orum n.pl.	the citadel of Troy	*arrigo, -ere, -exi, -ctus*	I lift, raise
dextra, -ae f.	right hand	*auris, -is* f.	ear
defendo, -ere	I defend	*asto, -are*	I stand
sacrum, -i n.	sacred object	*seges, -etis* f.	cornfield, corn
commendo, -are	I entrust		crop
penates, -ium m.pl.	Penates,	*veluti*	just like, just as
	household gods	*furo, -ere*	I rage
comes, -itis m.	295 companion	*Auster, -tri* m.	South Wind
pererro, -are, -avi, -atus	I wander across	*incido, -ere*	305 I fall upon
statuo, -ere	I establish, build	*rapidus, -a, -um*	swift
denique	at last	*montanus, -a, -um*	of a mountain
Vesta, -ae f.	Vesta	*torrens, -entis* m.	torrent
potens, -ntis	powerful	*sterno, -ere*	I flatten
aeternus, -a, -um	everlasting	*sata, -orum* n.pl.	crops
adytum, -i n.	shrine	*bos, bovis* m.	ox
penetralis, -e	innermost	*praeceps, -ipitis*	headlong
diversus, -a, -um	various	*stupeo, -ere*	I am dazed
misceo, -ere	I throw into	*inscius, -a, -um*	unaware
	confusion	*saxum, -i* n.	rock
secretus, -a, -um	set apart, isolated	*vertex, -icis* m.	top, head
parens, -ntis m./f.	parent	*pastor, -oris* m.	shepherd

287 **ille nihil:** supply *respondit*: he offered no reply to Aeneas' questions.

289 **nate dea:** lit. 'o one born from a goddess', and so 'son of a goddess'. **heu . . . dea:** note the fast rhythm of these words. **his . . . flammis:** the ghost gestures to the flames.

290 **alto a culmine:** lit. 'from the high summit (of the city)', i.e. 'from its highest point'.

291 **datum:** supply *est a te*. **Pergama:** here the citadel stands for the whole city of Troy. See synecdoche. **dextra:** 'by a (right) hand', i.e. by the sword-hand, and so 'by deeds of valour'.

292 **hac:** supply *dextra*: 'by this right hand (of mine)'. **fuissent:** a stronger alternative to *essent* in a past unfulfilled condition; what he is implying is that if he himself could not defend Troy successfully, no one else could, because he was the greatest warrior. Note the sibilance.

293 **sacra:** the sacred vessels, images and equipment that were sacred to the cult of the city's gods (detailed in line 296 below). **suos . . . penates:** although usually the tutelary gods of individual families, here they represent the spiritual essence of the city; they took tangible form as statuettes. If they were lost, Troy could not be resurrected in a new home. Romans believed that these very Penates were brought over to Italy by Aeneas. Note how *sacra* and *penates* enclose *tibi*, reflecting the fact that Aeneas is now burdened with them (see enclosing word order).

294 **comites:** 'as companions'. **hos . . . his:** polyptoton for rhetorical effect. **his:** probably dative.

295 **quae:** bring forward: *quae, pererrato ponto, denique statues*. This is the first inkling Aeneas has of his role following the destruction of Troy: to found a new Troy overseas.

296 **vittas Vestamque:** these, together with the *ignis*, are the *sacra* mentioned in line 293; Vesta was the goddess of the hearth, home and fire, and so her cult was parallel to that of the Penates; here it is the image of Vesta that is brought from her shrine; the headband either adorns the image, or it is the one worn by her priest and so sacred to her.

297 **aeternum . . . ignem:** in Virgil's time the sacred flame was kept permanently alight in Vesta's temple, symbolic of the continuity and survival of Rome; here he suggests it was originally brought from Troy to Rome to forge the continuity from one city to the other. Note the chiastic order, with the two accusatives framing the two ablatives. **effert:** we are to imagine that the ghost leaves Aeneas to fetch the *sacra*.

298 **interea:** this marks the transition from the dream to waking reality.

299–300 **parentis Anchisae domus:** clearly Aeneas had been sleeping in his father's house. Aeneas emphasises the house's seclusion, to explain why he had not been woken earlier.

301 **ingruit:** supply *nobis*.

302 **summi fastigia tecti:** 'the summit of the top of the roof', i.e. 'the highest point of the roof'.

303 Note the very strong assonance and alliteration of *a*, expressing Aeneas' heightened emotion. **arrectis auribus:** 'with ears pricked'.

304 **veluti cum:** 'just as when' introduces an extended simile. Note the strongly dactylic rhythm of this and the other lines of the simile, to emphasise the speed of the destruction.

306 **sternit . . . sternit:** the anaphora emphasises the destruction. **laeta:** here 'joy-giving'. **boum labores:** the hard work of the oxen in drawing the plough to prepare the ground for sowing.

307 **inscius:** he is 'unaware' of the cause of the ruin, as he has never seen its like before.

308 **sonitum:** i.e. the noise of the wind and fire or the torrent. Perhaps Aeneas imagines they happen during the night, when the shepherd would be more aware of the sound than the sight.

Questions

1 How does Hector's ghost make his message to Aeneas urgent and persuasive?

2 Why were the *sacra* (line 293) so important to Hector and Aeneas?

3 What use does Virgil make of sound effects in lines 298–301?

4 The simile (lines 304–308) is reckoned to be one of Virgil's finest. What makes it so good?

Then indeed the trickery of the Greeks became clear. Nearby houses were on fire. Out of my mind, I grabbed my armour and rushed down into the street, where I learned from a priest who was trying to escape how Sinon and the wooden horse had brought about the downfall of Troy. I soon joined up with some comrades and we attacked and killed a party of marauding Greeks. On impulse we donned their armour, hoping to deceive other bands of Greeks. After some success, an attempt to rescue Cassandra, who was being led away to captivity, saw us outnumbered, and most of my comrades were killed. I and a couple of others got away and made for Priam's palace, which was now the focus of the Greek attack. Using a back entrance, I climbed on to the roof and helped some defenders to send a wooden tower crashing down on the Greeks below, who were trying to break down the main door.

vestibulum ante ipsum primoque in limine Pyrrhus	
exsultat telis et luce coruscus aëna;	470
qualis ubi in lucem coluber mala gramina pastus,	
frigida sub terra tumidum quem bruma tegebat,	
nunc, positis novus exuviis nitidusque iuventa,	
lubrica convolvit sublato pectore terga	
arduus ad solem, et linguis micat ore trisulcis.	475
ipse inter primos correpta dura bipenni	479
limina perrumpit postesque a cardine vellit	480
aeratos; iamque excisa trabe firma cavavit	
robora et ingentem lato dedit ore fenestram.	
apparet domus intus et atria longa patescunt;	
apparent Priami et veterum penetralia regum,	
armatosque vident stantes in limine primo.	485
at domus interior gemitu miseroque tumultu	
miscetur, penitusque cavae plangoribus aedes	
femineis ululant; ferit aurea sidera clamor.	

vestibulum, -i n.	entrance hall	*cardo, -inis* m.	hinge
Pyrrhus, -i m.	Pyrrhus	*vello, -ere*	I tear
exsulto, -are	470 I prance, swagger	*aeratus, -a, -um*	bronze-plated
coruscus, -a, -um	gleaming	*excido, -ere, -cidi, -cisus*	I cut out, cut down
aënus, -a, -um	(made of) bronze		
coluber, -bri m.	snake	*trabs, -bis* f.	beam, panel
gramen, -inis n.	grass	*firmus, -a, -um*	strong
pascor, -i, pastus sum	I feed upon	*cavo, -are, -avi, -atus*	I pierce
frigidus, -a, -um	cold	*fenestra, -ae* f.	window
tumidus, -a, -um	swollen	*appareo -ere*	I become visible
bruma, -ae f.	winter	*intus*	inside, within
exuviae, -arum f.pl.	old skin	*atrium, -i* n.	hall
nitidus, -a, -um	shining, bright	*patesco, -ere*	I am opened up
iuventa, -ae f.	youthfulness	*vetus, -eris*	old
lubricus, -a, -um	smooth, slippery	*penetralia, -ium* n.pl.	inner rooms
convolvo, -ere	I roll up, coil up	*interior, -oris*	486 inner, inside of
arduus, -a, -um	475 high up	*tumultus, -us* m.	uproar, agitation
sol, solis m.	sun	*plangor, -oris* m.	wailing
mico, -are	I flash	*aedes, -is* f.	house, room
trisulcus, -a, -um	three-forked	*femineus, -a, -um*	of women
corripio, -ere	I seize	*ululo, -are*	I howl
bipennis, -is f.	two-edged axe	*ferio, -ire*	I strike
perrumpo, -ere	480 I break through	*aureus, -a, -um*	golden
postis, -is m.	door, post, pillar		

469 **vestibulum:** Virgil imagines the palace entrance door to be set back from the front wall in a recess, and calls the space so created a *vestibulum*; **primo . . . limine:** 'on the outer threshold', i.e. the outer part of the *vestibulum*: Pyrrhus moves from the street over the threshold and into the entrance hall, and then attacks the door itself. **Pyrrhus:** the son of the late Achilles.

470 **telis et luce . . . aëna:** both nouns are dependent on *coruscus*; *telis et luce* are an example of <u>hendiadys</u>, and may be translated as 'with weapons of flashing bronze'; Virgil has inverted the natural expression to give 'bronze light'.

471 **qualis ubi:** these words introduce another extended <u>simile</u>, in which Pyrrhus is compared with a snake, with similar emphasis on light (note the promoted position of *in lucem*, which belongs with *convolvit.*) **mala gramina:** Virgil is alluding to a belief that snakes had to eat poisonous plants in order to acquire venom. He implies that Pyrrhus was equally venomous.

472 **tumidum:** the idea is that, during hibernation underground, the snake swells until it casts its old skin. Note the scansion, which shows that *frigida* agrees with the subject, *bruma*.

473 Note the very fast rhythm, which reflects the renewed activity of the rejuvenated snake. **positis . . . exuviis:** 'after casting off its old skin'. The parallel is perhaps with the notion that Pyrrhus emerged from the shadow of his father after the latter's death, inheriting his reputation as a ferocious and pitiless fighter. **iuventa:** causal ablative.

474 **terga:** plural for singular.

475 **ad solem:** like all reptiles, the snake needs the warmth of the sun to give it energy. **linguis micat ore trisulcis:** lit. 'from its mouth it flashes with three-furrowed tongue', i.e. 'its forked tongue flashes from its mouth'. **trisulcis:** an exaggerated description of a snake's tongue.

479 The very slow rhythm marks the return to the narrative. **dura:** the scansion shows that this agrees with *limina*, not *bipenni*, despite its position; the bronze plating makes the doors hard.

480 **limina:** here used loosely to mean 'doors'. **postes:** these are the stout posts that formed the vertical edges of the double doors, strengthened with bronze because, projecting at top and bottom, where they fitted into sockets, they served as hinges.

481 **excisa trabe:** the *trabs* is probably the cross-beam that ran from side to side of the door, giving it strength; with this cut out, the thinner but still strong oak panel (*firma robora*) could be easily smashed through, to create a 'window'.

482 **lato . . . ore:** 'with wide mouth' and so 'gaping'.

483 A <u>chiasmus</u> is used together with <u>tautology</u> to emphasise the exposure of the palace interior. This is reinforced by the repetition of *apparent* in the next line, introducing a further tautology. The three parallel ideas form an <u>ascending tricolon</u>, an effective rhetorical device.

485 **armatos vident:** 'they' must be the Trojans inside the palace; the *armatos* are the Greeks.

486 The very fast rhythm reflects the panic of the Trojans when they see the Greeks.

487 **miscetur:** a favourite word of Virgil's, used to indicate confusion; here it is given emphasis by <u>enjambement</u>, and it adds its initial letter to the succession of *m* sounds in the previous line.

488 **ululant:** it is the women who 'howl', but Virgil turns the image upside down, making the 'hollow (and so echoing) rooms' howl. **aurea sidera:** the stars are described as 'golden' to emphasise their brightness, contrasting with the gloom and horror inside the palace.

Questions

1 How appropriate is the simile in lines 471–475?

2 What impression of Pyrrhus does the simile give?

3 What are the stages in Pyrrhus' attack on the palace?

4 In lines 483–488, how does Virgil bring out the horror of the people inside the palace?

tum pavidae tectis matres ingentibus errant
amplexaeque tenent postes atque oscula figunt.   490
instat vi patria Pyrrhus; nec claustra nec ipsi
custodes sufferre valent; labat ariete crebro
ianua, et emoti procumbunt cardine postes.
fit via vi; rumpunt aditus primosque trucidant
immissi Danai et late loca milite complent.   495
non sic, aggeribus ruptis cum spumeus amnis
exiit oppositasque evicit gurgite moles,
fertur in arva furens cumulo camposque per omnes
cum stabulis armenta trahit. vidi ipse furentem
caede Neoptolemum geminosque in limine Atridas,   500
vidi Hecubam centumque nurus Priamumque per aras
sanguine foedantem quos ipse sacraverat ignes.
quinquaginta illi thalami, spes ampla nepotum,
barbarico postes auro spoliisque superbi
procubuere; tenent Danai qua deficit ignis.   505

You may ask what happened to King Priam. When he realised the enemy were inside the palace, he armed himself and set off to defend his family, old though he was. His wife called him back and they sought refuge at a sacred altar in the middle of the palace.

pavidus, -a, -um	frightened	gurges, -itis m.	raging water
erro, -are	I wander, stray	moles, -is f.	massive work
osculum, -i n.	490 kiss	furens, -ntis	raging
figo, ere	I plant (a kiss)	cumulus, -i m.	mass
claustrum, -i n.	the bolt of a door	campus, -i m.	plain, field
custos, -odis m.	guard	stabulum, -i n.	stall
suffero, -ferre	I withstand	armentum, -i n.	herd
valeo, -ere	I am strong enough	caedes, -is f.	500 slaughter
labo, -are	I totter	Neoptolemus, -i m.	Neoptolemus, Pyrrhus
aries, -etis f.	battering ram	Atridae, -arum m.pl.	sons of Atreus
creber, -bra, -brum	frequent	Hecuba, -ae f.	Hecuba
emoveo, -ere, -movi, -motus	I pull out	nurus, -us f.	daughter-in-law
procumbo, -ere	I fall forward	sacro, -are	I consecrate
rumpo, -ere	I force, burst through	quinquaginta	fifty
aditus, -us m.	entrance	thalamus, -i m.	bed-chamber
trucido, -are	I slaughter	amplus, -a, -um	plentiful, great
late	495 far and wide	nepos, -otis m.	grandson, descendant
compleo, -ere	I fill	barbaricus, -a, -um	foreign
agger, -is m.	bank, embankment	aurum, -i n.	gold
		spolia, -orum n.pl.	spoils
spumeus, -a, -um	foaming	superbus, -a, -um	505 proud
amnis, -is m.	river	procumbo, -ere, -cubui, -itus	I fall in ruin
oppono, -ere, -sui, -situs	I place against	qua	where
evinco, -ere, -vici, -victus	I overwhelm	deficio, -ere	I am absent

489 matres: i.e. the mothers of Priam's grandchildren; this word evokes more pathos than *mulieres*. **tectis . . . ingentibus:** ablative of place; note the <u>enclosing word order</u>: the huge building encloses the mothers.

490 amplexae: probably 'having embraced the pillars' rather than 'each other'. **postes:** here probably 'pillars' rather than doorposts. **oscula figunt:** probably 'kissed the pillars (goodbye)' rather than 'each other'. This line is full of ambiguities.

491 instat: the promoted position emphasises the force and speed of Pyrrhus' attack. **vi patria:** 'with the violence of his father'. **claustra:** these were strong wooden bars that were held in place across the door, secured to both doorposts, preventing the door from being pushed open.

492 ariete crebro: ablative of cause: 'because of the frequent blows of the battering ram'. What is not clear is why a battering ram should be necessary at this late stage, when Pyrrhus had already broken through the doors.

493 procumbunt . . . postes: Pyrrhus appeared to achieve this already, in line 480. Perhaps this repetition is evidence that the *Aeneid* as we have it is Virgil's first draft, unrevised at his death.

494 rumpunt aditus: 'they burst through the entrance'. **primos:** supply 'men'.

495 immissi: probably a 'middle' use of the passive: 'having sent themselves in' and so 'charging in'. **milite:** a collective singular: 'with (a troop of) soldiers'.

496 non sic . . . cum: an abbreviated way of introducing a <u>simile</u>: lit. 'not so when' and so 'it is less destructive when'.

497 exiit: 'has overflowed'. **oppositas moles:** perhaps 'the embankments built to stop the river flooding'; some interpret *moles* to be the same as *aggeribus*, making the phrase redundant.

498 cumulo: 'in a mass', i.e. 'in a flood' (ablative of manner).

499 trahit: 'sweeps away'. **furentem:** parallels *furens* in the simile.

500 caede: take with *furentem*: 'revelling in the slaughter'. **Neoptolemum:** another name for Pyrrhus. **geminos . . . Atridas:** 'the twin (i.e. two) sons of Atreus' were Agamemnon, the commander of the Greeks, and Menelaus, the husband of the abducted Helen.

501 Hecubam: the wife of Priam. **centum nurus:** Priam and Hecuba had fifty sons and fifty daughters; here therefore *nurus* comprises both the daughters and daughters-in-law.

502 sanguine foedantem: Aeneas refers briefly to the slaying of Priam, before describing the events leading up to it. **quos ipse sacraverat ignes:** 'the fires which he himself had consecrated': fires were kept on the altars of the city's gods; Priam would have been high priest of these cults. The spilling of human blood on these altars was a sacrilege. See line 297 and note.

504 barbarico . . . auro spoliisque: <u>hendiadys</u>: 'with foreign spoils of gold'.

505 procubuere: an alternative for *procubuerunt*; note the <u>enjambement</u>, which provides a neat contrast with the promoted *tenent*; the switch of tenses is important: the ruin of the palace is complete, while the occupation of the surviving parts is ongoing.

Questions

1 In lines 489–490, how does Virgil emphasise the desperate situation of the women?

2 In lines 491–495, what are the stages in the Greek conquest of the palace?

3 How does Virgil emphasise the speed of the Greek conquest?

4 The simile in lines 496–499 is used to emphasise the thoroughness of the destruction of the palace. How successful is the simile in achieving this?

5 In lines 500–501, Virgil mentions four names. Why do you think he does this?

6 In lines 501–505, how does Virgil show the extent of the destruction of the royal family?

ecce autem elapsus Pyrrhi de caede Polites,   526
unus natorum Priami, per tela, per hostes
porticibus longis fugit et vacua atria lustrat
saucius. illum ardens infesto vulnere Pyrrhus
insequitur, iam iamque manu tenet et premit hasta.   530
ut tandem ante oculos evasit et ora parentum,
concidit ac multo vitam cum sanguine fudit.
hic Priamus, quamquam in media iam morte tenetur,
non tamen abstinuit nec voci iraeque pepercit:
"at tibi pro scelere," exclamat, "pro talibus ausis   535
di, si qua est caelo pietas quae talia curet,
persolvant grates dignas et praemia reddant
debita, qui nati coram me cernere letum
fecisti et patrios foedasti funere vultus.
at non ille, satum quo te mentiris, Achilles   540
talis in hoste fuit Priamo; sed iura fidemque
supplicis erubuit corpusque exsangue sepulcro
reddidit Hectoreum meque in mea regna remisit."
sic fatus senior telumque imbelle sine ictu
coniecit, rauco quod protinus aere repulsum,   545
et summo clipei nequiquam umbone pependit.
cui Pyrrhus: "referes ergo haec et nuntius ibis
Pelidae genitori. illi mea tristia facta
degeneremque Neoptolemum narrare memento.

elabor, -i, elapsus sum	I escape	*cerno, -ere*	I see, observe
Polites, -ae m.	Polites	*letum, -i* n.	death
porticus, -us f.	colonnade	*satus, -a, -um* + abl.	540 descended from
vacuus, -a, -um	empty	*mentior, -iri*	I lie, say falsely
lustro, -are	I pass through	*ius, iuris* n.	right
infestus, -a, -um	hostile	*erubesco, -ere, -rubui*	I respect
insequor, -i	530 I follow	*sepulcrum, -i* n.	tomb
premo, -ere	I press, threaten	*Hectoreus, -a, -um*	of Hector
evado, -ere, -vasi	I emerge	*regnum, -i* n.	kingdom
concido, -ere, -cidi	I collapse	*remitto, -ere, -misi, -missus*	I send back
fundo, -ere, fudi, fusus	I pour, pour out	*senior, -oris* m.	old man
abstineo, -ere, -ui, -entus	I refrain, hold back	*imbellis, -e*	harmless
ira, -ae f.	anger	*ictus, -us* m.	545 blow, strike
parco, -ere, peperci + dat.	I spare	*conicio, -ere, -ieci, -iectus*	I throw
pro + abl.	535 in return for, for	*raucus, -a, -um*	clanging
talis, -e	such	*protinus*	immediately
ausum, -i n.	daring attempt	*aes, aeris* n.	bronze
qui, qua, quod (after *si*)	any	*repello, -ere, -ppuli, -pulsus*	I repel, parry
caelum, -i n.	sky, heaven	*clipeus, -i* m.	shield
pietas, -atis f.	righteousness	*nequiquam*	in vain
curo, -are	I take care of	*umbo, -onis* m.	boss
persolvo, -ere	I give (thanks)	*pendeo, -ere, pependi*	I hang
grates f.pl.	thanks	*refero, -ferre*	I relate
dignus, -a, -um	worthy, suitable	*nuntius, -i* m.	messenger
praemium, -i n.	reward, recompense	*Pelides, -ae* m.	son of Peleus
reddo, -ere	I give back	*genitor, -oris* m.	father
debeo, -ere, -ui, -itus	I owe	*degener, -eris*	disgraceful
coram	with (my) own eyes	*memini, -isse*	I remember

526 Note the very slow rhythm, as Aeneas turns to a new and heart-breaking episode.
elapsus: the 'escape' was only temporary. **Pyrrhi:** subjective genitive: 'killing by Pyrrhus'.
528 Now the rhythm is fast to reflect the flight of Polites through the palace. **porticibus longis:** ablative of the route taken, akin to a local ablative.
529 **saucius:** the <u>enjambement</u> gives dramatic weight to this adjective. **infesto vulnere:** 'with hostile wound' may be rendered as 'threatening a hostile wound' (his weapon is ever poised to strike).
530 **iam iamque:** the doubling of this word is commonly used to indicate how close an action is to fulfilment: 'he is on the point of holding', etc. **manu tenet et premit hasta:** a perfect <u>chiasmus</u>, with the short parallel phrases emphasising how close Polites is to death.
531 **ut:** 'when'.
532 **multo:** with *sanguine*. **vitam fudit:** we have to imagine that Pyrrhus finally caught up with Polites and delivered the fatal blow, just as he reached his parents.
533 **hic:** 'at this point' or simply 'then'. **in media iam morte tenetur:** 'he was held in the very midst of death', i.e. his death was imminent.
534 **voci iraeque:** <u>hendiadys</u> for 'angry voice' and so 'angry words'.
535–8 The basic order is *at di persolvant tibi grates dignas, et reddant praemia debita*; the subjunctives express wishes, like prayers; **at tibi:** *at* is often used to introduce a curse, with the object of the curse immediately following. **grates:** sarcastic. **quae talia curet:** generic subjunctive: 'of the sort that may take care of such things'. **praemia debita:** also sarcastic: the 'rewards' he has in mind are death and punishment in the underworld. Note the very slow rhythm of line 537.
538 **qui:** the antecedent is *tibi*. **coram:** adverbial rather than prepositional, governing *me*, since the pronoun is required as the object of *fecisti* (here meaning 'made' in the sense of 'forced').
539 Note the heavy <u>alliteration</u> of *f*, expressing outrage. **foedasti:** = foedavisti. **patrios:** 'of a father' because he was forced to observe the death of his son.
540 **at:** introducing a strong contrast between Pyrrhus and his father, Achilles. **ille:** has the force of 'the famous'. **satum:** supply *esse*. **quo:** 'from whom' (ablative of origin). **mentiris:** 'you falsely claim' because Pyrrhus lacks his father's qualities.
541 **talis:** 'like you are'.
541–3 After Achilles killed Hector, Priam visited him at night to beg for the return of Hector's body; Achilles pitied the old king, gave him food and sent him safely back to Troy with the body (Homer, *Iliad* 24). **sepulcro:** 'for burial'.
544 **fatus:** supply *est*. **sine ictu:** 'without striking (him)'.
545 **repulsum:** supply *est*; the spear was parried by Pyrrhus' bronze shield and the tip just pierced and hung from the edge of the leather that coated the central boss of the shield.
547 **cui Pyrrhus:** supply *dixit*. **referes . . . ibis:** the future tenses are equivalent to imperatives. **haec:** 'this message' (i.e. what Priam has just said). **nuntius:** 'as messenger'.
548–9 **tristia . . . degenerem:** an ironic refence to Priam's accusations in lines 540ff. Supply *esse* with *degenerem*. **memento:** imperative; note the sarcastic tone.

Questions

1 In lines 526–530, how does Virgil bring out the pathos of Polites' flight?

2 In lines 533–534, what shows Priam's determination and courage?

3 How does Virgil make Priam's speech full of bitterness?

4 In lines 547–549, what is the tone of Pyrrhus' reply? How is this shown?

nunc morere." hoc dicens altaria ad ipsa trementem   550
traxit et in multo lapsantem sanguine nati,
implicuitque comam laeva, dextraque coruscum
extulit ac lateri capulo tenus abdidit ensem.
haec finis Priami fatorum, hic exitus illum
sorte tulit Troiam incensam et prolapsa videntem   555
Pergama, tot quondam populis terrisque superbum
regnatorem Asiae. iacet ingens litore truncus,
avulsum umeris caput et sine nomine corpus.
at me tum primum saevus circumstetit horror.
obstipui; subiit cari genitoris imago,   560
ut regem aequaevum crudeli vulnere vidi
vitam exhalantem; subiit deserta Creusa
et direpta domus et parvi casus Iuli.

*As I began to make my way to my house, I caught sight of Helen trying to hide from both
Greeks and Trojans. My first thought was to kill her because it was because of her that Troy
was now in ruins. But my mother appeared before me in all her glory and stayed my hand.
She allowed me to see the gods working to tear the city apart, and made me realise that there
was nothing left for me but to escape with my family. When I reached my home, my father
refused all my pleas to depart with us: he had decided to stay and await his fate. I had just
made up my mind to ignore my mother's advice and return to the battle. Creusa appealed to
me to stay to defend the family.*

talia vociferans gemitu tectum omne replebat,   679
cum subitum dictuque oritur mirabile monstrum.   680
namque manus inter maestorumque ora parentum
ecce levis summo de vertice visus Iuli
fundere lumen apex, tactuque innoxia molles
lambere flamma comas et circum tempora pasci.

morior, -i, mortuus sum	I die	*carus, -a, -um*	560 dear
altaria, -ium n.pl.	550 altar	*imago, -inis* f.	image, picture
lapso, -are	I slip	*aequaevus, -a, -um*	of similar age
coma, -ae f.	hair	*exhalo, -are*	I breathe out
laeva, -ae f.	left hand	*desero, -ere, -ui, -tus*	I abandon
capulus, -i m.	hilt	*Creusa, -ae* f.	Creusa
tenus + abl.	as far as	*diripio, -ere, -ui, -reptus*	I plunder, ransack
abdo, -ere, -didi, -ditus	I plunge	*casus, -us* m.	misfortune, fate
ensis, -is m.	sword	*Iulus, -i* m.	Iulus
finis, -is m./f.	end	*vociferor, -ari, -atus sum*	I shout
exitus, -us m.	death	*repleo, -ere, -evi, -etus*	I fill
incendo, -ere, -di, -sus	555 I burn	*subitus, -a, -um*	680 sudden
prolabor, -i, -lapsus sum	I fall in ruin	*orior, -iri, ortus sum*	I arise, appear
populus, -i m.	people, race	*mirabilis, -e*	wonderful
regnator, -oris m.	ruler	*namque*	for
Asia, -ae f.	Asia (i.e. Asia Minor)	*levis, -e*	light
		lumen, -inis n.	light
truncus, -i m.	trunk, body	*apex, -icis* m.	top, point of flame
avello, -ere, -vulsi, vulsus	I tear off		
umerus, -i m.	shoulder	*tactus, -us* m.	touch
circumsto, -are, -steti	I take possession of	*innoxius, -a, -um*	harmless
		mollis, -e	soft
obstipesco, -ere, -stipui	I am stupefied	*tempus, -oris* n.	temple

550 **morere:** imperative. **trementem:** supply *eum* (i.e. Priam); it is his age that makes him tremble.

551 **in multo . . . nati:** a poignant and graphic detail.

552–3 **implicuit . . . extulit:** a perfect chiasmus: verb – object – ablative; ablative – object – verb. **coruscum:** agrees with *ensem*; the separation of the adjective from its noun, together with its position at the end of the line, gives it particular force, emphasising the light reflected off the sword as the blade swings through the air (note also the fully dactylic rhythm of the line, emphasising the speed with which Pyrrhus moves). **lateri:** dative of goal of motion, poetic for *in latus*. **capulo tenus:** *tenus* always follows its noun. The enjambement of *extulit* and the enclosing of *capulo tenus* inside *lateri abdidit*, reflecting the action, add to the poetical intensity of this line.

554 **haec:** supply *erat*. Note the slow rhythm of the line, to underline the solemnity.

555 **sorte tulit:** 'befell him by fate'. **videntem:** a key word, given extra importance by its position at the end of the line; the episode is made so much more poignant by the fact that he was looking upon the destruction of his city as he died.

556–7 **tot populis terrisque:** ablative of cause dependent on *superbum*: 'proud with so many peoples and lands'. **regnatorem:** probably in apposition to *illum* rather than *Pergama*; either way, Aeneas reminds his audience that Troy had been the major power in Asia Minor, making its downfall a greater contrast.

557–8 **iacet:** Virgil uses the present tense perhaps for two reasons: firstly it suggests that Aeneas is reliving the horror of the moment as he retells it; secondly it reminds Virgil's contemporaries of the death of Pompey the Great, who, fleeing from Julius Caesar, was murdered and beheaded as he stepped ashore in Egypt. Note the heavy assonance of *u* in this sentence, indicating the grief Aeneas feels; this continues through lines 559 and 560.

559 **circumstetit horror:** Aeneas depicts the horror as an external force that seized hold of him. Note the heavy spondaic rhythm to match his dazed state.

560 **genitoris:** i.e. Anchises.

561–2 **ut:** 'when', followed by the indicative. Note the spondaic rhythm again. **vulnere vidi vitam:** heavy alliteration. **Creusa:** Aeneas' wife.

563 **direpta:** in his imagination, his house has already been ransacked by the Greeks. **Iuli:** Aeneas' son had two names: Iulus and Ascanius.

679 **talia vociferans:** the subject is Creusa, while *talia* refers to her appeal to Aeneas.

680 **dictu:** the ablative supine, to be taken with *mirabile*: 'wonderful to relate'. Note the repeated use of *m* in this and neighbouring lines, reflecting Aeneas' deep emotions.

681 The order is *namque inter manus oraque maestorum parentum*. We are to picture Creusa holding up Iulus to reinforce her appeal to Aeneas.

682 **levis:** agrees with *apex*: 'a thin tongue of flame'. **visus:** supply *est*.

683–4 The order is *flammaque, innoxia tactu, (visa est) lambere molles comas et pasci circum tempora*.

Questions

1 In lines 550–553, how does Virgil increase the horror of Priam's killing?

2 In lines 554–558, how does Aeneas emphasise the loss that he feels?

3 How does line 559 mark a transition from one phase of Aeneas' story to another?

4 In lines 560–563, there are six adjectives: identify each one and explain how each one makes an important contribution to Aeneas' story.

5 In lines 679–684, what makes the scene dramatic?

nos pavidi trepidare metu crinemque flagrantem   685
excutere et sanctos restinguere fontibus ignes.
at pater Anchises oculos ad sidera laetus
extulit et caelo palmas cum voce tetendit:
"Iuppiter omnipotens, precibus si flecteris ullis,
aspice nos, hoc tantum, et si pietate meremur,   690
da deinde augurium, pater, atque haec omina firma."
vix ea fatus erat senior, subitoque fragore
intonuit laevum, et de caelo lapsa per umbras
stella facem ducens multa cum luce cucurrit.
illam summa super labentem culmina tecti   695
cernimus Idaea claram se condere silva
signantemque vias; tum longo limite sulcus
dat lucem et late circum loca sulphure fumant.
hic vero victus genitor se tollit ad auras
adfaturque deos et sanctum sidus adorat.   700
"iam iam nulla mora est; sequor et qua ducitis adsum,
di patrii; servate domum, servate nepotem.
vestrum hoc augurium, vestroque in numine Troia est.
cedo equidem nec, nate, tibi comes ire recuso."

At once I lifted my father onto my shoulders, took my son's hand in mine and told my wife
to follow behind as we hurriedly began our escape from the blazing city. My father carried
the sacred objects that Hector's ghost had entrusted to me. Every movement and sound now
terrified me. Just as we approached the edge of the city, we heard the sound of running feet,
and my father urged me to run, as he could see light reflecting off Greek armour.

trepido, -are	685 I quake, tremble	*labor, -i, lapsus sum*	I glide, fall
metus, -us m.	fear	*umbra, -ae* f.	shadow, darkness
flagro, -are	I blaze	*stella, -ae* f.	star
excutio, -ere	I beat out	*fax, facis,* f.	torch, fiery trail
sanctus, -a, -um	sacred	*Idaeus, -a, -um*	695 of Mt Ida
restinguo, -ere	I extinguish	*clarus, -a, -um*	bright
fons, fontis m.	fountain, water	*condo, -ere*	I hide, bury
laetus, -a, -um	joyful, happy	*silva, -ae* f.	wood
effero, -ferre, -tuli, -latus	I raise	*signo, -are*	I mark, indicate
palma, -ae f.	palm, hand	*limes, -itis* m.	track, path
tendo, -ere, tetendi, tensus	I stretch out	*sulcus, -i* m.	furrow, trail
Iuppiter, Iovis m.	Jupiter	*sulphur, -uris* n.	sulphur
omnipotens, -ntis	all-powerful	*fumo, -are*	I smoke, reek
prex, precis f. (no nom.)	prayer	*aura, ae* f.	air, breeze
flecto, -ere	I influence	*adfor, -ari, -fatus sum*	700 I address
ullus, -a, -um	any	*adoro, -are*	I worship
mereor, -eri, -itus sum	690 I deserve	*sequor, -i, secutus sum*	I follow
augurium, -i n.	augury, omen	*qua*	where
omen, -inis n.	omen, portent	*servo, -are*	I save, protect
firmo, -are	I confirm	*cedo, -ere*	I yield, give way
fragor, -oris m.	crash, loud noise	*equidem*	indeed
intono, -are, -ui	I thunder	*recuso, -are*	I refuse

685–6 **trepidare, excutere, restinguere:** these are historic infinitives, here equivalent to inceptive and conative imperfect indicatives: 'we began to quake . . . we tried to beat out . . . and extinguish'. **sanctos:** the fire is sacred because it was supernatural and so caused by the gods.

687 **at:** this word usually indicates a strong contrast in Virgil; here it marks the reversal of Anchises' decision to stay in Troy.

690 **hoc tantum:** 'this alone (I pray)'. **si pietate meremur:** 'if by our righteousness we deserve (your help)'. Virgil makes clear that Aeneas is already marked out by his dutifulness to gods, country and family; this quality underpins the whole poem.

691 **deinde:** 'then' in the sense of 'next', i.e. 'now'. **augurium:** Anchises prays for a second omen to confirm the first as being a deliberate sign from the gods. **pater:** a term of respect for the king of the gods.

692 **subitoque:** translate *-que* as 'when' here. Note the fast rhythm of this line, to emphasise the speed of the divine response.

693 **laevum:** 'on the left' (an adverbial accusative); the left side was considered favourable in Roman augury.

694 **stella facem ducens:** 'a star leaving a fiery trail' is a shooting-star or meteor.

695 **summa . . . culmina tecti:** 'the highest part of the roof'.

696 **claram:** this can be translated as an adverb: 'brightly'. **Idaea . . . silva:** ablative of place; Ida was a forested mountain close to Troy towards the east.

697 **signantemque vias:** a phrase of uncertain meaning: possibly 'lighting up the streets (of the city)'; 'showing the way (for us to go)' (Servius); or 'leaving the trace of its path' (Williams).

697–8 Note the <u>alliteration</u> and frequent appearance of *l* in these lines, a soft sound usually associated with peace and tranquillity; here perhaps it is suggestive of the lingering afterglow. **late circum loca sulphure fumant:** 'and everywhere for a great distance all round was reeking with the smell of sulphur'.

699 **hic:** 'at this point'. **victus:** 'defeated' in the sense that his opposition to escaping had been ended by the signs from the gods. **se tollit ad auras:** 'raised himself up to the air', i.e. he stood up to his full height.

700 **et sanctum sidus adorat:** 'and showed his reverence for the sacred star'; for *sanctum* see line 686.

701 **iam iam:** the repetition of *iam* emphasises the immediacy of the need for action.

702 **domum:** not the physical house, but the family who had lived in it. **nepotem:** his grandson Iulus is the most important member of the family, as he will carry the bloodline furthest forward.

703 **vestrum . . . vestro:** the repetition emphasises the importance he attaches to the role of the gods, reminding them of their responsibility. **numine:** here 'power'.

704 **tibi comes:** 'as your companion'.

Questions

1 In lines 685–688, in what different ways did the adults react to the strange flame? Explain this difference.

2 In lines 689–691, why does Anchises pray for a second omen?

3 How does Virgil bring out the drama of the episode of the shooting star?

4 In lines 699–704, how does Virgil show the new-found determination of Anchises?

hic mihi nescio quod trepido male numen amicum   735
confusam eripuit mentem. namque avia cursu
dum sequor et nota excedo regione viarum,
heu misero coniunx fatone erepta Creusa
substitit, erravitne via seu lassa resedit,
incertum; nec post oculis est reddita nostris.   740
nec prius amissam respexi animumve reflexi
quam tumulum antiquae Cereris sedemque sacratam
venimus: hic demum collectis omnibus una
defuit, et comites natumque virumque fefellit.
quem non incusavi amens hominumque deorumque,   745
aut quid in eversa vidi crudelius urbe?
Ascanium Anchisemque patrem Teucrosque penates
commendo sociis et curva valle recondo;
ipse urbem repeto et cingor fulgentibus armis.
stat casus renovare omnes omnemque reverti   750
per Troiam et rursus caput obiectare periclis.

I retraced my steps to my house, only to find the Greeks had set fire to it. In the centre of the city treasure was being piled high, and captive boys and women were standing in line.

ausus quin etiam voces iactare per umbram   768
implevi clamore vias, maestusque Creusam
nequiquam ingeminans iterumque iterumque vocavi.   770
quaerenti et tectis urbis sine fine ruenti
infelix simulacrum atque ipsius umbra Creusae
visa mihi ante oculos et nota maior imago.

trepidus, -a, -um	735 alarmed	*incuso, -are, -avi, -atus*	745 I accuse
numen, -inis n.	divine power	*amens, -entis*	out of one's mind
confusus, -a, -um	confused	*everto, -ere, -verti, -versus*	I ruin, overthrow
avium, -i n.	by-way	*crudelis, -e*	cruel
cursus, -us m.	run, running	*Teucrus, -a, -um*	Trojan
excedo, -ere	I depart	*vallis, -is* f.	valley
regio, -onis f.	region, district	*recondo, -ere, -didi, -ditus*	I hide
coniunx, -iugis m./f.	husband, wife	*repeto, -ere*	I seek again
subsisto, -ere, -stiti	I stop	*cingo, -ere, cinxi, cinctus*	I surround
seu	or	*fulgeo, -ere*	I shine, gleam
lassus, -a, -um	weary	*renovo, -are*	750 I renew
resideo, -ere, -sedi, -sessus	I stay behind	*revertor, -i, -versus sum*	I return
incertus, -a, -um	740 uncertain	*rursus*	again
amitto, -ere, -misi, -missus	I lose	*obiecto, -are*	I expose
respicio, -ere, -spexi, -ctus	I look back for	*periclum, -i* n.	danger
reflecto, -ere, -flexi, -flexus	I turn back	*audeo, -ere, ausus sum*	768 I dare
tumulus, -i m.	burial mound	*quin*	indeed
antiquus, -a, -um	ancient	*vox, vocis* f.	voice, shout
Ceres, -eris f.	Ceres	*iacto, -are*	I throw
demum	at last	*impleo, -ere, -evi, -etus*	I fill
colligo, -ere, -legi, -lectus	I gather together	*ingemino, -are*	770 I repeat
desum, -esse, -fui	I am missing	*umbra, -ae* f.	ghost
fallo, -ere, fefelli, falsus	I fail to meet		

735 **hic:** 'at this point'. **mihi . . . trepido:** dative of disadvantage: 'from me in my alarm'. **nescio quod . . . numen:** 'I don't know what divine power', and so 'some divine power'. **male . . . amicum:** 'unfriendly'.

736 **cursu:** ablative of manner: 'at a run'.

738 **misero:** dative qualifying *mihi* understood, rather than ablative with *fato*; a dative of disadvantage, like *mihi* in line 735: 'snatched away from me in my misery'. **fatone:** the suffix *-ne* introduces the first of three direct questions (the second beginning with *erravitne* and the third with *seu*); the presence of *incertum* might have called for indirect questions ('it is uncertain whether . . . or'), but the whole sentence is disjointed, reflecting Aeneas' confused emotional response to the bitter memory of this event, for which he was responsible. We may translate 'did she stop . . . or did she wander . . . or did she sit down . . .? It is uncertain.' Certain it is that Aeneas made an error of judgement when he told Creusa to walk behind them.

739 **substitit:** the enjambement introduces a pause, which reflects the sense. **via:** ablative of separation: 'from the path'.

740 **post:** adverb: 'afterwards'.

741 **prius:** to be taken with *quam* in the next line: 'until'. **amissam:** 'the missing woman'.

742 **tumulum, sedem:** Aeneas had arranged to meet his attendants at these well-known places, sacred to the goddess Ceres.

743 **omnibus una:** a powerful antithesis: everyone else had reached the shrine, and just the one woman was missing.

744 **fefellit:** *fallo* is a strong verb, indicating a failure to meet the expectations of the others.

745 The polysyndeton of *-que . . . -que* gives a hypermetric syllable at the end of the line, which must be elided before the vowel at the start of the next line. This feature, together with the other elision and the slow rhythm, makes this line particularly striking.

747 **Teucros penates:** the statues of the national gods of Troy; see line 293.

748 **commendo:** here Aeneas switches to the historic present, to give greater immediacy to his actions, now that he has discovered the loss of his wife. **curva valle:** local ablative; presumably the mound and shrine of Ceres were in this valley. Note the chiastic structure.

749 **cingor:** a use of the passive that is parallel to the Greek middle voice, being equivalent to *me cingo*: 'I surround myself with', i.e. 'I put on'. We must assume that Aeneas had given his armour to his servants to carry, since to wear them would have drawn attention to him and placed his family in danger.

750 **stat:** lit. 'it stands', i.e. 'the decision stands', i.e. 'I resolved'. **renovare omnes omnemque reverti:** a fine chiasmus to emphasise the dangers he deliberately faced.

769 **Creusam:** i.e. Creusa's name.

770 **iterumque iterumque:** the anaphora of *iterum*, together with the polysyndeton, emphasise his desperate repetition of Creusa's name.

771 **quaerenti . . . furenti:** agree with *mihi* in line 773. **tectis:** local ablative: 'among the buildings'.

772–3 **simulacrum . . . umbra . . . imago:** all three words here have the same meaning; the tautology reinforces the unwelcome truth that Creusa was dead. **visa:** supply *est*. **nota:** ablative of comparison dependent on *maior*: 'greater than the woman I knew'.

Questions

1 In lines 735–751, how does Aeneas try to explain the loss of his wife? Do you believe him? How far do you think Aeneas himself was to blame?

2 In lines 768–773, how does Aeneas emphasise the pathos of this episode?

obstipui, steteruntque comae et vox faucibus haesit.
tum sic adfari et curas his demere dictis: 775
"quid tantum insano iuvat indulgere dolori,
o dulcis coniunx? non haec sine numine divum
eveniunt; nec te hinc comitem asportare Creusam
fas aut ille sinit superi regnator Olympi.
longa tibi exsilia et vastum maris aequor arandum,   780
et terram Hesperiam venies, ubi Lydius arva
inter opima virum leni fluit agmine Thybris.
illic res laetae regnumque et regia coniunx
parta tibi; lacrimas dilectae pelle Creusae.
non ego Myrmidonum sedes Dolopumve superbas   785
aspiciam aut Grais servitum matribus ibo,
Dardanis et divae Veneris nurus;
sed me magna deum genetrix his detinet oris.
iamque vale et nati serva communis amorem."
haec ubi dicta dedit, lacrimantem et multa volentem   790
dicere deseruit, tenuesque recessit in auras.
ter conatus ibi collo dare bracchia circum;
ter frustra comprensa manus effugit imago,
par levibus ventis volucrique simillima somno.
sic demum socios consumpta nocte reviso.'   795

fauces, -ium f.pl.	throat	*lacrima, -ae* f.	tear
haereo, -ere, haesi, haesus	I stick	*dilectus, -a, -um*	beloved
cura, -ae f.	775 anxiety, sorrow	*pello, -ere*	I drive away
demo, -ere	I take away	*Myrmidones, -um* m.pl.	785 Myrmidons
dictum, -i n.	word	*sedes, -is* f.	home
insanus, -a, -um	mad, frantic	*Dolopes, -um* m.pl.	Dolopians
iuvo, -are	I please	*Graius, -a, -um*	Greek
indulgeo, -ere + dat.	I indulge in	*servio, -ire, -ii, -itus*	I am a slave
dolor, -oris m.	grief	*Dardanis, -idis* f.	a Trojan woman
dulcis, -e	sweet	*diva, -ae* f.	goddess
evenio, -ire	I happen	*Venus, -eris* f.	Venus
hinc	from here	*genetrix, -icis* f.	mother
asporto, -are	I take away	*detineo, -ere*	I keep back
fas n. indecl.	right, allowed	*vale*	farewell
sino, -ere	I allow	*communis, -e*	shared
superus, -a, -um	above	*lacrimo, -are*	790 I cry
Olympus, -i m.	Olympus	*tenuis, -e*	thin
exsilium, -i n.	780 exile	*recedo, -ere, -cessi, -cessus*	I depart, recede
vastus, -a, -um	enormous	*ter*	three times
aequor, -oris n.	level surface, sea	*conor, -ari, -atus sum*	I try
aro, -are	I plough	*bracchium, -i* n.	arm
Hesperius, -a, -um	Western	*frustra*	in vain
Lydius, -a, -um	Lydian	*comprendo, -ere, -ndi, -nsus*	I clutch at, grasp
opimus, -a, -um	rich, fertile	*par* + dat.	just like
lenis, -e	smooth, gentle	*ventus, -i* m.	wind
Thybris, -is m.	River Tiber	*volucer, -cris, -cre*	fleeting
illic	there	*similis, -e* + dat.	795 similar (to)
regius, -a, -um	royal	*consumo, -ere, -psi, -ptus*	I spend
pario, -ere, peperi, partus	I obtain	*reviso, -ere*	I visit again

774 obstipui: see line 560 for the same word, used in a similar context. **steterunt:** 'stood on end'.

775 adfari, demere: historic infinitives, which can be translated as 'she began to address (me) . . . and tried to take away . . .'.

776 quid: here 'why'. **iuvat:** here impersonal: 'does it please (you)'.

777 haec: i.e. the capture of Troy and Creusa's own death. **divum:** = *divorum*.

778–9: the order is *nec fas (est) te asportare hinc Creusam comitem*. **fas:** this word refers to the law of the gods. **comitem:** 'as your companion'. **aut:** here = *nec*. **ille regnator:** 'he, the ruler': we are to imagine Creusa pointing up towards heaven. Creusa is almost saying the same thing twice, the difference being that the first statement refers to an impersonal divine prohibition, the second that Jupiter has taken a personal interest in preventing her escape. Virgil needs the death of Creusa at this point because, as she goes on to say, it is Aeneas' destiny to marry again when he reaches Italy.

780 exsilia: supply 'erunt'. **aequor arandum:** supply 'erit'; *aequor* can be used to refer to any flat or level surface, including farmland, whence the farming metaphor here.

781 terram Hesperiam: accusative of goal of motion. *Hesperiam* is either an adjective, meaning 'the Western land'; or a noun, meaning 'the land of Hesperia'; both amount to the same thing: Italy. This is the point in the *Aeneid* where Aeneas first learns of his destination in exile (all Hector's ghost had told him in line 295 was that he would have to cross the sea).

781–2 Lydius . . . Thybris: most of the river Tiber flowed through Etruria, the inhabitants of which were widely believed to be immigrants from Lydia in Asia Minor. **opima virum:** 'rich in men; *virum* = *virorum*. **agmine:** here 'course'.

783 res laetae: concrete for abstract: 'happiness'. **regia coniunx:** i.e. Lavinia, the daughter of king Latinus. Note that Aeneas does not shrink from telling Dido this.

784 parta: supply *sunt*; these rewards have been 'obtained' for him in the sense that Fate has already decreed them.

785 Myrmidonum, Dolopum: these were two tribes of Greeks living in Thessaly; the Myrmidons in particular were associated with Achilles, who had been the greatest warrior in the Greek army at Troy. Creusa is trying to soften the blow for Aeneas by saying she will not share the fate of most of the surviving Trojan woman: being enslaved.

786 servitum: the supine, used to express purpose.

787 Dardanis . . . nurus: in apposition to *ego* (line 785). This line was never completed by Virgil.

788 magna de(or)um genetrix: the 'great mother of the gods' is Cybele, a local goddess.

790–1: note the heavy <u>alliteration</u> of *d*. Supply *me* with the participles. Note the fast rhythm.

792–3 ter . . . ter: a favourite number of Virgil, borrowed from Homer. **conatus:** supply *sum*. **dare . . . circum:** this is the compound verb *circumdare* ('to place . . . round'), split and reversed.

794: the repetition of soft *l*, *m* and *s* sounds emphasises the insubstantial nature of the ghost.

Questions

1 How does Creusa's ghost try to lighten the burden of loss felt by Aeneas? In your answer you should divide up her speech into different arguments.

2 How important do you think the episode of Creusa's ghost is for Aeneas?

3 In lines 790–795, how does Aeneas allow his emotions to show through his words?

4 How much difference has it made to your understanding and reaction to the events described in Book 2 that they have been narrated by Aeneas himself?

Book 3

'The gods had decreed that Troy should fall. We, the survivors, were forced to sail away in search of a new home. After building ships we set sail. Our first attempt to build a new city failed when we learned that the place we had chosen was cursed. We prepared to sail again.'

'inde ubi prima fides pelago, placataque venti
dant maria et lenis crepitans vocat Auster in altum,   70
deducunt socii naves et litora complent.
provehimur portu terraeque urbesque recedunt.
sacra mari colitur medio gratissima tellus
Nereidum matri et Neptuno Aegaeo,
quam pius arquitenens oras et litora circum   75
errantem Mycono e celsa Gyaroque revinxit,
immotamque coli dedit et contemnere ventos.
huc feror, haec fessos tuto placidissima portu
accipit; egressi veneramur Apollinis urbem.
rex Anius, rex idem hominum Phoebique sacerdos,   80
vittis et sacra redimitus tempora lauro
occurrit; veterem Anchisen agnovit amicum.

inde	from there, then	*circum* + acc.	around
fides, -ei f.	trust	*erro, -are*	I wander
pelagus, -i n.	sea	*Myconos, -i* f.	Myconos
placo, -are, -avi, -atus	I calm	*celsus, -a, -um*	lofty, high
ventus, -i m.	wind	*Gyaros, -i* f.	Gyaros
mare, -is n. 70	sea	*revincio, -ire, -nxi*	I bind fast
lenis, -e	gentle	*immotus, -a, -um*	immovable
crepito, -are	I rustle	*colo, -ere, colui, cultus*	I inhabit
Auster, -tri m.	South Wind	*contemno -ere*	I despise, defy
altum, -i n.	the deep, sea	*huc*	to this place
deduco, -ere	I take down,	*fessus, -a, -um*	weary, tired
	launch	*tutus, -a, -um*	safe
socius -i m.	companion	*placidus, -a, -um*	peaceful
navis, -is f.	ship	*accipio -ere*	I receive
litus, -oris n.	shore, coast	*egredior, -i, -ssus sum*	I disembark
compleo, -ere	I fill	*veneror, -ari*	I pay reverence to
provehor, -i	I sail forth	*Apollo, -inis* m.	Apollo
portus, -us m.	harbour	*Anius, -i* m. 80	Anius
terra, -ae f.	land	*idem, eadem, idem*	the same
recedo, -ere	I recede	*homo, -inis* m.	man
sacer, -cra, -crum	sacred	*Phoebus, -i* m.	Phoebus (Apollo)
colitur	there exists	*sacerdos, -otis* m.	priest
medius, -a, -um	the middle of	*vitta, -ae* f.	headband
gratus, -a, -um	pleasing, dear	*redimio, -ire, -ivi, -itus*	I bind round
tellus, -uris f.	land	*tempus, -oris* n.	temple
Nereis, -idis f.	Nereid	*laurus, i* f.	laurel
Neptunus, -i m.	Neptune	*occurro, -ere*	I meet
Aegaeus, -a, -um	Aegean	*vetus, -eris*	old
pius, -a, -um 75	dutiful	*Anchises, -ae* (acc. *-en*)	Anchises
arquitenens, -ntis	carrying a bow	*agnosco, -ere, -ovi*	I recognise
ora, -ae f.	shore		

69 prima fides pelago: supply *est*: (when) the first trust was (given)' to the sea, i.e. 'as soon as we could place our trust in the sea'. Aeneas is continuing the story of his adventures to Dido (see Introduction).

70 dant, vocat, etc.: Virgil begins this episode with the historic present. **lenis:** this adjective is best translated as an adverb. **Auster:** Virgil is fond of personifying the winds; unfortunately the South Wind is the least favourable for the southward journey the Trojans need to make.

71 deducunt: lit. 'take down (to the sea)', because the ships had been drawn up on to the beach. This line has a slower rhythm than the preceding two, perhaps to reflect the slow process of launching and manning the ships.

72 portu: probably no more than a section of beach used for storing the ships.

73 sacra . . . tellus: the delayed subject gives an air of mystery and suspense to the beginning of this new episode in the Trojans' journey. **colitur:** lit. 'there is inhabited', and so in effect simply 'there is'. Note the position of *colitur*, enclosed between *mari* and *medio*, reflecting the reality. The 'sacred land' is the island of Delos.

74 matri et Neptuno: dependent on *gratissima*. The Nereids were sea-nymphs, the daughters of Doris and the sea-god Nereus. Neptune is described as 'Aegean' because the Aegean Sea was in effect the Greeks' own sea, and they naturally associated Neptune with it. The metre of the line is highly unusual: there is no elision before *et* or *Aegaeo*, and the fifth foot is spondaic.

75–6 quam . . . errantem: these link to *tellus*. **pius arquitenens:** the 'dutiful bow-carrier' is Apollo, the Archer god, who, out of respect for his mother, Latona, who gave birth to him and Diana on the island, fixed the position of the island, which until then had been 'wandering' across the sea. Wandering islands featured in several Greek myths. **oras . . . circum:** the order is *circum oras et litora*, dependent on *errantem*. There is no distinction between *oras* and *litora*. **Mycono . . . Gyaro:** these were two neighbouring islands. Myconos is described as *celsa* but is in fact a low island. **e Mycono:** Latin has a different perspective from English; we would say he bound the island fast 'to Myconos'.

77 dedit: here 'he allowed'. **contemnere ventos:** the island could 'defy the winds' because, being fixed, it could no longer be blown about.

78 haec: supply *insula*. **fessos:** supply *nos*. **tuto portu:** local ablative.

79 Apollinis urbem: Delos was the centre of worship of Apollo.

80 idem: used to emphasise the fact that Anius had two responsibilities, as king and priest; translate as 'both'. **rex hominum Phoebique sacerdos:** note the chiasmus. **Phoebus:** another name for Apollo.

81 vittis: plural for singular; priests were distinguished by the sacred headband they always wore. **redimitus tempora:** lit. 'having been bound round his temples (with headbands)', and so 'with a headband bound round his temples'; this is one of Virgil's favourite constructions for describing people, modelled on the Greek middle verb. **sacra:** belongs with *lauro*.

82 occurrit: supply *nobis*. **Anchisen agnovit:** Anchises was Aeneas' elderly father, who had visited king Anius before the Trojan War.

Questions

1 In lines 69–70, how does Aeneas emphasise that conditions were right for sailing?

2 In lines 73–82, how does Aeneas emphasise the special nature of Delos?

iungimus hospitio dextras et tecta subimus.
templa dei saxo venerabar structa vetusto:
"da propriam, Thymbrace, domum; da moenia fessis   85
et genus et mansuram urbem; serva altera Troiae
Pergama, reliquias Danaum atque immitis Achilli.
quem sequimur? quove ire iubes? ubi ponere sedes?
da, pater, augurium atque animis inlabere nostris."
vix ea fatus eram: tremere omnia visa repente,   90
liminaque laurusque dei, totusque moveri
mons circum et mugire adytis cortina reclusis.
summissi petimus terram et vox fertur ad aures:
"Dardanidae duri, quae vos a stirpe parentum
prima tulit tellus, eadem vos ubere laeto   95
accipiet reduces. antiquam exquirite matrem.
hic domus Aeneae cunctis dominabitur oris
et nati natorum et qui nascentur ab illis."
haec Phoebus; mixtoque ingens exorta tumultu
laetitia, et cuncti quae sint ea moenia quaerunt,   100
quo Phoebus vocet errantes iubeatque reverti.

iungo, -ere, -nxi, -nctus	I join, yoke	*repente*	suddenly
hospitium, -i n.	friendship	*limen, -inis* n.	threshold, doorway
dextra, -ae f.	right hand		
tectum, -i n.	roof, building	*laurus, -i* f.	laurel tree
subeo, -ire	I approach, enter	*moveo, -ere*	I move
templum, -i n.	temple	*mons, -ntis* m.	mountain
saxum, -i n.	stone, rock	*circum*	around
veneror, -ari	I regard reverently	*mugio, -ire*	I bellow, rumble
		adytum, -i n.	shrine, sanctuary
struo, -ere, -xi, -ctus	I build	*cortina, -ae* f.	cauldron
vetustus, -a, -um	ancient	*recludo, -ere, -si, -sus*	I open
proprius, -a, -um 85	one's own, permanent	*summissus, -a, -um*	humble
		auris, -is f.	ear
Thymbracus, -i m.	Apollo	*Dardanidae, -arum* m.pl.	Trojans
moenia, -um n.pl.	city walls	*durus, -a, -um*	hard, long-suffering
genus, -eris n.	race, offspring		
maneo, -ere, -nsi, -nsus	I remain, endure	*stirps, -pis* f.	stock, lineage
servo, -are	I keep, keep safe	*parens, -ntis* m.f.	parent, ancestor
alter, -era, -erum	the other, a second	*idem, eadem, idem* 95	the same
		uber, -eris n.	bosom
Troia, -ae f.	Troy	*accipio, -ere*	I receive
Pergama, -orum n.pl.	Pergama, citadel	*redux, -cis*	returning
reliquiae, -arum f.pl.	remnants	*antiquus, -a, -um*	ancient
Danai, -orum m.pl.	the Greeks	*exquiro, -ere*	I seek out
immitis, -e	cruel	*Aeneas, -ae* m.	Aeneas
Achilles, -i m.	Achilles	*cunctus, -a, -um*	all
sequor, -i	I follow	*dominor, -ari*	I hold power
quove	or whither	*natus, -i* m.	son
sedes, -is f.	home	*nascor, -i*	I am born
augurium, -i n.	omen	*mixtus, -a, -um*	confused
animus, -i m.	mind, heart	*exorior, -iri, -ortus sum*	I arise
inlabor, -i + dat.	I steal into	*tumultus, -us* m.	outburst
vix 90	scarcely	*laetitia, -ae* f. 100	joy
for, fari, fatus sum	I speak	*quo*	whither, to where
tremo, -ere	I quake, quiver	*revertor, -i*	I return
videor, -eri, visus sum	I seem		

83 **hospitio:** ablative of manner. **tecta subimus:** not 'we went up to the roof' as some have taken it, but 'we approached the buildings' or even 'we entered the buildings'.

84 **saxo . . . vetusto:** 'built of ancient stone': ablative of material.

85 **da:** supply *nobis.* **Thymbrace:** Apollo had a sanctuary at Thymbra, near Troy. **fessis:** having already used this word in line 78, Aeneas is emphasising how long-suffering the Trojans are.

86–7 **altera Troiae Pergama:** 'Troy's second citadel'; most editors take this to be symbolically referring to the surviving Trojans (in which case *reliquias* is in apposition to *Pergama*); Pergama had been the central citadel of Troy, now destroyed by the Greeks. It is possible however that Aeneas is referring to the new city and citadel he assumes he is about to found on Naxos, which he wishes Apollo to keep safe; in that case the *reliquias* would be a separate object of *serva.* **reliquiae:** the people (and possibly their possessions) left unharmed by the Greeks; the genitives are subjective. **Achilli:** Achilles was the most feared warrior in the Greek army.

88 **quem sequimur:** 'whom do we follow (as our guide)?' **ponere:** depends on *iubes.*

89 **inlabere:** imperative.

90 **tremere omnia visa:** '(when) everything suddenly seemed to quake'; **visa:** supply *sunt.*

91 **laurus:** the laurel, or bay, tree was sacred to Apollo; such trees were likely to adorn his shrines.

91–2 **moveri . . . mugire:** both are dependent on *visa (sunt)*; *mugire* represents an unearthly sound heralding the approach of the god. **mons:** Mt Cynthus overlooked the town. **cortina:** in oracular shrines, a cauldron was set on top of a tripod; here the priestess would receive the god's replies to her questions. **adytis . . . reclusis:** ablative absolute; the god was believed to dwell in the inner sanctuary of his temple; here he announces his appearance by throwing open the doors of the sanctuary.

93 **petimus:** 'we made for' and so 'we fell to'.

94–6 The order is *eadem tellus, quae prima tulit vos a stirpe parentum, accipiet vos reduces ubere laeto.* **Dardanidae duri:** vocative; by calling the Trojans 'Dardanians', the god is subtly pointing to their lineage, which could be traced back to Dardanus, who came to Troy from Italy. Unfortunately the Trojans missed this cue. Note the heavy alliteration of *d.* This prophecy, unusually delivered by the god in person rather than through his intermediary, gives Aeneas the first hint of his ultimate destiny. **ubere:** this word has two meanings: 'a mother's breast' and 'fertility of the land'. **antiquam . . . matrem:** if the Trojans can trace their ancestry back to Italian Dardanus, then Italy is their 'ancient mother'.

97–8 **hic:** i.e. in Italy. **cunctis . . . oris:** local ablative. **dominabitur:** this has three subjects: *domus, nati* and *qui* ('those who . . .'); it is singular because attached to the number of the first subject. Note the slow rhythm of lines 98 and 99, reflecting the awe caused by the prophecy.

99 **haec:** supply *dixit.* **tumultu:** the outburst of excited shouting that the prophecy evoked.

100 **laetitia:** note the enjambement.

Questions

1 In lines 85–89, how does Aeneas strengthen his prayer to Apollo?

2 In lines 90–93, how do Aeneas' words emphasise the supernatural nature of what happened?

3 In lines 94–98, how clear is the information given to the Trojans?

tum genitor veterum volvens monimenta virorum
"audite, o proceres," ait "et spes discite vestras.
Creta Iovis magni medio iacet insula ponto,
mons Idaeus ubi et gentis cunabula nostrae.   105
centum urbes habitant magnas, uberrima regna,
maximus unde pater, si rite audita recordor,
Teucrus Rhoeteas primum est advectus in oras,
optavitque locum regno. nondum Ilium et arces
Pergameae steterant; habitabant vallibus imis.   110
hinc mater cultrix Cybeli Corybantiaque aera
Idaeumque nemus, hinc fida silentia sacris,
et iuncti currum dominae subiere leones.
ergo agite et divum ducunt qua iussa sequamur:
placemus ventos et Cnosia regna petamus.   115
nec longo distant cursu: modo Iuppiter adsit,
tertia lux classem Cretaeis sistet in oris."

So saying, my father made sacrifices to Neptune, Apollo and the winds. We left the harbour
of Delos and sailed quickly across the sea. A following wind helped us to reach the shores
of Crete.

genitor, -oris m.	father	*imus, -a, -um*	the bottom of
volvo, -ere	I roll, consider	*hinc*	from here
monimentum, -i n.	tradition	*cultrix, -icis* f.	female inhabitant
procer, -eris m.	chieftain, lord	*Cybelus, -i* m.	Mt Cybelus
ait	he says	*Corybantius, -a, -um*	of the Corybantes
spes, -ei f.	hope	*aes, aeris* n.	bronze, cymbal
disco, -ere	I learn	*nemus, -oris* n.	grove
Creta, -ae f.	Crete	*fidus, -a, -um*	faithful
Iuppiter, Iovis m.	Jupiter	*silentium, -i* n.	silence
medius, -a, -um	the middle of	*sacra, -orum* n.pl.	sacred rites
insula, -ae f.	island	*currus, -us* m.	chariot
pontus, -i m.	sea	*domina, -ae* f.	mistress
Idaeus, -a, -um 105	of Mt Ida	*subeo, -ire*	I submit to
gens, -ntis f.	race, people	*leo, -onis* m.	lion
cunabula, -orum n.pl.	cradle	*ergo*	therefore
uber, -eris	rich	*agite*	come!
regnum, -i n.	kingdom, realm	*divus, -i* m.	god
unde	from where	*qua*	where
rite	rightly	*iussum, -i* n.	command
recordor, -ari	I remember	*placo, -are* 115	I win the favour
Teucrus, -i m.	Teucer		of
Rhoeteus, -a, -um	Rhoetean	*Cnosius, -a, -um*	Cretan
adveho, -ere, -exi, -ectus	I convey (to)	*disto, -are*	I am distant
opto, -are, -avi, -atus	I choose, wish for	*cursus, -us* m.	course, voyage
locus, -i m.	place	*modo*	only, if only
nondum	not yet	*adsum, -esse*	I am favourable
Ilium, -i n.	Ilium, Troy	*tertius, -a, -um*	third
arx, arcis f.	citadel	*lux, lucis* f.	light, dawn
Pergameus, -a, -um 110	of Pergama	*classis, -is* f.	fleet
sto, -are, steti, status	I stand	*Cretaeus, -a, -um*	Cretan
vallis, -is f.	valley	*sisto, -ere*	I bring to rest

102 **genitor:** Aeneas' aged father, Anchises, would have a greater knowledge of traditions than most. Note the <u>alliteration</u> of *v*.

103 **spes . . . vestras:** these hopes of course are for a permanent home.

104 **Creta Iovis magni:** Crete was the island 'of great Jupiter' because he was born there, on Mt Ida. **medio iacet insula ponto:** note the <u>enclosing</u> of the *insula* between *medio* and *ponto*, reflecting reality.

105 **mons Idaeus:** Anchises clearly believed that the Mt Ida on Crete gave its name to the Mt Ida near Troy; it is this apparent connection that persuaded him that Crete was the 'cradle of our race'. **ubi:** to be taken first in the line; supply *sunt*.

106 **habitant:** the subject is 'they', i.e. the Cretans. **uberrima regna:** in apposition to *centum urbes*; the number of cities is proof of the richness of the island.

107–8 **maximus . . . pater . . . Teucrus:** Teucer was, according to one tradition, the first founder of Troy, arriving from Crete before Dardanus came from Italy. Unfortunately for the Trojans, it is the Dardanus tradition which Apollo intended. **unde:** to be taken first in the line. **audita:** 'things having been heard' means 'the tradition'. **Rhoeteas:** Virgil is demonstrating his knowledge of the topography of Troy: Rhoeteum was a headland near Troy.

109 **regno:** 'for his kingdom' (dative of purpose). **arces:** plural for singular.

110 **steterant:** lit. 'had not (yet) stood', i.e. 'had not yet been built'. **vallibus:** local ablative.

111 **hinc:** i.e. from Crete; supply *venerunt*. **mater:** this could be Rhea, the mother of Jupiter, who bore him on the island; it is more likely, however, to refer to Cybele, widely known as the *Magna Mater*, whose cult was connected with that of Rhea and spread from Asia Minor to Rome. Anchises appears to be merging the two goddesses, so as to suggest that the cult of Cybele spread from Crete to the Trojan area. **cultrix Cybeli:** 'the dweller on (Mt) Cybelus'; there must have been a mountain near Troy with the same name as the goddess. **corybantia . . . aera:** 'the cymbals of the Corybantes'; these were worshippers of Rhea, who clashed their bronze cymbals to drown the cries of the infant Jupiter and so keep his existence a secret from his father, Saturn.

112 **Idaeum . . . nemus:** i.e. the Trojan Ida took its name from the Cretan one. **fida silentia sacris:** 'the silences faithful to her rites'; the cult of Cybele involved mysteries which must not be divulged.

113 **iuncti . . . leones:** the 'yoked lions' drew the chariot carrying the statue of Cybele during her rites; the use of lions proved her power over all nature. **subiere:** = *subierunt*.

114–15 **divum . . . sequamur:** the order is *sequamur qua iussa divum ducunt*. **sequamur:** jussive subjunctive, as also are *placemus* and *petamus*. **placemus:** i.e. by sacrifice. **Cnosia:** literally 'of Knossos'; Knossos was the main town of Minoan Crete.

116 **nec longo distant cursu:** '(the Cretan realms) are not distant by a long voyage'; ablative of measure of difference. The distance from Delos to the coast of Crete is just over 140 miles as the crow flies. **adsit:** subjunctive in a proviso clause: 'provided that Jupiter is with us'; Jupiter was the god of weather, and so his support would be vital.

Questions

1 In this section, how does Anchises make Crete sound attractive?

2 What are the arguments Anchises puts forward for choosing Crete? How persuasive do you think these arguments would appear to the Trojans?

3 How far could a ship reasonably be expected to travel in a day?

ergo avidus muros optatae molior urbis   132
Pergameamque voco, et laetam cognomine gentem
hortor amare focos arcemque attollere tectis.
iamque fere sicco subductae litore puppes;   135
conubiis arvisque novis operata iuventus;
iura domosque dabam; subito cum tabida membris
corrupto caeli tractu miserandaque venit
arboribusque satisque lues et letifer annus.
linquebant dulces animas aut aegra trahebant   140
corpora; tum steriles exurere Sirius agros,
arebant herbae et victum seges aegra negabat.
rursus ad oraclum Ortygiae Phoebumque remenso
hortatur pater ire mari veniamque precari,
quam fessis finem rebus ferat, unde laborum   145
temptare auxilium iubeat, quo vertere cursus.
    nox erat et terris animalia somnus habebat:
effigies sacrae divum Phrygiique Penates,
quos mecum ab Troia mediisque ex ignibus urbis
extuleram, visi ante oculos astare iacentis   150
in somnis multo manifesti lumine, qua se

avidus, -a, -um	eager	*Sirius, -i* m.	Sirius, the Dog
molior, -iri	I toil at building		Star
cognomen, -inis n.	old name, name	*ager, agri* m.	field
hortor, -ari	I encourage, urge	*areo, -ere*	I am parched
focus, -i m.	hearth, home	*herba, -ae* f.	grass, plant
attollo, -ere	I raise	*victus, -us* m.	sustenance
fere	135 about	*seges, -etis* f.	crop(s)
siccus, -a, -um	dry	*nego, -are*	I deny, refuse
subduco, -ere, -xi, -ctus	I draw up	*rursus*	again
puppis, -is f.	stern, ship	*oraclum, -i* n.	oracle
conubium, -i n.	marriage	*Ortygia, -ae* f.	Ortygia, Delos
arvum, -i n.	arable field	*remetior, -iri, -nsus sum*	I cross again
operor, -ari, -atus sum	I am busy	*venia, -ae* f.	pardon,
iuventus, -utis f.	youth, young men		forgiveness
iura, -um n.pl.	laws	*precor, -ari, -atus sum*	I pray for, pray to
tabidus, -a, -um	wasting	*finis, -is* f.	145 end
membrum, -i n.	limb	*labor, -oris* m.	toil, trouble
corruptus, -a, -um	tainted, infected	*tempto, -are*	I try, try to obtain
caelum, -i n.	sky	*auxilium, -i* n.	help
tractus, -us m.	region	*verto, -ere*	I turn
miserandus, -a, -um	pitiable	*animal, -is* n.	animal
arbos, -oris f.	tree	*somnus, -i* m.	sleep
sata, -orum n.pl.	crops	*effigies, -ei* f.	image
lues, -is f.	pestilence	*Phrygius, -a, -um*	Phrygian, Trojan
letifer, -era, -erum	deadly	*Penates, -ium* m.pl.	Penates
annus, -i m.	year, season	*effero, -ferre, extuli*	150 I carry out
linquo, -ere	140 I give up, lose	*oculus, -i* m.	eye
dulcis, -e	sweet	*asto, -are*	I stand
anima, -ae f.	breath, life	*iaceo, -ere*	I lie
aeger, -gra, -grum	sick, diseased	*manifestus, -a, -um*	plain, clear
traho, -ere	I drag	*lumen, -inis* n.	light
sterilis, -e	barren	*qua*	where
exuro, -ere	I burn, scorch		

132 **avidus:** best translated as 'eagerly'. **muros:** the city walls. **optatae:** 'longed for'.
133 **Pergameam:** the adjective agrees with *urbem*, understood from the previous line.
Literally 'I called it (the city) of Pergama', it may better be translated 'I called it Pergama'.
The logic is that the first requirement for a new city was a defensive central citadel, fortified
with walls. Once Aeneas has built these walls, he resurrected Troy's citadel by using the same
name. **cognomine:** ablative of cause, dependent on *laetam*.
134 **amare, attollere:** the infinitives after *hortor* are a poetic usage. **arcemque attollere tectis:**
'and to raise (the height of) the citadel with buildings'. Note the chiasmus.
135 **subductae:** supply *erant*. **puppes:** Virgil frequently uses the name of the part to represent
the whole; this is known as synecdoche. **litore:** local ablative.
136 **conubiis arvisque:** ablatives of respect. **operata:** supply *erat*.
137 **dabam:** Aeneas was establishing laws and allocating houses.
137–9 The order is *cum subito (e) corrupto tractu caeli venit tabida miserandaque lues
membris et letifer annus arboribusque satisque*. The past indicative is used in the 'inverse
cum construction': 'I was giving . . . when suddenly there came . . .'. **membris:** either dative of
disadvantage with *tabida* or dative of goal of motion with *venit*. **corrupto caeli tractu:** each
region of the sky was the source of a wind, one of which brought pestilence. **letifer annus:** a
'season of death'. The complex word order suggests that both the *lues* and the *letifer annus*
infected all three things: the people's limbs, the trees and the crops.
140 **linquebant:** the subject is Aeneas' people.
141 'Then Sirius scorched the fields and made them barren.' **steriles:** this use of the adjective
is called 'proleptic', showing the result of the action. **exurere:** historic infinitive. **Sirius:** the
rise of this star in July heralded the arrival of the hottest and most damaging season.
142 Note the chiastic word order, with the verbs at either end of the line.
143–4 The order is *pater hortatur (me), mari remenso, ire rursus ad oraclum Ortygiae
precarique Phoebum veniam*. **remenso . . . mari:** ablative absolute. **Ortygia:** Virgil uses this
name as an alternative to Delos. **veniam precari:** Anchises assumes the pestilence is the result
of their having offended the god in some way. *Precari* takes two accusatives.
145–6 **quam, quo, unde:** the three indirect questions depend on the notion of 'asking',
inferred from the previous lines. **fessis finem . . . ferat:** the heavy alliteration reveals Anchises'
despair. **fessis . . . rebus:** 'weary concerns'. **laborum:** objective genitive dependent on
auxilium; translate 'help for our troubles'. **cursus:** poetic plural.
147 **terris:** local ablative. **habebat:** 'held in its grip'.
148 **divum:** genitive plural; the 'gods' are the protective deities, including Vesta, whose
images were entrusted to Aeneas by the ghost of Hector in Book 2 (see notes on lines 293
and 296); **Penates:** the Household Gods of Troy.
149 **ab Troia:** poetic use of the preposition. Aeneas' account of the end of Troy is in Book 2.
150 **extuleram:** these images of the deities Aeneas had brought with him from Troy. **visi:**
supply *sunt*. **iacentis:** genitive to agree with *mei* (understood): 'before my eyes as I lay'.
151 **somnis:** poetic plural. **manifesti:** this agrees with both *effigies* and *Penates*; note the
position of this word, enclosed between *multo* and *lumine* (see enclosing word order); the
phrase, literally 'clear with much light', may be translated 'clearly and brightly lit'.

Questions

1 In lines 132–137, how does Aeneas paint an optimistic picture?

2 How do lines 137–142 present a picture that contrasts sharply with the preceding
lines?

3 In lines 143–146, what does Anchises think has happened, and what does he think
should be done about it?

plena per insertas fundebat luna fenestras;
tum sic adfari et curas his demere dictis:
"quod tibi delato Ortygiam dicturus Apollo est,
hic canit et tua nos en ultro ad limina mittit.   155
nos te Dardania incensa tuaque arma secuti,
nos tumidum sub te permensi classibus aequor,
idem venturos tollemus in astra nepotes
imperiumque urbi dabimus. tu moenia magnis
magna para longumque fugae ne linque laborem.   160
mutandae sedes. non haec tibi litora suasit
Delius aut Cretae iussit considere Apollo.
est locus, Hesperiam Grai cognomine dicunt,
terra antiqua, potens armis atque ubere glaebae;
Oenotri coluere viri; nunc fama minores   165
Italiam dixisse ducis de nomine gentem:
hae nobis propriae sedes, hinc Dardanus ortus
Iasiusque pater, genus a quo principe nostrum.
surge age et haec laetus longaevo dicta parenti
haud dubitanda refer: Corythum terrasque requirat   170
Ausonias; Dictaea negat tibi Iuppiter arva."

When my father heard my dream, he recalled an earlier prophecy that the destiny of the Trojans would lie in Italy. 'Let us trust Apollo,' he said, 'and follow a better course.'

plenus, -a, -um	full	*consido, -ere*	I settle
insertus, -a, -um	unshuttered	*Hesperia, -ae* f.	Hesperia
fundo, -ere	I pour	*Grai, -orum* m.pl.	the Greeks
luna, -ae f.	moon	*dico, -ere*	I say, call, name
fenestra, -ae f.	window	*potens, -ntis*	powerful
adfor, -fari	I speak to	*uber, -eris* n.	richness
cura, -ae f.	anxiety	*glaeba, -ae* f.	soil
demo, -ere	I take away	*Oenotrus, -a, -um*	165 Oenotrian
dictum, -i n.	word	*fama, -ae* f.	report, rumour
defero, -re, -tuli, -latus	I carry (down)	*minores, -um* m.pl.	younger people
cano, -ere	155 I sing, prophesy	*Italia, -ae* f.	Italy
en	look!	*dux, ducis* m.	leader
ultro	voluntarily	*nomen, -inis* n.	name
Dardania, -ae f.	Troy	*proprius, -a, -um*	proper
incendo, -ere, -di, -sus	I burn, set on fire	*Dardanus, -i* m.	Dardanus
arma, -orum n.pl.	arms	*orior, -iri, ortus sum*	I originate
tumidus, -a, -um	swelling	*Iasius, -i* m.	Iasius
sub + abl.	under (the protection of)	*princeps, -ipis* m.	chief, founder
		surgo, -ere	I rise
permetior, -iri, -nsus sum	I cross over	*age*	come!
aequor, -oris n.	sea	*laetus, -a, -um*	happy
tollo, -ere	I exalt, raise up	*longaevus, -a, -um*	aged
astrum, -i n.	star	*haud*	170 not
nepos, -otis m.	descendant	*dubito, -are*	I doubt
imperium, -i n.	power, dominion	*refero, -ferre*	I report
fuga, -ae f.	160 flight	*Corythus, -i* m.	Corythus
linquo, -ere	I shrink from	*requiro, -ere*	I seek
muto, -are	I change	*Ausonius, -a, -um*	Ausonian, Italian
suadeo, -ere, -si, -sus	I commend	*Dictaeus, -a, -um*	of Dicte, Cretan
Delius, -a, -um	Delian		

152 The order is *qua plena luna se fundebat per insertas fenestras*. **insertas:** the meaning of this word is uncertain; 'unshuttered' gives the best sense.

153 **adfari, demere:** historic infinitives. The spondaic rhythm adds solemnity to the words.

154 **quod:** supply *id*: 'that which', and so 'what'. **tibi delato:** 'to you when you reach'. **dicturus Apollo est:** 'Apollo is intending to say'.

155 **hic:** 'here'. **tua nos:** note the <u>antithesis</u>, frequent with personal pronouns. **ultro:** rather than waiting for the Trojans to sail back to Delos, Apollo takes the initiative.

156–7 **nos . . . nos:** the <u>anaphora</u> of *nos* and the continuing <u>antithesis</u> make their words more vivid. **Dardania incensa:** ablative absolute. **secuti:** since the deities were believed to reside in their statues, which Aeneas had with him on his ship, *secuti* may be translated here as 'having accompanied'. **classibus:** poetic plural.

158–9 **idem (= eidem):** as the subject of a 1st person plural verb, this may be translated as 'we also'. **tollemus in astra:** this is a promise to confer divinity on Aeneas' *nepotes*. **nepotes:** Virgil intends the reader to think of Julius Caesar and Augustus: after his death the former was deified, and during Virgil's lifetime the latter was known as *divi filius*. **imperiumque urbi:** 'and dominion to your city': Rome (not, strictly speaking, Aeneas' city but the one to be founded by his descendant, Romulus) will have dominion over the world. This prophecy is one of several in the *Aeneid* to herald the greatness of the future Rome and its Julio-Claudian rulers (see Introduction). Of course Aeneas has yet to learn the identities of these *nepotes* (he learns in Book 6), but the intention here is to boost his perseverance and hopes. This prophecy is an abbreviated version of that given by Jupiter to Venus in Book 1 (lines 261ff.).

159–60 Note the heavy <u>alliteration</u> of *m* and *l*, together with the internal alliteration of *-gn-*, *-ng-* and *-g-*; also the <u>polyptoton</u> of *magnis magna;* these all add weight to their exhortation. **magnis:** the sense is unclear; it is probably dative (of advantage) and means 'for your great destiny' or 'for your great descendants'. **ne linque:** poetical alternative for *noli linquere*.

161 **mutandae:** supply *sunt*. **haec:** emphatic after *non*: 'it was not these shores that . . .'.

162 **Delius:** qualifies *Apollo*. **Cretae:** locative.

163 **Hesperiam:** literally 'the Land of the Evening', i.e 'in the West'.

164 **armis, ubere:** ablatives of respect.

165–6 **Oenotri . . . viri:** the Oenotrians were an ancient race of Southern Italy. **coluere:** = *coluerunt*. **minores:** the accusative of an indirect statement introduced by *fama*: 'there is a rumour that younger people called it Italy . . .'. **ducis:** according to one legend, Italy gained its name from a hero named Italus.

167 **hae . . . sedes:** supply *sunt*; plural for singular, as usually with *sedes*. **hinc Dardanus ortus (est) Iasiusque pater:** although singular, *ortus* has two subjects; according to some legends, Dardanus and his brother Iasius set out from Italy to found Troy.

168 **genus nostrum:** supply a verb such as *ortum est*; most versions of the legend make Dardanus rather than Iasius the founder of Troy; probably Virgil intended *a quo principe* to refer to *Dardanus*, with *Iasiusque pater* added in parenthesis.

169 **laetus:** translate as an adverb: 'joyfully'.

170–1 **Corythum:** an Italian town supposedly founded by Corythus, the father or step-father of Iasius and Dardanus. **Ausonias terras:** a common poetic name for Italy.

Questions

1 How does Virgil make lines 154–160 dramatic and effective?

2 Why do you think Virgil includes so many proper names in these lines?

3 How would you expect Aeneas to react to this speech?

Once again we set sail. A mighty storm drove us blindly across the sea. After three days of this we sighted a mountainous island. This was the adopted home of the dreaded Harpies, monstrous birds with the faces of women and talons on their hands.

huc ubi delati portus intravimus, ecce	219
laeta boum passim campis armenta videmus	220
caprigenumque pecus nullo custode per herbas.	
inruimus ferro et divos ipsumque vocamus	
in partem praedamque Iovem; tum litore curvo	
exstruimusque toros dapibusque epulamur opimis.	
at subitae horrifico lapsu de montibus adsunt	225
Harpyae et magnis quatiunt clangoribus alas,	
diripiuntque dapes contactuque omnia foedant	
immundo; tum vox taetrum dira inter odorem.	
rursum in secessu longo sub rupe cavata	229
instruimus mensas arisque reponimus ignem;	231
rursum ex diverso caeli caecisque latebris	
turba sonans praedam pedibus circumvolat uncis,	
polluit ore dapes. sociis tunc arma capessant	
edico, et dira bellum cum gente gerendum.	235

defero, -re, -tuli, -latus	I bring to land	*contactus, -us* m.	touch
ecce	see, look	*foedo, -are*	I befoul, mutilate
bos, -vis m./f.	220 ox, cow	*immundus, -a, -um*	filthy
passim	everywhere	*taeter, -tra, -trum*	loathsome
campus, -i m.	plain	*dirus, -a, -um*	dreadful
armentum, -i n.	herd	*odor, -oris* m.	smell, stench
caprigenus, -a, -um	goat-born	*rursum*	again
pecus, -oris n.	flock	*secessus, -us* m.	sheltered area
custos, -odis m.	guard, herdsman	*rupes, -is* f.	rock, cliff
inruo, -ere	I rush upon	*cavatus, -a, -um*	hollowed out
ferrum, -i n.	iron, sword	*instruo, -ere*	231 I set up
pars, -tis f.	part, share	*mensa, -ae* f.	table
praeda, -ae f.	booty	*ara, -ae* f.	altar
curvus, -a, -um	curved	*repono, -ere*	I place again
exstruo, -ere	I pile up	*ignis, -is* m.	fire
torus, -i m.	couch, cushion	*diversus, -a, -um*	different
daps, -is f.	feast, banquet	*caecus, -a, -um*	blind, hidden
epulor, -ari	I feast	*latebra, -ae* f.	hiding place
opimus, -a, -um	sumptuous	*turba, -ae* f.	crowd, flock
subitus, -a, -um	225 sudden	*sono, -are*	I sound, screech
horrificus, -a, -um	dreadful	*pes, pedis* m.	foot, talon
lapsus, -us m.	swoop	*circumvolo, -are*	I fly round
mons, -ntis m.	mountain	*uncus, -a, -um*	hooked
adsum, -esse	I am present	*polluo, -ere*	I defile
Harpya, -ae f.	a Harpy	*os, oris* n.	mouth
quatio, -ere	I shake, flap	*tunc*	then
clangor, -oris m.	flapping noise	*capesso, -ere*	I seize
ala, -ae f.	wing	*edico, -ere*	235 I order, proclaim
diripio, -ere	I tear apart	*gero, -ere*	I wage (war)

219 **portus:** plural for singular.

220 **laeta . . . armenta:** 'contented herds'. **boum:** genitive plural. **videmus:** the first of many historic presents.

221 **caprigenum pecus:** a poetical way of saying 'a flock of goats'.

222–3 **ferro:** 'with iron', and so 'with swords'. **ipsum:** qualifies *Iovem*. **vocamus:** 'we invite' (by means of prayer). **in partem praedamque:** 'to a share of the booty': an example of hendiadys. **litore curvo:** local ablative.

224 **-que . . . -que:** 'both . . . and'. **toros:** these may be couches to recline upon in Roman style for the feast, but equally they may be simply cushions retrieved from the oar benches in the ships. **dapibus:** ablative of instrument with *epulamur*: 'we feasted on . . .'.

225 **subitae:** this adjective, agreeing with *Harpyae*, is best translated as an adverb: 'suddenly'. **adsunt:** 'were present' and so 'were upon us', appearing out of nowhere.

226 **Harpyae:** note the enjambement, holding back the subject of the previous line for dramatic suspense. In Greek mythology the Harpies, as well as devouring and befouling the food of travellers, also carried off evil-doers to Tartarus.

228 **immundo:** note the enjambement again, emphasising the word. Note also the rhythm of the line, which is heavily spondaic, to underscore the horror of the scene. **vox . . . dira:** a 'dreadful screech'. The synchysis of *vox taetrum dira inter odorem* mingles together the sound and the smell of the birds.

229 **secessu:** we are probably to imagine a section of cliff which had been undercut by the sea.

230 This line has been omitted because it is out of place here, belonging in Book 1.

231 **aris:** local ablative. **ignem:** this is the fire used to cook the meat that is to be offered to the gods.

232 **rursum:** the repetition of this word from line 229 is intended to mark the rapidity of the action: the men quickly prepared a second feast, and immediately it too was attacked. **ex diverso caeli:** 'from a different (part) of the sky'; *diverso* is used as a neuter abstract noun. This line too is heavily spondaic, for the same reason as line 228.

233 **praeda:** the 'booty' is of course the food that has been set out; note the alliteration.

234–5 **ore:** singular for plural. The word order for the next sentence is *tunc edico sociis (ut) arma capessant, et (edico) bellum gerendum (esse) cum dira gente.* **edico:** this verb is used with two different constructions: the first, with the meaning 'order' is followed by an indirect command (with *ut* understood); the second, with the meaning 'proclaim', is followed by an indirect statement (with *esse* understood). **gerendum:** gerundive of obligation. The rhythm of line 235 is again heavily spondaic, to reflect the gravity of his instructions, that they should prepare to wage war on supernatural creatures.

Questions

1 What kind of scene is described in lines 219–221?

2 In lines 222–224, how does Aeneas emphasise the speed with which the Trojans acted?

3 In lines 225–235, how does Virgil create a vivid and dramatic scene?

4 List all the words and phrases that Virgil uses to describe the Harpies; from these descriptions, how easy is it to picture the creatures in your mind?

haud secus ac iussi faciunt tectosque per herbam
disponunt enses et scuta latentia condunt.
ergo ubi delapsae sonitum per curva dedere
litora, dat signum specula Misenus ab alta
aere cavo. invadunt socii et nova proelia temptant,   240
obscenas pelagi ferro foedare volucres.
sed neque vim plumis ullam nec vulnera tergo
accipiunt, celerique fuga sub sidera lapsae
semesam praedam et vestigia foeda relinquunt.
una in praecelsa consedit rupe Celaeno,   245
infelix vates, rumpitque hanc pectore vocem:
"bellum etiam pro caede boum stratisque iuvencis,
Laomedontiadae, bellumne inferre paratis
et patrio Harpyias insontes pellere regno?
accipite ergo animis atque haec mea figite dicta,   250
quae Phoebo pater omnipotens, mihi Phoebus Apollo
praedixit, vobis Furiarum ego maxima pando.
Italiam cursu petitis ventisque vocatis:
ibitis Italiam portusque intrare licebit.
sed non ante datam cingetis moenibus urbem   255
quam vos dira fames nostraeque iniuria caedis
ambesas subigat malis absumere mensas."

haud secus ac	just as	*consido, -ere, -sedi*	I settle
tego, -ere, texi, tectus	I conceal	*Celaeno, -us* f.	Celaeno
dispono, -ere	I distribute, spread	*infelix, -icis*	unfortunate
		vates, -is f.	prophetess
ensis, -is m.	sword	*rumpo, -ere*	I break, utter
scutum, -i n.	shield	*pectus, -oris* n.	heart, breast
lateo, -ere	I lie hidden	*pro* + abl.	in return for
condo, -ere	I hide, store	*caedes, -is* f.	slaughter
delabor, -i, -lapsus sum	I swoop down	*sterno, -ere, stravi, stratus*	I fell
sonitus, -us m.	noise, cry	*iuvencus, -i* m.	bullock
signum, -i n.	signal, sign	*Laomedontiades, -ae* m.	Trojan
specula, -ae f.	look-out position	*infero, -re*	I begin (a war)
Misenus, -i m.	Misenus	*patrius, -a, -um*	ancestral, father's
aes, aeris n.	240 bronze, trumpet	*insons, -ntis*	innocent
cavus, -a, -um	hollow	*pello, -ere*	I drive
invado, -ere	I attack	*figo, -ere*	250 I fix
proelium, -i n.	battle	*omnipotens, -ntis*	all-powerful
obscenus, -a, -um	disgusting	*praedico, -ere, -dixi, -dictus*	I foretell
volucris, -is f.	bird	*Furiae, -arum* f.pl.	the Furies
vis, acc. *vim* f.	force, violence	*pando, -ere*	I reveal
pluma, -ae f.	feather	*cursus, -us* m.	speed
vulnus, -eris n.	wound	*intro, -are*	I enter
tergum, -i n.	back	*licet*	it is allowed
celer, -eris, -ere	swift	*cingo, -ere*	255 I surround
sidus, -eris n.	star	*fames, -is* f.	hunger
labor, -i, lapsus sum	I glide, soar, fall	*iniuria, -ae* f.	injustice, outrage
semesus, -a, -um	half-eaten	*ambedo, -ere, -edi, -esus*	I gnaw round
vestigium, -i n.	trace, mark, step	*subigo, -ere*	I compel
foedus, -a, -um	foul	*mala, -ae* f.	jaw
relinquo, -ere	I leave behind	*absumo, -ere*	I consume, eat
praecelsus, -a, -um	245 very high		

236–7 tectos, latentia: the <u>proleptic</u> use of these two adjectives gives the result of the two verbs: 'they spread out their swords concealed . . .' and 'hid their shields so as to be out of sight'. Note the <u>chiastic</u> word order in line 237.

238 delapsae: the participle agrees with the subject of *dedere* (= *dederunt*): the Harpies.

239 specula Misenus ab alta: presumably Misenus (the helmsman of Aeneas' ship) had been sent up on to the top of the cliff to give warning of the Harpies' next attack.

240 aere cavo: ablative of instrument. **invadunt:** the promoted position emphasises the speed of the attack. **nova:** 'strange', because they have never fought birds before.

241 obscenas . . . volucres: the strong adjective and noun <u>enclose</u> the line, giving maximum emphasis. **ferro foedare:** 'to mutilate with the sword'; the <u>alliteration</u> reflects Aeneas' disgust. In line 227, *foedant* was used of the Harpies fouling the food; here the tables are turned. **foedare:** the infinitive, in apposition to *proelia*, explains what the battle was about.

242–3 plumis, tergo: local ablatives. **accipiunt:** the subject is the Harpies. **sub sidera:** 'up to the stars', i.e. 'up into the sky'.

244 praedam: the 'booty' is of course the meal. **vestigia:** the birds' excrement. Note the <u>chiasmus</u>: adjective – noun – noun – adjective.

245 una . . . Celaeno: 'Celaeno alone'; Celaeno was the leader of the Harpies.

245–6 Both lines are heavily spondaic to slow the action in preparation for the prophecy.

246 infelix vates: 'prophetess of doom'; as the Harpies were supernatural beings, they had the gift of prophecy. **rumpit:** literally 'bursts out (with)', a very unusual usage intended to suggest Celaeno's strong indignation. **hanc vocem:** 'these words'. **pectore:** the words issue 'from her breast' as the heart was believed to be the seat of intelligence and thought.

247–8 The order is *paratisne inferre bellum etiam pro caede boum stratisque iuvencis, Laomedontiadae?* **bellum:** placed first, repeated and strengthened by *etiam*, all to emphasise Celaeno's outrage at the Trojans' actions. **pro:** 'in defence of'. Her argument is that, not only was it wrong of the Trojans to kill cattle belonging to the Harpies, but to then make ready to wage war on the owners of the cattle in order to protect the stolen meat was an even bigger crime. **Laomedontiadae:** 'Descendants of Laomedon'; this is a scornful name, as Laomedon, an early king of Troy, was notorious for his dishonesty and treachery.

249 patrio . . . regno: ablative of separation; since the Harpies had only recently moved to the Strophades, this is exaggeration born of indignation.

250 animis: local ablative to be taken with both verbs.

251 quae: the object both of *praedixit* and *pando* (supply *et*). **pater omnipotens:** i.e. Jupiter.

252 praedixit: to be translated twice – firstly with Jupiter as subject and then Apollo. **Furiarum ego maxima:** in the mythology the Furies were distinct from the Harpies, and so Virgil must be using the name in a general sense, to indicate the class of spirits created by the gods to punish wicked humans; also the Furies were generally more terrifying than the Harpies, and so perhaps Celaeno uses the name to strike fear into the Trojans.

253 cursu: ablative of manner: 'with speed'. **petitis:** 2nd person plural present. **ventisque vocatis:** the *-que* links *cursu* and *ventis vocatis* (ablative absolute).

254 Italiam: accusative of the goal of motion; the repetition is for rhetorical effect.

255 ante . . . quam: to be taken together. **datam:** 'promised'.

256 nostrae iniuria caedis: 'the wrong in (trying to) kill us': genitive of definition.

257 ambesas . . . absumere: 'to gnaw round and eat'. This terrible-sounding prophecy is fulfilled in Book 7, lines 109ff., when the Trojans eat thin cakes they have used as 'tables'.

Questions

1 How does Virgil make Celaeno's prophecy dramatic and effective?

*Horrified by these words, we rushed to sail away from the island. After passing the winter
on the west coast of Greece, we continued our journey along the shore of the Adriatic till we
came to Buthrotum. Here we learnt that Helenus, a son of Priam, had become king and had
married Andromache, the widow of Hector. Amazed at this news, I hurried to greet Helenus;
on the way I came upon Andromache herself, who was making an offering to the spirit of
Hector. She could scarcely believe I was real.*

labitur et longo vix tandem tempore fatur:	309
"verane te facies, verus mihi nuntius adfers,	310
nate dea? vivisne? aut, si lux alma recessit,	
Hector ubi est?' dixit, lacrimasque effudit et omnem	
implevit clamore locum. vix pauca furenti	
subicio et raris turbatus vocibus hisco:	
'vivo equidem vitamque extrema per omnia duco;	315
ne dubita, nam vera vides.	
heu! quis te casus deiectam coniuge tanto	
excipit, aut quae digna satis fortuna revisit,	
Hectoris Andromache? Pyrrhin conubia servas?"	
deiecit vultum et demissa voce locuta est:	320
"o felix una ante alias Priameia virgo,	
hostilem ad tumulum Troiae sub moenibus altis	
iussa mori, quae sortitus non pertulit ullos	
nec victoris heri tetigit captiva cubile!"	

*Andromache described her fate as a slave of Pyrrhus, who was later killed trying to carry
off another man's wife. She then became mated to Helenus, who, although also a slave of
Pyrrhus, inherited part of the kingdom after Pyrrhus' death. Just as Andromache started to
ask after Aeneas' son, Helenus himself arrived, overjoyed to recognise me and my comrades.
We enjoyed his hospitality for several days. Before we set sail again, I asked Helenus, who
had the gift of prophecy, for his advice on how to survive the rest of our journey. He led me
to Apollo's shrine, sacrificed to the god and began his prophecy.*

verus, -a, -um	310 true	*deicio, -ere, -ieci, -iectus*		I lower, deprive
facies, -ei f.	face, appearance	*excipio, -ere*		I catch, await
nuntius, -i m.	messenger	*dignus, -a, -um*		worthy
adfero, -re	I bring	*reviso, -ere*		I see again
vivo, -ere	I live, am alive	*Pyrrhus, -i* m.		Pyrrhus
almus, -a, -um	kindly	*demissus, -a, -um*	320 lowered
recedo, -ere, -cessi	I depart	*felix, -icis*		fortunate
lacrima, -ae f.	tear	*Priameius, -a, -um*		of Priam
effundo, -ere, -fudi	I pour forth	*virgo, -inis* f.		maiden
impleo, -ere, -plevi	I fill	*hostilis, -e*		of the enemy
clamor, -oris m.	scream, cry	*tumulus, -i* m.		burial mound
furens, -entis	raving, distraught	*morior, -i*		I die
subicio, -ere	I interpose	*sortitus, -us* m.		drawing of lots
rarus, -a, -um	infrequent,	*perfero, -re, -tuli*		I endure
	disjointed	*victor, -oris*		victorious
turbo, -are, -avi, -atus	I trouble, upset	*herus, -i* m.		master
hisco, -ere	I gape, stammer	*tango, ere, tetigi*		I touch
equidem	315 truly, indeed	*captiva, -ae* f.		(female) captive
extremus, -a, -um	extreme, utmost	*cubile, -is* n.		bed
heu	alas			
casus, -us m.	fall, fate,			
	misfortune			

309 labitur: i.e. 'she fainted'; note the dactyl to show the speed of Andromache's collapse, followed by spondees to indicate her slow recovery. **longo . . . tempore:** 'after a long time'.

310 tene . . . adfers: 'do you bring yourself', i.e. 'do you come'. **vera facies, verus nuntius:** these are in apposition to the understood *tu*: 'as a true face', etc. Andromache can scarcely believe her eyes, and begins to wonder why, if this is a ghost, it is not that of her beloved Hector that has come to visit her rather than Aeneas.

311 nate dea: *nate* is vocative and *dea* is ablative of origin; translate 'son of a goddess'. **lux:** the 'light of life', and so the clause represents 'if you are dead'.

313–4 pauca furenti subicio: 'I interject a few (words) to her raving', i.e. 'I interrupted her distraught speech with a few words.' **turbatus:** this indicates that Aeneas was just as moved as Andromache was. **raris . . . vocibus hisco:** 'I gaped with disjointed words,' indicating that his mouth opened but could only utter disjointed words.

315 extrema: 'extreme dangers'.

316 This is one of many incomplete lines in the *Aeneid* that were still awaiting completion when Virgil died. **ne dubita:** = *noli dubitare*. **vera vides:** 'what you see is real'.

317 quis: adjectival, with *casus*. **coniuge tanto:** ablative of separation: 'deprived of so great a husband. Note the heavily spondaic line to underline the wretchedness of her situation.

318 digna satis: supply *te*: 'sufficiently worthy of you'. **revisit:** supply *te* again; the question seems to be asking what kind of fortune has befallen her this time round, i.e. in relation to her enforced second marriage to Pyrrhus.

319 Hectoris Andromache: these gentle words remind her of her rightful place as wife of Hector, and then the immediate *Pyrrhin* (short for *Pyrrhi-ne*) gives a harsh contrast.

320 deiecit, demissa: both words indicate her sadness or humility, as does the heavily spondaic rhythm.

321 Priameia virgo: Polyxena was the 'maiden daughter of Priam', who was sacrificed by Pyrrhus on the tomb of Achilles. Andromache envies her her quick death, preferable to slavery.

323 iussa mori: 'ordered to die', i.e. 'ordered to be killed' (to be translated before line 322).

324 sortitus: accusative plural; the surviving female Trojan captives were divided up among the victorious Greeks by lot; Polyxena avoided this humiliation.

325 captiva: 'as a captive' (in apposition to *quae*).

Questions

1 What makes line 309 effective poetry?

2 How do Andromache's words in lines 310–312 show her surprise and lack of comprehension?

3 In lines 313–314, how does Aeneas show his own emotions?

4 Do you think Aeneas' words in lines 315–319 are sympathetic or unfeeling? What is the evidence to support your conclusion?

5 How do lines 321–324 support the description of Andromache as 'downcast' (line 320)?

"pauca tibi e multis, quo tutior hospita lustres   377
aequora et Ausonio possis considere portu,
expediam dictis: prohibent nam cetera Parcae
scire Helenum farique vetat Saturnia Iuno.   380
principio Italiam, quam tu iam rere propinquam
vicinosque, ignare, paras invadere portus,
longa procul longis via dividit invia terris.
ante et Trinacria lentandus remus in unda
et salis Ausonii lustrandum navibus aequor   385
infernique lacus Aeaeaeque insula Circae,
quam tuta possis urbem componere terra.
signa tibi dicam, tu condita mente teneto:
cum tibi sollicito secreti ad fluminis undam
litoreis ingens inventa sub ilicibus sus   390
triginta capitum fetus enixa iacebit
alba solo recubans, albi circum ubera nati,
is locus urbis erit, requies ea certa laborum.
nec tu mensarum morsus horresce futuros:
fata viam invenient aderitque vocatus Apollo.   395
has autem terras Italique hanc litoris oram,
proxima quae nostri perfunditur aequoris aestu,
effuge: cuncta malis habitantur moenia Grais."

Helenus gave me instructions about the best course to follow, and how to avoid the monsters that lay in wait for unwary voyagers, especially Scylla and Charybdis. He told me to offer sacrifice to Juno before reaching Cumae and the prophetess who lived there.

quo	= *ut*	*Circe, -ae* f.	Circe
hospitus, -a, -um	strange, foreign	*compono, -ere*	I build
lustro, -are	I pass through	*mens, -ntis* f.	mind
expedio, -ire	I explain	*sollicitus, -a, -um*	anxious
prohibeo, -ere	I forbid	*secretus, -a, -um*	secluded
Parcae, -arum f.pl.	the Fates	*litoreus, -a, -um*	390 on the bank
Helenus, -i m.	380 Helenus	*invenio, -ire, -veni, -ventus*	I find
veto, -are	I forbid	*ilex, -icis* f.	holm-oak
Saturnius, -a, -um	of Saturn	*sus, suis* f.	sow
Iuno, -onis f.	Juno	*triginta*	thirty
principium, -i n.	beginning	*fetus, -us* m.	litter
reor, reri, ratus sum	I think	*enitor, -i, enixus sum*	I give birth to
propinquus, -a, -um	near	*albus, -a, -um*	white
vicinus, -a, -um	close, nearby	*solum, -i* n.	ground
ignarus, -a, -um	ignorant	*recubo, are*	I lie, recline
procul	far off	*uber, -eris* n.	teat
divido, -ere	I separate	*requies, -etis* f.	rest
invius, -a, -um	pathless	*certus, -a, -um*	sure, definite
Trinacrius, -a, -um	Sicilian	*morsus, -us* m.	biting, chewing
lento, -are	I bend	*horresco, -ere*	I dread
remus, -i m.	oar	*fatum, -i* n.	395 fate
unda, -ae f.	wave, water	*proximus, -a, -um*	nearest
sal, -is m.	385 salt, sea	*perfundo, -ere*	I bathe
infernus, -a, -um	infernal	*aestus, -us* m.	tide
lacus, -us m.	lake	*effugio, -ere*	I escape (from)
Aeaeus, -a, -um	of Aea, Colchian		

377 **pauca:** the neuter plural adjective is used as a noun, forming the object of *expediam*: supply 'details'. **e multis:** 'of many'; Helenus omits to mention most of the adventures that will befall the Trojans on their journey. **tutior:** best translated as an adverb: 'more safely'.

378 **Ausonio . . . portu:** local ablative: 'in an Italian harbour'.

379 **dictis:** instrumental ablative: 'in words'. **nam:** to be taken first. **Parcae:** these were three immortal sisters who allocated life spans and destinies to all mortals.

380 **Helenum:** referring to himself in the third person gives a more formal tone to his prediction. **farique vetat:** supply *eum* (Helenus). **Saturnia Iuno:** Juno was the daugher of Saturn; she had been hostile to the Trojans ever since the Trojan prince Paris chose Aphrodite over her as the most beautiful goddess.

381 **principio:** 'in the beginning', and so 'firstly'. **Italiam:** the object of *dividit*. **rere:** = *reris*. **propinquam:** supply *esse*.

382 **vicinos . . . portus:** supply *cuius*; the separation of these words gives them emphasis. The argument is 'you think Italy is nearby and the harbours close by; you are wrong'.

383 **longa . . . longis via . . . invia:** there is a play on words here, typical of prophetic utterances; the way is 'pathless' because it is across the sea. **dividit:** supply *a te* (or *a vobis*). **longis . . . terris:** 'past long coastlines'.

384 **ante:** to be held back and linked to *quam* in line 387. **lentandus remus:** supply *est*; '(your) oar(s) must be bent', i.e. 'you must row'.

385 **salis Ausonii . . . aequor:** 'the waters of the Ausonian Sea': the southern part of the Tyrrhenian Sea, between Sicily and the west coast of Italy. **lustrandum:** supply *est*.

386 Supply *lustrandi sunt* and *lustranda est* with the two subjects. **inferni lacus:** the 'infernal lakes' are Lakes Lucrinus and Avernus, joined in Virgil's day; the latter was believed to be the entrance to the underworld and lay near Cumae. **Aeaeaeque insula Circae:** Circe was an enchantress who, in the *Odyssey*, turned Odysseus' men into pigs; the Greek tradition places her island in the East, but later tradition linked it with a promontory (now Monte Circeo) half way between Cumae and Rome. Aeaea was the name of the island in the *Odyssey*.

387 **tuta . . . terra:** 'on safe ground'. **possis:** subjunctive of purpose.

388 **tu . . . teneto:** 'see that you keep'; *teneto* is a formal form of the imperative, used here to make his instruction more weighty. **condita mente:** '(the signs) fixed in your mind'.

389–90 The basic order is *cum . . . ingens sus . . . inventa (est) . . . tibi*. **tibi:** 'by you' (dative of the agent). **secreti ad fluminis undam:** 'by the waters of a secluded river'; this river will prove to be the Tiber, which flows through Rome. **litoreis . . . sub ilicibus:** 'under the holm-oaks along the bank'.

391 **triginta capitum fetus:** 'a litter of thirty heads', i.e. thirty individuals. **iacebit:** supply *et*.

392 **alba solo recubans:** 'reclining white on the ground'; the word *alba* would remind readers of Alba Longa, the city that, according to the legend, Aeneas' son Ascanius would found thirty years later. **albi . . . nati:** supply *et erunt*.

393 **laborum:** '(rest) from your labours'. This prophecy is fulfilled in Book 8.

394 **morsus . . . futuros:** 'future bites'; this refers to Celaeno's prophecy (see lines 256–7).

395 **vocatus:** 'when called'.

396–8 **has . . . terras . . . hanc . . . oram:** the objects of *effuge*. **proxima quae:** take *quae* first: 'which is the nearest (shore bathed)'. **nostri . . . aequoris:** i.e. the Ionian Sea, between Southern Italy and Greece. **malis . . . Grais:** 'by evil Greeks' (dative of the agent).

Questions

1 How does Helenus make his prophecy formal and solemn?

2 If you were Aeneas, how would you have reacted to this prophecy, and why?

We left Helenus and Andromache. Soon we sighted Italy and pulled into a harbour by a temple to Minerva. We made sacrifice there to Minerva and Juno and then sailed on, narrowly avoiding the whirlpool Charybdis before drifting towards the coast of the Cyclopes.

portus ab accessu ventorum immotus et ingens	570
ipse: sed horrificis iuxta tonat Aetna ruinis,	
interdumque atram prorumpit ad aethera nubem	
turbine fumantem piceo et candente favilla,	
attollitque globos flammarum et sidera lambit,	
interdum scopulos avulsaque viscera montis	575
erigit eructans, liquefactaque saxa sub auras	
cum gemitu glomerat fundoque exaestuat imo.	
fama est Enceladi semustum fulmine corpus	
urgeri mole hac, ingentemque insuper Aetnam	
impositam ruptis flammam exspirare caminis,	580
et fessum quotiens mutet latus, intremere omnem	
murmure Trinacriam et caelum subtexere fumo.	
noctem illam tecti silvis immania monstra	
perferimus, nec quae sonitum det causa videmus.	
nam neque erant astrorum ignes nec lucidus aethra	585
siderea polus, obscuro sed nubila caelo,	
et lunam in nimbo nox intempesta tenebat.	

accessus, -us m.	570 approach, access	*gemitus, -us* m.	groan, roar
ventus, -i m.	wind	*glomero, -are*	I roll up
immotus, -a, -um	undisturbed	*fundus, -i* m.	bottom
horrificus, -a, -um	terrifying	*exaestuo, -are*	I boil up
iuxta	nearby	*Enceladus, -i* m.	Enceladus
tono, -are	I thunder	*semustus, -a, -um*	half-burned
Aetna, -ae f.	Mt Etna	*fulmen, -inis* n.	thunderbolt
ruina, -ae f.	shower of ash	*urgeo, -ere*	I crush, confine
interdum	sometimes	*moles, -is* f.	mass
ater, atra, atrum	black, dark	*insuper*	above
prorumpo, -ere	I fling out	*exspiro, -are*	580 I breath out
aether, -eris (acc. *-era*) m.	sky	*caminus, -i* m.	furnace
nubes, -is f.	cloud	*quotiens*	as often as
turbo, -inis m.	whirlwind	*latus, -eris* n.	side
fumo, -are	I reek, smoke	*intremo, -ere*	I tremble
piceus, -a, -um	pitchy, black	*murmur, -uris* n.	rumbling
candens, -ntis	white-hot	*Trinacria, -ae* f.	Sicily
favilla, -ae f.	ash, cinders	*subtexo, -ere*	I veil
attollo, -ere	I raise up	*fumus, -i* m.	smoke
globus, -i m.	mass	*immanis, -e*	monstrous, awful
flamma, -ae f.	flame	*monstrum, -i* n.	monster, portent
sidus, -eris n.	star	*perfero, -ferre*	I bear, endure
lambo, -ere	I lick	*lucidus, -a, -um*	585 bright, clear
scopulus, -i m.	575 rock	*aethra, -ae* f.	clear sky
avello, -ere, -vulsi, -vulsus	I tear out	*sidereus, -a, -um*	starry
viscera, -um n.pl.	insides	*polus, -i* m.	sky
erigo, -ere	I raise up	*obscurus, -a, -um*	dark
eructo, -are	I belch forth	*nubila, -orum* n.pl.	clouds
liquefactus, -a, -um	molten	*nimbus, -i* m.	cloud
aura, -ae f.	air, sky	*intempestus, -a, -um*	timeless

570 **portus:** this is the harbour that gave access to the community of the Cyclopes, the one-eyed giants who were employed by Vulcan to work at his forges in Mt Etna. Odysseus' imprisonment by the Cyclops Polyphemus was one of the central episodes of Homer's *Odyssey*. **ab accessu ventorum:** 'away from the approach of winds', i.e. sheltered from the winds.

571 **ipse:** this gives a contrast: the harbour itself is secure, but Etna is close by.

572–3 **turbine fumantem piceo:** the 'black cloud' is 'reeking with (i.e. 'of') a pitchy whirlwind', i.e. it reeks of black, swirling smoke. **piceo et candente:** note the <u>antithesis</u>: 'pitch black and white hot'.

574 **sidera lambit:** the subject of all these verbs is *Aetna*; the volcano 'licks the stars' in that the 'masses' or tongues of fire reach high into the sky (an example of <u>hyperbole</u>).

575–6 **avulsa viscera montis erigit eructans:** a very vivid description of an eruption. **erigit eructans:** 'belches forth and flings upwards'; note the <u>alliteration</u> and <u>assonance</u>.

576–7 **sub auras:** 'up into the sky'. **fundo . . . imo:** 'from its deepest depths'.

578 **fama est:** 'the story goes that'. **Enceladi . . . corpus:** Enceladus was one of the Titans who fought a war against the gods; when they were defeated by Jupiter's thunderbolt, they were imprisoned under various mountains.

579–80 **urgeri:** indirect statement dependent on *fama est* (also *exspirare*, *intremere* and *subtexere*). **mole hac:** 'under this mass' (the mountain). **insuper . . . impositam:** 'when placed on top (of him)'. **ruptis . . . caminis:** 'when its furnaces burst open'; the idea is that the thunderbolt that struck Enceladus tried to break out from his body, and the mountain could not contain it.

581 **mutet latus:** i.e. whenever he turned over. The idea is that the volcano erupted each time Enceladus changed his position.

583–4 **noctem illam:** 'for the duration of that night'. **monstra:** the 'portents' are the unearthly noises issuing from the mountain. **quae . . . causa:** 'what cause (produced the noise)', i.e. 'what caused the noise'.

585–6 **astrorum . . . ignes:** 'fires of stars', i.e. light from the stars. **lucidus aethra siderea polus:** '(nor was there) a bright sky with a clear, starry sky'; the <u>tautology</u> makes the description more vivid.

587 **nox intempesta:** 'timeless night', i.e. 'the dead of night'. **tenebat:** 'wrapped'.

Questions

1 How accurately does Virgil describe a volcanic eruption in these lines?

2 How does Virgil use language and imagery to make his description of Mt Etna more vivid?

3 Why do you think a number of mythical monsters were thought to lie beneath volcanoes?

4 What is the effect of the <u>enjambement</u> of *perferimus* in line 584?

postera iamque dies primo surgebat Eoo
umentemque Aurora polo dimoverat umbram,
cum subito e silvis macie confecta suprema   590
ignoti nova forma viri miserandaque cultu
procedit supplexque manus ad litora tendit.
respicimus. dira inluvies immissaque barba,
consertum tegimen spinis: at cetera Graius,
et quondam patriis ad Troiam missus in armis.   595
isque ubi Dardanios habitus et Troia vidit
arma procul, paulum aspectu conterritus haesit
continuitque gradum; mox sese ad litora praeceps
cum fletu precibusque tulit: "per sidera testor,
per superos atque hoc caeli spirabile lumen,   600
tollite me, Teucri; quascumque abducite terras:
hoc sat erit. scio me Danais e classibus unum
et bello Iliacos fateor petiisse penates.
pro quo, si sceleris tanta est iniuria nostri,
spargite me in fluctus vastoque immergite ponto;   605
si pereo, hominum manibus periisse iuvabit."
dixerat et genua amplexus genibusque volutans
haerebat. qui sit fari, quo sanguine cretus,
hortamur, quae deinde agitet fortuna fateri.

posterus, -a, -um	next	*aspectus, -us* m.	appearance
Eous, -i m.	Morning Star	*conterritus, -a, -um*	terrified
umens, -ntis	damp, moist	*haereo, -ere, -si, -sus*	I hesitate, cling
Aurora, -ae f.	Dawn	*contineo, -ere, -ui, -entus*	I check
dimoveo, -ere, -vi, -tus	I disperse	*gradus, -us* m.	step
umbra, -ae f.	shadow, ghost	*praeceps, -cipitis*	headlong
subito	590 suddenly	*fletus, -us* m.	weeping
macies, -ei f.	emaciation	*prex, -cis* f.	prayer, plea
confectus, -a, -um	worn out	*testor, -ari, -atus sum*	I declare
supremus, -a, -um	last	*superi, -orum* m.pl.	600 the gods above
ignotus, -a, -um	unknown	*spirabilis, -e*	vital
forma, -ae f.	shape, figure	*Teucri, -orum* m.pl.	the Trojans
miseror, -ari, -atus sum	I pity	*qui-, quae-, quod-cumque*	whichever
cultus, -us m.	dress	*sat*	enough
procedo, -ere	I come forward	*scio, -ire*	I know
supplex, -icis	begging	*Iliacus, -a, -um*	Trojan
tendo, -ere	I stretch out	*fateor, -eri*	I confess
respicio, -ere	I look back	*scelus, -eris* n.	crime
inluvies, -ei f.	filth	*spargo, -ere*	605 I scatter
immissus, -a, -um	straggly	*fluctus, -us* m.	wave
barba, -ae f.	beard	*vastus, -a, -um*	immense
consero, -ere, -erui -ertus	I fasten together	*immergo, -ere*	I plunge into
tegimen, -inis n.	covering	*pereo, -ire*	I die
spina, -ae f.	thorn	*iuvo, -are*	I please
Graius, -a, -um	Greek	*genu, -us* n.	knee
quondam	595 once	*amplector, -i, -xus sum*	I embrace
Dardanius, -a, -um	Trojan	*voluto, -are*	I hover
habitus, -us m.	dress	*cresco, -ere, -evi, -etus*	I grow
paulum	a little	*agito, -are*	I pursue

588 primo . . . Eoo: 'at the first appearance of the Morning Star'; this may signify the planet Venus or the Sun itself. **surgebat:** 'was rising', i.e. 'was dawning'.

589 umentem . . . umbram: 'the moist shadows (of night)'. **polo:** 'from the sky'.

590–2 cum . . . nova forma . . . procedit: 'when the strange figure (of a man) came forward' ('inverse *cum*' + indicative). **macie confecta suprema:** 'worn out with the last stages of emaciation'. **miseranda cultu:** 'piteous in dress'. **supplex:** 'begging', i.e. 'in supplication'.

593 respicimus: 'we looked back', because they were turning their backs on the shore to make their departure. **dira inluvies:** supply *erat*.

594 at cetera Graius: 'but in all other respects (he was) Greek'; *cetera* is accusative of respect. What these other indicators of nationality were is not stated.

595 The Trojans would not have known this until the man spoke and told them, unless they actually recognised him from the war.

597 procul: 'from afar'. **paulum . . . haesit:** 'he hesitated for a moment'.

598–9 sese . . . tulit: lit. 'he carried himself', and so 'he rushed'; *sese* = *se*.

599–601 per sidera testor: 'by the stars I implore you'. **hoc caeli spirabile lumen:** lit. '(and by) this breathable light of the sky', and so 'this vital light of the sky'; Virgil is conflating light and air, the two vital requirements for life, in a poetic <u>metaphor</u>.

601 quascumque . . . terras: 'to whichever lands (you wish)'. **abducite:** supply *me*.

602–3 scio: the -*o* is short (normally this verbal ending is long); Virgil takes this liberty only with *scio* and *nescio*, though later poets spread the practice. **me:** supply *esse*. **Danais e classibus unum:** 'that I am one (of the men) from the Greek fleet' (plural for singular). **Iliacos fateor petiisse penates:** 'I confess that I attacked Trojan homes'; supply *me* after *fateor*; *penates* are literally the household gods, and here stand for the houses in which these gods were worshipped (an example of <u>metonymy</u> and <u>synecdoche</u>). Note the bitterness of the <u>alliteration</u>, which carries over into the next line.

604 sceleris . . . nostri: 'of our crime'; whether for reasons of personal survival or from genuine remorse, this Greek admits that his people's waging of the Trojan War was a crime.

605 spargite me: understand 'cut me in pieces and then . . .'. **in fluctus:** 'onto the waves', and so 'over the sea'. **vasto . . . ponto:** ablative of place.

606 pereo, hominum: normally the -*o* would elide before *hom*-, but here there is a hiatus, i.e. a pause before the key word *hominum*. **hominum manibus:** 'at the hands of men', i.e. not at the hands of the Cyclopes; he is terrified of suffering the same fate as Odysseus' men when trapped in the cave of Polyphemus (*Odyssey* Book 9). **iuvabit:** supply *me*: 'it will please me'.

607–8 dixerat: the pluperfect is often used by Virgil to mark the conclusion of a speech; translate as 'he finished speaking'. **genua . . . genibus:** supply *mea* and *meis*; the repetition of *genu* in different forms (<u>polyptoton</u>) emphasises the desperation of the man. Clasping a person's knees was the standard way of seeking that person's help in the heroic world. **genibus volutans haerebat:** 'he clung to my knees hovering', i.e. 'grovelling'.

608–9 The order is *hortamur (eum) fari*, with the infinitive instead of the usual indirect command construction. **qui sit:** = the prose *quis sit*. **quo sanguine cretus:** supply *sit*: 'from what blood he had grown', and so 'from what parentage he had sprung'. **deinde . . . fateri:** the order is *deinde (hortamur eum) fateri quae fortuna (eum) agitet*. **fortuna:** 'evil fortune'.

Questions

1 In lines 588–595, how does Virgil emphasise the poor state of the man?

2 In lines 596–609, what impression do you gain of the man's character? Can you explain his behaviour?

Encouraged to tell his story, the man introduced himself as Achaemenides, one of the men who accompanied Odysseus into Polyphemus' cave. In the rush to escape, he had been left behind. He went on to describe the Cyclops as enormous and unapproachable.

"visceribus miserorum et sanguine vescitur atro.   622
vidi egomet duo de numero cum corpora nostro
prensa manu magna medio resupinus in antro
frangeret ad saxum, sanieque aspersa natarent   625
limina; vidi atro cum membra fluentia tabo
manderet et tepidi tremerent sub dentibus artus –
haud impune quidem, nec talia passus Ulixes
oblitusve sui est Ithacus discrimine tanto.
nam simul expletus dapibus vinoque sepultus   630
cervicem inflexam posuit, iacuitque per antrum
immensus saniem eructans et frusta cruento
per somnum commixta mero, nos magna precati
numina sortitique vices una undique circum
fundimur, et telo lumen terebramus acuto   635
ingens quod torva solum sub fronte latebat,
Argolici clipei aut Phoebeae lampadis instar,
et tandem laeti sociorum ulciscimur umbras."

Achaemenides explained how he survived by hiding in the woods, terrified of being found by one of the other Cyclopes. When he saw Aeneas' ship, the first that had come within sight, he decided that death from Trojans would be preferable to being eaten by a Cyclops.

vescor, -i + abl.	I feed on	*sepelio, -ire, -ivi, -ultus*	I bury
egomet	= *ego*	*cervix, -icis* f.	neck
numerus, -i m.	number	*inflexus, -a, -um*	bowed, drooping
prendo, -ere, -di, -sus	I seize	*pono, -ere, -sui, -situs*	I place, rest
resupinus, -a, -um	lying on the back	*immensus, -a, -um*	huge
antrum, -i n.	cave	*frustum, -i* n.	piece of food
frango, -ere	625 I smash, break	*cruentus, -a, -um*	blood-stained
sanies, -ei f.	gore	*commisceo, -ere, -ui, -ixtus*	I mix together
aspergo, -ere, -si, -sus	I splash, spatter	*merum, -i* n.	undiluted wine
nato, -are	I swim, am awash	*numen, -inis* n.	god
fluo, -ere	I flow	*sortior, -iri, -itus sum*	I draw lots
tabum, -i n.	gore	*vicem, -is* f.	turn, part
mando, -ere	I chew, crush	*una*	together
tepidus, -a, -um	warm	*undique*	from all sides
dens, dentis m.	tooth	*telum, -i* n.	635 weapon
artus, -us m.	limb	*lumen, -inis* n.	light, eye
impune	without punishment	*terebro, -are*	I bore
		acutus, -a, -um	sharp
quidem	however	*torvus, -a, -um*	fierce, grim
talis, -e	such	*frons, -ntis* f.	forehead, brow
patior, -i, passus sum	I suffer, endure	*Argolicus, -a, -um*	Greek
Ulixes, -is m.	Ulysses	*clipeus, -i* m.	shield
obliviscor, -i, -litus sum	I forget	*Phoebeus, -a, -um*	of Apollo
Ithacus, -i m.	the Ithacan	*lampas, -adis* f.	lamp
discrimen, -inis n.	crisis	*instar* + gen.	just like
simul = *simulac*	630 as soon as	*ulciscor, -i, ultus sum*	I avenge
expleo, -ere, -evi, -etus	I fill up, gorge		

622 **miserorum:** this belongs with both *visceribus* and *atro sanguine*.

623–5 **vidi egomet cum:** 'with my own eyes I saw when . . .'. The order from here on is *(Cyclops), resupinus in medio antro, prensa magna manu duo corpora de nostro numero frangeret ad saxum*. **duo . . . corpora . . . prensa . . . frangeret:** '(when) he smashed two having been seized bodies', i.e. 'he seized two bodies and smashed them'. **manu magna medio:** note the heavy <u>alliteration</u>. **resupinus:** note the <u>enclosing word order</u> used here. **ad saxum:** here 'against a rock'.

625–6 **sanie aspersa:** 'spattered with gore'. **natarent:** the subjunctive is dependent on *cum*. **limina:** plural for singular; note the <u>enjambement</u>.

626–7 **vidi . . . cum:** 'I saw when', as in line 623. **atro . . . tabo:** the ablative depends on *fluentia*; note the <u>enclosing word order</u> again. **tremerent:** the subjunctive is dependent on *cum*; the subject is *tepidi . . . artus*. **tepidi:** the limbs are still warm from being alive.

628–9 **haud impune:** supply a verb such as 'he did (all this)'. **passus:** supply *est*; the idea is that Ulysses did not allow these actions to go unpunished. **Ulixes:** the Roman name of Homer's Odysseus. **oblitusve sui est Ithacus:** 'nor did the Ithacan forget himself': he remained true to himself , i.e. to his leadership and heroic qualities. Ulysses was the king of Ithaca, a small island off the west coast of Greece, and famed for his cunning. **tanto discrimine:** ablative of time.

630–1 **expletus . . . sepultus:** these participles agree with the unexpressed subject, the Cyclops. Note the <u>chiasmus</u>, neatly balancing *expletus dapibus* with *vino sepultus*. **simul . . . cervicem . . . posuit:** 'as soon as he rested his neck', i.e. laid his head on the ground.

631–3 **per antrum:** 'all across the cave'. **eructans:** a strong word; it has two objects: *saniem* and *frusta*. **frusta:** the order is *frusta commixta cruento mero*; the *frusta* are the chunks of human flesh. **per somnum:** 'during his sleep', to be taken with *eructans*.

633–5 **sortitique vices:** 'and having drawn lots for the (different) tasks', following Homer's account. **una . . . fundimur:** 'and all together from all sides we rushed to surround him'; *fundimur* is literally 'we are poured', standing for the active used intransitively. Note the heavy <u>assonance</u> of *-u-* in these lines.

635–6 **telo . . . acuto:** Homer describes how Odysseus' men sharpened a wooden stake and heated it in the fire. **lumen terebramus . . . ingens:** 'we drilled through his huge eye'; in Homer's version the Greeks coiled a rope round the stake and used it like a traditional drill, with some men keeping the stake vertical while others rotated it with the rope. Note the <u>enjambement</u> of *ingens*, giving the word great emphasis. **quod . . . solum . . . latebat:** 'his only one, which was deep set'. **torva . . . sub fronte:** 'beneath his grim brow'; the *frons* is the pronounced eyebrow ridge.

637–8 **instar:** to be taken first, as *clipei* and *lampadis* are dependent on it. **Argolici clipei:** a Greek shield was large and round. **Phoebeae lampadis:** as Apollo was god of the sun, the *lampas* is the sun. **tandem:** i.e. after a long period of suffering.

Questions

1 How does Achaemenides make his account of the events in the cave dramatic and vivid? Try to include sound effects, choice of words and word order in your analysis.

2 Read if you can a translation of Homer's *Odyssey*, Book 9, lines 375–394; compare the two versions of the blinding of the Cyclops. Which do you prefer, and why?

vix ea fatus erat summo cum monte videmus   655
ipsum inter pecudes vasta se mole moventem
pastorem Polyphemum et litora nota petentem,
monstrum horrendum, informe, ingens, cui lumen ademptum.
trunca manum pinus regit et vestigia firmat;
lanigerae comitantur oves; ea sola voluptas   660
solamenque mali.

He waded out into the sea to wash the blood from the ruin of his eye. As we sailed away, we
saw the whole tribe of Cyclopes rushing to the harbour. Although they saw us, they could
not wade far enough out to stop us. We sailed along the coast of Sicily, reaching a harbour
finally at Drepanum.

hic pelagi tot tempestatibus actus   708
heu, genitorem, omnis curae casusque levamen,
amitto Anchisen. hic me, pater optime, fessum   710
deseris, heu, tantis nequiquam erepte periclis!
nec vates Helenus, cum multa horrenda moneret,
hos mihi praedixit luctus, non dira Celaeno.
hic labor extremus, longarum haec meta viarum;
hinc me digressum vestris deus appulit oris.'   715
sic pater Aeneas intentis omnibus unus
fata renarrabat divum cursusque docebat.
conticuit tandem factoque hic fine quievit.

pecus, -udis f.	656 sheep	ago, -ere, egi, actus	I drive
pastor, -oris m.	shepherd	levamen, -inis n.	comforter
Polyphemus, -i m.	Polyphemus	amitto, -ere	710 I lose
notus, -a, -um	known, familiar	desero, -ere	I abandon, desert
horrendus, -a, -um	horrible	nequiquam	in vain
informis, -e	shapeless, hideous	eripio, -ere, -ui, ereptus	I rescue
adimo, -ere, -emi, -emptus	I take away	periclum, -i n.	danger
truncus, -a, -um	lopped, cut down	vates, -is m.	prophet
pinus, -us f.	pine-tree	moneo, -ere	I warn of
rego, -ere	I rule, guide	luctus, -us m.	grief, sorrow
firmo, -are	I support	meta, -ae f.	goal
laniger, -era, -erum	660 wool-bearing	digredior, -i, -ssus sum	715 I depart
comitor, -ari	I accompany	appello, -ere, -puli, pulsus	I drive … to
ovis, -is f.	sheep	intentus, -a, -um	eager
voluptas, -atis f.	pleasure	renarro, -are	I relate
solamen, -inis n.	solace	doceo, -ere	I tell of
malum, -i n.	trouble	conticesco, -ere, -ticui	I fall silent
tempestas, -atis f.	storm	quiesco, -ere, -evi, -etus	I rest

655 **summo . . . monte:** local ablative. **cum . . . videmus:** inverse *cum* construction, taking the indicative, here the historic present. Note the long sequence of <u>alliterations</u> of *m*, with <u>consonance</u> and <u>assonance</u>, here and in the next few lines.

656–7 **ipsum:** to be taken with *pastorem Polyphemum*. **vasta . . . mole:** ablative of description: 'with his vast bulk'. **se . . . moventem:** 'moving himself', and so the intransitive 'moving'.

658 Note the very unusual triple elision with <u>asyndeton</u> and the spondaic rhythm, all designed to heighten the dramatic intensity of the description. **cui lumen ademptum:** supply *erat*: 'whose eye had been removed'; *cui* is dative of disadvantage.

660–1 **ea sola voluptas solamenque mali:** supply *erat*; *ea* agrees with *voluptas* but refers to the sheep. Note the similar sound of *sola* and *solamen*, heightening the pathos.

708 **pelagi:** dependent on *tempestatibus*.

709–10 **genitorem . . . Anchisen:** the two nouns are in apposition, separated for dramatic effect. **levamen:** in apposition to *Anchisen*.

710–11 **hic, heu:** note the repetition, to emphasise the pathos. **pater optime:** an example of <u>apostrophe</u>, increasing the pathos. **erepte:** vocative in apposition to *pater*. **tantis . . . periclis:** note the <u>enclosing word order</u>.

712 **vates Helenus:** see lines 377ff. **cum:** 'although'.

713 **hos . . . luctus:** plural for singular. **dira Celaeno:** see lines 245ff.

714–15 **hic . . . haec . . . hinc:** Aeneas finishes his tale with a rhetorical flourish, using <u>anaphora</u> with <u>polyptoton</u>. **hic labor extremus:** supply *erat*: 'this was my last anguish', i.e. before reaching Carthage. **longarum haec meta viarum:** supply *erat* again; *meta* here is generally taken to mean the 'goal' or 'destination' of his long voyage; in this case *haec* must mean his arrival in Carthage. This is unlikely to suggest that Aeneas is already thinking of staying permanently in Carthage, rather than continuing to Italy, as he has been told to do; rather he is simply stating that his journey so far has come to an end in Carthage. **hinc me digressum:** 'me departing from here', i.e. from Sicily. The difficulty with this interpretation is that *hic, haec, hinc* must refer to his father's death in Sicily, his arrival in Carthage, and his departure from Sicily, respectively. This seems an unlikely progression; much better would be to take *haec meta* as also referring to events in Sicily; this would render the <u>tricolon</u> properly ascendant (i.e. building to a climax).

716 **intentis omnibus:** 'to all his eager listeners'. **omnibus unus:** note the <u>antithesis</u> for emphasis.

717 **divum:** genitive plural, dependent on *fata*. **cursus:** 'his travellings' (accusative plural).

718 **hic:** 'at this point'.

Questions

1 In lines 655–658, how does Aeneas emphasise the monstrous nature of the Cyclops?

2 In lines 659–661, what may suggest that Aeneas felt some pity for the Cyclops?

3 In lines 708–715, how does Aeneas show his emotions at his father's death?

Book 4

Aeneas, while being entertained to dinner by queen Dido of Carthage, finished his account of his adventures after leaving Troy.

at regina gravi iamdudum saucia cura
vulnus alit venis et caeco carpitur igni.
multa viri virtus animo multusque recursat
gentis honos; haerent infixi pectore vultus
verbaque, nec placidam membris dat cura quietem.   5
postera Phoebea lustrabat lampade terras
umentemque Aurora polo dimoverat umbram,
cum sic unanimam adloquitur male sana sororem:
'Anna soror, quae me suspensam insomnia terrent!
quis novus hic nostris successit sedibus hospes,   10
quem sese ore ferens, quam forti pectore et armis!
credo equidem, nec vana fides, genus esse deorum.

regina, -ae f.	queen	*umens, -ntis*	damp, moist
gravis, -e	heavy	*Aurora, -ae* f.	Dawn
iamdudum	for a long time	*polus, -i* m.	sky
saucius, -a, -um	wounded	*dimoveo, -ere*	I dispel
cura, -ae f.	anxiety, trouble	*umbra, -ae* f.	shadow, ghost
vulnus, -eris n.	wound	*unanimus, -a, -um*	like-minded
alo, -ere	I nourish	*adloquor, -i*	I address
vena, -ae f.	vein	*male*	badly, barely
caecus, -a, -um	hidden	*sanus, -a, -um*	sane
carpo, -ere	I wear down	*soror, -oris* f.	sister
ignis, -is m.	fire	*Anna, -ae* f.	Anna
virtus, -utis f.	courage, virtue	*suspensus, -a, -um*	anxious
animus, -i m.	mind	*insomnium, -i* n.	dream
recurso, -are	I keep occurring	*terreo, -ere*	I frighten
gens, -ntis f.	race, lineage	*novus, -a, -um* 10	new
honos, -oris m.	glory	*succedo, -ere, -ssi, -ssus*	I come to
haereo, -ere, haesi	I remain fixed	*sedes, -is* f.	home
infixus, -a, -um	fixed	*hospes, -itis* m.	guest
pectus, -oris n.	breast, heart	*sese*	= *se*
vultus, -us m.	face	*os, oris* n.	face, mouth
verbum, -i n. 5	word	*fortis, -e*	brave, strong
placidus, -a, -um	peaceful	*arma, -orum* n.pl.	arms
membrum, -i n.	limb	*credo, -ere*	I believe
quies, -tis f.	rest	*equidem*	I for my part
posterus, -a, -um	next	*vanus, -a, -um*	empty, vain
Phoebeus, -a, -um	of Apollo	*fides, -ei* f.	belief, trust
lustro, -are	I illuminate	*genus, -eris* n.	race, descent
lampas, -adis f.	lamp, torch	*deus, -i* m.	god

1 **at regina:** *at* is Virgil's way of indicating a change of theme. In the previous two books, Aeneas has been recounting his adventures to queen Dido of Carthage (see Introduction). Now Virgil turns to Dido's reaction to this: as she listened she found herself falling hopelessly in love with Aeneas. **gravi . . . cura:** ablative of instrument dependent on *saucia*; the *cura* is the anxious suffering induced by love.

2 **vulnus alit venis:** 'she nourishes the wound in her veins', i.e. she keeps the wound unhealed because of her growing obsession with Aeneas. Love was often described as coursing through the veins. **caeco . . . igni:** the fire (of passion) is unseen – whether Dido kept it hidden from herself or from others is unclear.

3–4 **multa viri virtus:** 'the great courage of the man'; note the alliteration and assonance, following the similar alliteration in line 2. **animo . . . recursat:** 'continually runs through her mind'; *animo* is probably local ablative. **multusque . . . gentis honos:** 'and the great glory of his lineage'; Aeneas was the son of the goddess Venus, and so could not have been of more noble birth.

4–5 **infixi:** agrees with both *vultus* and *verba*. **pectore:** local ablative. Note that Dido is impressed by both Aeneas' qualities and his physical appearance.

6–7 The order is *postera Aurora lustrabat terras Phoebea lampade dimoveratque umentem umbram polo*. **postera Aurora:** 'the next day's dawn'. **terras:** 'lands', i.e. the Earth. **Phoebea lampade:** 'with Phoebus' lamp', i.e. the sun, as Phoebus Apollo was the sun god. **umentem umbram:** 'the moist shadow (of night)'; the darkness is moist because of the dew. **polo:** 'from the sky' (ablative of separation).

8 **cum . . . adloquitur:** this is the 'inverse *cum*' construction. **unanimam . . . sororem:** the meaning of *unanimam* here is uncertain: it could mean 'sympathetic', 'like-minded' (i.e. Anna also found Aeneas attractive) or 'loving'. **male sana:** Dido is 'barely sane' because her love is driving her mad.

9 **me suspensam:** 'my anxious heart'.

10 **quis novus hic . . . hospes:** 'what a man this new guest is who . . .'.

11 **quem sese ore ferens:** lit. 'bearing himself what a man in face', a difficult phrase generally translated as 'how noble in appearance'. **quam forti pectore at armis:** either 'with what strong chest and shoulders' or 'with what brave heart and military prowess': *armis* could be either from *arma, -orum* weapons or from *armus, -i* shoulder; both have found favour with editors. The two phrases combined make this one of the most difficult lines in the whole of the *Aeneid*, even though the basic thought process is clear enough.

12 **nec vana fides:** supply *est*. **genus esse deorum:** 'that he is of divine parentage'. Dido of course is correct in her appraisal; for Aeneas was the son of Venus.

Questions

1 How do lines 1–2 show the extent of Dido's infatuation?

2 In lines 3–5, what aspects of Aeneas does Dido keep thinking about?

3 In lines 6–7, why do you think Virgil devotes two whole lines to indicate 'next morning'?

4 In lines 9–12, how does Dido show her tormented feelings?

degeneres animos timor arguit. heu, quibus ille
iactatus fatis! quae bella exhausta canebat!
si mihi non animo fixum immotumque sederet   15
ne cui me vinclo vellem sociare iugali,
postquam primus amor deceptam morte fefellit;
si non pertaesum thalami taedaeque fuisset,
huic uni forsan potui succumbere culpae.
Anna, fatebor enim, miseri post fata Sychaei   20
coniugis et sparsos fraterna caede penates
solus hic inflexit sensus animumque labantem
impulit. agnosco veteris vestigia flammae.
sed mihi vel tellus optem prius ima dehiscat
vel pater omnipotens adigat me fulmine ad umbras,   25
pallentes umbras Erebo noctemque profundam,
ante, pudor, quam te violo aut tua iura resolvo.
ille meos, primus qui me sibi iunxit, amores
abstulit; ille habeat secum servetque sepulcro.'
sic effata sinum lacrimis implevit obortis.   30

degener, -eris	base, ignoble	sensus, -us m.	feelings
timor, -oris m.	fear	labo, -are	I waver
arguo, -ere	I show up, prove	impello, -ere, -puli, -pulsus	I stir
heu!	alas!	agnosco, -ere	I recognise
iacto, -are, -avi, -atus	I harass	vetus, -eris	old
fatum, -i n.	fate	vestigium, -i n.	trace, sign
exhaurio, -ire, -si, -stus	I drain, endure	flamma, -ae f.	flame, passion
cano, -ere	I sing, recount	vel ... vel	either ... or
fixus, -a, -um 15	fixed	tellus, -uris f.	earth, ground
immotus, -a, -um	immovable	opto, -are	I wish, pray
sedeo, -ere	I sit, am settled	prius	sooner
vinclum, -i n.	chain, bond	imus, -a, -um	the depths of
socio, -are	I ally, unite	dehisco, -ere	I gape open
iugalis, -e	of marriage	omnipotens, -ntis 25	all-powerful
amor, -oris m.	love	adigo, -ere	I drive, hurl
decipio, -ere, -cepi, -ceptus	I deceive	fulmen, -inis n.	thunderbolt
mors, mortis f.	death	pallens, -ntis	pale
fallo, -ere, fefelli, falsus	I cheat, deceive	Erebus, -i m.	Erebus
pertaedet, -ere, -taesum est	it wearies	nox, noctis f.	night
thalamus, -i m.	marriage bed	profundus, -a, -um	deep
taeda, -ae f.	marriage-torch	ante ... quam	before
forsan	perhaps	pudor, -oris m.	chastity, honour
succumbo, ere	I give way	violo, -are	I violate
culpa, -ae f.	fault	ius, iuris n.	law
fateor, -eri 20	I confess	resolvo, -ere	I break
miser, -era, -erum	poor	iungo, -ere, iunxi, iunctus	I join
Sychaeus, -i m.	Sychaeus	aufero, -re, abstuli, ablatus	I take away
coniunx, -ugis m.	husband	servo, -are	I keep
spargo, -ere, -rsi, -rsus	I bespatter	sepulcrum, -i n.	tomb
fraternus, -a, -um	of a brother	effor, -fari, -fatus sum 30	I speak out
caedes, -is f.	murder	sinus, -us m.	bosom
penates, -ium m.pl.	household gods	lacrima, -ae f.	tear
solus, -a, -um	only, alone	impleo, -ere, -evi, -etus	I fill
inflecto, -ere, -xi, -xus	I sway	oborior, -iri, -ortus sum	I rise, well up

13 Dido's argument is that only people of low birth show fear; Aeneas shows no fear, and so must be nobly born.

13–14 **quibus . . . fatis:** ablative of instrument. **iactatus:** supply *est*. **quae bella exhausta:** 'what wars that he endured'. Note the contrasting rhythm of the two lines: line 12 is entirely dactylic, while line 13 is (apart from the fifth foot) entirely spondaic; perhaps the idea is to reflect Dido's varying speed of thought, hastening over the low-born men but lingering over Aeneas' adventures; it may also heighten the contrast between the low-born and Aeneas.

15 **mihi . . . animo:** 'in my mind' (local ablative). **fixum immotumque sederet:** 'it were (not) settled, fixed and unmoveable'; the <u>tautology</u> is an attempt to convince Anna and herself that her vow not to remarry is unbreakable.

16 **ne . . . vellem:** 'not to want' or 'that I should not want'; *ne* may be viewed as equivalent to a purpose clause or an indirect command. **cui:** indefinite after *ne*: 'to anyone'. **vinclo . . . iugali:** ablative of instrument. The largely spondaic rhythm adds solemnity to her vow.

17 **primus amor:** this was her husband Sychaeus (see Introduction). **deceptam morte fefellit:** supply *me*: lit. 'cheated (me) having been deceived by his death', i.e. 'cheated and deceived me with his death'. She is not blaming Sychaeus, but lamenting the fact that his death cheated her of their happy life together.

18 **pertaesum . . . fuisset:** this is an impersonal construction, using a semi-deponent verb; *fuisset* is a stronger alternative to *esset* for the pluperfect subjunctive in a past unfulfilled condition; supply *me* as the object: lit. 'if it had not wearied me', and so 'if I had not been weary'. What she really means is less clear, as her marriage to Sychaeus had been a happy one; either she is weary of the idea of marriage after all the marriage proposals she has received since arriving in Africa; or she is saying that her one marriage to Sychaeus was enough for her. **thalami taedaeque:** the two genitives are dependent on *pertaesum fuisset*, giving the cause; the two items are symbolic of marriage and examples of <u>metonymy</u>.

19 **forsan potui:** 'perhaps I could have . . .'; the indicative is common in such conditional sentences where a possibility is expressed. **huic uni . . . culpae:** 'to this one weakness', i.e. to letting herself fall in love with Aeneas; however, the word also suggests wrongness or guilt.

20 **fatebor enim:** *enim* is used conversationally to reinforce the verb: 'yes, I will confess it'. **post fata:** 'after the death'.

21 **sparsos fraterna caede penates:** this enlarges on *fata*: 'the bespattering of my household gods (lit. 'the bespattered household gods') with blood shed by a brother'. *Fraterna* can be taken in two ways: 'by my brother' or 'by his brother(-in-law)'; in either case the reference is to Pygmalion. See Introduction for the story.

22–3 **hic:** Aeneas. Note the <u>enjambement</u> of *impulit*. **vestigia veteris flammae:** she is reminded of her old passion for Sychaeus.

24–7 **optem:** potential subjunctive: 'I could wish'. **prius:** this is redundant, because *ante* repeats it. **tellus . . . ima:** 'the depths of the earth', i.e. the underworld. **dehiscat, adigat:** jussive subjunctives dependent on *optem*. **pater omnipotens:** Jupiter, whose weapon was the thunderbolt. **ad umbras:** the shades of the dead, repeated for emphasis. **Erebo:** the underworld (local ablative). **ante . . . quam:** to be taken as one word. **pudor:** here 'conscience'; the use of <u>apostrophe</u> makes her plea more vivid.

28–9 **ille:** Sychaeus (note the <u>anaphora</u>). **amores abstulit:** he has taken her love away with him to the grave. **habeat, servet:** subjunctives to express wishes; their object is her love. Note the heavy <u>sibilance</u>. **sepulcro:** local ablative.

Questions

1 How successfully does Virgil portray Dido's conflicting emotions?

Anna replied,' Do you think the dead really care what you do? Have you forgotten how many hostile tribes surround us? You have rejected many suitors that you did not want; why can you not now accept one that you do want?' Anna continued:

'dis equidem auspicibus reor et Iunone secunda	45
hunc cursum Iliacas vento tenuisse carinas.	
quam tu urbem, soror, hanc cernes, quae surgere regna	
coniugio tali! Teucrum comitantibus armis	
Punica se quantis attollet gloria rebus!	
tu modo posce deos veniam, sacrisque litatis	50
indulge hospitio causasque innecte morandi,	
dum pelago desaevit hiems et aquosus Orion,	
quassataeque rates, dum non tractabile caelum.'	
his dictis incensum animum flammavit amore	
spemque dedit dubiae menti solvitque pudorem.	55

Dido and Anna visited all the temples to make sacrifices in the hope of receiving the gods' favour.

heu! vatum ignarae mentes! quid vota furentem,	65
quid delubra iuvant? est molles flamma medullas	
interea et tacitum vivit sub pectore vulnus.	

auspex, -icis m./f.	45 guide, leader	*desaevio, -ire*	I rage fully
reor, reri, ratus sum	I think	*hiems, -emis* f.	winter
Iuno, -onis f.	Juno	*aquosus, -a, -um*	watery, rainy
secundus, -a, -um	favourable	*Orion, -onis* m.	Orion
cursus, -us m.	course	*quasso, -are, -avi, -atus*	I batter
Iliacus, -a, -um	Trojan	*ratis, -is* f.	raft, ship
ventus, -i m.	wind	*tractabilis, -e*	manageable
carina, -ae f.	keel, ship	*caelum, -i* n.	sky
cerno, -ere	I see	*incendo, -ere, -di, -sus*	I inflame
surgo, -ere	I rise, grow	*animus, -i* m.	mind
regnum, -i n.	realm, kingdom	*flammo, -are, -avi, -atus*	I set on fire
coniugium, -i n.	marriage	*spes, -ei* f. 55	hope
talis, -e	such	*dubius, -a, -um*	wavering
Teucri, -orum m.pl.	Trojans	*mens, -ntis* f.	mind, intention
comitor, -ari	I accompany	*solvo, -ere, -i, -utus*	I dispel, set free
Punicus, -a, -um	Carthaginian	*pudor, -oris* m.	shame
attollo, -ere	I raise	*vates, -is* m. 65	prophet
gloria, -ae f.	glory	*ignarus, -a, -um*	ignorant
modo	50 only, just	*votum, -i* n.	prayer
posco, -ere	I demand, ask	*furo, -ere*	I rage, am mad
venia, -ae f.	indulgence	*delubrum, -i* n.	shrine
sacra, -orum n.pl.	sacrifice, emblems	*iuvo, -are*	I help, please
lito, -are, -avi, -atus	I perform correctly	*edo, esse*	I eat
		mollis, -e	tender, kind
indulgeo, -ere + dat.	I indulge in	*flamma, -ae* f.	flame
hospitium, -i n.	hospitality	*medulla, -ae* f.	marrow
causa, -ae f.	reason	*interea*	meanwhile
innecto, -ere	I weave	*tacitus, -a, -um*	silent
moror, -ari	I delay	*vivo, -ere*	I live
pelagus, -i n.	sea	*vulnus, -eris* n.	wound

45 dis ... auspicibus, Iunone secunda: ablatives absolute: 'with the guidance of the gods and with the approval of Juno'. Anna did not know it, but it was Venus, rather than Juno, who sowed the seeds of love in Dido's breast (Book 1); Juno had created a storm to try to shipwreck the Trojans. The storm had blown them towards the coast of Africa.

46 hunc cursum: i.e. to Carthage. **Iliacas ... carinas:** lit. 'the Trojan keels', and so 'the Trojan ships' (an example of <u>synecdoche</u>). **vento:** ablative of instrument.

47–8 quam ... urbem ... hanc cernes ... surgere: 'what a city you will see this grow into'; *surgere* is to be taken both with *urbem* and with *regna*. **coniugio tali:** causal ablative.

48–9 Teucrum: = *Teucrorum*. **comitantibus armis:** ablative absolute. **quantis ... rebus:** 'with what great things', and so 'with what great achievements' (instrumental ablative); an alternative is to take it as dative: 'to what great achievements'. **se ... attollet:** 'will raise itself', and so 'will rise'. Anna's argument is that, if Dido encourages the Trojans to stay and help, Carthage will achieve greater glory than if the Carthaginians have to proceed alone.

50–1 posce deos veniam: 'ask the gods for indulgence' (*posco* takes two direct objects), i.e. 'ask for forgiveness for breaking your oath of loyalty to the memory of Sychaeus'. **sacrisque litatis:** ablative absolute. **indulge hospitio:** 'indulge in hospitality', i.e. 'allow yourself to offer (the Trojans) hospitality'. **causasque innecte morandi:** 'and weave reasons of delaying', i.e. 'invent excuses to keep him here'.

52 pelago: local ablative. **aquosus Orion:** the setting of the constellation Orion in November heralded the beginning of wintry weather, when sailors tried to avoid sailing.

53 quassataeque rates: supply *dum* and *sunt*: 'and while ships have been battered', the idea being that they are under repair and not fit for sailing. **non tractabile caelum:** supply *est*; *caelum*, lit. 'sky', here signifies 'weather'.

54–5 Note the <u>alliteration</u> and <u>consonance</u> of *m* here, indicating the high emotional content.

55 solvitque pudorem: there are several ways of interpreting these words: 'she dispelled her shame', i.e. she persuaded Dido that there was no reason for her to feel ashamed of her love for Aeneas; alternatively 'she set her shame free from all restraints', i.e. she persuaded Dido to indulge in her shameful behaviour. In both cases her arguments persuaded Dido to allow herself to fall in love with Aeneas.

65–6 vatum ignarae mentes: the prophets are priests who carry out sacrifices and inspect the victims' organs to predict the future; they are 'ignorant' because they do not realise Dido's destructive mental disorder is beyond their power to cure. **quid ... quid:** 'what (help do they give)?' The <u>anaphora</u> adds emphasis to the poet's observation. Virgil often stands back from the narrative to make his own comments. This would suggest that **furentem** refers not specifically to Dido (as some take it) but to anyone in a similar situation.

66–7 est: an alternative to *edit*, from *edo*, not *sum*. **molles ... medullas:** 'her soft marrow', and so 'her tender heart'; *medulla*, literally 'marrow' came to be used by poets to mean the essential core of the being, where we would use 'heart'. **tacitum ... vulnus:** by 'silent wound', Virgil means the wound inflicted by her love, that for the moment is unobserved.

Questions

1 What arguments does Anna use to try to persuade Dido?

2 How does Anna make these arguments persuasive?

3 In lines 54–55, how does Virgil emphasise the depth of Dido's passion?

4 What makes lines 65–67 ominous?

uritur infelix Dido totaque vagatur
urbe furens, qualis coniecta cerva sagitta,
quam procul incautam nemora inter Cresia fixit   70
pastor agens telis liquitque volatile ferrum
nescius: illa fuga silvas saltusque peragrat
Dictaeos; haeret lateri letalis harundo.
nunc media Aenean secum per moenia ducit
Sidoniasque ostentat opes urbemque paratam,   75
incipit effari mediaque in voce resistit;
nunc eadem labente die convivia quaerit,
Iliacosque iterum demens audire labores
exposcit pendetque iterum narrantis ab ore.
post ubi digressi, lumenque obscura vicissim   80
luna premit suadentque cadentia sidera somnos,
sola domo maeret vacua stratisque relictis
incubat. illum absens absentem auditque videtque,
aut gremio Ascanium genitoris imagine capta
detinet, infandum si fallere possit amorem.   85

uro, -ere	I burn	effor, -fari, -fatus sum	I speak
infelix, -icis	unhappy	resisto, -ere	I stop
furo, -ere	I rage	labor, -i	I sink, slip away
vagor, -ari	I wander	convivium, -i n.	banquet
qualis, -e	just like	quaero, -ere	I seek
conicio, -ere, -ieci, -iectus	I throw, shoot	demens, -ntis	mad, foolish
cerva, -ae f.	doe, hind	labor, -oris m.	toil, trouble
sagitta, -ae f.	arrow	exposco, -ere	I demand
procul 70	from afar, far away	pendeo, -ere	I hang
		narro, -are 80	I relate, tell
incautus, -a, -um	unwary	digredior, -i, -gressus sum	I separate
nemus, -oris n.	grove	lumen, -inis n.	light, eye
Cresius, -a, -um	Cretan	obscurus, -a, -um	dark
figo, -ere, fixi, fixus	I wound	vicissim	in turn
pastor, -oris m.	shepherd	luna, -ae f.	moon
ago, -ere	I chase, hunt	premo, -ere	I veil, suppress
telum, -i n.	weapon, arrow	suadeo, -ere	I urge
linquo, -ere, liqui, lictus	I leave	cado, -ere	I fall, set
volatilis, -e	flying, winged	sidus, -eris n.	star
ferrum, -i n.	iron, sword	somnus, -i m.	sleep
nescius, -a, -um	unaware	maereo, -ere	I grieve, lament
fuga, -ae f.	flight	vacuus, -a, -um	empty
silva, -ae f.	wood	stratum, -i n.	blanket, couch
saltus, -us m.	glade	relinquo, -ere, -liqui, -lictus	I abandon, leave
peragro, -are	I wander through	incubo, -are + dat.	I lie on
Dictaeus, -a, -um	of Mt Dicte	absens, -ntis	absent
latus, -eris n.	side	gremium, -i n.	lap
letalis, -e	deadly	Ascanius, -i m.	Ascanius
harundo, -inis f.	reed, arrow	genitor, -oris m.	father
moenia, -ium n.pl.	walls, city	imago, -inis f.	image, ghost
Sidonius, -a, -um 75	Sidonian	detineo, -ere 85	I hold
ostento, -are	I show, point out	infandus, -a, -um	unspeakable
opes, -um f.pl.	wealth	fallo, -ere	I deceive, cheat
incipio, -ere	I begin		

68–9 uritur: Dido 'burns' with passion. **tota ... urbe:** 'throughout the whole city' (local ablative).

69–73 qualis: this word is regularly used to introduce an extended <u>simile</u>; here the love-stricken Dido is compared to a deer that has been shot by an arrow. Note the careful elaboration of the simile with all the points of comparison.

69 coniecta ... sagitta: ablative absolute; the scansion shows that *coniecta* agrees with *sagitta,* not *cerva.* However, natural English requires 'a doe shot by an arrow'.

70 quam ... fixit pastor: 'which a shepherd has wounded'. **incautam:** like Dido, the doe is unwary. **nemora inter Cresia:** Virgil uses 'Cretan' to add colour and because the Cretans were famous for their archery; he may also be thinking of the fact that Aeneas too has come from Crete (where he had hoped to found a new city – Book 3).

71–2 liquitque: supply *in qua.* **ferrum:** 'iron', i.e. any weapon made of iron, such as the arrow-head. **nescius:** the <u>enjambement</u> gives extra weight to this word, which is a key part of the simile, because Aeneas was equally unaware of his effect on Dido.

72–3 illa: the deer. **fuga:** ablative of manner. **Dictaeos:** Dicte is a mountain in Crete.

74 media ... per moenia: 'through the middle of her city'; *moenia,* literally 'city-walls', is often used to refer to the buildings enclosed by the city-walls.

75–6 Sidonias ... opes: 'Phoenician treasures'; Sidon was one of the two harbour cities on the Phoenician coast (the other being Tyre), from which Dido and her people emigrated to found Carthage. Virgil uses the two names indiscriminately. The 'treasures' are presumably sacred objects and valuables that they brought with them. **paratam:** the city is ready and waiting to accommodate the Trojans. **mediaque in voce:** 'in mid-speech'.

77 eadem ... convivia: she sought 'the same banquets', i.e. a repeat of the banquet at which Aeneas recounted his adventures (Books 2 and 3) and during which she began to fall in love.

78 Iliacos labores: i.e. the adventures of the Trojans, as told by Aeneas in Books 2 and 3. **demens:** 'foolishly' or 'in her mad passion'; note the position of the word, in the middle of the lines, surrounded by the Trojan adventures.

79 pendet ... ab ore: she 'hangs from his lips', a graphic <u>metaphor</u> emphasising the close attention she pays to Aeneas. **iterum:** note the repetition of this word, indicating that she was not satisfied with a single telling. **narrantis:** 'of the narrator', i.e. Aeneas.

80–1 digressi: supply *sunt.* **obscura ... luna:** the moon dims as dawn approaches. **cadentia sidera:** the stars too are setting, in the sense that they are fading as dawn approaches. Note the <u>sibilance</u> in line 81, suggesting sleep, along with the <u>assonance</u> of *dent.*

82 domo ... vacua: local ablative; everyone else has gone to bed. **maeret:** the subject is Dido. **stratis relictis:** the dining couch on which Aeneas had reclined.

83 Note the slow rhythm of this line, reflecting the amount of time Dido spends moping. **absens absentem:** the repetition emphasises the physical separation of Dido and Aeneas. **auditque videtque:** in her imagination she hears and sees him; the <u>polysyndeton</u> gives extra force to the two activities.

84–5 gremio: local ablative. **Ascanium:** Ascanius, also called Iulus, is Aeneas' son who has travelled with him from Troy (see Introduction); his age is hard to determine: young enough to sit on Dido's lap but old enough to go hunting (lines 156–9). In Book I Venus persuaded her son, Cupid, to take the place of Ascanius to stir Dido's love for Aeneas the more quickly. **genitoris imagine capta:** 'captivated by his likeness to his father', **detinet:** she pets him in her imagination. **infandum si fallere possit amorem:** '(to see) if she could deceive her love'; what Virgil means by this is unclear – perhaps that she hopes to satisfy the pangs of love by fondling Ascanius.

Questions

1 How effective is the simile? What makes it so effective?

non coeptae adsurgunt turres, non arma iuventus
exercet portusve aut propugnacula bello
tuta parant: pendent opera interrupta minaeque
murorum ingentes aequataque machina caelo.   89

*When the goddess Juno saw how hopelessly in love Dido had fallen, she approached Venus
and suggested that they cooperate in encouraging Dido and Aeneas to marry. Although
Venus realised that Juno's real motive was to snare Aeneas and the Trojans in Africa so that
they would never fulfil their destiny of founding the Roman race, she nevertheless decided
to agree to the plan, on the condition that Juno would seek her husband Jupiter's approval.
Juno revealed to Venus a plan she had formed to separate Dido and Aeneas from all the
others during a storm while on a hunting trip.*

Oceanum interea surgens Aurora reliquit.   129
it portis iubare exorto delecta iuventus,   130
retia rara, plagae, lato venabula ferro,
Massylique ruunt equites et odora canum vis.
reginam thalamo cunctantem ad limina primi
Poenorum exspectant, ostroque insignis et auro
stat sonipes ac frena ferox spumantia mandit.   135
tandem progreditur magna stipante caterva
Sidoniam picto chlamydem circumdata limbo;
cui pharetra ex auro, crines nodantur in aurum,
aurea purpuream subnectit fibula vestem.

coepi, -isse, coeptus	I began	*vis, - f.*	force, power
adsurgo, -ere	I rise up	*thalamus, -i* m.	bedroom
turris, -is f.	tower	*cunctor, -ari*	I delay, linger
iuventus, -utis f.	young men	*limen, -inis* n.	doorway
exerceo, -ere	I practise	*Poeni, -orum* m.pl.	Carthaginians
portus, -us m.	harbour	*ostrum, -i* n.	purple
propugnaculum, -i n.	battlement	*insignis, -e*	conspicuous
tutus, -a, -um	safe	*aurum, -i* n.	gold
pendeo, -ere	I am suspended	*sonipes, -pedis* m.	135 horse
opus, -eris n.	work	*frenum, -i* n.	bridle, bit
interrumpo, -ere, -rupi, -ruptus	I interrupt	*ferox, -ocis*	fierce, spirited
mina, -ae f.	threat	*spumo, -are*	I foam
murus, -i m.	89 wall	*mando, -ere*	I chew, champ at
aequo, -are, -avi, -atus	I make equal	*progredior, -i*	I proceed
machina, -ae f.	machine, crane	*stipo, -are*	I surround
Oceanus, -i m.	129 Ocean	*caterva, -ae* f.	crowd
Aurora, -ae f.	Dawn	*pictus, -a, -um*	embroidered
iubar, -aris n.	130 sunlight	*chlamys, -ydis* f.	cloak
exorior, -iri, -ortus sum	I arise	*cirdumdatus, -a, -um*	wearing
deligo, -ere, -legi, -lectus	I choose	*limbus, -i* m.	border
rete, -is n.	net	*pharetra, -ae* f.	quiver
rarus, -a, -um	wide-meshed	*crinis, -is* m.	hair
plaga, -ae f.	net	*nodo, -are*	I knot
venabulum, -i n.	hunting spear	*aureus, -a, -um*	made of gold
Massylus, -a, -um	Massylian	*purpureus, -a, -um*	purple
ruo, -ere	I rush	*subnecto, -ere*	I fasten
eques, -itis m.	horseman	*fibula, -ae* f.	brooch, clasp
odorus, -a, -um	keen-scented	*vestis, -is* f.	clothes

86–8 non . . . non: qualify *adsurgunt* and *exercet*; note the emphatic positioning of these words as well as the <u>anaphora</u>. **coeptae . . . turres:** 'the towers that had been begun'; these are defensive towers at intervals along the city walls. Virgil begins a list of building projects that are left unfinished because Dido is too distracted to pay attention to them. **iuventus:** this word, literally the abstract 'youth', is regularly used by Virgil in the singular to mean 'young men'. **-ve aut:** 'either . . . or'. **parant:** supply *non* from line 86; the subject is the men of the city. **bello tuta:** 'providing safety in war'; *bello* is ablative of respect.

88–9 pendent: this verb has three subjects: *opera, minae* and *machina*; if *machina* means 'crane' (as most editors assume), rather than the 'structure (of the walls)', then *pendent* must have the meaning 'stands idle'. **minae murorum ingentes:** lit. 'the huge threats of the walls', and so 'the huge threatening walls'. **aequata . . . caelo:** 'reaching up to the sky'.

129 Oceanum: the Greeks thought of a single ocean surrounding the inhabited world. The sun, rising in the East, would begin its journey by rising above the part of the ocean that bounded the eastern extremity of the Earth.

130 portis: ablative of route. **iubare exorto:** ablative absolute. **delecta iuventus:** see note on line 66; these young men are 'chosen' (a favourite word of Virgil) because they have been invited to take part in the hunt.

131 plagae: these are narrow-meshed nets; supply a verb such as *sunt*. **lato ferro:** 'with broad iron (heads)', i.e. 'broad-bladed'. Hunting spears were clearly different from those used in warfare.

132 Massyli . . . equites: the Massylians were a tribe living to the west of Carthage; their inclusion in the hunt suggests that Dido had developed good relations with at least some of her neighbours. **odora canum vis:** 'the keen-scented power of dogs' – a poetic, ultimately Homeric, way of saying 'powerful, keen-scented dogs'. Contrast the fast rhythm of this line, matching the rushing of the horsemen and dogs, with that of the next line, where the queen is lingering in her room.

133–5 reginam: the direct object of *exspectant* is promoted to make Dido the focus of attention. **thalamo:** local ablative. **cunctantem:** Virgil makes her linger in her room to heighten the sense of expectation. **ad limina:** 'by the doorway'. **primi Poenorum:** *primi* is here a noun: 'the leading men'; note the <u>alliteration</u>. **ostro . . . auro:** these two colours were the prerogative of royalty; they are ablatives of respect. **stat . . . mandit:** note the heavy <u>alliteration</u> and <u>assonance</u> in line 135, emphasising the impatience of Dido's horse.

136–7 progreditur: the subject is Dido. **magna stipante caterva:** ablative absolute. **Sidoniam . . . chlamydem circumdata:** this is one of Virgil's favourite constructions for describing people, modelled on the Greek middle verb; Dido is (lit.) 'surrounded with respect to a Sidonian cloak', and so 'wrapped in a Sidonian cloak'. **Sidoniam:** see note on line 75. **picto . . . limbo:** ablative absolute.

138–9 cui: 'her'; this is the connecting relative, with the dative (of advantage) replacing the simpler genitive. **ex auro . . . in aurum . . . aurea:** the repetition of 'gold' emphasises Dido's regal status and brilliance. Throughout this episode there is heavy emphasis on royal colours. **pharetra:** supply *est*.

Questions

1 In lines 86–89, what shows that Dido is neglecting her duties as queen?

2 In lines 130–139, how does Virgil add drama and interest to the scene?

Aeneas' Trojan companions and his son Iulus also set off. Aeneas had all the grace of the god Apollo.

postquam altos ventum in montes atque invia lustra,	151
ecce ferae saxi deiectae vertice caprae	
decurrere iugis; alia de parte patentes	
transmittunt cursu campos atque agmina cervi	
pulverulenta fuga glomerant montesque relinquunt.	155
at puer Ascanius mediis in vallibus acri	
gaudet equo iamque hos cursu, iam praeterit illos,	
spumantemque dari pecora inter inertia votis	
optat aprum, aut fulvum descendere monte leonem.	
interea magno misceri murmure caelum	160
incipit, insequitur commixta grandine nimbus,	
et Tyrii comites passim et Troiana iuventus	
Dardaniusque nepos Veneris diversa per agros	
tecta metu petiere; ruunt de montibus amnes.	
speluncam Dido dux et Troianus eandem	165
deveniunt. prima et Tellus et pronuba Iuno	
dant signum; fulsere ignes et conscius aether	
conubiis, summoque ulularunt vertice Nymphae.	

invius, -a, -um	pathless	*leo, -onis* m.	lion
lustrum, -i n.	forest	*misceo, -ere*	160 I mix, disturb
ecce	behold, see	*murmur, -uris* n.	rumbling
ferus, -a, -um	wild	*incipio, -ere*	I begin
saxum, -i n.	rock	*insequor, -i*	I follow
deicio, -ere, -ieci, -iectus	I dislodge	*commisceo, -ere, -ui, -ixtus*	I mix, mingle
vertex, -icis m.	summit, peak	*grando, -inis* f.	hail
capra, -ae f.	goat	*nimbus, -i* m.	rain-storm
decurro, -ere, -i, -cursus	I run down	*Tyrius, -a, -um*	Carthaginian,
iugum, -i n.	ridge		Tyrian
pars, partis f.	part, direction	*passim*	in all directions
pateo, -ere	I lie open	*Dardanius, -a, -um*	Trojan
transmitto, -ere	I cross	*nepos, -otis* m.	grandson
cursus, -us m.	running	*Venus, -eris* f.	Venus
campus, -i m.	plain	*diversus, -a, -um*	various
agmen, -inis n.	moving herd	*tectum, -i* n.	shelter, building
cervus, -i m.	deer	*metus, -us* m.	fear
pulverulentus, -a, -um	155 dusty	*peto, -ere, -ii, -itus*	I seek, make for
fuga, -ae f.	flight	*ruo, -ere*	I rush
glomero, -are	I mass together	*amnis, -is* m.	river
vallis, -is f.	valley	*spelunca, -ae* f.	165 cave
acer, acris, acre	spirited	*dux, ducis* m.	leader
gaudeo, -ere	I delight	*devenio, -ire*	I reach, come to
praetereo, -ire	I overtake	*Tellus, -uris* f.	Earth
spumo, -are	I foam	*pronuba, -ae* f.	bride's attendant
pecus, -oris n.	herd, cattle	*signum, -i* n.	sign
iners, -rtis	timid	*fulgeo, -ere, fulsi*	I flash
opto, -are	I wish for	*conscius, -a, -um*	aware
aper, apri m.	wild boar	*aether, -eris* m.	sky, heaven
fulvus, -a, -um	tawny	*conubium, -i* n.	marriage
descendo, -ere	I descend	*ululo, -are, -avi, -atus*	I howl, shriek

151 **ventum:** supply *est*; impersonal passive construction; translate as 'after they came'. There are three elisions in this line; combined with the slow rhythm, they emphasise the stately progress of the hunting party.

152–3 **ferae ... caprae:** wild goats frequent mountain crags. **deiectae vertice:** 'dislodged' (by the beaters) 'from the summit' (ablative of separation). **decurrere iugis:** 'ran down along the ridges'; *decurrere = decurrerunt*; *iugis* is ablative of route.

153–4 **transmittunt:** the subject is *cervi*. **patentes ... campos:** these are the open plains at the foot of the mountains. **cursu:** 'by running' and so 'at great speed'.

155 This is one of Virgil's most famous lines, because its heavily pulsating dactylic rhythm suggests the drumming of the hooves on the ground as the deer run. **agmina ... pulverulenta ... glomerant:** they 'mass together their dusty herds'. **fuga:** ablative of instrument.

156–7 **at:** this strong word emphasises the difference between the adult hunters and Ascanius, who has to stay on lower ground. **hos ... illos:** = *alios ... alios:* probably herds of deer rather than other hunters.

158–9 **spumantemque dari ... optat aprum:** 'and wishes for a foaming boar to be granted (to him); the boar would be 'foaming' either from rage or from running very quickly. **pecora ... inertia:** i.e. the deer. **votis:** 'in his prayers', probably ablative of instrument.

160 Note the heavy <u>alliteration</u> of *m*, reflecting the rumbling of the thunder and the ominous atmosphere (an example of <u>onomatopoeia</u>). **misceri:** one of Virgil's favourite verbs, suggesting turmoil and confusion.

161 **incipit, insequitur:** the <u>enjambement</u>, combined with the <u>asyndeton</u> and <u>alliteration</u>, emphasises the rapid development of the storm. **commixta grandine:** ablative absolute.

162 **et ... et:** 'both ... and'.

163 **Dardaniusque nepos Veneris:** i.e. Ascanius.

164 **metu:** causal ablative. **petiere:** = *petiverunt*.

165 Note the slow rhythm of this line, to bring the focus down to Dido and Aeneas after describing the dash for shelter of everyone else. **speluncam ... eandem:** note the <u>enclosing word order</u>, enclosing Dido and Aeneas inside the 'same cave'. **Dido dux et Troianus:** *et* is placed after *dux* instead of before it, perhaps to suggest that it was Dido that actually took the lead in seeking out the cave.

166 **prima ... Tellus:** either 'first of all Earth' or 'primeval Earth'; Mother Earth was the oldest of the deities in the Greek pantheon. **et ... et:** 'both ... and' again. **pronuba Iuno:** since Juno was the goddess of marriage it was natural for her to oversee the 'wedding'. She and Venus had already planned this anyway.

167–8 **dant signum:** i.e. to begin the supposed wedding ceremony. **fulsere ignes:** = *fulserunt ignes*; the lightning flashes served as the wedding torches that were a standard accompaniment to Roman weddings. **conscius aether conubiis:** either supply *fuit* or take *aether* as a second subject of *fulsere*; the sky served as witness to the wedding. **ulularunt:** = *ululaverunt*; this verb, here taking the place of the wedding hymn sung at Roman weddings, is usually associated with horror or terror. **vertice:** local ablative, referring to the mountain peak above them. Is this a genuine wedding or a travesty of one? The participation of the gods could be taken as a sign of divine approval for the union, but the imagery and choice of words could suggest that the whole episode is delusional thinking on the part of Dido.

Questions

1 In lines 151–159, how does Virgil make his description of the hunt vivid and realistic?

2 From lines 160–168, discuss the arguments for and against this being a real wedding.

ille dies primus leti primusque malorum
causa fuit; neque enim specie famave movetur   170
nec iam furtivum Dido meditatur amorem:
coniugium vocat, hoc praetexit nomine culpam.
extemplo Libyae magnas it Fama per urbes,
Fama, malum qua non aliud velocius ullum:
mobilitate viget viresque adquirit eundo,   175
parva metu primo, mox sese attollit in auras
ingrediturque solo et caput inter nubila condit.   177

nocte volat caeli medio terraeque per umbram   184
stridens, nec dulci declinat lumina somno;   185
luce sedet custos aut summi culmine tecti
turribus aut altis, et magnas territat urbes,
tam ficti pravique tenax quam nuntia veri.
haec tum multiplici populos sermone replebat
gaudens, et pariter facta atque infecta canebat: 190
venisse Aenean Troiano sanguine cretum,
cui se pulchra viro dignetur iungere Dido;
nunc hiemem inter se luxu, quam longa, fovere
regnorum immemores turpique cupidine captos.
haec passim dea foeda virum diffundit in ora.   195
protinus ad regem cursus detorquet Iarban
incenditque animum dictis atque aggerat iras.

letum, -i n.	death	*fictus, -a, -um*	false
causa, -ae f.	170 cause	*pravus -a, -um*	crooked, bad
species, -ei f.	appearance	*tenax, -acis*	gripping
fama, -ae f.	reputation,	*nuntia, -ae* f.	reporter
	rumour	*verum, -i* n.	truth
furtivus, -a, -um	secret	*multiplex, -icis*	various
meditor, -ari	I contemplate	*populus, -i* m.	people
praetexo, -ere	I hide, cover	*sermo, -onis* m.	speech, gossip
extemplo	immediately	*repleo, -ere*	I fill
Libya, -ae f.	Libya	*pariter*	190 equally
velox, -ocis	swift	*infectus, -a, -um*	not done
mobilitas, -atis f.	175 swiftness	*cano, -ere*	I sing, sing of
vigeo, -ere	I thrive	*sanguis, -inis* m.	blood
vires, -ium f.pl.	strength	*cretus, -a, -um*	sprung
adquiro, -ere	I gain	*dignor, -ari*	I think right
aura, -ae f.	breeze, air	*luxus, -us* m.	extravagance
ingredior, -i	I move along	*foveo, -ere*	I keep warm
solum, -i n.	ground	*regnum, -i* n.	kingdom
nubilum, -i n.	cloud	*immemor, -oris*	forgetful
condo, -ere	I hide	*turpis, -e*	foul, shameful
volo, -are	184 I fly	*cupido, -inis* f.	lust
strido, -ere	185 I shriek	*foedus, -a, -um*	195 foul
dulcis, -e	sweet	*diffundo, -ere*	I spread
declino, -are	I droop	*protinus*	at once
lux, lucis f.	daylight	*detorqueo, -ere*	I turn aside
custos, -odis m./f.	sentinel	*Iarbas, -ae* (acc. *-an*) m.	Iarbas
summus, -a, -um	highest, top of	*dictum, -i* n.	word
culmen, -inis n.	top, roof	*aggero, -are*	I swell
territo, -are	I terrify	*ira, -ae* f.	anger
tam . . . quam	as much . . . as		

169–70 **primus . . . primus:** treat as adverbs: 'that day first . . .'. The repetition emphasises the significance for the future that the events of that day would have. **leti:** Dido's death is here foreshadowed. **malorum:** the 'troubles' are the Punic Wars that would lead to the destruction of Carthage by Rome in the second century BC. Virgil interrupts his narrative to focus on the idea of destiny: the wars were major episodes in Rome's history, and Virgil has constructed this storyline partly at least to provide a root cause of hostilities that would break out many centuries later.

170–1 **specie famave:** Dido was moved by 'neither appearances nor reputation': i.e. she gave no thought to what others might think of her relationship with Aeneas. **furtivum . . . amorem:** she no longer entertained the idea of keeping her affair secret.

172 **coniugium vocat:** 'she called (their union) marriage'. **culpam:** her 'sin' is breaking her vows to Sychaeus; a second marriage would be less shameful in her eyes than an affair. Notice that Virgil makes no mention here of Aeneas' views of what happened in the cave.

173–4 **Fama:** Virgil personifies Rumour here and elsewhere, describing her as a monstrous goddess dedicated to the spreading of news, whether true or false. **malum . . . non aliud . . . ullum:** 'no other evil'; supply *est*. **qua:** 'than whom' (ablative of comparison).

175 Note the <u>chiasmus</u>: ablative – verb – verb – ablative. Rumour gets stronger the faster she goes, unlike most creatures.

176–7 **metu:** 'because of fear'; until she grows by spreading, she is timid. **sese:** = *se*. **solo:** 'on the ground' (local ablative). These words suggest the monstrous size of Rumour, with her feet on the ground and her head in the clouds.

178–83 The omitted lines describe Rumour's parentage and appearance.

184–5 **nocte:** 'by night' (ablative of time and contrasted with *luce* in line 186). **medio:** here a noun: 'mid-way between'. **lumina:** 'eyes', as frequently in poetry.

186–7 **luce:** 'by day'. **custos:** '(like) a sentinel', i.e. on the lookout for new rumours **summi culmine tecti:** poetic for 'on the highest rooftop'. **turribus aut altis:** take *aut* first.

188 **ficti pravique tenax:** 'greedy for the false and crooked'; *ficti*, *pravi* and the later *veri* are all neuter adjectives used as abstract nouns, and are all objective genitives.

189–90 **haec:** i.e. *Fama*. **tum:** i.e. 'on this occasion'. **populos:** i.e. the peoples living around Carthage. **replebat:** inceptive imperfect: 'began to fill'. **facta atque infecta:** this explains *multiplici* in the preceding line: 'things done and things not done', i.e. 'fact and fiction'.

191–2 **venisse Aenean:** accusative and infinitive, introduced by *canebat*. **sanguine:** ablative of origin. **viro:** in apposition to *cui*: 'as her husband'. **dignetur:** subjunctive because it is in a subordinate clause in indirect speech.

193–4 **hiemem:** some take this as the direct object of *fovere*, meaning 'to spend the winter', but there is no evidence that *fovere* can have this meaning; it is simpler to take it as accusative of duration of time, with *inter se* becoming the effective object of *fovere*. In either case, *eos* must be supplied as the subject of *fovere* (continuing the indirect statement). **luxu:** ablative of manner. **quam longa:** supply *sit*: 'however long it was', i.e. for its entire duration. **regnorum:** i.e. of Carthage and Troy.

195 **haec:** supply *verba*. **virum:** = *virorum*. **in ora:** Rumour puts the words into the mouths of men.

196–7 **ad regem . . . Iarban:** Iarbas was king of a neighbouring tribe and had been the most determined of Dido's suitors, but she had rejected him.

Questions

1 Do you think Virgil is blaming Dido for allowing herself to love Aeneas?

2 What makes the description of *Fama* and her actions effective?

Iarbas was the son of Jupiter and an African nymph. Bitterly angry at the news of the marriage, he complained in prayer to his father. Jupiter heard his son's prayer and summoned Mercury, the messenger god; he ordered him to visit Aeneas and remind him that his destiny was not to stay in Carthage but to found a new city in Italy. Mercury strapped on his winged sandals and picked up his wand which could control the winds. He flew straight to Carthage.

ut primum alatis tetigit magalia plantis,	259
Aenean fundantem arces ac tecta novantem	260
conspicit. atque illi stellatus iaspide fulva	
ensis erat Tyrioque ardebat murice laena	
demissa ex umeris, dives quae munera Dido	
fecerat, et tenui telas discreverat auro.	
continuo invadit: 'tu nunc Carthaginis altae	265
fundamenta locas pulchramque uxorius urbem	
exstruis, heu regni rerumque oblite tuarum?	
ipse deum tibi me claro demittit Olympo	
regnator, caelum et terras qui numine torquet;	
ipse haec ferre iubet celeres mandata per auras:	270
quid struis? aut qua spe Libycis teris otia terris?	
si te nulla movet tantarum gloria rerum,	
Ascanium surgentem et spes heredis Iuli	
respice, cui regnum Italiae Romanaque tellus	275
debetur.' tali Cyllenius ore locutus	
mortales visus medio sermone reliquit	
et procul in tenuem ex oculis evanuit auram.	

alatus, -a, -um	winged	uxorius, -a, -um	fond of a wife
tango, -ere, tetigi, tactus	I touch	exstruo, -ere	I build
magalia, -um n.pl.	huts	heu	alas
planta, -ae f.	sole (of foot)	oblitus, -a, -um + gen.	forgetful (of)
fundo, -are	260 I found, build	clarus, -a, -um	bright
arx, arcis f.	citadel, defence	demitto, -ere	I send down
novo, -are	I renew, change	Olympus, -i m.	Mt Olympus
conspicio, -ere	I catch sight of	regnator, -oris m.	ruler, king
stellatus, -a, -um	starred	numen, -inis n.	divine will, god
iaspis, -idis f.	jasper	torqueo, -ere	I direct, guide
ensis, -is m.	sword	celer, -eris, -ere	270 swift
ardeo, -ere	I blaze, am keen	mandatum, -i n.	command
murex, -icis m.	purple	struo, -ere	I build, plan
laena -ae f.	cloak	spes, -ei f.	hope
demissus, -a, -um	hanging	Libycus, -a, -um	African
umerus, -i m.	shoulder	tero, -ere	I waste
dives, -itis	wealthy	otium, -i n.	leisure
munus, -eris n.	gift	heres, -edis m.	heir
tenuis, -e	fine, thin	Iulus, -i m.	Julus, Ascanius
tela, -ae f.	warp	respicio, -ere	275 I consider
discerno, -ere	I interweave	debeo, -ere	I owe
continuo	265 at once	Cyllenius, -i m.	Mercury
invado, -ere	I attack	mortalis, -e	mortal
Carthago, -inis f.	Carthage	visus, -us m.	sight
fundamentum, -i n.	foundation	oculus, -i m.	eye
loco, -are	I place, lay	evanesco, -ere, -nui	I vanish

259 **ut primum:** 'as soon as'. **magalia:** a Carthaginian word; its use suggests that some at least of the population were still living in temporary huts while the more important buildings were erected.

260–1 **fundantem arces:** 'putting up defences' – presumably city walls. **tecta novantem:** 'renewing buildings', i.e. replacing temporary structures with permanent ones. Note the slow rhythm of line 260 and the enjambement of *conspicit*, with *Aenean* set at the beginning of the line; the overall intent is to indicate that Aeneas was doing things he should not have been doing.

261–4 **atque:** Mercury immediately notices a second thing that betrays Aeneas' destiny: his appearance. **illi:** 'for him'; treat as if genitive: 'Aeneas' (sword)'. **stellatus:** 'starred', i.e. 'studded'. **Tyrio . . . murice:** 'with Tyrian purple'; *murex* was literally a species of shellfish, from which the purple dye was harvested; the species was found off the coast of Phoenicia. Purple was an expensive dye to produce, and so was restricted to royalty; Dido had brought some with her from Tyre and bestowed it upon Aeneas as a token of her love. **dives . . . fecerat:** the order is *munera quae dives Dido fecerat*. **telas discreverat:** 'she had interwoven the warp' with gold; the warp is the longitudinal threads on a loom; the gold thread would have been the weft.

265–7 **invadit:** a strong word, emphasising the speed with which Mercury delivered his message. **uxorius:** this word carries a note of censure: Aeneas is 'too fond of his wife', and not interested enough in what he should be doing. **rerum . . . tuarum:** 'of your own affairs', i.e. his destiny to sail to Italy to found a new city there.

268–9 **deum . . . regnator:** 'the ruler of the gods', i.e. Jupiter; *deum = deorum*. **claro . . . Olympo:** 'from bright Olympus' (ablative of separation). **numine:** 'with his will' (instrumental ablative).

270 **ipse:** the anaphora of *ipse* emphasises the fact that the orders he is there to deliver come from the highest authority.

271 **teris . . . terris:** note the play on words. **terris:** local ablative.

272 **tantarum . . . rerum:** 'so great a destiny'. These words and many of Mercury's other words are close echoes of those expressed to him by Jupiter (lines 232–7).

273 This line has been omitted as it is rejected as an interpolation by all editors.

274–5 **Ascanium . . . Iuli:** both names of Aeneas' son are used probably to indicate that Iulus is to become the more important name as he will be the founder of the Julian *gens* (see Introduction). **spes:** like *Ascanium*, the object of *respice*; the 'hopes of Julus' are either 'the hopes you have for Julus' or 'the hopes Julus has'; editors are divided as to which to choose.

275–6 **debetur:** the enjambement of this verb, following the similar positioning of *respice*, gives extra weight to the verb, to persuade Aeneas to accept the arguments. Interestingly, Mercury at no point directly orders Aeneas to depart, although Jupiter had ended his instructions with the similarly enjambed *naviget* (line 237).

276–8 **tali . . . ore:** 'with such words'. **Cyllenius:** according to the myth, Mercury was born and brought up on Mt Cyllene in Greece, and so 'the Cyllenian' is a poetic alternative name for him. **medio sermone:** lit. 'in mid-speech', which is clearly not true, and so best rendered as 'while he was still speaking'.

Questions

1 In lines 259–264, what impression of Aeneas does Virgil give?

2 What arguments does Mercury use to persuade Aeneas to depart from Carthage?

3 How effective are Mercury's arguments?

at vero Aeneas aspectu obmutuit amens,
arrectaeque horrore comae et vox faucibus haesit.   280
ardet abire fuga dulcesque relinquere terras,
attonitus tanto monitu imperioque deorum.
heu quid agat? quo nunc reginam ambire furentem
audeat adfatu? quae prima exordia sumat?
atque animum nunc huc celerem nunc dividit illuc   285
in partesque rapit varias perque omnia versat.
haec alternanti potior sententia visa est:
Mnesthea Sergestumque vocat fortemque Serestum,
classem aptent taciti sociosque ad litora cogant,
arma parent et quae rebus sit causa novandis   290
dissimulent; sese interea, quando optima Dido
nesciat et tantos rumpi non speret amores,
temptaturum aditus et quae mollissima fandi
tempora, quis rebus dexter modus. ocius omnes
imperio laeti parent et iussa facessunt.   295
at regina dolos (quis fallere possit amantem?)
praesensit, motusque excepit prima futuros
omnia tuta timens. eadem impia Fama furenti
detulit armari classem cursumque parari.

vero	indeed	*Serestus, -i* m.	Serestus
aspectus, -us m.	sight	*classis, -is* f.	fleet
obmutesco, -ere, -mutui	I am struck dumb	*apto, -are*	I make ready
amens, -ntis	frantic	*litus, -oris* n.	shore
arrectus, -a, -um	280 stood on end	*cogo, -ere*	I assemble
horror, -oris m.	horror	*dissimulo, -are*	290 I hide
coma, -ae f.	hair	*quando*	since
fauces, -ium f.pl.	throat	*nescio, -ire*	I do not know
attonitus, -a, -um	stunned	*rumpo, -ere*	I break, shatter
monitus, -us m.	warning	*spero, -are*	I hope, expect
imperium, -i n.	power, command	*tempto, -are*	I try
ambio, -ire	I placate	*aditus, -us* m.	approach
audeo, -ere	I dare	*for, fari, fatus sum*	I speak
adfatus, -us m.	address	*dexter, -tra, -trum*	right, suitable
exordium, -i n.	beginning	*modus, -i* m.	way, method
sumo, -ere	I take, choose	*ocius*	(more) swiftly
huc	285 this way	*pareo, -ere* + dat.	295 I obey
divido, -ere	I divide	*iussum, -i* n.	command
illuc	that way	*facesso, -ere*	I do eagerly
rapio, -ere	I seize, hurry	*dolus, -i* m.	deceit, trick
varius, -a, -um	various	*amans, -ntis* f.	lover
verso, -are	I turn	*praesentio, -ire, -sensi*	I learn first
alterno, -are	I hesitate	*motus, -us* m.	movement
potior, -ius	preferable	*excipio, -ere, -cepi, -ceptus*	I hear of, rescue
sententia, -ae f.	opinion	*impius, -a, -um*	wicked
videor, -eri, visus sum	I seem	*defero, -re, -tuli, -latus*	I inform
Mnestheus, -ei (acc. *-ea*) m.	Mnestheus	*armo, -are*	I arm, equip
Sergestus, -i m.	Sergestus		

279 **at vero:** these words represent a strong contrast, like the start of a new chapter in a novel. **aspectu:** ablative of cause, dependent on *amens*. Note the heavy, spondaic rhythm.

280 **arrectae:** supply *sunt*. **faucibus:** local ablative.

281 **fuga:** ablative of manner: 'in flight', i.e. quickly. **dulces ... terras:** the fact that Carthage is 'pleasant' makes it all the more difficult for him to leave.

282 **deorum:** plural because Mercury was relaying the will of Jupiter.

283–4 **heu quid agat:** a deliberative question: 'Alas, what was he to do?' **quo ... adfatu:** 'with what address'. **furentem:** Aeneas foresees Dido's reaction to the news of his departure. **quae ... sumat:** another deliberative question. **exordia:** he is asking himself how he can begin to explain to the queen.

285–6 **animum ... celerem ... dividit:** 'he divided his swift mind' is a poetic way of emphasising how thoroughly Aeneas considered all possibilities. **in partes ... varias:** '(and he rapidly directs his mind) in different directions'. **perque omnia versat:** 'and turns (his mind) through all (possibilities)'. Virgil uses three different expressions to repeat the same idea, that Aeneas tried desperately to find some way of telling Dido.

287 **alternanti:** supply *ei*: 'to him hesitating'. **haec ... sententia:** i.e. the plan that follows.

288 The three men are all close companions of Aeneas.

289–91 **aptent, cogant, parent, dissimulent:** supply *eis imperavit ut* to give indirect commands. **quae ... sit causa:** 'what was the reason' (indirect question dependent on *dissimulent*). **rebus ... novandis:** 'for the change of plan'.

291–4 **sese ... tempturum:** supply *esse*: indirect statement dependent on *dixit* (understood). **tantos ... amores:** 'such great love' (between herself and Aeneas). **aditus:** 'a way to approach her' (poetic plural). **quae ... tempora:** supply *sint*. **fandi:** 'for speaking'. **quis ... modus:** supply *sit* again. **rebus:** 'for the circumstances'.

294–5 **ocius:** emphatic at the start of the sentence; this adverb is sometimes used without a comparative meaning. **laeti:** note the contrast between the other men and Aeneas.

296–7 **at regina:** the use of *at* indicates a complete change of focus, from Aeneas to Dido. **possit:** potential subjunctive.

297–8 Note the slow rhythm of line 297, contrasted with the fast rhythm of line 298. **prima:** either 'at once' or 'before anyone else'. **motus ... futuros:** 'future movements', i.e. activities that were about to occur. **omnia tuta timens:** 'fearing everything, even when it was safe'. Perhaps these words are intended to indicate Dido's sense of insecurity.

298–9 **eadem impia Fama:** see 173ff. **furenti:** supply *ei*. **cursumque parari:** 'and that a voyage was being prepared'.

Questions

1 In lines 279–282, how does Virgil emphasise the horror felt by Aeneas?

2 In lines 282–286, what impression do you receive of Aeneas?

3 In lines 287–295, does your impression of Aeneas change? If so, in what way and why?

4 If you were Dido, how would you react to Aeneas' choice of action?

5 In lines 296–299, how do Virgil's choice of words and his use of word order and sound effects support the meaning?

saevit inops animi totamque incensa per urbem   300
bacchatur, qualis commotis excita sacris
Thyias, ubi audito stimulant trieterica Baccho
orgia nocturnusque vocat clamore Cithaeron.
tandem his Aenean compellat vocibus ultro:
'dissimulare etiam sperasti, perfide, tantum   305
posse nefas tacitusque mea decedere terra?
nec te noster amor nec te data dextera quondam
nec moritura tenet crudeli funere Dido?   308
mene fugis? per ego has lacrimas dextramque tuam te   314
(quando aliud mihi iam miserae nihil ipsa reliqui),   315
per conubia nostra, per inceptos hymenaeos,
si bene quid de te merui, fuit aut tibi quicquam
dulce meum, miserere domus labentes et istam,
oro, si quis adhuc precibus locus, exue mentem.
te propter Libycae gentes Nomadumque tyranni   320
odere, infensi Tyrii; te propter eundem
exstinctus pudor et, qua sola sidera adibam,
fama prior. cui me moribundam deseris, – hospes
(hoc solum nomen quoniam de coniuge restat)?
quid moror? an mea Pygmalion dum moenia frater   325
destruat aut captam ducat Gaetulus Iarbas?

saevio, -ire, -ii	300 I rage, am furious	*quicquam*	anything
inops, -opis	helpless	*misereor, -eri, -itus sum*	I pity
incensus, -a, -um	inflamed, on fire	*iste, ista, istud*	that of yours
bacchor, -ari, -atus sum	I roam frenziedly	*oro, -are*	I beg
commoveo, -ere, -vi, -tus	I shake, wave	*si quis*	if any
excitus, -a, -um	excited	*adhuc*	still
Thyias, -adis f.	Bacchante	*prex, precis* f.	prayer, plea
stimulo, -are	I rouse, excite	*locus, -i* m.	place
trietericus, -a, -um	triennial	*exuo, -ere*	I put off, drop
Bacchus, -i m.	Bacchus	*propter* + acc.	320 because of
orgia, -orum n.pl.	orgies	*Nomas, -adis* m./f.	Numidian
nocturnus, -a, -um	nocturnal	*tyrannus, -i* m.	king, ruler
Cithaeron, -onis m.	(Mt) Cithaeron	*odi, odisse*	I hate
compello, -are	I address	*infensus, -a, -um*	hostile
vox, vocis f.	voice, word	*exstinguo, -ere, -nxi, -nctus*	I destroy
ultro	spontaneously	*adeo, -ire*	I reach
dissimulo, -are	305 I hide, conceal	*prior, -oris*	former, previous
perfidus, -a, -um	treacherous	*moribundus, -a, -um*	doomed to die
nefas n. (indecl.)	crime	*desero, -ere*	I abandon
decedo, -ere	I depart	*quoniam*	since
dext(e)ra, -ae f.	right hand	*resto, -are*	I am left
quondam	once, previously	*an*	= *-ne*
morior, -i, mortuus sum	I die	*Pygmalion, -onis* m.	325 Pygmalion
funus, -eris n.	309 death	*frater, -tris* m.	brother
hymenaeus, -i m.	316 marriage	*destruo, -ere*	I destroy
mereo, -ere, -ui, -itus	I deserve	*Gaetulus, -a, -um*	Gaetulian

300–1 **saevit:** the subject is Dido. **animi:** locative case: 'in her mind'. **bacchatur:** this verb is formed from *Bacchus*, the Roman god of wine, and suggests the frenzied, intoxicated madness experienced by his worshippers.

301–3 Note the slow rhythm of line 301. **qualis:** as before, the word introduces a <u>simile</u>, in which Dido is compared to a Bacchante, or female worshipper of Bacchus. **commotis . . . sacris:** '(excited) by the waved emblems', i.e. 'by the waving of the sacred emblems; these emblems, comprising statues of the god and other items related to his worship, would have been carried in procession at his festivals. **audito . . . Baccho:** 'when (the name) "Bacchus" was heard' (ablative absolute). **orgia:** these are the orgiastic rites in which women lost all inhibitions and rampaged through the countryside. **stimulant, vocat:** supply *eam* as their object. **nocturnus . . . Cithaeron:** 'Cithaeron by night'; Cithaeron was a mountain in central Greece famous for the orgiastic worship of Bacchus.

304 **his . . . vocibus:** 'with these words'. **ultro:** i.e. she accosted him first.

305–6 The order is *etiam sperasti, perfide, (te) posse dissimulare tantum nefas*. **sperasti:** = *speravisti*. **tantum . . . nefas:** i.e. leaving her. **perfide:** i.e. 'you traitor'. **tacitus:** 'in silence'.

307–8 An ascending <u>tricolon</u>. **data dextera quondam:** the clasping of right hands signified a pledge. **moritura . . . Dido:** Dido is indicating that she will kill herself if he leaves her; note the position in the line of *Dido*. **tenet:** i.e. 'stop you leaving'; the verb has three subjects.

314 **ego . . . te:** supply *oro* from line 319, with *te* as its object; such misplacement of words is common in prayers.

315 **aliud . . . nihil . . . reliqui:** 'I have left nothing else'. **mihi . . . miserae:** 'to my poor self'.

316 **conubia . . . hymenaeos:** *conubia* is the state of wedlock, while *hymenaeos* is the wedding itself. Logically therefore, it should be the *conubia* that has been 'begun', rather than the *hymenaeos*. It is possible that *inceptos* should be taken with both nouns.

317–19 **si . . . quid:** 'if in any way'. **quicquam . . . meum:** 'anything of mine'. **miserere:** singular imperative, deponent. **domus labentes:** 'a house falling into ruin': Dido means her dynasty, which is destined for collapse if Aeneas leaves. **istam . . . exue mentem:** 'put aside that intention of yours'.

320–1 **te propter:** inverted word order. **odere:** alternative for *oderunt*; the local tribal chiefs, who sought her hand in marriage when she first arrived in Africa, but were rejected by her. **infensi Tyrii:** supply *sunt*; most editors take these words to mean that her Carthaginian subjects are now hostile to her, which is not the impression given previously. An alternative is to take the words as a reference to her brother Pygmalion and the people in Tyre who did not accompany Dido to Carthage. Pygmalion had killed her husband and would kill her too. **Nomadum:** a North-African tribe.

321–3 **te . . . eundem:** 'the same you', i.e. 'you also'. **exstinctus pudor:** supply *est*; *pudor* is her reputation for chastity. **fama prior:** 'my previous reputation', amplifying *pudor*; supply *exstincta est*. **qua sola sidera adibam:** 'by which alone I could reach the stars'; if her soul could ascend to the stars after her death, she would achieve immortality.

323–4 **moribundam:** this repeats the idea of *moritura* (line 308). **hospes:** Aeneas is no more than a visitor or guest, now that he can't be called a husband. **quoniam:** bring forward. **de coniuge:** 'from (the name of) husband'.

325–6 The order is *an dum frater Pygmalion destruat mea moenia*. **Gaetulus Iarbas:** Iarbas was king of the Gaetulians and had sought Dido's hand in marriage.

Questions

1 Explain the simile in lines 301–303; how effective is it?

2 How does Virgil emphasise Dido's bitterness in her speech?

saltem si qua mihi de te suscepta fuisset
ante fugam suboles, si quis mihi parvulus aula
luderet Aeneas, qui te tamen ore referret,
non equidem omnino capta ac deserta viderer.'   330
dixerat. ille Iovis monitis immota tenebat
lumina et obnixus curam sub corde premebat.
tandem pauca refert: 'ego te, quae plurima fando
enumerare vales, numquam, regina, negabo
promeritam, nec me meminisse pigebit Elissae   335
dum memor ipse mei, dum spiritus hos regit artus.
pro re pauca loquar. neque ego hanc abscondere furto
speravi (ne finge) fugam, nec coniugis umquam
praetendi taedas aut haec in foedera veni.
me si fata meis paterentur ducere vitam   340
auspiciis et sponte mea componere curas,
urbem Troianam primum dulcesque meorum
reliquias colerem, Priami tecta alta manerent,
et recidiva manu posuissem Pergama victis.
sed nunc Italiam magnam Gryneus Apollo,   345
Italiam Lyciae iussere capessere sortes;
hic amor, haec patria est. si te Carthaginis arces
Phoenissam Libycaeque aspectus detinet urbis,
quae tandem Ausonia Teucros considere terra
invidia est? et nos fas extera quaerere regna.   350

desine meque tuis incendere teque querelis;   360
Italiam non sponte sequor.'

saltem	at least	fingo, -ere	I imagine
suscipio, -ere, -cepi, -ceptus	I bear	praetendo, -ere	I hold out
suboles, -is f.	child	foedus, -eris n.	pact
parvulus, -a, -um	tiny	patior, -i, passus sum	340 I allow
aula, -ae f.	palace	auspicium, -i n.	auspice
ludo, -ere	I play	sponte mea	of my own accord
refero, -ferre	I recall, answer	compono, -ere	I settle, allay
omnino	330 entirely	reliquiae, -arum f.pl.	relics
Iuppiter, Iovis m.	Jupiter	colo, -ere	I look after
moneo, -ere, -ui, -itus	I warn	Priamus, -i m.	Priam
obnitor, -i, -nixus sum	I struggle (against)	recidivus, -a, -um	restored
		Pergama, -orum n.pl.	Pergama
cura, -ae f.	love, anxiety	Gryneus, -a, -um	345 Grynian
cor, cordis n.	heart	Apollo, -inis m.	Apollo
enumero, -are	I recite	Lycia, -ae f.	Lycia
valeo, -ere	I can	capesso, -ere	I make for, seek
nego, -are	I deny	sors, sortis f.	oracle
promereor, -eri, -itus sum	335 I deserve	patria, -ae f.	fatherland
memini, -isse + gen.	I remember	Phoenissus, -a, -um	Phoenician
piget, -ere, -uit	it disgusts, annoys	Ausonius, -a, -um	Italian
Elissa, -ae f.	Dido	consido, -ere	I settle
memor, -oris	mindful	invidia, -ae f.	350 envy, grudge
spiritus, -us m.	breath, life	fas n.(indecl.)	lawful, right
rego, -ere	I control	exterus, -a, -um	foreign
artus, -us m.	limb	desino, -ere	360 I stop, cease
abscondo, -ere	I hide	querela, -ae f.	complaint
furtum, -i n,	stealth		

327–8 **si qua ... suboles:** 'if some child'. **suscepta fuisset:** = *suscepta esset*. **mihi:** dative of the agent after a passive verb. **de te:** 'fathered by you'.

328–9 **si quis ... parvulus ... Aeneas:** 'if some tiny Aeneas'. **mihi:** dative of advantage: 'for me'. **qui ... referret:** 'to recall' or 'who would recall' (purpose). **ore:** 'in looks'.

330 **capta ac deserta:** 'deceived and abandoned'. Note the strong passion of Dido's appeal.

331–2 **dixerat:** the pluperfect is often used by Virgil to mark the conclusion of a speech; translate as 'she finished speaking'. **ille:** Aeneas. **monitis:** causal ablative: 'because of the warnings'. **immota tenebat lumina:** i.e. he did not lower his eyes as an admission of shame. **obnixus:** 'having struggled', and so 'with a great effort'. **curam ... premebat:** i.e. he refused to acknowledge (or give way to) his love for Dido. **sub corde:** 'deep in his heart'.

333–5 **tandem:** i.e. after he had considered what to say. **pauca:** i.e. out of all the things he might have said, he chose only a few. The order of the next words is probably *ego numquam negabo te, regina, promeritam (esse) plurima quae vales enumerare fando*; most editors take this to mean 'I shall never deny that you, o queen, have deserved (well of me) in respect of the very many things that you can recite in words'; other editors have interpreted the words differently. Another possibility perhaps is to take *quae* as agreeing with *te* instead of *plurima*; the sense would then be 'I shall never deny that you, o queen, who can recite in words very many things (you have done), have deserved (well of me)'. Both interpretations would amount to 'I shall never deny my great debt to you for all you have done'.

335–6 **Elissae:** Elissa was Dido's original name. **dum memor:** supply *sum*. **mei:** objective genitive, dependent on *memor*: 'as long as I am mindful of myself', i.e. 'as long as my memory still functions'. Aeneas' words sound very feeble today, but in the context of Stoic virtue, where emotions are repressed, they would indicate strength.

337–9 **pro re pauca loquar:** these are the emotionless words of a lawyer. **furto:** 'by stealth' (ablative of manner) and so 'furtively'. **hanc ... fugam:** 'this flight'. **ne finge:** poetic for *noli fingere*. **praetendi taedas:** 'nor did I hold out the marriage torch': the *taeda* was carried at weddings and so became a symbol of marriage; *praetendi* carries two meanings: 'hold out in front (of me)' and 'put forward as a pretence'. He is disclaiming any marriage pact between them; Dido's interpretation of the cave scene was entirely her own. Such a claim was hardly likely to satisfy Dido. **haec ... foedera:** i.e. marriage. Note the slow rhythm of line 339.

340–1 **meis ... auspiciis:** i.e. 'according to my own desires'; the auspices were omens of the future taken by Roman magistrates and generals to determine their actions.

342–4 Note the slow rhythm of line 342. **reliquias:** either the ruins of Troy or the ashes of his dead countrymen. **manerent:** 'would still be there', in the sense that he would have rebuilt the city. **posuissem:** 'I would have founded'. **manu:** 'by my own hand'. **victis:** 'for the conquered'. **Pergama:** the citadel of Troy.

345–6 **nunc:** 'as it is'. **Gryneus Apollo:** Apollo had a shrine at Gryneum in Asia Minor. **Lyciae ... sortes:** 'the Lycian oracles': Apollo was the god of prophecy and he had a shrine in Lycia (Asia Minor) where he delivered them. **iussere:** = *iusserunt*.

347 **hic amor, haec patria est:** i.e. it is Italy, not Dido and Carthage, that Aeneas has to love.

347–50 **te ... Phoenissam:** 'you, a Phoenician' (from Tyre). **arces:** supply *detinent* from the next line. **quae ... invidia est:** 'what grudge is there', i.e. 'how can you begrudge'. **Ausonia ... terra:** local ablative: 'in the land of Italy'. His argument is that, if Dido, an exile from Tyre, can settle in a foreign land, why can't he? **fas:** supply *est*.

360 **meque ... teque:** 'both me and you'. **tuis ... querelis:** 'with your complaints'.

Question

1 Evaluate Aeneas' response to Dido. Is he fair to her? What sort of man does he seem?

talia dicentem iamdudum aversa tuetur
huc illuc volvens oculos totumque pererrat
luminibus tacitis et sic accensa profatur:
'nec tibi diva parens generis nec Dardanus auctor,   365
perfide, sed duris genuit te cautibus horrens
Caucasus Hyrcanaeque admorunt ubera tigres.
nam quid dissimulo aut quae me ad maiora reservo?
num fletu ingemuit nostro? num lumina flexit?
num lacrimas victus dedit aut miseratus amantem est?   370
quae quibus anteferam? iam iam nec maxima Iuno
nec Saturnius haec oculis pater aspicit aequis.
nusquam tuta fides. eiectum litore, egentem
excepi et regni demens in parte locavi.
amissam classem, socios a morte reduxi   375
(heu furiis incensa feror!): nunc augur Apollo,
nunc Lyciae sortes, nunc et Iove missus ab ipso
interpres divum fert horrida iussa per auras.
scilicet is superis labor est, ea cura quietos
sollicitat. neque te teneo neque dicta refello: 380
i, sequere Italiam ventis, pete regna per undas.
spero equidem mediis, si quid pia numina possunt,
supplicia hausurum scopulis et nomine Dido
saepe vocaturum.   384

averto, -ere, -ti, -sus	I turn away	antefero, -ferre	I put … before
tueor, -eri, tutus sum	I watch	Saturnius, -a, -um	of Saturn
huc illuc	this way and that	aspicio, -ere	I observe, see
volvo, -ere	I roll	aequus, -a, -um	impartial
pererro, -are	I scan, survey	nusquam	nowhere
accendo, -ere, -di, -sus	I inflame	eicio, -ere, -ieci, -iectus	I cast up
profor, -fari, -fatus sum	I speak out	egeo, -ere	I am in need
divus, -a, -um	365 divine	amitto, -ere, -misi, -missus	I lose
parens, -ntis m./f.	parent	reduco, -ere, -xi, -ctus	375 I bring back
Dardanus, -i m.	Dardanus	furiae, -arum f.pl.	madness
auctor, -oris m.	ancestor	augur, -uris m.	augur, prophet
durus, -a, -um	hard	Lycius, -a, -um	Lycian
gigno, -ere, genui, genitus	I beget	interpres, -etis m.	messenger
cautes, -is f.	rock	divus, -i m.	god
horrens, -ntis	rough	horridus, -a, -um	dreadful
Caucasus, -i m.	Caucasus	scilicet	to be sure
Hyrcanus, -a, -um	Hyrcanian	superi, -orum m.pl.	the gods
admoveo, -ere, -movi, -motus	I move … to	quietus, -a, -um	quiet
uber, -eris n.	udder	sollicito, -are	380 I trouble
tigris, -idis f.	tigress	refello, -ere	I refute
reservo, -are	I keep back	unda, -ae f.	wave
fletus, -us m.	weeping	pius, -a, -um	righteous, dutiful
ingemo, -ere, -ui, -itus	I groan	supplicium, -i n.	punishment
flecto, -ere, -xi, -xus	I bend, turn	haurio, -ire, -si, -s(t)us	I drink, swallow
miseror, -ari, -atus sum	370 I pity	scopulus, -i m.	rock

362 **talia dicentem:** supply *eum*. **iamdudum:** i.e. since he started speaking. **aversa tuetur:** supply *Dido* as subject: 'she watched him while turned away', i.e. she looked at him askance.
363–4 **huc illuc volvens oculos:** this is indicative of her frenzy. **totum:** supply *eum*: she surveyed 'his whole body'. **luminibus tacitis:** 'with silent eyes', i.e. 'with expressionless eyes'.
365 **diva parens:** the reference is to Venus; supply *erat*. **Dardanus auctor:** Dardanus was a son of Jupiter and the founder of the royal line of Troy, and so an ancestor of Aeneas. Dido's scathing comments here are in direct contrast to her words to her sister Anna (line 12). **tibi . . . generis:** i.e. 'of your line'.
366–7 **duris . . . cautibus:** either ablative of description (qualifying *horrens*) or local ablative. **Caucasus:** a mountainous region between the Black and Caspian Seas; it is unlikely that Dido would have known anything about the area, other than its reputation as being at the furthest corner of the known world. **Hyrcanaeque . . . tigres:** Hyrcania was a region close to the Caucasus and known for its tigers. **admorunt ubera:** supply *tibi*; *admorunt* = *admoverunt*; translate as 'suckled you'.
368 **quid:** 'why'. **dissimulo:** supply *iram* or similar. **quae . . . ad maiora:** 'for what more important matters'. She means that nothing can have such a profound effect on her life as Aeneas' departure. Note the sequence of <u>rhetorical questions</u> using the vivid indicative rather than the subjunctive.
369–70 **num . . . num . . . num:** the use of a <u>tricolon</u> indicates her use of a highly rhetorical style of speech. **ingemuit:** the change to the 3rd person expresses contempt.
371–2 **quae quibus anteferam:** deliberative subjunctive: 'what should I mention first?' **iam iam:** 'right now'. **Saturnius . . . pater:** not 'the father of Saturn' but 'the father (of us all, who is the son) of Saturn'; this is an unusual term for Jupiter. **oculis . . . aequis:** i.e. they will be angered by Aeneas' treatment of her; Dido ignores for the moment the fact that Aeneas has already told her that it is Jupiter who ordered him to leave.
373–4 **nusquam tuta fides:** supply *est*. **eiectum, egentem:** supply *eum*. **eiectum litore:** i.e. 'shipwrecked'. **regni . . . in parte locavi:** i.e. 'I gave him a share of the kingdom'.
375–6 **amissam classem:** supply *reduxi* with this object as well as with *socios*. Note the <u>consonance</u> of *-m-* sounds in this line, all indicating high emotion. **furiis . . . feror:** 'I am being carried away by madness'.
376–8 **nunc . . . nunc . . . nunc:** another <u>ascending tricolon</u> used for rhetorical effect. **augur Apollo:** Apollo was the god of prophecy. **Lyciae sortes:** Dido repeats Aeneas' catalogue of excuses (lines 345–6). **et:** 'too'. **divum:** = *divorum*.
379–80 **scilicet:** this word generally introduces sarcasm, as here; Dido in fact rejects the notion that the gods take any interest in human affairs. **quietos:** supply *eos* (the gods). Note the fast rhythm of line 380, followed by the almost-as-quick line 381: she urges him to leave, sarcastically.
381 **sequere:** 'make for' (imperative). **ventis:** 'on the winds'.
382–4 **mediis . . . scopulis:** i.e. in a shipwreck. **si quid . . . possunt:** 'if (they) have any power'. **hausurum, vocaturum:** supply *te* as the subject of the indirect statements introduced by *spero*. **supplicia hausurum:** a clever <u>metaphor</u>, as she hopes he will drown; *hausurum* is a rare alternative to the normal *hausturum*. **Dido:** a Greek accusative.

Questions

1 In 362–364, how does Virgil indicate the fury of Dido?

2 What different arguments does Dido use in her speech?

3 Discuss the range of emotions revealed by this speech.

4 Who is the more deserving of our pity: Dido or Aeneas?

```
        sequar atris ignibus absens                                    384
et, cum frigida mors anima seduxerit artus,                            385
omnibus umbra locis adero. dabis, improbe, poenas.
audiam et haec manes veniet mihi fama sub imos.'
his medium dictis sermonem abrumpit et auras
aegra fugit seque ex oculis avertit et aufert,
linquens multa metu cunctantem et multa parantem               390
dicere. suscipiunt famulae conlapsaque membra
marmoreo referunt thalamo stratisque reponunt.
at pius Aeneas, quamquam lenire dolentem
solando cupit et dictis avertere curas,
multa gemens magnoque animum labefactus amore                 395
iussa tamen divum exsequitur classemque revisit.
tum vero Teucri incumbunt et litore celsas
deducunt toto naves.
```

The Trojans hurried from all over the city to the harbour like ants on the march. Dido made one last appeal to Aeneas, sending her sister Anna to plead with him to stay. Aeneas remained steadfast to his divine orders, as unmoveable as a mighty oak-tree in a gale. Dido now prayed only for death. After determining the time and method of her death, she tricked Anna into building a pyre on which she would destroy all the possessions left behind by Aeneas, including the bed they had shared. After a sleepless night, dawn revealed to her the empty harbour. Cursing Aeneas and the Trojans, she climbed to the top of the pyre and spoke her last words.

```
'dulces exuviae, dum fata deusque sinebat,                     651
accipite hanc animam meque his exsolvite curis.
vixi et quem dederat cursum Fortuna peregi,
et nunc magna mei sub terras ibit imago.
urbem praeclaram statui, mea moenia vidi,                      655
ulta virum poenas inimico a fratre recepi,
felix, heu nimium felix, si litora tantum
numquam Dardaniae tetigissent nostra carinae.'
```

ater, atra, atrum		black	*exsequor, -i, -secutus sum*	I carry out
frigidus, -a, -um	385	cold	*reviso, -ere*	I revisit
anima, -ae f.		breath, life	*incumbo, -ere*	I set to work
seduco, -ere, -duxi, -ductus		I separate	*celsus, -a, -um*	tall
adsum, -esse		I am present	*deduco, -ere*	I take down, launch
improbus, -a, -um		wicked, vile		
poenas do, dare		I am punished	*exuviae, -arum* f.pl.	651 spoils, arms
manes, -ium m.pl.		spirits, shades	*sino, -ere*	I allow
imus, -a, -um		the lowest	*exsolvo, -ere*	I release
abrumpo, -ere		I break off	*Fortuna, -ae* f.	Fortune
aeger, -gra, -grum		sick	*perago, -ere, -egi, -actus*	I complete
famula, -ae f.	390	maid-servant	*praeclarus, -a, -um*	655 famous
conlabor, -i, -lapsus sum		I collapse, faint	*statuo, -ere, -ui, -utus*	I found
marmoreus, -a, -um		of marble	*ulciscor, -i, ultus sum*	I avenge
lenio, -ire		I soothe	*inimicus, -i* m.	enemy
doleo, -ere		I grieve	*recipio, -ere, -cepi, -ceptus*	I exact
solor, -ari		I console	*felix, -icis*	happy
gemo, -ere	395	I sigh	*nimium*	too (much)
labefacio, -ere, -feci, -factus		I shake	*tantum*	only

384–6 **sequar:** supply *te*. **atris ignibus:** 'with smokey flames': there is a double meaning here: the torches carried by the avenging Furies as they chase after sinners; but also the smoke and flames from her funeral pyre, which she hopes Aeneas will look back and see. **absens:** 'though I shall be far away'. **anima:** ablative of separation. **omnibus umbra locis:** 'everywhere as a ghost', i.e. there will be no escape for Aeneas from her spiritual pursuit of him.

387 **audiam:** i.e. that he has been duly punished. **haec . . . fama:** i.e. the report of his punishment. **manes . . . sub imos:** 'down to the deepest depths of Hades'; she means that, whichever part of the underworld she inhabits, the news will reach her.

388–9 **medium . . . sermonem:** i.e. 'in mid-speech'; Virgil suggests that she had more to say. **auras:** object of *fugit*: 'the open air'. **ex oculis:** 'from his sight'. **aufert:** supply *se*.

390–1 **cunctantem, parantem:** supply *eum*. **multa . . . multa:** the first is adverbial: 'deeply (uncertain)'; the second is the object of *dicere*. Note the heavy <u>alliteration</u> and <u>consonance</u> of -*m* in line 390, emphasising Dido's emotional turmoil.

391–2 **marmoreo . . . thalamo:** poetic for *ad marmoreum thalamum*. **stratis:** local ablative.

393–4 **at pius Aeneas:** *at* introduces a change of subject or theme; *pius* is an interesting choice of word at this point: although Aeneas is not at all dutiful towards his lover, it is precisely because he is so dutiful to his people, his gods and his destiny that he abandons her.

395–6 **animum labefactus:** lit. 'shaken with respect to his heart', and so 'his heart shaken'; *animum* is most simply construed as an accusative of respect or adverbial accusative. Note the heavy <u>alliteration</u> and <u>consonance</u> of -*m* again in line 395, showing that his emotional upset was as great as Dido's. **divum:** = *divorum*.

397–8 **litore . . . toto:** local ablative: 'all along the shore'. Aeneas' ships would have been drawn up onto a sandy beach.

651–2 **dulces exuviae:** these would be everything left behind by Aeneas, including clothing and his sword; she calls them 'sweet' because her love for Aeneas has welled up inside her again. **dum fata deusque sinebat:** i.e. the *exuviae* were sweet 'as long as fate and the god allowed', that is until they forced Aeneas to leave; the 'god' is probably intended to be Jupiter.

653–4 Dido begins a catalogue of her achievements, such as a Roman of Virgil's day would expect to find as an epitaph on a tombstone – a fitting memorial to Dido. The order is *vixi et peregi cursum quem Fortuna dederat*. Fortune is here personified. **magna mei . . . imago:** 'my great spirit'; she describes her spirit as great partly because ghosts were regularly thought of as larger than life, and perhaps partly because of her high status as queen. **sub terras:** i.e. to the underworld.

655–6 She continues her list of achievements. **ulta virum:** 'having avenged my husband'; see lines 17 and 21 and the Introduction for the story. **poenas . . . recepi:** 'I exacted punishment', i.e. 'I punished'.

657–8 **felix:** supply *fuissem*: 'I would have been happy'. **heu nimium felix:** 'alas too happy': she perhaps means that too much happiness would inevitably be followed by a fall. **si . . . tantum:** 'if only'. **Dardaniae . . . carinae:** 'Trojan ships', an example of <u>synecdoche</u>.

Questions

1 What emotions does Dido display in the last four lines of her speech to Aeneas?

2 In 388–392, how are Dido and Aeneas contrasted?

3 In 393–396, why does a modern reader finds this account of Aeneas hard to accept?

4 What impression of Dido are we given by her final speech?

dixit, et os impressa toro, 'moriemur inultae,
sed moriamur' ait. 'sic, sic iuvat ire sub umbras.   660
hauriat hunc oculis ignem crudelis ab alto
Dardanus, et nostrae secum ferat omina mortis.'
dixerat, atque illam media inter talia ferro
conlapsam aspiciunt comites, ensemque cruore
spumantem sparsasque manus.   665

*News of Dido's suicide spread quickly through the city. Juno, taking pity on the dying
woman, sent Iris, goddess of the Rainbow, to take a lock of hair from Dido's head as an
offering to Pluto, and so the queen died.*

imprimo, -ere, -pressi, pressus	I press . . . on	*omen, -inis* n.	omen, portent
inultus, -a, -um	unavenged	*mors, mortis* f	death
aio (defective verb)	I say	*comes, -itis* m./f.	companion
haurio, -ire	660 I drink in	*cruor, -oris* m.	blood, gore
crudelis, -e	cruel	*spumo, -are*	665 I foam

659–60 **os impressa:** the passive participle is treated as if from a deponent verb, in imitation of a Greek middle verb: 'having pressed her mouth'. **toro:** dative after the compound verb. **moriemur ... moriamur:** plural for singular; her argument is that, even though her death will be unavenged, she must die anyway. **sic, sic:** as she says these words, she plunges the sword into her body. **ire sub umbras:** a poetic phrase meaning 'to die'.

661–2 **hauriat ... oculis:** 'let him drink in with his eyes', i.e. 'let him see'. **hunc ... ignem:** as she says these words, she sets fire to the pyre. **ab alto:** 'from far out to sea'. **nostrae ... omina mortis:** 'portents of my death', i.e. 'evidence of my death'; the smoke rising from the pyre above the roof of the palace will, she hopes, make him realise what she has done.

663–5 **media inter talia:** 'in the midst of such words'. **ferro conlapsam:** 'collapsed upon the sword'; *ferro* is probably ablative, which could be construed as instrumental, causal or local. **cruore:** to be taken both with *ensem spumantem* and *sparsas manus*.

Questions

1 How do lines 659–662 show Dido's anguish?

2 How is Dido's death described?

3 Do you find this a suitable ending for the book?

4 Who do you think was to blame for death of Dido?

Book 5

Bidden by the gods, Aeneas and his Trojans had sailed away from Carthage in their quest for a new home in Italy. Aeneas was unaware that his departure had induced queen Dido to kill herself.

interea medium Aeneas iam classe tenebat
certus iter fluctusque atros Aquilone secabat
moenia respiciens, quae iam infelicis Elissae
conlucent flammis. quae tantum accenderit ignem
causa latet; duri magno sed amore dolores   5
polluto, notumque furens quid femina possit,
triste per augurium Teucrorum pectora ducunt.
ut pelagus tenuere rates nec iam amplius ulla
occurrrit tellus, maria undique et undique caelum,
olli caeruleus supra caput astitit imber   10
noctem hiememque ferens et inhorruit unda tenebris.
ipse gubernator puppi Palinurus ab alta:
'heu quianam tanti cinxerunt aethera nimbi?

interea	meanwhile	*duco, -ere*	I lead
medius, -a, -um	middle (of)	*ut* + indic.	when
classis, -is f.	fleet	*pelagus, -i* n.	the open sea
teneo, -ere	I hold	*ratis, -is* f.	boat, ship
certus, -a, -um	certain	*amplius*	any more
iter, itineris n.	course	*ullus, -a, -um*	any
fluctus, -us m.	wave	*occurro, -ere, -ri, -rsus*	I appear to
ater, atra, atrum	black, dark	*tellus, -uris* f.	land
Aquilo, -onis m.	North-Wind	*mare, -is* n.	sea
seco, -are	I cut, cleave	*undique*	on all sides
moenia, -ium n.pl.	city, city walls	*caelum, -i* n.	sky
respicio, -ere	I look back at	*caeruleus, -a, -um* 10	dark, blue
infelix, -icis	ill-fated, unlucky	*supra* + acc.	above
Elissa, -ae f.	Dido	*caput, -itis* n.	head
conluceo, -ere	I glow	*asto, -are, -stiti*	I stand
flamma, -ae f.	flame	*imber, -ris* m.	rain cloud
tantus, -a, -um	so great	*nox, noctis* f.	night, darkness
accendo, -ere, -ndi, -nsus	I light, kindle	*hiems, -mis* f.	storm
ignis, -is m.	fire	*inhorresco, -ere, -ui*	I shiver
causa, -ae f. 5	cause, reason	*unda, -ae* f.	wave
lateo, -ere	I am hidden	*tenebrae, -arum* f.pl.	darkness
durus, -a, -um	hard, harsh	*gubernator, -oris* m.	helmsman
amor, -oris m.	love	*puppis, -is* f.	stern
dolor, -oris m.	pain, grief	*Palinurus, -i* m.	Palinurus
polluo, -ere, -ui, -utus	I desecrate	*altus, -a, -um*	high
notum, -i n.	knowledge	*heu*	alas
furo, -ere	I rage, am mad	*quianam*	why?
tristis, -e	sad	*cingo, -ere, -nxi, -nctus*	I surround
augurium, -i n.	foreboding	*aether, -eris* (acc. *-era*) m.	sky
Teucri, -orum m.pl.	the Trojans	*nimbus, -i* m.	storm cloud
pectus, -oris n.	heart		

1–2 **interea:** i.e. while Dido was committing suicide. **medium . . . tenebat . . . iter:** Aeneas 'was maintaining the middle part of his course'; this is a poetic way of saying that he was already well on his way. **classe:** 'with his fleet' (ablative of attendant circumstances). **certus:** 'certain', i.e. 'determined' to complete his journey. **atros Aquilone:** the waves are '(made) dark by the North Wind'. The Trojans need to sail north-eastwards to reach their destination, and so the North Wind will slow their progress considerably.

3–4 **moenia:** i.e. Carthage. **Elissae:** the original Phoenician name of Dido (see Introduction). **flammis:** 'with the flames' (causal ablative); these are the flames of the funeral pyre on which Dido has killed herself.

4–5 **quae . . . accenderit . . . causa latet:** lit. 'what cause kindled . . . is unknown', i.e. 'it was unkknown (to Aeneas) what caused the fire'. Note the change to the historic present, the norm in Virgil's narrative.

5–7 **sed:** bring to the front. **magno . . . amore . . . polluto:** ablative absolute: 'when a great love has been desecrated'; *polluto* is a strong word, implying that the breaking off of a love-pact is a violation of a sacred oath; its emphasis is strengthened by the <u>enjambement</u>. **dolores . . . notumque:** these are the two subjects of *ducunt*. **duri . . . dolores:** the 'severe distress' now realised by the Trojans, who in Book IV (with the exception of Aeneas) had given no thought to Dido's likely reaction to their abandonment of her. **notumque . . . quid:** 'and the knowledge (of) what'. **triste per augurium:** the thought of Dido's distress and her likely response led the hearts of the Trojans 'through sad foreboding', i.e. they developed a grim foreboding of what Dido had done.

8–9 **tenuere:** = *tenuerunt*. **occurrit:** i.e. 'could be seen'. **maria . . . caelum:** note the <u>chiasmus</u> in these five words; supply *erant* with *maria* and *erat* with *tellus*.

10–11 **olli:** this is an archaic form of *illi* (dative singular, dative of possession), to be taken with *caput*. **inhorruit unda:** i.e. the surface of the sea became choppy in the prelude to the storm. **tenebris:** 'in the darkness' (local ablative). Note the fast rhythm of line 11, mirroring the speed of the storm's approach.

12 **gubernator . . . Palinurus:** Palinurus had been the helmsman on Aeneas' ship since leaving Troy. The helmsman stood on the deck at the stern of the ship, which towered above the rest of the ship. His job was to watch where they were headed and to handle the steering oar, which dipped into the sea behind the ship. Supply *dixit*.

13 **quianam:** an archaic word.

Questions

1 Why do you think Virgil describes Aeneas as *certus* (line 2)?

2 *Moenia respiciens* (line 3): why might Aeneas have done this?

3 In lines 1–7, what impression are we given of Aeneas and the Trojans?

4 In lines 8–11, how effective is the description of the approaching storm?

5 Find one example of <u>alliteration</u> and one of <u>assonance</u> from lines 1–13; what effect do they have?

quidve, pater Neptune, paras?' sic deinde locutus
colligere arma iubet validisque incumbere remis,   15
obliquatque sinus in ventum ac talia fatur:
'magnanime Aenea, non, si mihi Iuppiter auctor
spondeat, hoc sperem Italiam contingere caelo.
mutati transversa fremunt et vespere ab atro
consurgunt venti, atque in nubem cogitur aër.   20
nec nos obniti contra nec tendere tantum
sufficimus. superat quoniam Fortuna, sequamur,
quoque vocat vertamus iter. nec litora longe
fida reor fraterna Erycis portusque Sicanos,
si modo rite memor servata remetior astra.'   25
tum pius Aeneas: 'equidem sic poscere ventos
iamdudum et frustra cerno te tendere contra.
flecte viam velis. an sit mihi gratior ulla,
quove magis fessas optem demittere naves,
quam quae Dardanium tellus mihi servat Acesten   30

Neptunus, -i m.	Neptune	*quoniam*	since
paro, -are	I prepare	*Fortuna, -ae* f.	Fortune
deinde	then	*sequor, -i, secutus sum*	I follow
loquor, -i, locutus sum	I speak	*quo*	whither
colligo, -ere 15	I gather, take in	*verto, -ere*	I turn
arma, -orum n.pl.	arms, tackle	*litus, -oris* n.	shore
iubeo, -ere	I order	*longe*	far away, far
validus, -a, -um	strong	*fidus, -a, -um*	safe
incumbo, -ere + dat.	I bend to, lean on	*reor, -eri, ratus sum*	I think
remus, -i m.	oar	*fraternus, -a, -um*	a brother's
obliquo, -are	I set aslant	*Eryx, -ycis* m.	Eryx
sinus, -us m.	fold	*portus, -us* m.	harbour
ventus, -i m.	wind	*Sicanus, -a, -um*	Sicilian
talis, -e	such	*modo* 25	only
for, fari, fatus sum	I speak	*rite*	correctly
magnanimus, -a, -um	great-hearted	*memor, -oris*	remembering
Iuppiter, Iovis m.	Jupiter	*servo, -are, -avi, -atus*	I observe, save
auctor, -oris m.	guarantor	*remetior, -iri, -mensus sum*	I calculate back
spondeo, -ere	I promise	*astrum, -i* n.	star
spero, -are	I hope	*pius, -a, -um*	dutiful
Italia, -ae f.	Italy	*equidem*	I for my part
contingo, -ere	I reach	*posco, -ere*	I demand
muto, -are, -avi, -atus	I change	*iamdudum*	long since
transversa	sideways-on	*frustra*	in vain
fremo, -ere	I roar	*cerno, -ere*	I observe
vesper, -eris m.	the West	*flecto, -ere*	I turn
consurgo, -ere 20	I rise	*velum, -i* n.	sail
nubes, -is f.	cloud	*an*	or
cogo, -ere	I gather, thicken	*gratus, -a, -um*	pleasing
aër, -eris m.	air	*magis*	rather
obnitor, -i, -nixus sum	I struggle against	*fessus, -a, -um*	weary
contra + acc.	against	*opto, -are*	I wish, choose
tendo, -ere	I struggle, go	*demitto, -ere*	I bring to land
sufficio, -ere	I am able	*Dardanius, -a, -um* 30	Trojan
supero, -are	I overpower	*Acestes, ae* m. (acc. *-en*)	Acestes

14–15 **quidve:** 'or what'. **Neptune:** Neptune was the god of the sea, and so was believed to be responsible for storms at sea. **iubet:** supply *viros* or similar as object. **colligere arma:** 'to take in the tackle': a poetic expression to indicate the shortening of the sails so that they would withstand the onslaught of the wind.

16 **obliquatque sinus:** 'and he set the folds (of the sails) aslant', i.e. he changed the angle of the sails so that they could catch the wind as it changed. **in ventum:** '(in relation) to the wind'.

17–18 **magnanime Aenea:** vocative case; the adjective is used as an indication of respect. **Iuppiter auctor:** 'Jupiter as guarantor'; his argument is that he wouldn't be optimistic of reaching Italy even if Jupiter promised to guarantee their safety. **hoc . . . caelo:** 'with this (stormy) sky'. **contingere:** prose would require accusative and future infinitive.

19–20 **mutati . . . venti:** 'the winds have changed direction and . . .'. **vespere ab atro:** 'from the dark West'; the Trojans had departed from Carthage at dawn; although the wind is now more favourable for their planned route, its violence threatens their safety. **in nubem cogitur:** a poetic idea: the air 'is thickening into cloud'.

21–2 The order is *nos sufficimus nec obniti nec tendere contra tantum.* **obniti, tendere:** the difference is that *obniti* means to struggle against the storm, while *tendere* means to make headway against it. **tantum:** 'such a great (storm)', dependent on *contra*.

22–3 **quoniam:** to be taken first. **sequamur:** 'let us follow', i.e. they should go where the wind wants to blow them and not fight it. **quoque vocat:** 'and (let us change our course) to where (Fortune) summons us'.

23–5 **longe:** supply *abesse.* **litora . . . fida . . . fraterna:** 'the safe shores of your brother'. **Erycis:** Eryx and Aeneas shared the same mother, Venus. **portusque Sicanos:** Eryx lived in Sicily. **servata remetior astra:** 'I (can) calculate (our route) back (by) the stars I observed': that is, if he can remember how the stars were positioned when their ships were blown off course to Carthage (Book I), he should be able to work backwards using the same stars.

26–7 **pius Aeneas:** supply *dixit*; Virgil frequently describes Aeneas as *pius*, to remind the reader that he is always motivated by his sense of duty towards his family, his people and his gods. The order is *equidem cerno ventos iamdudum sic poscere et te tendere contra (eos) frustra.* **sic ventos poscere:** 'that the winds demand thus', i.e. 'that this (a change of course) is what the winds demand of us'. **iamdudum:** this could be taken with *cerno* but is simpler if taken with *poscere* and *tendere*.

28 **flecte viam:** 'change course'. **velis:** 'using the sails' (instrumental ablative).

28–30 **an:** lit. 'or', usually introducing the second of two alternative possibilities, but here very unusually used to introduce the first of two. We are probably to suppose that the train of thought is, 'change course; or if you don't wish to, can you imagine any other land more dear to me?' It is simpler to omit it in translation here. **sit, optem;** most simply to be taken as potential subjunctives ('could there be', 'I could wish'), but possibly virtual indirect questions, the logic being '(tell me) whether there is . . . or whether I could wish'. **ulla . . . tellus:** these words are unusually far apart. **quove:** 'or to where'. **fessas:** it is really the men who are tired: an example of <u>hypallage</u>. **quam:** dependent on *magis*. **quae:** '(the land) which'. **Dardanium . . . Acesten:** Acesten was a prince of Trojan ancestry whose mother had settled in Sicily. In Book 1 we are told that he had previously given hospitality to the Trojans.

Questions

1 Explain the actions described in lines 15–16.

2 What impression of Palinurus' role and importance can be gained from his speech?

3 What does Aeneas say about Sicily?

et patris Anchisae gremio complectitur ossa?'
haec ubi dicta, petunt portus et vela secundi
intendunt Zephyri; fertur cita gurgite classis,
et tandem laeti notae advertuntur harenae.
at procul ex celso miratus vertice montis   35
adventum sociasque rates occurrit Acestes.   36
gratatur reduces et gaza laetus agresti   40
excipit, ac fessos opibus solatur amicis.
postera cum primo stellas Oriente fugarat
clara dies, socios in coetum litore ab omni
advocat Aeneas tumulique ex aggere fatur:
'Dardanidae magni, genus alto a sanguine divum,   45
annuus exactis completur mensibus orbis,
ex quo reliquias divinique ossa parentis
condidimus terra maestasque sacravimus aras;
iamque dies, nisi fallor, adest, quem semper acerbum,
semper honoratum (sic di voluistis) habebo.   50
ergo agite et laetum cuncti celebremus honorem.   58

Anchises, -ae m.	Anchises	*Oriens, -ntis* m.	East, Dawn
gremium, -i n.	lap	*fugo, -are, -avi -atus*	I put to flight
complector, -i, -xus sum	I embrace, hold	*clarus, -a, -um*	bright
os, ossis n.	bone	*dies, -ei* m. or f.	day
peto, -ere	I make for	*coetus, -us* m.	assembly
portus, -us m.	harbour	*advoco, -are*	I summon
secundus -a, -um	favourable	*tumulus, -i* m.	mound, tomb
intendo, -ere	I stretch (out), bind	*agger, -eris* n.	mound
Zephyrus, -i m.	West Wind	*Dardanidae, -arum* m.pl. 45	Trojans
citus, -a, -um	swift	*genus, -eris* n.	race, people
gurges, -itis m.	sea	*sanguis, -inis* m.	blood
laetus, -a, -um	glad, happy	*divus, -i* m.	god
notus, -a, -um	familiar	*annuus, -a, -um*	annual
adverto, -ere + dat.	I turn towards	*exigo, -ere, -egi, -actus*	I complete
harena, -ae f.	sand, beach	*compleo, -ere*	I fill
procul 35	far	*mensis, -is* m.	month
celsus, -a, -um	high	*orbis, -is* m.	cycle
miror, -ari, -atus sum	I wonder (at)	*reliquiae, -arum* f.pl.	remains
vertex, -icis m.	top, peak, head	*divinus, -a, -um*	divine
mons, -ntis m.	mountain	*parens, -ntis* m./f.	parent
adventus, -us m.	approach	*condo, -ere, -didi, -ditus*	I bury
socius, -a, -um	allied, friendly	*maestus, -a, -um*	sad, gloomy
occurro, -ere	I run to meet	*sacro, -are, -avi, -atus*	I consecrate
grator, -ari, -atus sum 40	I congratulate	*ara, -ae* f.	altar
redux, -ucis	returned	*nisi*	unless, if not
gaza, -ae f.	treasure, wealth	*fallo, -ere*	I deceive
agrestis, -e	rustic	*adsum, -esse*	I am here
excipio, -ere	I welcome	*acerbus, -a, -um*	bitter
ops, opis f.	wealth, help	*honoro, -are, -avi, -atus* 50	I honour
solor, -ari, -atus sum	I comfort	*ergo* 58	therefore
amicus, -a, -um	friendly	*age, agite!*	come on!
posterus, -a, -um	next	*cunctus, -a, -um*	all
stella, -ae f.	star	*celebro, -are*	I celebrate
		honos, -oris m.	honour, tribute

31 patris Anchisae . . . ossa: Aeneas' father had died a year previously, just before the Trojans left Sicily and were blown off course to Carthage (Book III, 710ff.). **gremio:** 'in its bosom'.

32–3 dicta: supply *sunt*. **secundi . . . Zephyri:** the west winds are now favourable because, after their change of course, they are directly behind them.

33–4 gurgite: strictly, a whirlpool, but Virgil uses it regularly to mean simply 'the sea'; here local ablative. **notae . . . harenae:** since Acestes was the king of Segesta, at the western tip of Sicily, Virgil probably means that place; Anchises had died just along the coast, at Drepanum. Note the slow, spondaic rhythm of line 34, mirroring the Trojans' slowing to a halt.

35–6 miratus . . . Acestes: the sentence builds to a climax with the subject not named until the end. **occurrit:** supply *eis*. Acestes was the son of a Trojan woman.

37–9 These lines describe Acestes' wild appearance and ancestry.

40–1 gratatur reduces: Acestes 'congratulates them on their (safe) return'. **gaza . . . agresti:** 'with his rustic wealth'. **opibus:** the same as *gaza*: 'with his friendly riches'.

42–4 cum primo . . . Oriente: 'when at earliest dawn' (ablative of time). **postera . . . dies:** 'the following day'. **fugarat:** = *fugaverat*, standing for the prose *fugavisset*. **socios . . . litore ab omni:** most editors take this to mean 'his companions from all along the beach'; another possibility is 'his allies from all along the coast', i.e. all those previously visited and befriended by Aeneas before leaving Sicily. **tumulique ex aggere:** i.e. 'from a piled-up mound', like a general addressing his troops.

45 alto a sanguine divum: 'from the exalted blood of the gods'; *divum = divorum*; Aeneas' mother was Venus, who in turn was the daughter of Jupiter; Dardanus, the founder of Troy, was the son of Jupiter.

46 annuus . . . orbis: 'the annual cycle', i.e. the cycle of a year. **exactis . . . mensibus:** 'the months having been completed', i.e. a full year has passed. It was customary in Rome to mark the deaths of illustrious citizens with funerary games.

47–8 reliquias . . . ossa: 'the remains and bones', i.e. the remains consisting of the bones'. **divini . . . parentis:** i.e. his father Anchises; he is 'divine' because of his association with Venus. **terra:** local ablative. **maestasque sacravimus aras:** 'and we consecrated the gloomy altars'; altars were decorated with garlands of cypress, which were symbols of mourning.

49–50 dies: i.e. the anniversary. **habebo:** 'I shall consider'. **sic di voluistis:** an example of apostrophe, indicating that Aeneas turns his face to heaven as he speaks.

51–7 Aeneas says he would be honouring his father whatever their circumstances.

58 laetum . . . honorem: 'a joyful tribute'; his father is to be honoured not just with sadness but with joy.

Questions

1 How does Virgil show that Acestes welcomed the Trojans?

2 Why do you think Virgil chose to write the long clause *postera . . . dies* (lines 42–43) rather than a short phrase such as *prima luce*?

3 How does Aeneas show his reverence and love for his father?

poscamus ventos, atque haec me sacra quotannis
urbe velit posita templis sibi ferre dicatis.   60
bina boum vobis Troia generatus Acestes
dat numero capita in naves; adhibete penates
et patrios epulis et quos colit hospes Acestes.
praeterea, si nona diem mortalibus almum
Aurora extulerit radiisque retexerit orbem,   65
prima citae Teucris ponam certamina classis;
quique pedum cursu valet, et qui viribus audax
aut iaculo incedit melior levibusque sagittis,
seu crudo fidit pugnam committere caestu,
cuncti adsint meritaeque exspectent praemia palmae.   70
ore favete omnes et cingite tempora ramis.'

After placing wreaths of myrtle on their heads, the Trojans proceeded to the barrow
containing the remains of Anchises. There Aeneas prayed to the spirit of his father.

dixerat haec, adytis cum lubricus anguis ab imis   84
septem ingens gyros, septena volumina traxit   85
amplexus placide tumulum lapsusque per aras,

posco, -ere	I ask for	*iaculum, -i* n.	javelin
sacer, -ra, -rum	sacred	*incedo, -ere*	I step, go
quotannis	annually	*levis, -e*	light
pono, -ere, -sui, -situs 60	I place, set up	*sagitta, -ae* f.	arrow
templum, -i n.	temple	*seu*	or
dico, -are, -avi, -atus	I dedicate	*crudus, -a, -um*	raw
bini, -ae, -a	two each	*fido, -ere* + dat.	I trust (in), dare
bos, bovis m./f.	bull, cow, ox	*pugna, -ae* f.	fight
Troia, -ae f.	Troy	*committo, -ere*	I engage in
genero, -are, -avi, -atus	I beget	*caestus, -us* m.	boxing glove
numerus, -i m.	number	*cunctus, -a, -um* 70	all
adhibeo, -ere	I invite	*mereo, -ere, -ui, -itus*	I earn, deserve
penates, -ium m.pl.	household gods	*exspecto, -are*	I wait for
patrius, -a, -um	ancestral	*praemium, -i* n.	reward
epulae, -arum f.pl.	banquet	*palma, -ae* f.	prize, hand
colo, -ere	I worship	*os, oris* n.	mouth, face
praeterea	furthermore	*faveo, -ere*	I favour
nonus, -a, -um	ninth	*cingo, -ere*	I wreathe
mortalis, -is m.	mortal, human	*tempus, -oris* n.	temple
almus, -a, -um	kindly	*ramus, -i* m.	branch, twig
Aurora, -ae f. 65	Dawn	*adytum, -i* n. 84	shrine
effero, -re, extuli, elatus	I bring out	*lubricus, -a, -um*	slippery
radius, -i m.	ray	*anguis, -is* m.	snake
retego, -ere, -texi, -tectus	I reveal	*imus, -a, -um*	the base of
orbis, -is m.	world	*gyrus, - i* m. 85	coil
certamen, -inis n.	contest, race	*septenus, -a, -um*	seven
pes, pedis m.	foot	*volumen, -inis* n.	coil
cursus, -us m.	race	*amplector, -i, -plexus sum*	I encircle
valeo, -ere	I am strong, able	*placide*	peacefully
vires, -ium f.pl.	strength	*labor, -i, lapsus sum*	I glide, slip
audax, -acis	bold	*ara, -ae* f.	altar

59–60 **poscamus ventos:** 'let us ask (Anchises) for (favourable) winds'; Aeneas believes the spirit of his dead father can influence the gods to provide the winds needed to speed the Trojan ships towards their goal of Italy. The order for the rest is *atque urbe posita velit me ferre haec sacra quotannis templis sibi dicatis.* **urbe posita:** ablative absolute: 'when I have established the city'. **me ... velit ... ferre:** 'may he be willing for me to present'. **haec ... sacra:** 'these rites'; Virgil is alluding to the tradition that the annual nine-day festival of the *Parentalia*, beginning on 13 February in honour of a family's ancestors, was introduced to Rome by Aeneas. **templis ... dicatis:** local ablative: 'in a temple I have dedicated' (poetic plural). **sibi:** to be taken either with *ferre* ('to present to him') or with *dicatis* ('dedicated to him').

61–2 **bina boum ... capita in naves:** 'two head of cattle for each ship'. **numero:** ablative of respect, dependent on *bina*.

62–3 **penates et patrios ... et quos ...:** 'invite the household gods (to the ceremony), both our own native ones and those ...'. The *penates* were worshipped in the form of statuettes, and were believed to protect both the individual household and the state as a whole. One of Aeneas' principal responsibilities during his long journey was to convey the *penates* of Troy safely to the new city to be founded in Italy, thus preserving both divine protection and cultural continuity.

64–5 **si nona ... Aurora:** 'if the ninth Dawn (from now)'; Roman funeral solemnities lasted for nine days, as did the festival of the *Parentalia*; Dawn was conceived to be a goddess. **diem ... almum:** 'kindly day'; *almus* is a standard epithet of *dies*.

66 **prima ... certamina:** 'the first contests', and so 'first of all contests'. **citae ... classis:** 'for the swift fleet'.

67–70 **qui ... et qui:** the grammatical antecedent of the relative pronouns is *cuncti*: 'let all who ... and who ... be present'. **pedum cursu:** 'in a foot race'. **viribus audax:** 'bold in (respect of) strength', and so 'taking courage from their strength'; the phrase is to be taken with all the contests listed in the next two lines, all of which require physical strength. **iaculo incedit melior:** 'advances better with the javelin', a poetic trope for 'is better at the javelin'. **sagittis:** parallel to *iaculo* and clearly thought of by Aeneas as being the same kind of contest; in the event, no javelin contest takes place. **crudo ... caestu:** boxing gloves were made of untanned hide and sometimes weighted with metal. Note the heavily spondaic rhythm of line 69, reflecting the weighty gloves. **meritae ... palmae:** '(the rewards) of the prize they have earned'; the prize was in the form of a palm wreath.

71 **ore favete:** a religious formula, lit. 'be favourable with the mouth', i.e. 'say nothing unfavourable', and so 'be silent'. **ramis:** 'with twigs (of myrtle)', i.e. with wreaths of myrtle; the myrtle was sacred to Venus and worn here as a sign of religious devotion.

84–6 **dixerat:** the pluperfect of this verb is regularly used by Virgil to mark the end of a speech; translate as 'he finished speaking'. **cum ... anguis ... traxit:** 'inverted' *cum* construction with the indicative. **adytis ab imis:** 'from the depths of the shrine'; because Aeneas sees his dead father as being now one of the gods, he regards his tomb as also a temple to him. Snakes were often viewed as portents of good or evil. **septem ... gyros, septena volumina:** the same idea repeated; translate 'seven, yes seven, looping coils'. **per aras:** 'over the altars'.

Questions

1 In lines 59–60, what deal does Aeneas make with his father's spirit?

2 In lines 61–63, what is the purpose of the feast?

3 In lines 64–70, how does Virgil make Aeneas' announcement of the games more than simply a list?

4 Do you think this snake will be seen as a good or a bad omen?

caeruleae cui terga notae maculosus et auro
squamam incendebat fulgor, ceu nubibus arcus
mille iacit varios adverso sole colores.
obstipuit visu Aeneas. ille agmine longo   90
tandem inter pateras et levia pocula serpens
libavitque dapes rursusque innoxius imo
successit tumulo et depasta altaria liquit.

*Aeneas and his men, spurred on by the portent, sacrificed a large number of animals in
honour of Anchises. When the ninth day dawned, local people flocked to the shore to watch
or participate in the games. The first event was a boat race in which four ships from the
Trojan fleet took part. Aeneas presented the victorious captain with a wreath of bay leaves
and food and drink and other prizes to his crewmen. The losers also received prizes.*

hoc pius Aeneas misso certamine tendit   286
gramineum in campum, quem collibus undique curvis
cingebant silvae, mediaque in valle theatri
circus erat; quo se multis cum milibus heros
consessu medium tulit exstructoque resedit.   290
hic, qui forte velint rapido contendere cursu,
invitat pretiis animos, et praemia ponit.
undique conveniunt Teucri mixtique Sicani,
Nisus et Euryalus primi,

tergum, -i n.	back, hide	altaria, -ium n.pl.	altar
nota, -ae f.	spot, marking	linquo, -ere, liqui, lictus	I leave
maculosus, -a, -um	mottled	gramineus, -a, -um	287 grassy
aurum, -i n.	gold	campus, -i m.	plain
squama, -ae f.	scale	collis, -is m.	hill
incendo, -ere	I set ablaze	undique	from all sides
fulgor, -oris m.	gleam	curvus, -a, -um	curved
ceu	just as	cingo, -ere	I enclose
nubes, -is f.	cloud	silva, -ae f.	wood
arcus, -us m.	bow, rainbow	vallis, -is f.	valley
iacio, -ere	I throw, cast	theatrum, -i n.	theatre
varius, -a, -um	different	circus, -i m.	race-track, circle
adversus, -a, -um	opposite	mille, plur. milia, -ium	thousand
sol, solis m.	the sun	heros, -ois m.	hero
color, -oris m.	colour	consessus, -us m.	290 assembly
obstipesco, -ere, -ui	90 I am amazed	exstructum, -i n.	platform
visus, -us m.	sight	resido, -ere, -sedi	I sit down
agmen, -inis n.	line, host	forte	by chance
patera, -ae f.	bowl	rapidus, -a, -um	fast
lēvis, -e	smooth	contendo, -ere	I compete
poculum, -i n.	cup	invito, -are	I invite
serpo, -ere	I creep	pretium, -i n.	prize
libo, -are, -avi, -astus	I taste	animus, -i m.	spirit, mind
daps, dapis f.	feast, food	convenio, -ire	I come together
rursus	back	misceo, -ere, -ui, mixtus	I mix, mingle
innoxius, -a, -um	harmless	Sicani, -orum m.pl.	Sicilians
succedo, -ere, -essi + dat.	I approach	Nisus, -i m.	Nisus
depasco, -ere, -pavi, -pastus	I feed on	Euryalus, -i m.	Euryalus

87–8 The order is *cui terga caeruleae notae et squamam fulgor maculosus auro incendebat*. **cui:** 'whose'. **terga:** plural for singular. **squamam:** singular for plural. **incendebat:** although singular to agree with the nearer subject, it is to be taken with both subjects (*notae* and *fulgor*); it is used <u>metaphorically</u> to suggest a blaze of colour.

88–9 **mille . . . varios . . . colores:** an example of <u>hyperbole</u>. **nubibus:** probably dative showing the goal of the motion of casting. **adverso sole:** ablative absolute: 'the sun being opposite'.

90 **visu:** causal ablative.

90–4 **ille:** the snake, contrasted with *Aeneas*. **agmine longo:** 'in a long line', and so 'trailing its long body'. **pateras et levia pocula:** these are the vessels placed on the altars to hold the sacrificial offerings; the cups are 'smooth' because they have been burnished to improve their quality. **serpens:** here a participle rather than a noun. **depasta altaria:** 'the altars it had fed on'.

286–7 **hoc . . . certamine misso:** 'when this contest (i.e. the boat race) was concluded'.

287–9 **collibus . . . curvis:** 'on hills that curved round (the plain)'; local ablative. **theatri circus:** 'the circle of a theatre'; the ring of wooded hills provided slopes where the spectators could sit, as well as a rounded track for the races to take place on.

289–90 **quo:** 'to this place'. **se . . . heros . . . tulit:** 'the hero made his way'; Aeneas is of course the hero. **consessu medium:** *medium* agrees with *se*; 'so that he was in the middle of the seated crowd', with *consessu* being a local ablative. **exstructo:** a rare usage of the participle as a noun; again local ablative.

291–2 **qui:** supply *eorum* as possessors of *animos* and antecedent of *qui*. **velint:** generic subjunctive; translate as 'who might wish'. **animos:** he invited 'the spirits (of those who . . .)'; translate as 'he invited those of spirit who might wish . . .'. **pretiis, praemia:** the instrumental ablative suggests that Aeneas rewarded all those who were prepared to enter the race, as well as setting up prizes for the victor.

294 **Nisus et Euryalus:** these two young friends have their moment of glory in Book IX, lines 176ff., where they attempt to break through the besieging enemy lines to carry a message to Aeneas, and meet their deaths after killing many of the enemy. The incomplete line, one of many in the poem, is generally regarded as evidence that Virgil left the work partially unrevised when he died.

Questions

1 How does Virgil make the snake seem larger than life?

2 How did the actions of the snake suggest that it was supernatural?

3 Describe in your own words the location of the foot race.

4 Find out all you can about Nisus and Euryalus.

Euryalus forma insignis viridique iuventa,   295
Nisus amore pio pueri; quos deinde secutus
regius egregia Priami de stirpe Diores;
hunc Salius simul et Patron, quorum alter Acarnan,
alter ab Arcadio Tegeaeae sanguine gentis:
tum duo Trinacrii iuvenes, Helymus Panopesque,   300
adsueti silvis, comites senioris Acestae;
multi praeterea, quos fama obscura recondit.
Aeneas quibus in mediis sic deinde locutus:
'accipite haec animis laetasque advertite mentes.
nemo ex hoc numero mihi non donatus abibit.   305
Cnosia bina dabo levato lucida ferro
spicula caelatamque argento ferre bipennem;
omnibus hic erit unus honos. tres praemia primi
accipient flavaque caput nectentur oliva.
primus equum phaleris insignem victor habeto;   310
alter Amazoniam pharetram plenamque sagittis
Threiciis, lato quam circum amplectitur auro
balteus et tereti subnectit fibula gemma;
tertius Argolica hac galea contentus abito.'

forma, -ae f.	295 beauty	*bini, -ae, -a*	two each
insignis, -e	remarkable	*levo, -are, -avi, -atus*	I polish
viridis, -e	vigorous	*lucidus, -a, -um*	bright, gleaming
iuventa, -ae f.	youth(fulness)	*ferrum, -i* n.	iron
regius, -a, -um	princely	*spiculum, -i* n.	arrow-head
egregius, -a, -um	eminent	*caelo, -are, -avi, -atus*	I engrave
Priamus, -i m.	Priam	*argentum, -i* n.	silver
stirps, -is f.	lineage	*bipennis, -is* f.	two-headed axe
Diores, -is m.	Diores	*honos, -oris* m.	honour
Salius, -i m.	Salius	*flavus, -a, -um*	yellow
simul	at the same time	*necto, -ere*	I bind
Patron, -onis m.	Patron	*oliva, -ae* f.	olive
Acarnan, -anis	Acarnanian	*equus, -i* m.	310 horse
Arcadius, -a, -um	Arcadian	*phalerae, -arum* f.pl.	trappings
Tegeaeus, -a, -um	Tegean	*victor, -oris* m.	winner
gens, gentis f.	race, stock	*Amazonius, -a, -um*	of the Amazons
Trinacrius, -a, -um	300 Sicilian	*pharetra, -ae* f.	quiver
Helymus, -i m.	Helymus	*plenus, -a, -um* + abl.	full (of)
Panopes, -ae m.	Panopes	*sagitta, -ae* f.	arrow
adsuetus, -a, -um	accustomed	*Threicius, -a, -um*	Thracian
comes, -itis m.	companion	*latus, -a, -um*	broad, wide
senex, -is	old	*circum*	around, all round
fama, -ae f.	reputation, fame	*amplector, -i, -plexus sum*	I enclose
obscurus, -a, -um	obscure	*balteus, -i* m.	belt
recondo, -ere	I hide	*teres, -etis*	polished
accipio, -ere	I receive	*subnecto, -ere*	I fasten under
adverto, -ere	I turn . . . to	*fibula, -ae* f.	brooch, clasp
mens, mentis f.	mind	*gemma, -ae* f.	jewel
nemo -inis m.	305 no one	*tertius, -a, -um*	third
dono, -are, -avi, -atus	I reward	*Argolicus, -a, -um*	Argive
abeo, -ire	I go away	*galea, -ae* f.	helmet
Cnosius, -a, -um	of Knossos	*contentus, -a, -um*	satisfied

295–6 **forma, iuventa:** ablatives of respect. **Nisus:** supply *insignis* again. **amore pio:** also ablative of respect; *pio* here has the meaning of 'devoted'. **pueri:** i.e. love for Euryalus, whom Virgil portrays as younger than Nisus; *pueri* is objective genitive. The nature of this love has often been discussed; some see it as simply a deep friendship, others as homosexual love.

296–7 **regius . . . Diores:** Diores appears again in Book XII, when he is killed by Turnus; note the <u>chiastic</u> word order of line 297.

298–9 **Salius, Patron:** two Greeks. **hunc:** supply *secuti sunt*. **simul et:** = *et simul*. **Acarnan, Arcadia:** Acharnania and Arcadia were two regions of Greece. **Tegeaeae . . . gentis:** Tegea was a city in Arcadia.

300–1 Note the fast rhythm of line 300. **senioris Acestae:** *senior* often lacks a comparative sense: 'elderly' will suffice.

302 **multi praeterea:** 'and many more besides', too numerous to mention by name. **quos fama obscura recondit:** 'whose little-known reputations keep them in obscurity', i.e. they are ordinary men, not members of the nobility.

303 **quibus in mediis:** 'in the midst of these men'. **locutus:** supply *est*.

304 **haec:** supply *verba*. **animis:** local ablative.

305 **mihi:** dative of the agent dependent on *donatus*: 'rewarded by me'.

306–7 **Cnosia bina . . . spicula:** 'two Cretan arrow-heads each'; Knossos was the chief town of Crete, and the island was famous for its archers. **levato . . . ferro:** 'made of polished iron' (ablative of material); iron was a very rare metal at this time in the late Bronze Age, and so much prized. **argento:** dependent on *caelatam*: 'engraved with silver' (also ablative of material); the axe-heads would have been made of bronze. **ferre:** 'to take away' (epexegetic infinitive).

308–9 **unus honos:** 'a single honour', i.e. 'the same honour'. **caput nectentur:** 'their heads will be bound'; *caput* is an accusative of respect dependent on the passive verb, lit. 'they will be bound with respect to their head(s)'. **flava . . . oliva:** 'with (a garland of) yellow olive' (ablative of instrument); olive branches are a yellowish green.

310 **primus . . . victor:** 'the first, as victor'. **phaleris insignem:** 'remarkable for its trappings' (ablative of cause); the trappings were decorations placed on the horse's head. **habeto:** 'let (him) have': this is a rare 3rd person imperative.

311–13 **alter:** 'the one who comes second'. **Amazoniam:** the Amazons were a race of female warriors who lived at the edge of the known world. They and the Thracians were noted archers and also allied to Troy during the war. The order for the next section is *quam balteus amplectitur lato auro et fibula subnectit tereti gemma*. **balteus:** the shoulder strap from which the quiver was suspended. **circum:** this is almost redundant, adding little to the verb; translate 'encloses all round'. **lato . . . auro:** 'with (a) broad (band of) gold' (ablative of instrument); note the <u>enclosing</u> word order. **tereti . . . gemma:** instrumental ablative again.

314 **abito:** like *habeto* above. **Argolica hac galea:** 'with this Argive helmet'; we are to imagine Aeneas holding up the helmet as he speaks; Homer's regular name for the Greeks was 'Argives'; presumably this was a war trophy.

Questions

1 How does Virgil make the list of competitors more than a simple, repetitive list?

2 How does Aeneas make the prizes seem worth competing for?

haec ubi dicta, locum capiunt signoque repente   315
corripiunt spatia audito limenque relinquunt,
effusi nimbo similes. simul ultima signant,
primus abit longeque ante omnia corpora Nisus
emicat et ventis et fulminis ocior alis;
proximus huic, longo sed proximus intervallo,   320
insequitur Salius; spatio post deinde relicto
tertius Euryalus;
Euryalumque Helymus sequitur; quo deinde sub ipso
ecce volat calcemque terit iam calce Diores
incumbens umero, spatia et si plura supersint   325
transeat elapsus prior ambiguumve relinquat.
iamque fere spatio extremo fessique sub ipsam
finem adventabant, levi cum sanguine Nisus
labitur infelix, caesis ut forte iuvencis
fusus humum viridesque super madefecerat herbas.   330
hic iuvenis iam victor ovans vestigia presso
haud tenuit titubata solo, sed pronus in ipso
concidit immundoque fimo sacroque cruore.
non tamen Euryali, non ille oblitus amorum:

signum, -i n.	315 signal	*elabor, -i elapsus sum*	I slip ahead
repente	suddenly	*prior, prius*	in front
corripio, -ere	I speed over	*ambiguus, -a, -um*	doubtful
spatium, -i n.	course, track	*fere*	almost
limen, -inis n.	starting line	*extremus, -a, -um*	last
relinquo, -ere, -liqui, -lictus	I leave behind	*fessus, -a, -um*	tired
effundo, -ere, -fudi, -fusus	I stream, pour out	*finis, -is* f.	end
nimbus, -i m.	storm cloud	*advento, -are*	I approach
similis, -e + dat.	similar (to)	*lēvis, -e*	slippery
ultimus, -a, -um	last, final	*caedo, -ere, cecidi, caesus*	I slaughter
signo, -are	I note, observe	*iuvencus, -i* m.	bullock
longe	far	*fundo, -ere, fudi, fusus*	330 I pour, spill
ante + acc.	in front of	*humus, -i* f.	ground
emico, -are	I dart, dash forth	*super*	on the surface
fulmen, -inis n.	lightning	*madefacio, -ere, -feci, -factus*	I soak
ocior, ocius	swifter	*herba, -ae* f.	grass
ala, -ae f.	wing	*hic*	here
proximus, -a, -um	320 next	*ovo, -are*	I triumph, rejoice
intervallum, -i n.	interval	*vestigium, -i* n.	footstep
insequor, -i, -secutus sum	I follow	*premo, -ere, pressi, pressus*	I press, tread on
tertius, -a, -um	third	*haud*	not
sub + abl./acc.	close to, under	*titubo, -are, -avi, -atus*	I stagger, totter
ecce	look! behold!	*solum, -i* n.	ground
volo, -are	I fly	*pronus, -a, -um*	face-down
calx, calcis f.	heel	*concido, -ere, -i*	I fall
tero, -ere	I graze	*immundus, -a, -um*	filthy
umerus, -i m.	325 shoulder	*fimus, -i* m.	mire, muck
supersum, -esse	I am left, remain	*cruor, -oris* m.	gore
transeo, -ire	I overtake	*obliviscor, -i, -litus sum* + gen.	I forget

315–6 **dicta:** supply *sunt.* **signo … audito:** 'when they heard the signal'. **corripiunt spatia:** *spatia* were the sections of track that made up the course, rather like laps in a modern race.

317 **nimbo similes:** 'like a storm cloud', the idea being that storm clouds propelled by a strong wind seem to race across the sky. Note the strong <u>sibilance</u> in this line, emphasising the speed. **simul ultima signant:** this short sentence has been interpreted in several ways: 'together they (the competitors) mark the goal', 'at the same time they (the officials) mark out the finish', 'as soon as they (the competitors) notice the finish'. Probably *ultima* agrees with *spatia* (understood from line 316), meaning 'the final sections of the course'; *simul* could equally be the adverb ('together' or 'at the same time'), or short for *simulatque* ('as soon as'), in which case the comma is needed rather than the conventional full stop after *signant.* Williams suggests that Nisus broke away from the main body of runners as soon as that body came within sight of the end of the course; this seems to give the best meaning.

318–19 **primus abit:** 'was the first to draw away'. **omnia corpora:** i.e. 'before all the other competitors'. Note the delay of the subject to increase suspense. **ventis, alis:** ablatives of comparison. **fulminis … alis:** thunderbolts were sometimes represented as being winged.

320 **longo sed … intervallo:** 'but after a long interval'; note the very rare spondaic fifth foot, slowing the pace of the second-placed runner.

321–2 **spatio post deinde relicto:** 'next, a space having been left behind Salius, …'. **tertius Euryalus:** supply *insequitur*: 'Euryalus followed in third place'. For the incomplete line, see the note on line 294.

323–5 **quo … sub ipso:** 'close behind Helymus himself'. **calcemque terit … calce:** 'and grazed his heel with his foot'; the literal meaning of *calx* is fine for the first occurrence, but is not possible for the second, which must be an example of <u>synecdoche</u>.

325–6 **spatia et si plura:** = *et si plura spatia.* **supersint:** 'had remained'; the present subjunctive replaces the pluperfect subjunctive (for an unfulfilled condition) because Virgil is using the historic present for the whole episode. **transeat elapsus prior:** 'slipping ahead he would have passed him (to go) in front'. **ambiguumve relinquat:** 'or he would have left it (i.e. the outcome) doubtful'; the correct reading and meaning of these two words have been much debated; perhaps the most likely idea is that, if Diores failed to overtake Helymus, he would have drawn level with him, therefore leaving it uncertain who finished in fourth place.

327–30 **fere spatio extremo:** 'almost on the final stretch' (local ablative). **sub ipsam finem:** 'near to the actual finish'. **cum:** bring forward. **levi sanguine:** local ablative. **ut forte:** 'as by chance'. **caesis … iuvencis:** 'when some bullocks had been slaughtered'. **fusus:** supply *sanguis* and *erat*: 'the blood had spilled onto the ground'. **super:** an unusual use of the word.

331–3 **iam victor ovans:** 'already rejoicing as victor', i.e. 'already celebrating his victory'. **presso … solo:** 'the ground having been pressed', and so 'treading on the area (of the spill)'. **haud tenuit:** 'could not keep control of'. **vestigia … titubata:** 'his tottering footsteps'. **in ipso:** supply *solo* from above. **fimo:** this is the mud onto which the blood was spilt. **sacro cruore:** the blood is sacred because the animals had been killed as a sacrifice to the gods. There is a strong contrast between *immundo* and *sacro.*

334 The order is *ille tamen non oblitus (erat) Euryali, non (oblitus erat) amorum.* **Euryali, amorum:** Euryalus is defined as Nisus' 'love'; whether this indicates a homosexual relationship is debatable (cf. line 296).

Questions

1 How does Virgil make the description of the race interesting and exciting?

2 How is the fall of Nisus made vivid?

nam sese opposuit Salio per lubrica surgens,   335
ille autem spissa iacuit revolutus harena;
emicat Euryalus et munere victor amici
prima tenet, plausuque volat fremituque secundo.
post Helymus subit et nunc tertia palma Diores.
hic totum caveae consessum ingentis et ora   340
prima patrum magnis Salius clamoribus implet,
ereptumque dolo reddi sibi poscit honorem.
tutatur favor Euryalum lacrimaeque decorae,
gratior et pulchro veniens in corpore virtus.
adiuvat et magna proclamat voce Diores,   345
qui subiit palmae frustraque ad praemia venit
ultima, si primi Salio reddentur honores.
tum pater Aeneas 'vestra' inquit 'munera vobis
certa manent, pueri, et palmam movet ordine nemo;
me liceat casus miserari insontis amici.'   350
sic fatus tergum Gaetuli immane leonis
dat Salio villis onerosum atque unguibus aureis.
hic Nisus 'si tanta' inquit 'sunt praemia victis,
et te lapsorum miseret, quae munera Niso
digna dabis, primam merui qui laude coronam   355
ni me, quae Salium, fortuna inimica tulisset?'
et simul his dictis faciem ostentabat et udo
turpia membra fimo.

oppono, -ere, -posui, -itus	335	I place in the way	*moveo, -ere*	I move
surgo, -ere		I raise up	*ordo, -inis* m.	order, rank
spissus, -a, -um		thick	*licet, -ere*	350 it is allowed
iaceo, -ere, -ui		I lie	*casus, -us* m.	bad luck, fall
revolvo, -ere, -volvi, -utus		I roll over	*miseror, -ari, -atus sum* + gen.	I pity
munus, -eris n.		kind action, gift	*insons, -ontis*	innocent
plausus, -us m.		applause	*for, fari, fatus sum*	I say, speak
fremitus, -us m.		shouting	*Gaetulus, -a, -um*	Gaetulian
subeo, -ire, -ii, -itus		I come up	*immanis, -e*	immense
cavea, -ae f.	340	grandstand	*leo, -onis* m.	lion
consessus, -us m.		spectators	*villus, -i* m.	shaggy hair
clamor, -oris m.		shout	*onerosus, -a, -um*	heavy
impleo, -ere		I fill	*unguis, -is* m.	claw
eripio, -ere, -ui, -reptus		I snatch away	*aureus, -a, -um*	golden, gilded
dolus, -i m.		trick	*vinco, -ere, vici, victus*	I defeat
reddo, -ere		I give back	*miseret, -ere*	it distresses
tutor, -ari, -atus sum		I defend	*dignus, -a, -um*	355 worthy
favor, -oris m.		favour, support	*laus, laudis* f.	achievement, glory
lacrima, -ae f.		tear		
decorus, -a, -um		appealing	*corona, -ae* f.	crown, wreath
gratus, -a, -um		welcome	*ni*	if not
corpus, -oris n.		body	*inimicus, -a, -um*	hostile
virtus, -utis f.		courage	*facies, -ei* f.	face
adiuvo, -are	345	I help	*ostento, -are*	I display
proclamo, -are		I proclaim	*udus, -a, -um*	wet
vester, -tra, -trum		your	*turpis, -e*	filthy
maneo, -ere		I remain	*membrum, -i* n.	limb

335–6 Salio: dative of disadvantage after *opposuit.* **per lubrica:** neuter plural used as a noun: 'through the slippery mess'. **ille:** i.e. Salius. **spissa . . . harena:** 'on the thick patch of sand' (local ablative). **iacuit:** the perfect tense shows the suddenness of the action.

337–8 Euryalus: unusually, the final syllable is long. **munere victor amici:** the position of *victor* mirrors the fact that Euryalus is dependent on the kindness of Nisus. **prima tenet:** 'held first position'. **plausu, fremitu:** 'accompanied by applause and shouting'.

339 tertia palma: supply *erat.*

340–2 hic: 'at this point'. The order is *hic Salius implet totum consessum caveae et prima ora patrum magnis clamoribus.* **totum caveae consessum:** 'the whole mass of spectators assembled in the grandstand'; the *cavea* was the natural amphitheatre described in lines 287–90. **ora prima patrum:** lit. 'the first faces of the fathers', i.e. 'the faces of the fathers on the front rows'. The *patres* are either the fathers of the competitors, or (more likely) the elders; in Virgil's day senators (also called *patres*) had reserved seats in the front rows of the amphitheatre. **Salius . . . implet:** 'Salius filled (the ears of)', and so 'kept on appealing to'; note the delayed subject to increase the drama. **ereptumque dolo . . . honorem:** 'the honour (of winning the first prize), which had been snatched away (from him) by a trick'.

343–4 tutatur favor Euryalum: 'the support (of the spectators) favoured Euryalus'. **lacrimae, virtus:** secondary subjects of *tutatur.* **gratior et . . . virtus:** move *et* to the front; Euryalus' courage is all the more pleasing because it appears (*veniens*) in a beautiful body.

346–7 qui subiit palmae: 'who came up for a prize', and so 'who qualified for a prize'. **venit:** 'would have come'; the perfect indicative is used for vividness. **ad praemia . . . ultima:** 'for the last (i.e. third) prize'. **primi . . . honores:** 'the first prize'. **reddentur:** future indicative for vividness again: 'were to be given'.

348–50 certa: 'guaranteed'. **ordine:** 'in respect of your order', i.e. no one is changing the order of the prizes. **me liceat:** 'may I be allowed'.

351–2 tergum: 'back' and so 'hide'. **Gaetuli . . . leonis:** a lion from Gaetulia, in NW Africa.

354 te lapsorum miseret: 'you take pity on those who have slipped'.

355 laude: 'by my achievement' (instrumental ablative).

356 The order is *ni (eadem) inimica fortuna, quae Salium tulit, tulisset me.* **tulisset:** 'had not knocked me out (of the race); the logic of the condition is 'I deserved the prize (and would have received it), if . . .'.

357–8 simul his dictis: 'at the same time as he said these words'.

Questions

1 Describe what happened to each of the named competitors.

2 Why did Nisus act as he did?

3 Why did the crowd support Euryalus?

4 Do you think Salius would have been satisfied with Aeneas' gift?

5 What impression do you get of Nisus' character from this passage?

     risit pater optimus olli
et clipeum efferri iussit, Didymaonis artes,
Neptuni sacro Danais de poste refixum.   360
hoc iuvenem egregium praestanti munere donat.
post, ubi confecti cursus et dona peregit:
'nunc, si cui virtus animusque in pectore praesens,
adsit et evinctis attollat bracchia palmis.'
sic ait, et geminum pugnae proponit honorem,   365
victori velatum auro vittisque iuvencum,
ensem atque insignem galeam solacia victo.
nec mora; continuo vastis cum viribus effert
ora Dares magnoque virum se murmure tollit,
solus qui Paridem solitus contendere contra,   370
idemque ad tumulum quo maximus occubat Hector
victorem Buten immani corpore, qui se
Bebrycia veniens Amyci de gente ferebat,
perculit et fulva moribundum extendit harena.
talis prima Dares caput altum in proelia tollit,   375
ostenditque umeros latos alternaque iactat
bracchia protendens et verberat ictibus auras.
quaeritur huic alius; nec quisquam ex agmine tanto
audet adire virum manibusque inducere caestus.

rideo, -ere, risi, risus		I laugh	*murmur, -uris* n.	murmuring
clipeus, -i m.		shield	*tollo, -ere*	I raise, remove
effero, -re		I bring out, raise	*solus, -a, -um*	370 only, alone
Didymaon, -onis m.		Didymaon	*Paris, -idis* m.	Paris
ars, artis f.		art, skill	*soleo, -ere, -itus sum*	I am accustomed
Neptunus, -i m.	360	Neptune	*idem, eadem, idem*	the same
Danai, -orum m.pl.		the Greeks	*occubo, -are*	I lie buried
postis, -is m.		door post	*Hector, -oris* m.	Hector
refigo, -ere, -fixi, -fixus		I take down	*Butes, -ae* m. (acc. *-en*)	Butes
egregius, -a, -um		outstanding	*Bebrycia, -ae* f.	Bebrycia
praestans, -ntis		excellent	*Amycus, -i* m.	Amycus
dono, -are		I present	*percello, -ere, -culi, -culsus*	I knock down
conficio, -ere, -feci, -fectus		I complete	*fulvus, -a, -um*	yellow
donum, -i n.		gift	*moribundus, -a, -um*	dying
perago, -ere, -egi, -actus		I finish	*extendo, -ere, -ndi, -ntus*	I stretch out
praesens, -ntis		present, ready	*proelium, -i* n.	375 battle
evincio, -ire, -nxi, -nctus		I bind, tie	*ostendo, -ere, -ndi, -ntus*	I show, display
attollo, -ere		I raise	*alternus, -a, -um*	by turns
bracchium, -i n.		arm	*iacto, -are*	I toss, swing
geminus, -a, -um	365	twin	*protendo, -ere*	I stretch out
propono, -ere		I set out, offer	*verbero, -are*	I strike, punch
velo, -are, -avi, -atus		I cover, wrap	*ictus, -us* m.	blow
vitta, -ae f.		headband	*aura, -ae* f.	air
ensis, -is m.		sword	*quaero, -ere*	I seek
solacium, -i n.		consolation	*quisquam, quae-, quid-*	anyone
mora, -ae f.		delay	*audeo, -ere*	I dare
continuo		immediately	*adeo, -ire*	I approach
vastus, -a, -um		immense	*induco, -ere*	I pull on
Dares, -(et)is (acc. *-n/eta*) m.		Dares	*caestus, -us* m.	boxing glove

358 **pater:** i.e. Aeneas. **olli:** archaic form of *illi*: 'at him'.
359–60 **Didymaonis artes:** 'the workmanship of Didymaon'; *artes* is in apposition to
clipeum; Didymaon is an unknown craftsman. **refixum:** agrees with *clipeum*; the shield had
adorned a temple of Neptune, having been fixed there as an offering to the god by some
unknown sailor. **Danais:** all editors have taken this to be a dative of the agent with *refixum*,
i.e. it was the Greeks who had removed the shield, and presumably Aeneas had captured it
from them. Why the Greeks should have removed the shield is far from clear, and it seems
odd that Virgil should mention it. A possible alternative is to take it as a dative of the person
interested: 'sacred for the Greeks', i.e. 'considered sacred by the Greeks'; this would enhance
the significance of the shield more than the standard interpretation and so make it a more
worthy prize.
361 **donat:** this verb takes an accusative of the person and an ablative of the thing given.
362 **confecti:** supply *sunt*. **dona:** i.e. the prize-giving.
363–4 **si cui:** 'if for anyone (there is)'; supply *est*; the meaning is therefore 'if anyone has'.
attollat bracchia: 'let him raise his arms', ready to box. **evinctis ... palmis:** 'after binding his
hands', i.e. after putting on the boxing gloves.
365 **geminum ... honorem:** 'a pair of prizes'.
366 Note the heavy <u>alliteration</u> of *v*, together with the slow rhythm, the effect being to make
the prize appear more significant. **velatum auro vittisque:** when bullocks were prepared for
sacrifice, their heads were adorned with garlands (*vittis*) and their horns wrapped in gold.
367 **solacia:** 'as consolation', in apposition to *ensem* and *galeam*.
368–9 **nec mora:** supply *erat*. **effert ora Dares:** 'Dares brought out his mouth', and so 'thrust
out his jaw' (Williams), an act of defiance. **virum:** = *virorum*, referring to the crowd of
spectators. **se tollit:** 'stood up'. Dares was one of the best known and most successful boxers
of his day, according to the epic poets.
370 **solus qui:** = *qui solus*. **Paridem:** dependent on *contra*; Paris was the son of king Priam of
Troy, whose abduction of Helen caused the Trojan War. **solitus:** supply *erat*.
371–4 **idemque:** i.e. Dares; he is the subject of *perculit*. **ad tumulum quo:** 'at the tomb in
which'. **Hector:** the eldest son of king Priam of Troy, and their greatest warrior, killed towards
the end of the Trojan War by Achilles. His death was commemorated by funeral games at his
tomb, just as the Trojans are now holding games at the tomb of Anchises. **victorem Buten:** 'the
champion Butes'; he is not mentioned elsewhere. **immani corpore:** ablative of description. **se ...
ferebat:** there have been several interpretations of *se ferebat*: 'strode forth' and 'boasted' are the
most favoured, with 'boasted' perhaps giving the better sense: 'boasted (that he was) from the
race of Amycus in Bebrycia'; Amycus was a king of Bebrycia (in Asia Minor) who challenged
all visitors to a boxing match. **veniens:** either 'coming to the games' or 'coming from Bebrycia'.
fulva ... harena: local ablative.
375 **talis ... Dares:** 'such a man was Dares who...'. **prima ... in proelia:** 'for the first bout'.
376–7 **alterna iactat bracchia:** 'swung each arm in turn'. **verberat ictibus auras:** he
shadow-boxes.
378–9 **huic:** 'for him', i.e. 'to fight against him'. **caestus:** these consisted of leather thongs
weighted with lead to cause maximum damage.

Questions

1 What made Nisus' prize special?

2 How does Virgil make the two boxing prizes seem special?

3 How does Virgil emphasise the power and reputation of Dares?

ergo alacris cunctosque putans excedere palma   380
Aeneae stetit ante pedes, nec plura moratus
tum laeva taurum cornu tenet atque ita fatur:
'nate dea, si nemo audet se credere pugnae,
quae finis standi? quo me decet usque teneri?
ducere dona iube.' cuncti simul ore fremebant   385
Dardanidae reddique viro promissa iubebant.
hic gravis Entellum dictis castigat Acestes,
proximus ut viridante toro consederat herbae:
'Entelle, heroum quondam fortissime frustra,
tantane tam patiens nullo certamine tolli   390
dona sines? ubi nunc nobis deus ille, magister
nequiquam memoratus, Eryx? ubi fama per omnem
Trinacriam et spolia illa tuis pendentia tectis?'
ille sub haec: 'non laudis amor nec gloria cessit
pulsa metu; sed enim gelidus tardante senecta   395
sanguis hebet, frigentque effetae in corpore vires.
si mihi quae quondam fuerat quaque improbus iste
exsultat fidens, si nunc foret illa iuventas,
haud equidem pretio inductus pulchroque iuvenco
venissem, nec dona moror.' sic deinde locutus   400
in medium geminos immani pondere caestus
proiecit, quibus acer Eryx in proelia suetus
ferre manum duroque intendere bracchia tergo.

ergo	380 therefore	*memoro, -are, -avi, -atus*	I celebrate
alacris, -e	eager	*Trinacria, -ae* f.	Sicily
excedo, -ere	I withdraw	*spolia, -orum* n.pl.	spoils
moror, -ari, -atus sum	I delay, care for	*pendeo, -ere*	I hang
laeva, -ae f.	left hand	*tectum, -i* n.	house, roof
taurus, -i m.	bull	*sub* + acc.	after
cornu, -us n.	horn	*gloria, -ae* f.	glory, pride
natus, -i m.	son	*cedo, -ere, cessi, cessus*	I fail, give way
credo, -ere	I entrust	*pello, -ere, pepuli, pulsus*	395 I drive out, beat
sto, stare	I stand	*metus, -us* m.	fear
quo . . . usque	for how long	*gelidus, -a, -um*	cold
decet, -ere	it is proper	*tardo, -are*	I make slow
fremo, -ere	385 I shout, roar	*senecta, -ae* f.	old age
promissum, -i n.	promise	*hebeo, -ere*	I am sluggish
gravis, -e	heavy, stern	*frigeo, -ere*	I am cold, stiff
Entellus, -i m.	Entellus	*effetus, -a, -um*	worn out
castigo, -are	I rebuke	*improbus, -a, -um*	shameless
viridans, -ntis	green	*iste, ista, istud*	that of yours
torus, -i m.	couch, bank	*exsulto, -are*	I exult, boast
consido, -ere, -sedi	I settle	*iuventas, -atis* f.	youth
quondam	once, previously	*induco, -ere, -xi, -ctus*	I lead on
patior, -i, passus sum	390 I suffer	*pondus, -eris* n.	400 weight
sino, -ere	I allow	*proicio, -ere, -ieci, -iectus*	I throw forward
magister, -tri m.	teacher	*acer, acris, acre*	fierce, spirited
nequiquam	in vain	*suesco, -ere, suevi, suetus*	I am accustomed

380–2 **alacris:** supply *Dares*. **palma:** 'from (claiming) the prize'. **nec plura moratus:** 'without further delay'. **laeva:** 'with his left hand'. **cornu:** ablative: 'by the horn'. Note the slow rhythm of line 382, reflecting the fact that all the action has stopped.

383–4 **nate dea:** Aeneas is frequently addressed thus: lit. 'o one born from a goddess', and so 'son of a goddess'. **quae finis standi:** supply *est*; lit. 'what end (is there) of standing', i.e. 'how long must I stand here?' **teneri:** 'to be kept waiting'.

385 **ducere dona iube:** either 'order (men) to bring forth the gifts (i.e. prizes)' or 'order (me) to lead away the gifts'; the former fits the Latin better, but most editors prefer the latter, on the grounds that the prizes have already been brought out; however, the verb *proponit* (line 365) does not necessarily imply this.

385–6 **cuncti:** agrees with *Dardanidae*. **ore:** 'with their mouths', redundant here. **reddique . . . promissa:** 'that the promised prizes be awarded'.

387–8 **hic:** 'hereupon'. **Entellum:** this character does not appear elsewhere. The order for line 388 is *ut sederat proximus (ei) viridante toro herbae*. **viridante toro:** local ablative.

389–91 **frustra:** Acestes is suggesting that Entellus' previous bravery is of no use now, if he will not fight. The order for the rest is *sinesne tam patiens tanta dona tolli nullo certamine*. **tam patiens:** 'so patiently'. **tolli:** 'to be taken (from you)'. **dona:** i.e. the prizes.

391–3 **ubi:** supply *est*. **nobis:** a so-called ethic dative, identifying a person interested in the idea being expressed; translate as 'I ask you'. **deus:** Eryx, being a son of Venus, was considered semi-divine; he was supposedly a famous Sicilian boxer. **magister nequiquam memoratus:** Eryx was supposed to have taught Entellus; he was 'celebrated in vain' as a teacher if his pupil failed to accept a challenge. **ubi fama:** supply *est* again; the sense is almost 'what of'; the *fama* is that of Entellus. **tuis . . . tectis:** 'in your house' (local ablative).

394–6 **ille:** supply *dixit*. **pulsa metu:** *pulsa* should be taken with both *amor* and *gloria*: 'driven out by fear'. **sed enim:** 'but in fact'. **tardante senecta:** 'slowed down by old age'.

397–8 The order is *si mihi nunc foret illa iuventas, quae quondam fuerat, quaque iste improbus fidens exsultat*. **si mihi:** repeated for emphasis. **foret:** = *esset*. **quaque . . . fidens:** 'and trusting in which'. **iste improbus:** 'that shameless man (you speak of)', i.e. Dares.

399–400 **haud . . . pretio inductus:** 'I would have come (anyway), without the inducement of a reward'. **nec dona moror:** 'and I do not care for prizes'.

400–3 **geminos caestus . . . proiecit:** equivalent to throwing down the gauntlet to signify a challenge. **immani pondere:** ablative of description, qualifying *caestus*: 'enormously heavy'. **quibus:** '(armed) with which'. **suetus:** supply *erat*. **ferre manum:** 'to carry his hand' into fights; an odd expression, including singular for plural. **duro . . . tergo:** 'with the tough hide'. **intendere bracchia:** 'to bind his forearms'; presumably the gloves consisted mainly of broad leather straps that were wound round the hand and then the wrist; if they extended as far as the elbow, they would have served to protect the arms when parrying blows.

Questions

1 In lines 380–386, what sort of a character does Dares appear to be?

2 In lines 387–393, how did Acestes try to persuade Entellus to fight?

3 How did Entellus make his reply effective?

4 How did Entellus cast doubt on the truth of his arguments?

obstipuere animi: tantorum ingentia septem
terga boum plumbo insuto ferroque rigebant.   405
ante omnes stupet ipse Dares longeque recusat,
magnanimusque Anchisiades et pondus et ipsa
huc illuc vinclorum immensa volumina versat.
tum senior tales referebat pectore voces:
'quid, si quis caestus ipsius et Herculis arma   410
vidisset tristemque hoc ipso in litore pugnam?
haec germanus Eryx quondam tuus arma gerebat
(sanguine cernis adhuc sparsoque infecta cerebro),
his magnum Alciden contra stetit, his ego suetus,
dum melior vires sanguis dabat, aemula necdum   415
temporibus geminis canebat sparsa senectus.
sed si nostra Dares haec Troius arma recusat
idque pio sedet Aeneae, probat auctor Acestes,
aequemus pugnas. Erycis tibi terga remitto
(solve metus), et tu Troianos exue caestus.'   420
haec fatus duplicem ex umeris reiecit amictum
et magnos membrorum artus, magna ossa lacertosque
exuit atque ingens media consistit harena.
tum satus Anchisa caestus pater extulit aequos
et paribus palmas amborum innexuit armis.   425
constitit in digitos extemplo arrectus uterque
bracchiaque ad superas interritus extulit auras.

plumbum, -i n.	405 lead	*Troius, -a, -um*	Trojan
insuo, -ere, -ui, -utus	I sew in	*sedeo, -ere*	I am settled
rigeo, -ere	I am stiff	*probo, -are*	I approve
ante + acc.	before	*aequo, -are*	I make equal
stupeo, -ere	I am amazed	*remitto, -ere*	I give up
longe	from afar	*solvo, -ere*	420 I dismiss
recuso, -are	I refuse	*exuo, -ere*	I take off, bare
Anchisiades, -ae m.	son of Anchises	*duplex, -icis*	double
huc illuc	this way and that	*reicio, -ere, -ieci, -iectus*	I throw off
vinclum, -i n.	thong, binding	*amictus, -us* m.	cloak
immensus, -a, -um	huge	*artus, -us* m.	limb, joint
verso, -are	I revolve, spin	*lacertus, -i* m.	upper arm
refero, -ferre	I relate, speak	*consisto, -ere*	I stand
Hercules, -is m.	410 Hercules	*sero, -ere, sevi, satus*	I beget
germanus, -i m.	brother	*aequus, -a, -um*	equal
gero, -ere	I wear	*par, paris*	425 equal
adhuc	still	*ambo, -ae, -o*	both
spargo, -ere, sparsi, sparsus	I (be)spatter	*innecto, -ere, -xui, -xus*	I bind
inficio, -ere, -feci, -fectus	I stain	*digitus, -i* m.	toe
cerebrum, -i n.	brain	*extemplo*	immediately
Alcides, -ae m. (acc. *-en*)	Hercules	*arrigo, -ere, -rexi, -rectus*	I raise, lift
aemulus, -a, -um	415 jealous	*uterque, utraque, utrumque*	each, both
necdum	nor yet	*superus, -a, -um*	above
caneo, -ere	I am white	*interritus, -a, -um*	unafraid
senectus, -utis f.	old age		

404–5 obstipuere: = *obstipuerunt*. **animi:** 'the minds' (of the spectators). **tantorum . . . terga boum:** 'so great were the oxen whose . . . hides'.

406–8 ante omnes: i.e. 'more than anyone else'. **longeque:** i.e. 'and keeping his distance'. **et . . . et:** 'both . . . and'. **versat:** 'kept turning (them) over (in his hands)'. Note the <u>alliteration</u>.

409 senior: i.e. Entellus. **pectore:** '(words) from his heart', i.e. 'heartfelt words'.

410–11 quid: supply a verb such as *dixisset*: 'what (would he have said, if. . .'. **si quis:** 'if someone'; all best rearranged as 'what would someone have said, if he had. . .'. **Herculis:** Hercules, reputedly the strongest man on Earth, had captured the cattle of Geryon (one of his Twelve Labours); while leading them back home, he had been challenged by Eryx to a boxing match. Eryx lost and was killed. **et:** to be taken before *ipsius*. **arma:** this word may not indicate some other arms carried by Hercules, but simply explains *caestus*: 'the gloves, the actual arms'. **tristem . . . pugnam:** 'grim' because it brought about the death of Eryx.

412–13 haec . . . arma: i.e. the gloves now owned by Entellus. **germanus:** see line 24 note. **recusat:** i.e. 'refuses to face'. **infecta:** supply *ea (arma)* and *esse* to complete the indirect statement. **sanguine, cerebro:** from some boxers previously defeated by Eryx.

414–16 his: 'with these (gloves)'. **dum melior vires sanguis dabat:** 'as long as better blood gave me strength'; by 'better' he means 'more vigorous'. **aemula . . . senectus:** old age is 'jealous' because it jealously strives to diminish the vigour of youth, **canebat sparsa:** lit. 'had not become white having been sprinkled (on both temples)', and so 'had not (yet) flecked both temples with white'.

418–19 idque pio sedet Aeneae: lit. 'and that is settled for dutiful Aeneas', and so 'and if that is agreed by dutiful Aeneas'. **probat:** supply *-que*. **auctor:** Acestes was Entellus' sponsor or backer. **aequemus pugnas:** 'let us make the fight equal' (plural for singular).

419–20 tibi: 'for you'. **terga:** 'the hides', i.e. the gloves.

421–3 duplicem . . . amictum: the cloak was 'folded double', a common way of wearing them. Line 422 is unusual because of the so-called hypermetric *-que* at the end, which has to be elided before the vowel at the start of line 423 to avoid having one syllable too many in the line. Note also the heavy spondaic rhythm and <u>alliteration</u> of *m-*; the effect of all these features is to emphasise the enormous size of Entellus' body. **media . . . harena:** local ablative.

424–5 satus Anchisa: 'the one begotten by Anchises', and so 'the son of Anchises', i.e. Aeneas. **pater:** 'father' either because he is in the position of father to his people, or because he is the sponsor of the games. **paribus . . . armis:** note the <u>enclosing word order</u> and <u>alliteration</u>.

426–7 in digitos . . . arrectus: 'raised up on tip-toe'.

Questions

1 Describe Entellus' boxing gloves in as much detail as you can.

2 How does Virgil emphasise the huge size of the gloves?

3 Why does Entellus refer to Hercules?

4 How does Virgil make vivid the power and size of Entellus?

5 How was the boxing match made fair?

6 How do we know that both boxers were happy with the arrangement?

abduxere retro longe capita ardua ab ictu
immiscentque manus manibus pugnamque lacessunt,
ille pedum melior motu fretusque iuventa,   430
hic membris et mole valens; sed tarda trementi
genua labant, vastos quatit aeger anhelitus artus.
multa viri nequiquam inter se vulnera iactant,
multa cavo lateri ingeminant et pectore vastos
dant sonitus, erratque aures et tempora circum   435
crebra manus, duro crepitant sub vulnere malae.
stat gravis Entellus nisuque immotus eodem
corpore tela modo atque oculis vigilantibus exit.
ille, velut celsam oppugnat qui molibus urbem
aut montana sedet circum castella sub armis,   440
nunc hos, nunc illos aditus, omnemque pererrat
arte locum et variis adsultibus inritus urget.
ostendit dextram insurgens Entellus et alte
extulit; ille ictum venientem a vertice velox
praevidit celerique elapsus corpore cessit;   445
Entellus vires in ventum effudit et ultro
ipse gravis graviterque ad terram pondere vasto
concidit, ut quondam cava concidit aut Erymantho
aut Ida in magna radicibus eruta pinus.
consurgunt studiis Teucri et Trinacria pubes;   450

abduco, -ere, -duxi, -ductus	I draw back	*oculus, -i* m.	eye
retro	back	*vigilans, -ntis*	watchful
arduus, -a, -um	high	*exeo, -ire*	I avoid
immisceo, -ere	I mix, mingle	*velut*	just like
lacesso, -ere	I provoke	*celsus, -a, -um*	lofty, high
motus, -us m.	430 movement	*oppugno, -are*	I attack
fretus, -a, -um + abl.	relying on	*moles, -is* f.	war engine
moles, -is f.	bulk	*montanus, -a, -um*	440 mountain
tardus, -a, -um	slow	*castellum, -i* n.	fortress
tremo, -ere	I shake	*aditus, -us* m.	approach
genu, -us n.	knee	*pererro, -are*	I survey
labo, -are	I totter	*adsultus, -us* m.	assault
quatio, -ere	I shake	*inritus, -a, -um*	unsuccessful
aeger, -gra, -grum	painful	*urgeo, -ere*	I press forward
anhelitus, -us m.	panting	*dextra, -ae* f.	right hand
vulnus, -eris n.	heavy blow	*insurgo, -ere*	I rise up
cavus, -a, -um	hollow	*velox, -ocis*	swift
latus, -eris n.	side	*praevideo, -ere, -vidi, -visus*	I foresee
ingemino, -are	I repeat, redouble	*celer, -eris, -ere*	445 swift
sonitus, -us m.	435 noise	*elabor, -i, elapsus sum*	I slip aside
erro, -are	I miss	*ultro*	spontaneously
auris, -is f.	ear	*Erymanthus, -i* m.	Erymanthus
creber, -bra, -brum	frequent	*Ida, -ae* f.	Ida
crepito, -are	I rattle	*radix, -icis* f.	root
mala, -ae f.	jaw	*eruo, -ere, erui, erutus*	I tear out
nisus, -us m.	posture, effort	*pinus, -us* f.	pine tree
immotus, -a, -um	immovable	*studium, -i* n.	450 enthusiasm
telum, -i n.	missile, blow	*pubes, -is* f.	youth(s)
modo	only, merely		

428 **abduxere:** = *abduxerunt*. **retro longe ... ardua:** 'high and a long way back'.
429 **immiscent manus manibus:** 'they traded blows with their hands'; the <u>polyptoton</u> adds
to the <u>alliteration</u> and <u>consonance</u> of -*m*-, providing appropriate sound effects. **pugnamque
lacessunt:** 'and they provoked the fight', i.e. each blow called for retaliation. Note the
<u>chiasmus</u> in this line.
430 **ille:** Dares, as opposed to *hic* in line 431 (Entellus). **motu:** ablative of respect; note the
heavy <u>alliteration</u> of *m*-.
431–2 **membris, mole:** ablatives of respect. **trementi:** dative of disadvantage, most easily
translated as if genitive: 'the tottering man's (knees)'. **vastos ... artus:** note the <u>enclosing
word order</u>; similarly the two body parts enclose the line. Note the heavy <u>alliteration</u> of *a*-,
strengthened by even heavier <u>assonance</u> of the same letter throughout the line. Note also how
the rhythm, slow at *vastos*, speeds up in the rest of the line to reflect the rapid panting of the
aging boxer. All these effects make this a beautifully crafted line of poetry.
433 **multa ... vulnera:** not 'wounds', as these punches miss their targets, as *nequiquam*
indicates.
434–6 **multa:** supply *vulnera*. **cavo lateri:** dative of destination; the sides of the body are
'hollow' at the waist. **pectore:** local ablative. **dant:** the subject is *vulnera*. **erratque ... crebra
manus:** 'and their fists, punching thick and fast, miss their target'. Virgil alternates the blows:
first general misses (*nequiquam*), then blows to the sides, then misses round the head, and
finally blows to the jaw.
437–8 **stat gravis Entellus:** 'Entellus solidly stood his ground'. **nisu ... eodem:** 'with the same
effort'. **corpore tela ... exit:** 'avoided the blows with his body', i.e. by swaying his body from
side to side he made Dares' punches miss. **oculis vigilantibus:** i.e. as well as moving his body,
he used his eyes to anticipate and so avoid the blows. Note the fast rhythm of line 438, in
contrast with the much slower line 437, where the emphasis was on Entellus standing still;
in line 438 the emphasis is on his ducking and weaving his body.
439–40 **ille:** Dares. **velut ... qui:** 'like one who. . .'. **sedet circum ... sub armis:** i.e. 'is
besieging'.
441–2 **pererrat:** this verb has two objects: *aditus* and *locum*. **arte:** 'skilfully' (instrumental
ablative). **locum:** i.e. a place to aim a punch. **inritus urget:** 'he presses forward in vain';
the two key words are left until the last for emphasis: Dares is the one constantly pressing
forward his attack, but he is unsuccessful.
443–5 Note the slow rhythm of line 443, helping us to imagine Entellus, having so far fought
defensively, slowly rising up ready to deliver a powerful blow. **ostendit dextram:** i.e. he
brought his right hand out of its defensive role close to his body. **ille:** Dares. Note the heavy
alliteration of *v*- in line 444. **a vertice:** 'from (the blow's) high point'. **cessit:** 'he stepped back'.
446–8 **in ventum:** i.e. his punch hit only the air. **ultro:** i.e. without being hit by Dares; the air
punch overbalanced him. **gravis graviterque:** the <u>polyptoton</u> emphasises the heaviness of his
fall.
448–9 **ut:** 'just as' or 'just like', introducing a <u>simile</u>. **cava ... pinus:** pine trees grew thickly
on mountains such as Erymanthus (in Central Greece) and Ida (near Troy); the specific place
names are used to add colour to the simile; both nouns are local ablatives. **radicibus eruta:**
'torn out by the roots', by a storm.
450 **studiis:** 'enthusiastically' (ablative of manner).

Questions

1 How skilfully does Virgil describe the contest?

2 Discuss the use of sound effects in these lines.

it clamor caelo primusque accurrit Acestes
aequaevumque ab humo miserans attollit amicum.
at non tardatus casu neque territus heros
acrior ad pugnam redit ac vim suscitat ira:
tum pudor incendit vires et conscia virtus,   455
praecipitemque Daren ardens agit aequore toto
nunc dextra ingeminans ictus, nunc ille sinistra.
nec mora nec requies: quam multa grandine nimbi
culminibus crepitant, sic densis ictibus heros
creber utraque manu pulsat versatque Dareta.   460
tum pater Aeneas procedere longius iras
et saevire animis Entellum haud passus acerbis,
sed finem imposuit pugnae fessumque Dareta
eripuit mulcens dictis ac talia fatur:
'infelix, quae tanta animum dementia cepit?   465
non vires alias conversaque numina sentis?
cede deo.' dixitque et proelia voce diremit.

Entellus took the prize of an ox, which he killed with a single blow. There followed an archery contest and an equestrian parade. Meanwhile Juno sent her assistant Iris to cause trouble for the Trojans; she persuaded the womenfolk, who were tired of constantly journeying in search of a new home, to set fire to the Trojan ships, so that they would be forced to make their home in Sicily. Aeneas prayed to Jupiter, who sent a rain storm that saved all but four of the ships. The prophet Nautes advised Aeneas to leave most of the women and the elderly in Sicily with Acestes, while he led an elite band of warriors to Italy. That night the ghost of Anchises appeared to Aeneas to offer the same advice. He also warned his son that he must visit the underworld before continuing to Latium, where he would have to defeat a local army before he could build his new city. Aeneas founded a city for those who chose to stay behind, and ordered his men to repair the damaged ships. After nine days of feasting and prayers, Aeneas and his men set sail. On the journey, Aeneas' helmsman, Palinurus, fell asleep at the tiller and was flung overboard by the god of sleep. He was lost.

accurro, -ere	I run up	requies, -etis f.	rest
aequaevus, -a, -um	of the same age	grando, -inis f.	hail
vis, acc. vim f.	force, violence	culmen, -inis n.	roof, top, peak
suscito, -are	I rouse	densus, -a, -um	constant
ira, -ae f.	anger	procedo, -ere	461 I continue
pudor, -oris m.	455 shame	saevio, -ire	I rage
conscius, -a, -um	conscious	impono, -ere, -sui, -situs	I impose
praeceps, -ipitis	headlong	mulceo, -ere	I soothe
ardens, -ntis	furious	dementia, -ae f.	465 madness
ago, -ere	I drive, chase	converto, -ere, -ti, -sus	I turn, change
aequor, -oris n.	plain	numen, -inis n.	god
totus, -a, -um	all, whole	dirimo, -ere, -emi, -emptus	I put an end to
sinistra, -ae f.	left hand		

451–2 **caelo:** 'to the sky' (dative of destination). **aequaevumque . . . amicum:** both were old.
454 **vim suscitat ira:** this is generally taken to mean 'he rouses violence with his anger', i.e.
'he increases his violence because of his anger'; however, there is no reason why *ira* should
not be nominative: 'anger increases his violence'.
455 **pudor:** 'shame' at his failure. **conscia virtus:** 'his confident courage', and so 'confidence
in his courage'.
456–7 **aequore toto:** 'all over the levelled ground' (local ablative). Note the <u>assonance</u>.
sinistra: ablative, parallel to *dextra*. **ille:** redundant in English.
458–60 **nec mora:** supply *erat*. **quam multa grandine:** 'with how much hail', picked up by *sic
densis ictibus:* 'with as great a density of blows as the hail with which . . .' **culminibus:** local
ablative. **creber:** best translated as an adverb. **versat:** 'sends him spinning'. **Dareta:** this is an
alternative Greek accusative ending (cf. *Daren* in line 456), used here to complete the rhythm.
461–2 **pater:** Virgil often defines Aeneas with this word, to emphasise his role as patron of
the games and his *pietas*. The order is . . . *Aeneas haud passus (est) iras procedere longius
et (haud passus est) Entellum saevire acerbis animis*. **iras:** either Entellus' anger, or the angry
passions of both men. **animis . . . acerbis:** local ablative.
463–4 **pugnae:** dative after the compound verb.
465 **quae tanta . . . dementia:** 'what is this great madness that has . . .'.
466 **non . . . sentis:** 'don't you see that'. **vires alias:** supply *esse*; the probable meaning is
'that (his) strength has changed' (i.e. increased), because the gods have turned their backs on
Dares and supported Entellus. **conversaque numina:** supply *esse*: 'that the gods have changed
(their support)'.
467 **cede deo:** 'yield to the god'; *deo* is singular because Aeneas assumes that only one god
would have intervened in that contest; *numina* is plural because Aeneas was thinking in
more general terms at that point. As in Homer's works, fights, whether on the battlefield or
in contests, are determined not just by the relative skills or strength of the combatants, but
also by which gains the support of a god.

Questions

1 How does the contest end?

2 What impression do you form of Entellus in these lines?

3 How is this impression reinforced by Virgil's style of writing?

4 *pater Aeneas*: to what extent do Aeneas' actions and words justify this description
of him?

Book 6

The Trojans landed at Cumae on the west coast of Italy. Aeneas went at once to see Deiphobe, the Sibyl, who was a prophetess of the god Apollo. She first prophesied the troubles that the Trojans would face when they tried to settle in Latium. Aeneas then explained that he needed her help to enter the underworld (as the ghost of his father had bidden him to do). The entrance to this was very close to Cumae.

talibus orabat dictis arasque tenebat,
cum sic orsa loqui vates: 'sate sanguine divum,   125
Tros Anchisiade, facilis descensus Averno:
noctes atque dies patet atri ianua Ditis;
sed revocare gradum superasque evadere ad auras,
hoc opus, hic labor est. pauci, quos aequus amavit
Iuppiter aut ardens evexit ad aethera virtus,   130
dis geniti potuere. tenent media omnia silvae,
Cocytusque sinu labens circumvenit atro.
quod si tantus amor menti, si tanta cupido est
bis Stygios innare lacus, bis nigra videre
Tartara, et insano iuvat indulgere labori,   135
accipe quae peragenda prius.

talis, -e	such	*aequus, -a, -um*	fair
oro, -are	I beg	*Iuppiter, Iovis* m.	130 Jupiter
dictum, -i n.	word	*ardens, -ntis*	burning
ara, -ae f.	altar	*eveho, -ere, -vexi, -vectus*	I raise up
teneo, -ere	I hold	*aether, -eris* (acc. *-era*) m.	sky, heaven
ordior, -iri, orsus sum	125 I begin	*virtus, -utis* f.	virtue, courage
loquor, -i	I speak	*deus, -i* m.	god
vates, -is f.	prophetess	*gigno, -ere, genui, genitus*	I beget
sero, -ere, sevi, satus	I sow, bear	*medium, -i* n.	middle
sanguis, -inis m.	blood	*silva, -ae* f.	wood
divus, -i m.	god	*Cocytus, -i* m.	Cocytus
Tros, Trois m.	Trojan	*sinus, -us* m.	bend, fold
Anchisiades, -ae m.	Anchises' son	*labor, -i, lapsus sum*	I glide
facilis, -e	easy	*circumvenio, -ire*	I encircle
descensus, -us m.	descent	*quod si*	but if
Avernus, -i m.	Lake Avernus	*amor, -oris* m.	love
nox, noctis f.	night	*mens, mentis* f.	mind
dies, diei f.	day	*cupido, -inis* f.	desire
pateo, -ere	I am open	*bis*	twice
ater, atra, atrum	black, dark	*Stygius, -a, -um*	Stygian
ianua, -ae f.	door	*inno, innare*	I swim in
Dis, Ditis m.	Pluto, Hades	*lacus, -us* m.	lake
revoco, -are	I retrace	*niger, nigra, nigrum*	black
gradus, -us m.	step	*Tartara, -orum* n.pl.	135 Tartarus
superus, -a, -um	above, upper	*insanus, -a, -um*	insane
evado, -ere	I escape	*iuvat, -are*	it pleases
aura, -ae f.	air, gleam	*indulgeo, -ere* + dat.	I indulge in
opus, operis n.	toil, task	*accipio, -ere*	I receive, hear
labor, -oris m.	work, task	*perago, -ere*	I accomplish
pauci, -ae, -a	few	*prius*	first

124–6 **talibus . . . dictis**: 'with such words', i.e. with the words which Aeneas had addressed to the Sibyl. **arasque tenebat**: Aeneas grasped the altar (plural for singular) in supplication to Apollo. **orsa**: supply *est*; the indicative is needed by the 'inverse *cum*' construction. **sate**: 'o (man) born'; the vocative of the perfect passive participle used as a noun. **sanguine divum**: 'from the blood of the gods'. Aeneas was the son of the goddess Venus. The Sibyl addresses him with formal words in deference to his high status. **Anchisiade**: Anchises was Aeneas' father. **facilis**: supply *est*; to gain entry, all anyone had to do was die. **Averno**: 'to Avernus' (dative of destination); Avernus is a circular lake near Cumae, which fills the crater of a dormant volcano; because the poisonous fumes rising from the lake were strong enough to kill birds flying over it, it was regarded as an entrance to the underworld. Here Avernus is probably intended to mean the underworld itself, rather than just its entrance.

127 **noctes atque dies**: accusatives of duration of time. **patet . . . ianua**: the gateway to the underworld must always lie open to receive the souls of people as they die. **atri . . . Ditis**: Pluto (or Hades to give him his Greek name) was the brother of Jupiter and keeper of the underworld; he is described as 'black' to match the imagined darkness of his realm.

128 **superasque . . . ad auras**: 'to the air above', i.e. to the world of the living.

129–31 **opus, labor**: the same idea is repeated to emphasise the difficulty of escaping the underworld. **pauci**: the subject of *potuere*, separated from it for emphasis; in fact Greek mythology tells of only four living mortals who entered the underworld and were allowed to leave: Orpheus, Pollux, Theseus and Hercules. **aequus . . . Iuppiter**: 'fair-minded Jupiter'. **ardens . . . virtus**: 'fiery courage'. **dis geniti**: 'those begotten by gods', i.e. 'the sons of gods'; Pollux and Hercules were the sons of Jupiter. **potuere**: 'have been able (to escape)'; *potuere = potuerunt*.

131–2 **media omnia**: 'all the central parts (of the underworld)'. **Cocytus**: one of the five mythical rivers of the underworld. **sinu . . . atro**: 'with its black coiling' (ablative of manner).

133–5 **tantus amor . . . tanta cupido**: the same idea repeated for emphasis. **menti . . . est**: 'is in your mind'. **bis . . . innare**: 'to swim twice in', and so 'to sail twice across'; Aeneas would of course do this the second time when he died. **Stygios . . . lacus**: 'the Stygian lake' (plural for singular); the Styx was another of the rivers of the underworld, often described more as a lake or marsh than a river. **nigra . . . Tartara**: Tartarus was the sector of the underworld in which the souls of the wicked were condemned to reside. **insano . . . labori**: Aeneas' task (of entering the underworld) is 'insane' because of its dangers.

136 **quae**: = *ea quae*. **peragenda**: supply *sunt*.

Questions

1 What picture of the underworld does the Sibyl present?

2 How does her use of words make this picture more effective?

3 Lines 126–127 have often been quoted by other writers. Can you suggest a reason why this is so?

4 How does the Sibyl indicate that Aeneas' plan is a mad one?

latet arbore opaca
aureus et foliis et lento vimine ramus,
Iunoni infernae dictus sacer; hunc tegit omnis
lucus et obscuris claudunt convallibus umbrae.
sed non ante datur telluris operta subire   140
auricomos quam quis decerpserit arbore fetus.
hoc sibi pulchra suum ferri Proserpina munus
instituit. primo avulso non deficit alter
aureus, et simili frondescit virga metallo.
ergo alte vestiga oculis et rite repertum   145
carpe manu; namque ipse volens facilisque sequetur,
si te fata vocant; aliter non viribus ullis
vincere nec duro poteris convellere ferro.
praeterea iacet exanimum tibi corpus amici
(heu nescis) totamque incestat funere classem,   150
dum consulta petis nostroque in limine pendes.

lateo, -ere	I lie hidden	*virga, -ae* f.	twig, rod
arbos, -oris f.	tree	*metallum, -i* n.	metal
opacus, -a, -um	shady	*ergo*	145 therefore
aureus, -a, -um	golden	*alte*	high up
folium, -i n.	leaf	*vestigo, -are*	I search
lentus, -a, -um	pliant	*oculus, -i* m.	eye
vimen, -inis n.	twig	*rite*	duly
ramus, -i m.	branch, bough	*reperio, -ire, -pperi, -pertus*	I find
Iuno, -onis f.	Juno	*carpo, -ere*	I pluck
infernus, -a, -um	of the underworld	*manus, -us* f.	hand
dico, -ere, dixi, dictus	I say, speak	*namque*	for
sacer, sacra, sacrum	sacred	*volo, velle*	I wish, want
tego, -ere	I cover, hide	*sequor, -i, secutus sum*	I follow
lucus, -i m.	grove	*fatum, -i* n.	fate
obscurus, -a, -um	dark	*voco, -are*	I call
claudo, -ere	I enclose	*aliter*	otherwise
convallis, -is f.	valley	*vires, -ium* f.pl.	strength
umbra, -ae f.	shadow, shade	*ullus, -a, -um*	any
ante . . . quam	140 before	*vinco, -ere*	I win
do, dare	I give, allow	*durus, -a, -um*	hard
tellus, -uris f.	earth, ground	*convello, -ere*	I tear off
operta, -orum n.pl.	hidden places	*ferrum, -i* n.	iron
subeo, -ire	I enter	*praeterea*	furthermore
auricomus, -a, -um	golden-leaved	*iaceo, -ere*	I lie
decerpo, -ere, -rpsi, -rptus	I pluck off	*exanimus, -a, -um*	dead
fetus, -us m.	growth	*corpus, -oris* n.	body
pulcher, -ra, -rum	beautiful	*heu*	150 alas
fero, ferre	I bring, take, say	*nescio, -ire*	I do not know
Proserpina, -ae f.	Proserpina	*totus, -a, -um*	all, the whole
munus, muneris n.	gift, duty	*incesto, -are*	I pollute
instituo, -ere, -ui, -utus	I set up	*funus, -eris* n.	death
avello, -ere, -velli, -vulsus	I pluck off	*classis, -is* f.	fleet
deficio, -ere	I fail	*consultum, -i* n.	decree, oracle
alter, -era, -erum	a second	*peto, -ere*	I seek
similis, -e	similar	*limen, -inis* n.	threshold
frondesco, -ere	I sprout	*pendeo, -ere*	I linger

136–7 **arbore opaca**: local ablative. **aureus . . . ramus**: the famous Golden Bough; note how the two words <u>enclose</u> the line, occupying the key positions. **et . . . et**: 'both . . . and'; *foliis* and *lento vimine* are ablatives of respect, both qualifying *aureus*: 'golden in both leaves and pliant stem'.

138–9 **Iunoni infernae**: 'Juno of the underworld', i.e. Proserpina, who was the wife of Pluto and so queen of the underworld, just as Juno was the wife of Jupiter and so queen of heaven. **dictus**: 'said (to be)'. **claudunt . . . umbrae**: 'shadows enclose it'. **obscuris . . . convallibus**: local ablative. Note the <u>alliteration</u> and <u>consonance</u> of *c* in line 139.

140–1 **ante**: this is best deferred until it can be joined to *quam*. **non . . . datur**: 'it is not allowed'. **telluris operta**: i.e. the underworld. **auricomos quam**: the order of these two words is inverted; *auricomos* belongs with *fetus* (note again how these words <u>enclose</u> the line). **auricomos . . . fetus**: lit. 'the golden-haired offspring'. **quis**: after *antequam* this means 'anyone', i.e. 'someone'. **decerpserit**: future perfect indicative because the bough will have to have been plucked from the tree before entry to the underworld will be granted. **arbore**: ablative of separation.

142–3 **hoc . . . suum . . . munus**: 'this (golden bough) as her gift'. **instituit**: Proserpina 'set up' or 'established' the bringing of the bough to her as a kind of passport for entry to the underworld. Note the <u>enjambement</u>.

143–4 **primo avulso**: 'when the first bough is plucked off'. **non deficit**: a second branch 'does not fail (to grow in its place)'. **aureus**: supply *ramus*; note the <u>enjambement</u> again. **simili . . . metallo**: ablative of material; translate 'of similar metal'. Virgil repeats the idea using different words, as he frequently does, to fix it more securely in the reader's mind.

145–6 **alte vestiga**: almost antithetical, as *vestigare* normally indicates following tracks on the ground. **rite**: the idea is that, if Aeneas searches carefully, he will duly find the bough. **repertum**: supply *ramum*.

146–7 **ipse**: supply *ramus* again. **volens facilisque**: 'willingly and easily'. **si te fata vocant**: 'if the fates summon you', i.e. if it is Aeneas' destiny to visit the underworld.

147–8 **aliter**: i.e. if Aeneas is not fated to visit the underworld. **vincere**: i.e. win the bough. **duro . . . ferro**: i.e. no sword will cut it free from the tree.

149–50 **praeterea**: introduces a new task for Aeneas. **tibi**: a so-called ethic dative, which may be translated as '(a friend) of yours'. **heu nescis**: Aeneas is unaware that one of his friends has died. Aeneas might have assumed that the Sibyl was referring to Palinurus (see end of Book V), until these words. **totam . . . classem**: note how these words <u>enclose</u> the clause, emphasising the scale of the pollution. **incestat funere**: the dead man 'pollutes' the fleet 'with his death' because he lies unburied. It was a traditional belief that without burial rites, a dead person's soul could not gain access to the underworld and so would be condemned to pollute the site of his or her death.

151 **consulta**: i.e. while Aeneas is seeking an oracular response from the Sibyl.

Questions

1 Can you think of other talismans in mythology or literature like the Golden Bough?

2 How does the Sibyl emphasise the special qualities of the bough?

3 In what way will the Golden Bough be a test for Aeneas?

4 Why do you think the Sibyl wants Aeneas to bury his friend before seeking the Golden Bough?

Aeneas discovered that the musician, Misenus, had drowned, after foolishly challenging the gods to a contest. While his men prepared a funeral pyre for him, Aeneas prayed for help in finding the Golden Bough.

vix ea fatus erat geminae cum forte columbae	190
ipsa sub ora viri caelo venere volantes,	
et viridi sedere solo. tum maximus heros	
maternas agnovit aves laetusque precatur:	
'este duces, o, si qua via est, cursumque per auras	
derigite in lucos ubi pinguem dives opacat	195
ramus humum. tuque, o, dubiis ne defice rebus,	
diva parens.' sic effatus vestigia pressit	
observans quae signa ferant, quo tendere pergant.	
pascentes illae tantum prodire volando	
quantum acie possent oculi servare sequentum.	200
inde ubi venere ad fauces grave olentis Averni,	
tollunt se celeres liquidumque per aëra lapsae	
sedibus optatis gemina super arbore sidunt,	
discolor unde auri per ramos aura refulsit.	204
corripit Aeneas extemplo avidusque refringit	210
cunctantem, et vatis portat sub tecta Sibyllae.	

vix	190 scarcely	*signum, -i* n.	sign
for, fari, fatus sum	I speak	*quo*	whither
geminus, -a, -um	twin	*tendo, -ere*	I aim
forte	by chance	*pergo, -ere*	I proceed
columba, -ae f.	dove	*pasco, -ere*	I feed
os, oris n.	face, mouth	*prodeo, -ire*	I advance
caelum, -i n.	sky	*acies, -ei* f.	200 eyesight, blade
volo, -are	I fly	*servo, -are*	I keep
viridis, -e	green, fresh	*inde*	then
sedeo, -ere	I sit	*fauces, -ium* f.pl.	throat, jaws
solum, -i n.	ground	*gravis, -e*	heavy, serious
heros, -ois m.	hero	*oleo, -ere*	I smell
maternus, -a, -um	a mother's	*tollo, -ere*	I raise
agnosco, -ere, -novi, -nitus	I recognise	*celer, -eris, -ere*	swift
avis, -is f.	bird	*liquidus, -a, -um*	clear
laetus, -a, -um	glad, happy	*aër, aëris* m. (acc. *aera*)	air
precor, -ari, -atus sum	I pray	*sedes, sedis* f.	home, perch
dux, ducis m.	leader	*opto, -are, -avi, -atus*	I choose
cursus, -us m.	course	*super* + abl.	above, on
derigo, -ere	195 I direct, guide	*sido, -ere*	I settle
pinguis, -e	rich	*discolor, -oris*	204 of different hue
dives, -itis	rich	*unde*	from where
opaco, -are	I shade	*aurum, -i* n.	gold
humus, -i f.	ground	*refulgeo, -ere, -fulsi*	I shine
dubius, -a, -um	doubtful	*corripio, -ere*	210 I seize
divus, -a, -um	divine	*extemplo*	immediately
parens, -ntis m./f.	parent	*avidus, -a, -um*	eager
effor, -fari, -fatus sum	I speak out	*refringo, -ere*	I break off
vestigium, -i n.	step	*cunctor, -ari, -atus sum*	I delay, cling
premo, -ere, pressi, pressus	I press, check	*tectum, -i* n.	dwelling
observo, -are	I watch		

190–1 **ea:** i.e. his prayer. **geminae . . . columbae:** 'a pair of doves'; doves were considered sacred to Venus. **cum:** to be taken before *geminae columbae*; this is an example of an 'inverse *cum*', taking the indicative (*venere* = *venerunt*). **ipsa sub ora viri:** 'right in front of the man's (i.e. Aeneas') face'. **caelo:** 'from the sky' (ablative of origin).

192–3 **sedere:** this is the shortened form of the 3rd plural perfect (*sederunt*); cf. *venere* above. This form is frequent in poetry and will not be commented on again. **viridi . . . solo:** local ablative. **maximus heros:** Virgil often uses such epithets to remind the reader of Aeneas' heroic qualities.

194–6 **o:** a cry of joy and hope. **si qua via est:** 'if there is any way', i.e. if it is possible. **dives . . . ramus:** 'the rich bough'; note the position of *dives* next to the similar *pinguem*, reinforcing the idea. **opacat:** 'casts its shade' over the ground (a poetic image).

196–7 **ne defice:** a poetic form of prohibition. **dubiis . . . rebus:** 'at this critical time'.

197–8 **vestigia pressit:** 'he checked his steps'. **ferant:** the subject is *columbae*. **quo tendere pergant:** 'where they would proceed to aim for'. Note the slow rhythm of line 198.

199–200 **tantum . . . quantum:** 'as far as'. **prodire:** a historic infinitive. **possent:** the subjunctive expresses purpose. **oculi . . . sequentum:** 'the eyes of those following them', i.e. Aeneas and one or more companions he took with him, though these are not mentioned. **acie:** 'in sight'.

201 **fauces:** 'jaws' gives the image of a gaping mouth ready to swallow its victims. **grave:** an adverbial form, qualifying *olentis*: 'evil-smelling'.

202–3 **tollunt se:** 'they flew up'. **celeres:** best translated as an adverb. **gemina super arbore:** 'at the top of a tree of two forms', i.e. with two types of foliage, normal and golden (as defined in line 204).

204 **discolor . . . aura:** 'the contrasting-coloured gleam (of gold)'; the gold contrasted with the green of the rest of the tree. Note the <u>alliteration</u> and <u>assonance</u> of *auri . . . aura*.

205–9 The Golden Bough is likened to mistletoe growing on a tree.

210–1 **corripit:** supply *ramum*. **avidus:** best translated as an adverb. **cunctantem:** the bough resisted his grasp at first. Note the slow, spondaic rhythm of this word, which continues through the rest of the line.

Questions

1 Why are doves the appropriate birds to lead Aeneas to the bough?

2 How does Virgil use sound effects and choice of words in lines 190–192 to make the appearance of the doves dramatic?

3 Why might Virgil have chosen to describe Aeneas as *maximus heros* (192) at this point?

4 To whom does Aeneas address his prayers (lines 194–197)?

5 Why did Aeneas 'check his steps' (line 197)?

6 Describe in your own words the behaviour of the doves.

7 How does Virgil make the bough seem magical?

Meanwhile the rest of the Trojans prepared a pyre and gave Misenus a splendid funeral.
Aeneas, on his return from the wood, built a barrow to contain the ashes of his dead friend.
The barrow lies at the foot of a mountain, which is still called Misenus after him.

his actis propere exsequitur praecepta Sibyllae.	236
spelunca alta fuit vastoque immanis hiatu,	
scrupea, tuta lacu nigro nemorumque tenebris,	
quam super haud ullae poterant impune volantes	
tendere iter pennis: talis sese halitus atris	240
faucibus effundens supera ad convexa ferebat.	
quattuor hic primum nigrantes terga iuvencos	
constituit frontique invergit vina sacerdos.	244

The Sibyl prepared the animals and sacrificed them to the infernal gods.

ecce autem primi sub lumina solis et ortus	255
sub pedibus mugire solum et iuga coepta moveri	
silvarum, visaeque canes ululare per umbram	
adventante dea. 'procul, o procul este, profani,'	
conclamat vates, 'totoque absistite luco;	
tuque invade viam vaginaque eripe ferrum:	260
nunc animis opus, Aenea, nunc pectore firmo.'	
tantum effata furens antro se immisit aperto;	

ago, -ere, egi, actus	I do	sacerdos, -otis f.	priestess
propere	quickly	ecce	255 see!
exsequor, -i, -secutus sum	I carry out	lumen, -inis n.	light, eye
praeceptum, -i n.	order	sol, solis m.	sun
spelunca, -ae f.	cave	ortus, -us m.	rising
vastus, -a, -um	huge	pes, pedis m.	foot
immanis, -e	immense	mugio, -ire	I moo, bellow
hiatus, -us m.	gape, mouth	iugum, -i n.	mountain ridge
scrupeus, -a, -um	stony, rugged	coepi, -isse, coeptus	I began
tutus, -a, -um	safe, protected	moveo, -ere	I move
nemus, -oris n.	grove	canis, -is m./f.	dog
tenebrae, -arum f.pl.	darkness	ululo, -are	I howl
impune	safely	advento, -are	I approach
volans, -ntis f.	bird	procul	far away
iter, itineris n.	240 journey, route	profanus, -a, -um	uninitiated
penna, -ae f.	wing	conclamo, -are	I shout
halitus, -us m.	breath, vapour	absisto, -ere	withdraw
effundo, -ere	I pour out	invado, -ere	260 I enter
superus, -a, -um	above	vagina, -ae f.	scabbard
convexa, -orum n.pl.	vault, sky	ferrum, -i n.	iron, sword
hic	here	animus, -i m.	courage
nigrans, -ntis	black	opus (est)	(there is) need
tergum, -i n.	back, hide	pectus, -oris n.	heart
iuvencus, -i m.	ox, bullock	firmus, -a, -um	stout
constituo, -ere	I place, stand	furens, -ntis	mad, raging
frons, -ntis f.	forehead	antrum, -i n.	cave
invergo, -ere	I pour on	immitto, -ere, -misi, -missus	I send in
vinum, -i n.	wine	apertus, -a, -um	open

236 **his actis:** i.e. the burial rites for Misenus, which remove the pollution, allowing Aeneas
to enter the underworld.

237–8 **alta:** probably 'deep' rather than 'high up'. Note the heavy <u>assonance</u> of *a* in line 237,
reinforcing the image of a gaping mouth. **tuta lacu nigro:** 'safe from (because of) a black
lake', i.e. 'protected by a black lake'. **tenebris:** a second causal ablative. The lake is Avernus,
and the cave is not the Sibyl's but the entrance to the underworld.

239–40 **quam super** = *super quam*. **tendere iter pennis:** 'direct their course on wings' – little
more than 'fly'.

240–1 **talis . . . halitus:** 'such was the (poisonous) vapour that . . .'. Virgil is suggesting that
the name *Avernus* was derived from the similar Greek *Aornos*, meaning 'birdless'. **sese . . .
effundens:** 'pouring out' (the Latin verb is transitive and requires an object). **ferebat:** supply
sese from the line above: 'bore itself' and so 'rose'. Line 242 is considered spurious by all
editors, and so has been omitted.

243–4 The order is *hic primum sacerdos constituit quattuor iuvencos, nigrantes terga,
invergitque vina fronti.* **nigrantes terga:** 'black with respect to their hides, and so 'with black
hides'; *terga* is accusative of respect. Note the spondaic rhythm of line 243, appropriate to
the solemnity of the activity. **fronti:** dative of destination and singular for plural. This was
a ritual act, preceding the sacrifice of the animals. The sacrifice was considered an essential
prerequisite to a visit to the underworld, in order to win the favour of the infernal deities.

255 **sub lumina:** 'just before the light'. **primi . . . solis:** 'of the first sun'; an example of
<u>hypallage</u>. **et ortus:** 'and its rising' (genitive, parallel to *solis*). The whole phrase is a poetic
elaboration of 'just before dawn'.

256–9 **mugire:** historic infinitive: 'began to bellow'. **coepta:** supply *sunt*. **coepta moveri:**
'began to move'. **iuga . . . silvarum:** 'the ridges of woods' and so 'the wooded mountain
ridges'. **visaeque canes:** supply *sunt*; the dogs are female because they belong to Hecate,
a goddess associated with the underworld (referred to here simply as *dea*). **profani:** the
'uninitiated' are the Trojans who have accompanied Aeneas thus far; Virgil has not
mentioned them, but we must infer their presence. Only Aeneas has the Golden Bough and
so the right to participate in the unfolding mysteries; the rest must leave and not observe
what happens, as shown by *totoque absistite luco*.

260 **tuque:** the Sibyl turns to address Aeneas. **ferrum:** the sword will be of little use against
the monsters and spirits of the underworld but, as in Homer's account of Odysseus' visit to
the underworld in Book XI of the *Odyssey*, the swords will frighten the spirits enough to
keep them at bay.

261–2 **animis:** plural for singular. **opus:** supply *est*. **se immisit:** 'she dashed into'. **antro . . .
aperto:** note the <u>enclosing word order</u>, mirroring the action.

Questions

1 How does Virgil make the cave and the lake beside it seem eerie?

2 How does Virgil use the image of darkness in these lines?

3 In lines 255–262, how does Virgil create an atmosphere of horror?

4 Why do you think the Sibyl says the words *nunc animis opus*?

ille ducem haud timidis vadentem passibus aequat.   263

O gods of the underworld, let me tell what I learnt of the affairs under the earth. Aeneas and the Sibyl began their journey through the halls of Dis, passing all the assembled woes that trouble humankind. Grief, Disease, Fear, Hunger, Death and his twin Sleep, and War they passed, all waiting to prey upon mortals. Dreams clung like bats to the branches of a tree. Many were the other monsters they passed.

corripit hic subita trepidus formidine ferrum   290
Aeneas strictamque aciem venientibus offert,
et ni docta comes tenues sine corpore vitas
admoneat volitare cava sub imagine formae,
inruat et frustra ferro diverberet umbras.
hinc via Tartarei quae fert Acherontis ad undas.   295
turbidus hic caeno vastaque voragine gurges
aestuat atque omnem Cocyto eructat harenam.
portitor has horrendus aquas et flumina servat
terribili squalore Charon, cui plurima mento
canities inculta iacet, stant lumina flamma,   300
sordidus ex umeris nodo dependet amictus.
ipse ratem conto subigit velisque ministrat
et ferruginea subvectat corpora cumba,

timidus, -a, -um	timid	*aestuo, -are*	I seethe
vado, -ere	I go	*eructo, -are*	I spew out
passus, -us m.	step	*harena, -ae* f.	sand
aequo, -are	I keep pace with	*portitor, -oris* m.	ferryman
subitus, -a, -um	290 sudden	*horrendus, -a, -um*	dreadful
trepidus, -a, -um	alarmed	*aqua, -ae* f.	water
formido, -inis f.	panic	*flumen, -inis* n.	river
stringo, -ere, strinxi, strictus	I draw	*servo, -are*	I watch over
offero, -ferre	I present	*terribilis, -e*	terrible
ni	unless, if not	*squalor, -oris* m.	squalor, filth
doctus, -a, -um	wise	*Charon, -ontis* m.	Charon
tenuis, -e	insubstantial	*mentum, -i* n.	chin
sine + abl.	without	*canities, -ei* f.	300 greyness
vita, -ae f.	life	*incultus, -a, -um*	unkempt
admoneo, -ere	I advise, warn	*iaceo, -ere*	I lie
volito, -are	I flit about	*sto, stare*	I stand (out)
cavus, -a, -um	hollow	*flamma, -ae* f.	flame, fire
imago, -inis f.	image	*sordidus, -a, -um*	dirty
forma, -ae f.	shape, beauty	*umerus, -i* m.	shoulder
inruo, -ere	I rush upon	*nodus, -i* m.	knot
frustra	in vain	*dependeo, -ere*	I hang down
diverbero, -are	I cleave in two	*amictus, -us* m.	cloak
hinc	295 from here	*ratis, -is* f.	raft, boat
Tartareus, -a, -um	of Tartarus	*contus, -i* m.	pole
Acheron, -ontis m.	river Acheron	*subigo, -ere*	I push
unda, -ae f.	wave, water	*velum, -i* n.	sail
turbidus, -a, -um	wild	*ministro, -are*	I tend
caenum, -i n.	mud	*ferrugineus, -a, -um*	rusty
vorago, -inis f.	whirlpool	*subvecto, -are*	I transport
gurges, -itis m.	whirlpool	*cumba, -ae* f.	boat

263 **ille**: Aeneas. **vadentem**: 'as she went'.

290–1 **corripit**: the subject is *Aeneas* in the next line, held back to increase suspense. **hic**: 'at this point'. **offert**: 'pointed (the blade) at'. **venientibus**: 'at (the monsters) as they approached'.

292–4 **ni . . . moneat**: 'if (the *docta comes*) had not advised him'; the present subjunctive is used instead of the pluperfect because the whole passage is set in the historic present, and because the present subjunctive makes the actions more vivid. **tenues . . . vitas**: 'insubstantial lives', i.e. the monstrous forms that appear so threatening are bodiless entities that 'flutter about' (*volitare*) as if without purpose. **cava sub imagine formae**: 'under the hollow image of shape', and so 'giving the empty appearance of substance'; this repeats the idea of *tenues vitas*, to emphasise to Aeneas that they pose no physical threat. The fully dactylic rhythm of line 293 reflects their rapid movement. **inruat**: the apodosis of the unfulfilled condition, as is also *diverberet*: 'he would have rushed at them'.

295 **hinc via**: supply *est*. **quae fert**: 'which leads'. **Tartarei . . . Acherontis**: 'of Tartarean Acheron'; this was one of the five rivers of the underworld, like the Cocytus in lines 132 and 297. Virgil does not, of course, present a clear geographical description of the underworld, but merely helps the reader to build up a rough picture in his or her mind.

296–7 **hic**: the Acheron. **turbidus . . . gurges**: '(this) wild whirlpool'; note how the two words enclose the line. **caeno vastaque voragine**: 'with mud and a vast boiling mass of water'; *voragine* and *gurges* are more or less the same, both vivid words indicating seething masses of water. **omnem . . . harenam**: 'all its sand', i.e. all the sand that the speeding flow has scoured from the banks and river bed. **Cocyto**: dative of destination: 'into the Cocytus'.

298–9 **portitor . . . Charon**: Charon, whose job was to ferry souls of the dead across the Styx (according to some the Acheron), is one of the most familiar underworld characters; relatives used to place a coin in the mouth of the deceased to pay the fare. Note how the name is delayed for suspense. **horrendus**: in this, one of the most famous sections of the *Aeneid*, Virgil portrays Charon as a scarecrow-like figure. **aquas et flumina**: tautological. **servat**: he 'watches over' the rivers, in that it is his job to ferry across only those souls that have received burial rites, and to prevent all others from crossing. **terribili squalore**: ablative of description.

299–300 **cui . . . mento**: 'on whose chin'. **plurima . . . canities inculta**: 'very much unkempt greyness', i.e. 'a very long shaggy grey beard'. **stant lumina flamma**: there are various interpretations of this famous phrase; perhaps the literal 'his eyes stand in flame' is intended to mean 'his eyes are burning with fire'.

301 **sordidus . . . amictus**: note how once again the adjective + noun pair enclose the rest of the line. **nodo**: 'by means of a knot'.

302–3 **ratem, cumba**: different words for the same thing, a small boat; this one is fitted with both oars and sail. **velis**: this is either dative if *ministrat* is being used intransitively, or ablative if it is being used transitively; both are possible; 'attends to the sails' is simpler than 'attends to the boat with the sails'. **ferruginea . . . cumba**: 'in his rust-coloured boat'. **corpora**: 'the dead', not to be confused with living bodies which have substance.

Questions

1 In lines 290–297, how does Virgil create an atmosphere of horror?

2 What picture does Virgil present of Charon?

3 What makes this picture effective?

iam senior, sed cruda deo viridisque senectus.
huc omnis turba ad ripas effusa ruebat,   305
matres atque viri defunctaque corpora vita
magnanimum heroum, pueri innuptaeque puellae,
impositique rogis iuvenes ante ora parentum:
quam multa in silvis autumni frigore primo
lapsa cadunt folia, aut ad terram gurgite ab alto   310
quam multae glomerant aves, ubi frigidus annus
trans pontum fugat et terris immittit apricis.
stabant orantes primi transmittere cursum,
tendebantque manus ripae ulterioris amore.
navita sed tristis nunc hos nunc accipit illos,   315
ast alios longe summotos arcet harena.
Aeneas miratus enim motusque tumultu
'dic' ait, 'o virgo, quid vult concursus ad amnem?
quidve petunt animae? vel quo discrimine ripas
hae linquunt, illae remis vada livida verrunt?'   320
olli sic breviter fata est longaeva sacerdos:
'Anchisa generate, deum certissima proles,
Cocyti stagna alta vides Stygiamque paludem,
di cuius iurare timent et fallere numen.

senior, -oris	elderly	longe	far away
crudus, -a, -um	fresh	summoveo, -ere, -ovi, -otus	I remove
viridis, -e	vigorous	arceo, -ere	I keep off
senectus, -utis f.	old age	miror, -ari, -atus sum	I wonder at
huc	305 to this place	tumultus, -us m.	tumult
turba, -ae f.	crowd	aio (defective verb)	I say
ripa, -ae f.	bank	virgo, -inis f.	maiden
ruo, -ere	I rush	concursus, -us m.	gathering
defungor, -i, -nctus sum + abl.	I finish (with)	amnis, -is m.	river
magnanimus, -a, -um	great-hearted	anima, -ae f.	soul
innuptus, -a, -um	unmarried	vel	or
impono, -ere, -posui, -positus	I place on	discrimen, -inis n.	distinction
rogus, -i m.	pyre	linquo, -ere	320 I leave
ante + acc.	before	remus, -i m.	oar
autumnus, -i m.	autumn	vadum, -i n.	shallow water
frigus, -oris n.	cold, frost	lividus, -a, -um	dark
cado, -ere	310 I fall	verro, -ere	I sweep
glomero, -are	I gather	brevis, -e	brief
frigidus, -a, -um	cold	longaevus, -a, -um	long-lived
annus, -i m.	year	Anchises, -ae m.	Anchises
pontus, -i m.	sea	genero, -are, -avi, -atus	I beget
fugo, -are	I put to flight	certus, -a, -um	certain
apricus, -a, -um	sunny	proles, -is f.	offspring
transmitto, -ere	I cross	stagnum, -i n.	pool, marsh
tendo, -ere	I stretch out, go	palus, -udis f.	marsh
ulterior -oris	further	iuro, -are	I swear
navita, -ae m.	315 sailor	timeo, -ere	I fear
tristis, -e	sad	fallo, -ere	I deceive
accipio, -ere	I accept	numen, -inis n.	divine power
ast	but		

304 senior: the comparative of *senex* often means 'rather old'. **cruda . . . senectus:** supply *est.* **deo:** dative of possession.

305 turba: the crowd of souls wanting admission to the underworld. **effusa:** 'pouring out', i.e. from the entrance cave. Note the slow rhythm, contrasting with the rapidity of *effusa ruebat*; Virgil's intention was probably to prepare the reader for the fact that the souls, having reached the river bank, were held there for a long time; thus the main body of the crowd was actually static.

306–8 defunctaque corpora vita: 'and bodies that have finished with life'; *corpora*, as in line 303, does not mean bodies of substance but rather the souls of the dead that retain the form of their bodies in death. **magnanimum** = *magnanimorum*. **rogis:** local ablative. The list of the dead souls is intended to evoke pity, as the ones most likely to be there, the elderly, are not mentioned; the suggestion is that all these souls belong to people who died young.

309–12 This extended <u>simile</u> compares the number of souls awaiting transport to the number of falling leaves or migrating birds in autumn. **quam multa . . . folia:** 'as many as the leaves'. **frigore primo:** ablative of time. **gurgite ab alto:** 'from the churning sea'. **frigidus annus:** 'the cold season of the year'. **terris . . . apricis:** dative of destination.

313 Note the slow rhythm, reflecting the static scene. **primi transmittere cursum:** 'to be the first to direct their course across'; prose would have used *ut* + subjunctive.

314 A famous image, full of pathos. **amore:** causal ablative.

315–16 tristis: probably 'grim' rather than 'sad'. **longe summotos:** 'moving them far away'. **arcet harena:** 'keeps them off the sand'; ablative of separation.

317–18 enim: qualifies *miratus*: 'for he was wondering at (the events)'. **tumultu:** 'the chaotic scene' (ablative of instrument). **vult:** here 'mean' or 'signify'. Note the heavy <u>alliteration</u> and <u>consonance</u> of *m*, suggesting deep emotion.

319–20 quo discrimine: 'by what distinction' (causal ablative). **hae . . . illae:** we are to imagine Aeneas pointing to different groups of souls. **ripas . . . linquunt:** these are the souls driven away by Charon. **remis . . . verrunt:** 'sweep with the oars'; Charon makes the souls work for their crossing.

321 olli: an archaic form of *illi* (dative).

322 Anchisa: ablative of origin; the phrase means no more than 'son of Anchises'. **deum:** = *deorum*. **certissima proles:** 'most certain offspring', i.e. 'unquestionably the offspring'.

323 Stygiamque paludem: the Styx was regularly portrayed as a marsh rather than a river.

324 The order is *cuius numen di timent iurare et fallere*. **numen:** this is a difficult word to translate, as its meaning varies according to context; it may mean power invested in an object by the gods, or the will of the gods, or the god in person, or some less definable immortal spirit. Here it refers to the first of these meanings: even the gods feared to make an oath invoking the Styx and then break it. **iurare et fallere:** 'to break an oath by', taking a direct object.

Questions

1 In lines 305–308, what picture does Virgil draw of the souls on the river bank?

2 How appropriate is the simile in lines 309–312?

3 In lines 313–316, how does Virgil create a sense of pathos?

4 Suggest reasons why lines 306–324 are considered some of the greatest in the whole *Aeneid*.

haec omnis, quam cernis, inops inhumataque turba est;   325
portitor ille Charon; hi, quos vehit unda, sepulti.
nec ripas datur horrendas et rauca fluenta
transportare prius quam sedibus ossa quierunt.
centum errant annos volitantque haec litora circum;
tum demum admissi stagna exoptata revisunt.'   330
constitit Anchisa satus et vestigia pressit
multa putans sortemque animo miseratus iniquam.

*Aeneas saw several comrades who had died on the journey from Troy, including Palinurus,
who explained that he had been killed by tribesmen after swimming ashore. The Sibyl
promised him that the place where he died would bear his name for ever. As soon as Aeneas
and the Sibyl approached Charon, he scolded them for trying to enter the underworld whilst
alive; he feared some form of treachery, such as had been committed by the previous living
visitors. The Sibyl reassured him, showing him the Golden Bough. This was enough to
persuade him to convey the two visitors across the river.*

Cerberus haec ingens latratu regna trifauci   417
personat adverso recubans immanis in antro.
cui vates horrere videns iam colla colubris
melle soporatam et medicatis frugibus offam   420
obicit. ille fame rabida tria guttura pandens
corripit obiectam, atque immania terga resolvit
fusus humi totoque ingens extenditur antro.
occupat Aeneas aditum custode sepulto
evaditque celer ripam inremediabilis undae.   425

cerno, -ere	325 I see	*regnum, -i* n.	kingdom
inops, inopis	helpless	*trifaux, -aucis*	three-throated
inhumatus, -a, -um	unburied	*persono, -are*	I make resound
veho, -ere	I convey	*adversus, -a, -um*	opposite
sepelio, -ire, -ivi, -ultus	I bury	*recubo, -are*	I lie
raucus, -a, -um	roaring	*horreo, -ere*	I bristle
fluentum, -i n.	river	*collum, -i* n.	neck
transporto, -are	I transport	*coluber, -bri* m.	snake
prius quam	before, until	*mel, mellis* n.	420 honey
os, ossis n.	bone	*soporo, -are, -avi, -atus*	I make drowsy
quiesco, -ere, -evi, -etus	I rest	*medico, -are, -avi, -atus*	I drug
centum	a hundred	*frux, frugis* f.	fruit, grain
erro, -are	I wander	*offa, -ae* f.	morsel
litus, -oris n.	shore	*obicio, -ere, -ieci, -iectus*	I throw (to)
circum + acc.	around	*fames, -is* f. *-um*	mad
demum	330 at last	*guttur, -uris* n.	throat
admitto, -ere, -misi, -missus	I admit	*pando, -ere*	I open
exopto, -are, -avi, -atus	I long for	*resolvo, -ere*	I relax
reviso, -ere	I see again	*fundo, -ere, fudi, fusus*	I pour
consisto, -ere, -stiti, -stitus	I stop	*extendo, -ere*	I extend
puto, -are	I consider	*occupo, -are*	I occupy
sors, sortis f.	fate, destiny	*aditus, -us* m.	entrance
miseror, -ari, -atus sum	I pity	*custos, -odis* m.	guard
iniquus, -a, -um	unfair	*inremediabilis, -e*	425 irretraceable
Cerberus, -i m.	417 Cerberus		
latratus, -us m.	barking		

325 **inops:** the crowd is helpless because they are unburied, and so can do nothing.

326 **ille:** supply *est*. **vehit unda:** 'the water bears across'. **sepulti:** supply *sunt*.

327–8 **nec . . . datur:** 'and it is not allowed'. **ripas:** '(across) the banks', and so 'from bank to bank'. Note the chiasmus of *ripas horrendas et rauca fluenta*. **transportare:** supply *eos*. **sedibus:** 'in their resting places', i.e. tombs; local ablative. **quierunt** = *quieverunt*.

329 **haec litora circum** = *circum haec litora*.

330 **stagna exoptata:** 'the pools they have longed for', i.e. the Cocytus and the Styx. Note the slow rhythm of the line, emphasising the long wait for admission.

331–2 **Anchisa satus:** this is similar to *Anchisa generate* in line 322. **vestigia pressit:** repeated from line 197. **animo:** 'in his mind' (local ablative).

417–18 The order is *ingens Cerberus personat haec regna trifauci latratu, recubans immanis in adverso antro*. **Cerberus:** the three-headed monster dog, set to defend the entrance to the central part of the underworld (i.e. on the inner bank of the river), is one of the most famous underworld characters. **immanis:** agrees with *Cerberus*; notice the enclosing word order. **adverso . . . in antro:** the cave was opposite the bank on which the souls gathered, waiting to cross the river.

419–21 **cui:** it is simplest to take this as a possessive dative with *colla*. **colla collubris:** note the alliteration and assonance. The order for lines 420–1 is *obicit offam soporatam melle et medicatis frugibus*. **melle soporatam:** 'made drowsy with honey'; the honey alone of course would not induce sleep; rather it was the 'drugged meal' that sent Cerberus to sleep; the honey simply made the *offa* (any morsel of food) attractive to the hound. The Sibyl had prepared well for the journey.

421–3 **fame rabida:** 'with mad hunger': causal ablative and hypallage: it was the dog that was mad, not the hunger. **obiectam:** supply *offam*. Note the fast rhythm of line 421, reflecting the speed with which the dog pounced on the food. **fusus humi:** 'poured on the ground', and so 'sinking to the ground'. **totoque . . . antro:** 'across the whole cave'; note the enclosing word order.

424–5 **occupat Aeneas aditum:** 'Aeneas occupied the entrance', i.e. 'Aeneas moved quickly into the entrance (to the underworld)'. **sepulto:** 'buried (in sleep)'. **celer:** best translated as an adverb. **inremediabilis undae:** 'of the water across which none could retrace their steps'. *inremediabilis* is a rare word coined by Virgil.

Questions

1 Explain the differences between the two groups of souls.

2 In lines 315–330, why do you think Virgil devotes only half a line to one group of souls and all the rest to the other group?

3 In lines 331–332, what picture emerges of Aeneas?

4 Describe Cerberus.

5 How does Virgil make his description of Cerberus vivid and terrifying?

6 How did Aeneas get past the dog?

Aeneas and the Sibyl passed through the first sections of the underworld. These were reserved for the very young, those accused falsely of crimes, suicides, then the vast area occupied by those who died for love. Aeneas saw a number of famous women.

inter quas Phoenissa recens a vulnere Dido	450
errabat silva in magna; quam Troius heros	
ut primum iuxta stetit agnovitque per umbras	
obscuram, qualem primo qui surgere mense	
aut videt aut vidisse putat per nubila lunam,	
demisit lacrimas dulcique adfatus amore est:	455
'infelix Dido, verus mihi nuntius ergo	
venerat exstinctam ferroque extrema secutam?	
funeris heu tibi causa fui? per sidera iuro,	
per superos et si qua fides tellure sub ima est,	
invitus, regina, tuo de litore cessi.	460
sed me iussa deum, quae nunc has ire per umbras,	
per loca senta situ cogunt noctemque profundam,	
imperiis egere suis; nec credere quivi	
hunc tantum tibi me discessu ferre dolorem.	
siste gradum teque aspectu ne subtrahe nostro.	465
quem fugis? extremum fato quod te adloquor hoc est.'	
talibus Aeneas ardentem et torva tuentem	
lenibat dictis animum lacrimasque ciebat.	

Phoenissus, -a, -um	450 Phoenician	*regina, -ae* f.	queen
recens, -ntis	fresh	*cedo, -ere, cessi, cessus*	I depart
vulnus, -eris n.	wound	*iussum, -i* n.	command
Dido, -onis f.	Dido	*locus, -i* m.	place
Troius, -a, -um	Trojan	*sentus, -a, -um*	rough
iuxta + acc.	next to	*situs, -us* m.	decay, mould
surgo, -ere	I rise up	*cogo, -ere*	I compel, force
mensis, -is m.	month	*profundus, -a, -um*	deep
nubilum, -i n.	cloud	*imperium, -i* n.	command
luna, -ae f.	moon	*ago, -ere, egi, actus*	I drive
demitto, -ere, -misi, -ssus	455 I let fall	*credo, -ere*	I believe
lacrima, -ae f.	tear	*queo, -ere, -ivi*	I can
dulcis, -e	sweet, fond	*discessus, -us* m.	departure
infelix, -icis	unhappy	*dolor, -oris* m.	pain, grief
verus, -a, -um	true	*sisto, -ere*	465 I stop
nuntius, -ii m.	report	*aspectus, -us* m.	sight
exstinguo, -ere, -nxi, -nctus	I destroy	*subtraho, -ere*	I withdraw
extrema, -orum n.pl.	death	*fugio, -ere*	I flee
causa, -ae f.	cause, case	*extremus, -a, -um*	final
sidus, -eris n.	star	*adloquor, -i*	I speak to
iuro, -are	I swear	*torvus, -a, -um*	fierce, grim
superi, -orum m.pl.	gods above	*tueor, -eri, -itus sum*	I look (at)
fides, -ei f.	trust, honour	*lenio, -ire*	I soothe
imus, -a, -um	the depths of	*cieo, -ere*	I rouse
invitus, -a, -um	460 unwilling		

450–1 quas: i.e. the famous women. **Phoenissa . . . Dido:** in Books I–IV, the Trojans were given hospitality by Dido, queen of Carthage on the North African coast. She is called *Phoenissa* because she had sailed from her home in Tyre in Phoenicia (modern Lebanon). She fell in love with Aeneas and, although he reciprocated her love, he was ordered by the gods to leave Carthage, as this city was not the place destined to be the Trojans' new home. As a result Dido killed herself. **recens a vulnere:** she had only recently arrived in the underworld, having died as soon as the Trojans departed. **silva:** Virgil imagined the underworld to be similar in features to the upper world.

451–3 quam . . . iuxta = *iuxta quam*. **ut primum:** 'as soon as'. **obscuram:** Dido was 'dimly seen' because of the shadows cast by the trees; note the <u>enjambement</u>.

453–4 qualem . . . lunam: 'just like the moon'; *qualis* frequently introduces a <u>simile</u>. The order in full would be *qualem (is videt) lunam qui videt (lunam) surgere aut putas (se) vidisse (surgere) per nubila primo mense*; the language is very compressed. Translate as 'just like the moon that a man sees or thinks he has seen rising'. **primo . . . mense:** not 'in the first month' but 'at the beginning of the month' (ablative of time). Note the slow rhythm of line 453. **surgere:** possibly 'appear' would be more appropriate than 'rise'.

455 demisit lacrimas: the subject is *Troius heros* in line 451. **dulcique . . . amore:** this is Virgil's confirmation of the fact that Aeneas really did love Dido; Book IV leaves the reader in some doubt about that as, in the scene where Aeneas takes his leave, he comes across as lacking in emotion and empathy.

456–7 verus . . . nuntius: there has been no mention of a report of Dido's death reaching Aeneas; all we have been told, at the beginning of Book V, is that Aeneas looked back at Carthage and saw the smoke from Dido's funeral pyre, but did not know the cause, though he may have suspected it. **exstinctam:** supply *te* and *esse* (indirect statement). **extrema secutam:** supply *esse* again: 'sought death'.

459–60 et si qua fides . . . est: '(and I swear by) honour if there is any down in the depths of the earth'. **invitus:** it was only when the god Mercury, on the orders of Jupiter, visited Aeneas in Carthage and commanded him to leave that he abandoned the city and Dido.

461–3 iussa deum: *deum* = *deorum*; *iussa* is the subject of *egere* (= *egerunt*). **quae . . . egere:** supply *me* as object. **senta situ:** 'rough with decay' (causal ablative).

463–4 The order is *nec quivi credere me ferre hunc tantum dolorem tibi discessu*.

465 siste gradum: Dido is already walking away from him, unimpressed by his appeal. **aspectu . . . nostro:** 'from my sight' (ablative of separation).

466 quem fugis: echoes Dido's words in Book IV, line 314; just as he walked away from her, so now she walks away from him. **extremum fato:** 'the last (time allowed) by fate'. **quod:** 'that'.

467–8 talibus: with *dictis*. **torva tuentem:** 'looking at grim things', and so 'grim-eyed' a strange description of Dido's *animus* (here 'anger'). **lenibat, ciebat:** conative imperfects ('tried to soothe, tried to rouse'). He tried to rouse her tears as an indication that she still felt something for him and so might forgive him.

Questions

1 Read in English the relevant part of Book IV and then try to explain why Dido refuses to acknowledge Aeneas here.

2 How appropriate is the description of Aeneas as *heros* (451)?

3 Explain the simile in 453–454.

4 Does Aeneas make a good defence of his actions? Does he show remorse?

illa solo fixos oculos aversa tenebat
nec magis incepto vultum sermone movetur   470
quam si dura silex aut stet Marpesia cautes.
tandem corripuit sese atque inimica refugit
in nemus umbriferum, coniunx ubi pristinus illi
respondet curis aequatque Sychaeus amorem.
nec minus Aeneas casu concussus iniquo   475
prosequitur lacrimis longe et miseratur euntem.

They moved on to the most secluded area, reserved for those killed in war. Here he saw many old comrades, who thronged round him; in contrast the Greek warriors fled from him in fear. Next Aeneas saw Priam's son, Deiphobus, who had married Helen after the death of Paris. He explained how Helen had betrayed him to the Greeks after they gained entry to the city, and Menelaus, Helen's first husband, killed him and mutilated him.

hac vice sermonum roseis Aurora quadrigis   535
iam medium aetherio cursu traiecerat axem;
et fors omne datum traherent per talia tempus,
sed comes admonuit breviterque adfata Sibylla est:
'nox ruit, Aenea; nos flendo ducimus horas.
hic locus est, partes ubi se via findit in ambas: 540
dextera quae Ditis magni sub moenia tendit,
hac iter Elysium nobis; at laeva malorum
exercet poenas et ad impia Tartara mittit.'   543
respicit Aeneas subito et sub rupe sinistra   548
moenia lata videt triplici circumdata muro,

figo, -ere, fixi, fixus	I fix	aetherius, -a, -um	heavenly
averto, -ere, -rti -rsus	I turn away	traicio, -ere, -ieci, -iectus	I cross
magis	470 more	axis, -is m.	axle, heavens
incipio, -ere, -cepi, -ceptus	I begin	fors	perhaps
vultus, -us m.	face	traho, -ere	I drag, spend
sermo, -onis m.	speech	adfor, -fari, -fatus sum	I speak to
silex, -icis f.	flint	fleo, flere	I weep
Marpesius, -a, -um	of Marpesus	hora, -ae f.	hour
cautes, -is f.	rock	pars, partis f.	540 part
inimicus, -a, -um	hostile	findo, -ere	I divide, split
refugio, -ere, -fugi	I flee away	ambo, -ae, -o	both, two
umbrifer, -era, -erum	shady	dexter, -era, -erum	on the right
coniunx, -ugis m.	husband	moenia, -ium n.pl.	walls
pristinus, -a, -um	former	Elysium, -i n.	Elysium
respondeo, -ere	I respond (to)	laevus, -a, -um	on the left
cura, -ae f.	care, trouble	exerceo, -ere	I inflict
aequo, -are	I match	poena, -ae f.	punishment
Sychaeus, -i m.	Sychaeus	impius, -a, -um	unholy
minus	475 less	respicio, -ere	548 I look round
casus, -us m.	misfortune	subito	suddenly
concutio, -ere, -cussi, -cussus	I shake	rupes, -is f.	rock
prosequor, -i, -secutus sum	I follow	sinister, -tra, -trum	on the left
vicis f. (defective)	535 exchange	latus, -a, -um	wide, broad
roseus, -a, -um	rosy	triplex, -icis	triple
Aurora, -ae f.	Dawn	circumdo, -dare, -dedi, -datus	I surround
quadrigae, -arum f.pl.	chariot	murus, -i m.	wall

469 illa . . . aversa: 'Dido, turning away'.

470 nec . . . vultum . . . movetur: 'nor was she moved in respect of her face', i.e. 'nor did her expression change'; *vultum* is accusative of respect; alternatively it may be seen as a borrowing of the Greek middle construction, where the passive verb would have a reflexive meaning, with *vultum* its object. incepto . . . sermone: 'by the speech he had begun'.

471 quam si . . . stet: 'than if she were'; *stet* is a stronger alternative to *sit*, implying something fixed and unyielding – appropriate to the rock with which she is compared. Marpesia cautes: 'Marpesian rock' is marble; Marpessus was a mountain on the Greek island of Paros, famed for its marble.

472–4 corripuit sese: 'she snatched hold of herself', and so 'she set off quickly'. coniunx . . . pristinus . . . Sychaeus: Dido's 'previous husband, Sychaeus' had been murdered by her brother for his wealth and power; this was why Dido left Tyre to found Carthage. aequat . . . amorem: 'reciprocates her love'. Although Sychaeus did not die for love and so should not have been in this part of the underworld, Virgil places him there to provide a contrast with Aeneas: the husband who remained loyal, as opposed to the one who abandoned her.

475–6 nec minus . . . concussus: probably not to be taken together, as Dido was clearly not shaken at all by their meeting. Instead *nec minus* means no more than 'also'. casu . . . iniquo: probably 'by her unjust misfortune' rather than by misfortune in general. prosequitur lacrimis: 'trailed after her in tears'; supply *eam*.

535–6 hac vice: 'during this exchange'; ablative of time. roseis . . . quadrigis: 'in her rosy chariot'; local ablative. Aurora: the goddess of Dawn, represented in Greek myth as driving a four-horse chariot bearing the sun across the sky. Note the enclosing word order of *Aurora*. medium . . . traiecerat axem: 'had crossed the mid-point of the heavens', i.e. it was after mid-day. Most editors assume that Virgil is referring to the sun's passage across the sky in the upper world; but in the underworld they would be unaware of this. Another possibility is that Virgil imagines the sun moving across the sky of the underworld. A primitive but persistent belief was that the earth was flat; in this arrangement, a cave leading down from the surface of the upper world could be supposed to give access to the underside, which would be the location of the underworld. After setting in the west, the sun somehow had to make its unseen way back to the east ready to appear again at dawn. Virgil's underworld is illuminated, and the returning sun would naturally provide this illumination.

537–8 omne datum . . . tempus: 'all the time they had been granted'; Virgil does not tell us what the time limit was for Aeneas to leave. traherent: 'they would have spent'; *traherent* would be *traxissent* in prose, part of a virtual unfulfilled condition. per talia: 'engaged in such matters', i.e. conversing with old friends.

539 nox ruit: 'night is hastening on'. nos ducimus horas: 'we are spending hours'.

540 partes . . . in ambas: 'into two parts'.

541–2 dextera: supply *via est*: ' the right-hand one (is the road) which leads . . .'. sub moenia: 'up to the walls', that is the walls that surround the palace of Dis, or Pluto. hac iter Elysium nobis: 'by this (path is) our way to Elysium'. Elysium was the part of the underworld occupied by the souls of good people.

542–3 malorum: 'on the wicked' (objective genitive).

548–9 respicit: Aeneas has already started along the right-hand path to Elysium.

Questions

1 How does Virgil make lines 469–476 particularly moving and effective?

2 Describe the geography of the underworld as it has so far been introduced.

quae rapidus flammis ambit torrentibus amnis,   550
Tartareus Phlegethon, torquetque sonantia saxa.
porta adversa ingens solidoque adamante columnae,
vis ut nulla virum, non ipsi exscindere bello
caelicolae valeant; stat ferrea turris ad auras,
Tisiphoneque sedens palla succincta cruenta   555
vestibulum exsomnis servat noctesque diesque.
hinc exaudiri gemitus et saeva sonare
verbera, tum stridor ferri tractaeque catenae.
constitit Aeneas strepitumque exterritus hausit.
'quae scelerum facies? o virgo, effare; quibusve   560
urgentur poenis? quis tantus plangor ad auras?'
tum vates sic orsa loqui: 'dux inclute Teucrum,
nulli fas casto sceleratum insistere limen;
sed me cum lucis Hecate praefecit Avernis,
ipsa deum poenas docuit perque omnia duxit.   565
Cnosius haec Rhadamanthus habet durissima regna
castigatque auditque dolos subigitque fateri
quae quis apud superos furto laetatus inani
distulit in seram commissa piacula mortem.

rapidus, -a, -um	550 rapid	*haurio, -ire, hausi, haustus*	I drink in
ambio, -ire	I surround	*scelus, -eris* n.	560 crime, sin
torreo, -ere	I burn, seethe	*facies, -ei* f.	appearance
Phlegethon, -ontism	Phlegethon	*urgeo, -ere*	I oppress, beset
torqueo, -ere	I whirl around	*plangor, -oris* m.	wailing
sono, -are	I resound	*inclutus, -a, -um*	famous
saxum, -i n.	rock	*Teucri, -orum* m.pl.	Trojans
solidus, -a, -um	solid, strong	*fas* n. (indecl.)	right
adamas, -antis m.	adamant	*castus, -a, -um*	pure, chaste
columna, -ae f.	pillar, post	*sceleratus, -a, -um*	criminal
vis f. (defective noun)	force	*insisto, -ere*	I set foot on
exscindo, -ere	I destroy	*limen, -inis* n.	threshold
caelicola, -ae m.	god	*Hecate, -es* f.	Hecate
valeo, -ere	I am strong	*praeficio, -ere, -feci, -fectus*	I put in charge
	enough	*Avernus, -a, -um*	of Avernus
ferreus, -a, -um	of iron	*doceo, -ere, -ui, -ctus*	565 I teach
turris, -is f.	tower	*Cnosius, -a, -um*	of Knossos
Tisiphone, -es f.	555 Tisiphone	*Rhadamanthus, -i* m.	Rhadamanthus
palla, -ae f.	cloak	*castigo, -are*	I punish
succingo, -ere, -inxi, -inctus	I wrap	*dolus, -i* m.	deceit, trick
cruentus, -a, -um	blood-stained	*subigo, -ere*	I force
vestibulum, -i n.	entrance	*fateor, -eri, fassus sum*	I confess
exsomnis, -e	sleepless	*apud* + acc.	among
exaudio, -ire	I hear clearly	*furtum, -i* n.	theft
gemitus, -us m.	groan	*laetor, -ari, -atus sum*	I rejoice
saevus, -a, -um	cruel	*inanis, -e*	empty
verber, -eris n.	blow	*differo, -erre, distuli, dilatus*	I put off
stridor, -oris m.	clanking	*serus, -a, -um*	late
catena, -ae f.	chain	*committo, -ere, -misi, -missus*	I perform
strepitus, -us m.	din	*piaculum, -i* n.	atonement
exterreo, -ere, -ui, -itus	I terrify	*mors, -rtis* f.	death

550–1 **rapidus . . . amnis:** note the <u>enclosing word order</u>. **Phlegethon:** another of the five rivers of the underworld, made of fire.

552 Supply *est* with *porta* and *sunt* with *columnae*. **solido adamante:** 'made of solid adamant'; adamant was a name given to the hardest substance known. **columnae:** the door posts are so large they are like columns.

553–4 **ut:** to be taken first. **virum:** = *virorum*. **bello:** 'in war', probably instrumental ablative. **valeant:** to be taken with both *vis nulla* and *ipsi caelicolae*. **stat:** 'stands upright', and so 'points upwards'.

555–6 **Tisiphone:** one of the Furies – three sisters of Greek mythology whose task was to pursue criminals and sinners and drive them mad. **cruenta:** ablative to agree with *palla*. Note the <u>sibilance</u> in line 556, perhaps suggesting a hissing sound that the Fury might be supposed to make.

557–8 **hinc:** i.e. from inside the walls of Tartarus. **exaudiri, sonare:** historic infinitives. **ferri tractaeque catenae:** perhaps an example of <u>hendiadys</u>, meaning 'of iron chains being dragged'.

559 **strepitumque . . . hausit:** 'and drank in the din', i.e. 'listened to the din'.

560–1 **quae . . . facies:** this phrase could be singular or plural; supply therefore *est* or *sunt*. Perhaps the simplest translation is 'what forms of crimes are there'. **quis tantus plangor:** supply a verb such as *oritur*: 'what is this great wailing that rises to the air'.

562–3 **orsa:** supply *est*. **Teucrum** = *Teucrorum*. **nulli fas casto:** supply *est*: 'it is allowed to no one pure'.

564–5 **cum . . . praefecit:** the indicative after *cum* meaning 'when' shows that the clause is purely temporal, with no hint of causality. **lucis . . . Avernis:** dative dependent on *praefecit*. **deum:** = *deorum*.

566 **Cnosius . . . Rhadamanthus:** Rhadamanthus was the son of Zeus and brother of Minos. He was a king ruling part of Crete, whence the adjective *Cnosius*, which relates to Knossos, the most powerful city on the island. After his death, Rhadamanthus was appointed a judge of the dead. **haec . . . regna:** i.e. Tartarus.

567–9 **subigitque fateri:** supply *animas*: 'he compels souls to confess'. The meaning of lines 568–9 is obscure, and there have been many attempts to make sense of them. Perhaps the best interpretation is '(to confess) the crimes in respect of which (*quae*) anyone, rejoicing in fruitless deceit among the people of the upper world, has put off the atonements incurred until the late time of death'. The probable argument is that Rhadamanthus, by compelling souls to admit to their crimes, imposes an inescapable punishment on the guilty, no matter how long they prolong their lives. **quae:** object of *fateri* and an accusative of respect dependent on *laetatus*. **apud superos:** 'among the people of the upper world'. **quis:** 'anyone'. **commissa piacula:** commonly translated as 'crimes committed', which does not easily fit the sense of the rest. **in seram . . . mortem:** 'until the late time of death', i.e. until death, however late.

Questions

1 Describe Tartarus as Virgil depicts it.

2 In lines 550–558, how does Virgil emphasise the terrifying nature of Tartarus?

3 How and when did the Sibyl find out about Tartarus?

4 How is the judgement of the souls carried out?

continuo sontes ultrix accincta flagello   570
Tisiphone quatit insultans, torvosque sinistra
intentans angues vocat agmina saeva sororum.
tum demum horrisono stridentes cardine sacrae
panduntur portae. cernis custodia qualis
vestibulo sedeat, facies quae limina servet?   575
quinquaginta atris immanis hiatibus Hydra
saevior intus habet sedem. tum Tartarus ipse
bis patet in praeceps tantum tenditque sub umbras
quantus ad aetherium caeli suspectus Olympum.
hic genus antiquum Terrae, Titania pubes,   580
fulmine deiecti fundo volvuntur in imo.'

'Here too I saw others who made war on the gods or committed dreadful crimes; some had killed brothers or parents or hoarded wealth or fought unjust wars. All have committed a monstrous sin and are imprisoned within, waiting to be punished.'

haec ubi dicta dedit Phoebi longaeva sacerdos,   628
'sed iam age, carpe viam et susceptum perfice munus;
acceleremus' ait; 'Cyclopum educta caminis   630
moenia conspicio atque adverso fornice portas,
haec ubi nos praecepta iubent deponere dona.'
dixerat et pariter gressi per opaca viarum
corripiunt spatium medium foribusque propinquant.
occupat Aeneas aditum corpusque recenti   635
spargit aqua ramumque adverso in limine figit.

continuo	570 immediately	*pubes, -is* f.	man
sons, sontis	guilty	*fulmen, -inis* n.	thunderbolt
ultrix, -icis	avenging	*deicio, -ere, -ieci, -iectus*	I throw down
accingo, -ere, -nxi, -nctus	I arm	*fundus, -i* m.	bottom, depths
flagellum, -i n.	whip	*volvo, -ere*	I roll, writhe
quatio, -ere	I shake, harry	*Phoebus, -i* m.	628 Phoebus Apollo
insulto, -are	I leap upon	*carpo, -ere*	I pluck, seize
sinistra, -ae f.	left hand	*suscipio, -ere, -cepi, -ceptus*	I undertake
intento, -are	I threaten with	*perficio, -ere*	I complete
anguis, -is m.	snake	*accelero, -are*	630 I hasten
agmen, -inis n.	army, band	*Cyclops, -opis* m.	Cyclops
soror, -oris f.	sister	*educo, -ere, -duxi, -ductus*	I raise
horrisonus, -a, -um	horrible-sounding	*caminus, -i* m.	forge
strido, -ere	I creak	*conspicio, -ere*	I catch sight of
cardo, -inis m.	hinge	*fornix, -icis* m.	arch
custodia, -ae f.	guardian	*praecipio, -ere, -cepi, -ceptus*	I order
qualis, -e	574 what sort of	*iubeo, -ere*	I order
quinquaginta	fifty	*depono, -ere*	I lay down
Hydra, -ae f.	Hydra	*donum, -i* n.	gift
intus	inside	*pariter*	side by side
bis	twice	*gradior, -i, gressus sum*	I walk
praeceps, -itis n.	steep drop	*opacus, -a, -um*	dark
suspectus, -us m.	view upwards	*spatium, -i* n.	space
Olympus, -i m.	Olympus	*foris, -is* f.	door
genus, -eris n.	580 race, offspring	*propinquo, -are* + dat.	I approach
Titanius, -a, -um	of the Titans	*spargo, -ere*	636 I sprinkle

570–2 **intentans**: 'holding out (her snakes towards them)', and so 'threatening (them) with snakes'. Tisiphone was often associated with snakes. **agmina saeva sororum**: she had two sisters, Alecto and Megaera; *agmina* is therefore <u>hyperbolic</u>.

573–4 **sacrae . . . portae**: the gates of Tartarus are 'sacred' in that they give access to a part of the underworld. **horrisono . . . cardine**: singular for plural; probably causal ablative.

574–5 **cernis**: the Sibyl turns from her narrative description of Tartarus and its environs to address Aeneas, who can see Tisiphone because she is outside the gates, but presumably cannot see the Hydra, which is inside the gates. We should assume that Aeneas does not see the gates swing open. **custodia qualis**: 'what sort of guardian'; she refers to Tisiphone. **vestibulo**: local ablative. **facies quae**: parallel to *custodia qualis*: 'what shape'.

576–7 **Hydra saevior**: 'the (even) crueller Hydra', i.e. crueller than Tisiphone. The Hydra was a monster of Greek mythology, a giant serpent with many heads and poisonous breath and blood; it was killed by Hercules for his second labour. **quinquaginta atris immanis hiatibus**: 'huge with fifty black, gaping mouths'. Note the <u>assonance</u> of *a*, imitating the gaping mouths.

577–9 **patet in praeceps**: 'opens to a steep drop', i.e. 'gapes sheer downwards'; Virgil imagines Tartarus to be a huge gaping chasm. **tendit sub umbras**: 'reaches below the shades', i.e. below the rest of the underworld. **bis . . . tantum . . . quantum**: 'twice as much as'. **caeli suspectus**: supply *tendit*: 'a view up to the sky (extends)'. The sense is that Tartarus extends twice as far below Hades as Mount Olympus (the home of the gods) extends above a person on the surface of the earth.

580–1 **Titania pubes**: 'the male Titans'; the Titans were the offspring of Mother Earth (*Terra*); they fought against the gods and were defeated by Zeus (Jupiter) and thrown into Tartarus. **deiectis, volvuntur**: plural according to sense.

629 **sed iam age**: 'but come along now'. **carpe viam**: 'seize the way', and so 'get on with your journey'. **susceptum . . . munus**: this could refer to either the Golden Bough, a gift to Persephone, or the duty to see his father's spirit; perhaps Virgil meant both.

630–1 **moenia, portas**: these belong to Elysium, the home of the blessed, where Aeneas will find his father. **Cyclopum educta caminis**: 'built by the forges of the Cyclopes'; they were the one-eyed giants who worked for the blacksmith god, Vulcan. **adverso fornice**: 'with their archway facing us'.

632 **haec**: to be taken with *dona*: the Golden Bough. **praecepta**: the orders of the underworld deities, as issued to the Sibyl and told to Aeneas.

633–4 **per opaca viarum**: 'through the darkness of the ways'. **corripiunt spatium medium**: 'they hurried through the intervening space'. Note the fast rhythm of line 634, to reflect the increased speed of their journey.

635 **occupat . . . aditum**: 'reaches the threshold'. **recenti spargit aqua**: Aeneas purifies himself before proceeding.

Questions

1 In lines 570–581, how does the Sibyl use imagery and language to paint a terrifying picture of Tartarus?

2 In lines 550–558, what words and phrases indicate that the Sibyl wished to hurry?

3 Why did Aeneas place the Golden Bough inside the gates of Elysium?

his demum exactis, perfecto munere divae,
devenere locos laetos et amoena virecta
fortunatorum nemorum sedesque beatas.
largior hic campos aether et lumine vestit   640
purpureo, solemque suum, sua sidera norunt.

*Here souls were taking exercise or dancing, accompanied by Orpheus. Here too were the
ancient kings of Troy. The Sibyl asked Musaeus where they could find Anchises. Musaeus led
them to the top of a hill, from where they could see the plains of Elysium.*

at pater Anchises penitus convalle virenti
inclusas animas superumque ad lumen ituras   680
lustrabat studio recolens, omnemque suorum
forte recensebat numerum, carosque nepotes
fataque fortunasque virum moresque manusque.
isque ubi tendentem adversum per gramina vidit
Aenean, alacris palmas utrasque tetendit,   685
effusaeque genis lacrimae et vox excidit ore:
'venisti tandem, tuaque exspectata parenti
vicit iter durum pietas? datur ora tueri,
nate, tua et notas audire et reddere voces?
sic equidem ducebam animo rebarque futurum   690
tempora dinumerans, nec me mea cura fefellit.
quas ego te terras et quanta per aequora vectum
accipio! quantis iactatum, nate, periclis!
quam metui ne quid Libyae tibi regna nocerent!'

exigo, -ere, -egi, -actus		I complete	*gramen, -inis* n.		grass
diva, -ae f.		goddess	*alacris, -e*	685	eager
devenio, -ire, -veni, -ventus		I reach	*palma, -ae* f.		hand, palm
amoenus, -a, -um		pleasant	*uterque, -traque, -trumque*		both
virectum, -i n.		meadow	*gena, -ae* f.		cheek
fortunatus, -a, -um		blessed	*vox, vocis* f.		voice
beatus, -a, -um		happy	*excido, -ere, -idi*		I fall out, drop
largus, -a, -um	640	abundant	*exspecto, -are, -avi, -atus*		I wait for
campus, -i m.		plain	*pietas, -atis* f.		dutifulness
vestio, -ire		I clothe	*natus, -i* m.		son
purpureus, -a, -um		purple, brilliant	*notus, -a, -um*		familiar
nosco, -ere, novi, notus		I learn	*reddo, -ere*		I give back
penitus	679	deep within	*equidem*	690	I for my part
virens, ntis		green	*duco, -ere*		I think
includo, -ere, -si, -sus	680	I enclose	*reor, reri, ratus sum*		I think
lustro, -are		I survey	*dinumero, -are*		I count
studium, -i n.		zeal	*fallo, -ere, fefelli, falsus*		I deceive
recolo, -ere		I contemplate	*aequor, -oris* n.		sea
recenseo, -ere		I review	*veho, -ere, vexi, vectus*		I convey
numerus, -i m.		number	*iacto, -are, -avi, -atus*		I toss, buffet
carus, -a, -um		dear	*periclum, -i* n.		danger
nepos, -otis m.		descendant	*metuo, -ere, -ui*		I fear
fortuna, -ae f.		fortune	*Libya, -ae* f.		Africa
mos, moris f.		character, custom	*noceo, -ere* + dat.		I harm

637 munus divae: this could be either 'the gift (of the bough) to the goddess' or 'their duty to the goddess'. Note the chiastic order and slow rhythm of the line.

638–9 locos laetos: accusative of goal of motion. Note the chiasmus again. They have reached Elysium, the half of the underworld reserved for the souls of the good. **virecta . . . nemorum:** 'the green spaces of the groves' i.e. 'amid the groves'. **sedes beatas:** 'the happy homes', and so 'the homes of the blest; *fortunatorum* and *beatas* have been attached to the places rather than the souls that inhabited them, examples of hypallage. Note the chiastic word order again in line 639: adjective – noun – noun – adjective. In all three examples of chiasmus Virgil says more or less the same thing twice; his intention is to leave no doubt in the reader's mind that the travellers have reached the climax of their visit.

640–1 largior . . . aether: 'an ampler sky', i.e. than that over Tartarus. **et:** the sense is 'a sky ampler and (illuminated) with brilliant light'. **norunt** = noverunt: '(the souls here) know'. **solem . . . suum:** see note on 535–6.

679–83 at: this marks a change of subject. **penitus:** used here like a preposition with the ablative. **inclusas animas:** i.e. the souls enclosed in the valley, which borders the river Lethe, from which souls must drink to forget their previous lives before being reborn, after spending a thousand years in the underworld. **ituras:** 'destined to travel' to the world of the living. **studio recolens:** 'contemplating them with enthusiasm'. **omnem suorum . . . numerum:** 'the whole number of his family'. **virum** = *virorum*. **manusque:** 'and their workmanship', i.e. 'their achievements'. Note the chiastic word order of line 683, with balancing alliterative pairs at each end.

684–5 tendentem adversum: 'walking towards him'. **alacris:** best translated as an adverb: 'eagerly'.

686 effusae: supply *sunt*. **genis:** local ablative: **excidit ore:** 'fell from his mouth,' and so 'issued from his mouth'.

687–8 tuaque . . . pietas: 'and your dutifulness'; Aeneas' *pietas* is regularly pointed out by Virgil. **exspectata parenti:** 'awaited by your parent'; *parenti* is dative of the agent. **vicit:** i.e. has persuaded to complete.

688–9 datur: 'is it granted'. **reddere voces:** 'and to address you in return'.

690–1 animo: local ablative. **rebarque futurum:** supply *id . . . esse*: 'and I supposed it would be'. **tempora dinumerans:** 'calculating the passage of time'. **nec me mea cura fefellit:** 'nor has my anxiety deceived me', i.e. 'my anxiety has not caused me to miscalculate'.

692–3 The order is (*per*) *quas terras et per quanta aequora ego accipio te vectum* (*esse*). The sense is 'what a journey you must have had before I welcome you'. **iactatum:** supply *te . . . esse*.

694 ne quid: 'lest . . . in any way'. **Libyae . . . regna:** i.e. Carthage, where Aeneas stayed as the guest and lover of Dido.

Questions

1 In lines 637–41, how does Virgil make Elysium appear attractive?

2 Describe what Anchises was doing as Aeneas approached.

3 How does Anchises show his emotion on seeing his son? List as many ways as you can.

ille autem: 'tua me, genitor, tua tristis imago   695
saepius occurrens haec limina tendere adegit;
stant sale Tyrrheno classes. da iungere dextram,
da, genitor, teque amplexu ne subtrahe nostro.'
sic memorans largo fletu simul ora rigabat.
ter conatus ibi collo dare bracchia circum;   700
ter frustra comprensa manus effugit imago,
par levibus ventis volucrique simillima somno.

Aeneas noticed the river and the host of souls flitting round it. Shocked by the sight, he asked his father for an explanation.

tum pater Anchises: 'animae, quibus altera fato   713
corpora debentur, Lethaei ad fluminis undam
securos latices et longa oblivia potant.   715
has equidem memorare tibi atque ostendere coram,
iampridem hanc prolem cupio enumerare meorum,
quo magis Italia mecum laetere reperta.'

Aeneas asked Anchises to explain why some souls would want a second life. He said, 'All living creatures are imbued with spirit, but bodies pollute the spirit, and so after death all souls need to be purified before being allowed into Elysium. Then, after a thousand years, they are summoned to the river Lethe, so that when they re-enter a body they will do so without memory.' He now led Aeneas and the Sibyl into the midst of the gathered souls.

nunc age, Dardaniam prolem quae deinde sequatur   756
gloria, qui maneant Itala de gente nepotes,
inlustres animas nostrumque in nomen ituras,
expediam dictis, et te tua fata docebo.

genitor, -oris m.	695 father	debeo, -ere	714 I owe
occurro, -ere	I come to meet	Lethaeus, -a, -um	of the Lethe
adigo, -ere, -egi, -actus	I drive	securus, -a, -um	715 free from care
sal, salis m.	sea	latex, -icis m.	water
Tyrrhenus, -a, -um	Tyrrhenian	oblivium, -i n.	forgetfulness
iungo, -ere	I join	poto, -are	I drink
amplexus, -us m.	embrace	ostendo, -ere	I show
memoro, -are	I say, recount	coram	face to face
fletus, -us m.	weeping	iampridem	long since
simul	at the same time	cupio, -ere	I wish
rigo, -are	I moisten, wet	enumero, -are	I count
ter	700 three times	quo + comparative	so that
conor, -ari, -atus sum	I try	Dardanius, -a, -um	756 Trojan
bracchium, -i n.	arm	gloria, -ae f.	glory
comprendo, -ere, -ndi, -nsus	I grasp	maneo, -ere	I remain
effugio, -ere, -fugi	I escape	gens, gentis f.	race, stock
par, paris	equal, similar	inlustris, -e	famous
levis, -e	light	nomen, -inis n.	name
volucer, -cris, -cre	winged	expedio, -ire	I relate
somnus, -i m.	sleep		

695–6 ille: supply *dixit*. tua ... tua: the repetition shows heightened emotion. saepius: an exaggeration, as the ghost of his father only appeared to him twice. haec limina tendere: 'to make for these abodes'; *limina* is accusative of goal of motion.

697–8 stant: 'are secure'. sale Tyrrheno: 'in the Tyrrhenian Sea', that is the sea that borders the west coast of Italy; Aeneas is reassuring his father that the Trojan ships have safely reached their destination. da iungere dextram: either 'give (me) your right hand to clasp' or 'allow (me) to clasp your right hand'; the repetition of *da* shows his lack of success. amplexu ... nostro: 'from my embrace' (ablative of separation).

700–2 ter ... ter: the <u>anaphora</u> emphasises the failure to embrace. The lines are repeated from Book II, 792–4, where Aeneas tried unsuccessfully to embrace the ghost of his newly dead wife, Creusa. Perhaps Virgil intended the reader to realise that Aeneas' love for his father matched that for his wife. conatus: supply *est*. dare ... circum: this is the compound verb *circumdare* ('to place ... round'), split and reversed. The repetition of soft *l*, *m* and *s* sounds emphasises the insubstantial nature of the ghost.

713–15 Anchises: supply *dixit*. Lethaei ad fluminis undam: 'by the waters of the river Lethe'. securos latices: 'water that removes their cares', by making them forget. longa oblivia: '(water which causes) long-lasting forgetfulness'.

716–17 The order is *equidem iampridem cupio memorare tibi has (animas) atque ostendere (eas) coram, (et) enumerare hanc prolem meorum*. cupio: 'I have been wanting'; the present is regularly used after words like *iampridem* instead of the perfect. This verb has all three infinitives dependent upon it, of which *enumerare* amplifies the previous ones.

718 laetere: = *laeteris* (present subjunctive of purpose after *quo*). Italia ... reperta: 'now that you have found Italy'.

756–9 nunc age: 'come now'. The order is *expediam dictis quae gloria deinde sequatur Dardaniam prolem, (et) qui nepotes maneant de Itala gente, inlustres animas iturasque in nostrum nomen, et docebo te tua fata*. Dardaniam prolem: the descendants of the Trojans. deinde: 'in the future'. Itala de gente: 'of Italian stock', following intermarriage with the Trojans. animas: loosely in apposition to the two indirect questions, all the objects of *expediam*. These lines serve to introduce a long pageant of heroes from Roman history, i.e. from Aeneas' future but Virgil's past. Anchises' intention is to fire Aeneas with enthusiasm for the future, after becoming weary of travelling for years across the seas and anxious about the battles to come.

Questions

1 In lines 697–702, how does Virgil increase the pathos of the meeting of father and son? Discuss both the content and the style.

2 What does Anchises suggest happens to the souls of the dead?

3 What is Anchises' purpose in summoning Aeneas to the underworld?

Anchises pointed out the souls of all the kings of Alba Longa and Rome; all the great generals who would defeat Rome's enemies; and Julius Caesar and Augustus, who would trace their ancestry back through Aeneas' son, Iulus, to Aeneas himself.

'excudent alii spirantia mollius aera   847
(credo equidem), vivos ducent de marmore vultus,
orabunt causas melius, caelique meatus
describent radio et surgentia sidera dicent: 850
tu regere imperio populos, Romane, memento
(hae tibi erunt artes), pacique imponere morem,
parcere subiectis et debellare superbos.'

Anchises also pointed out two men who would be named Marcellus: one a great general who would defeat Carthaginian forces in the Second Punic War; the second a young man who died while Virgil was writing the Aeneid, *and whose death was widely mourned.*

quae postquam Anchises natum per singula duxit   888
incenditque animum famae venientis amore,
exim bella viro memorat quae deinde gerenda,   890
Laurentesque docet populos urbemque Latini,
et quo quemque modo fugiatque feratque laborem.
sunt geminae Somni portae, quarum altera fertur
cornea, qua veris facilis datur exitus umbris,
altera candenti perfecta nitens elephanto,   895
sed falsa ad caelum mittunt insomnia manes.
his ibi tum natum Anchises unaque Sibyllam
prosequitur dictis portaque emittit eburna.
ille viam secat ad naves sociosque revisit.
tum se ad Caietae recto fert litore portum,   900
ancora de prora iacitur; stant litore puppes.

excudo, -ere	I hammer out	fama, -ae f.	glory, fame
spiro, -are	I breathe	exim	890 then
mollis, -e	soft	gero, -ere	I manage
aes, aeris n.	bronze	Laurens, -ntis	of Laurentum
vivus, -a, -um	living	Latinus, -i m.	Latinus
marmor, -oris n.	marble	quisque, quaeque, quidque	each, every
meatus, -us m.	course	corneus, -a, -um	of horn
describo, -ere	850 I map, plot	exitus, -us m.	way out
radius, -i m.	rod, compass	candens, -ntis	895 shining, white
rego, -ere	I rule	nitens, -ntis	gleaming
populus, -i m.	people, nation	elephantus, -i m.	ivory
memini, -isse	I remember	falsus, -a, -um	false
ars, artis f.	art, skill	insomnium, -i n.	dream
pax, pacis f.	peace	una	together
impono, -ere	I impose	emitto, -ere	I send forth
parco, -ere + dat.	I spare	eburnus, -a, -um	(of) ivory
subicio, -ere, -ieci, -iectus	I conquer	seco, -are	I cut
debello, -are	I crush	Caieta, -ae f.	900 Caieta
superbus, -a, -um	proud	rectus, -a, -um	straight
singuli, -ae, -a	888 individual	ancora, -ae f.	anchor
incendo, -ere, -di, -sus	I inflame	prora, -ae f.	prow

847 **alii**: i.e. the Greeks, always respected by the Romans for their artistic and scientific skills. **spirantia . . . aera**: 'breathing bronze', i.e. lifelike sculptures. **mollius**: 'more softly', i.e. 'with softer lines' (than the Romans).

848 **ducent**: 'they will carve'.

849–50 **orabunt causas**: 'they will plead cases' (in the lawcourts). **caeli meatus**: 'the courses of the sky', i.e. 'the movements of the heavenly bodies'. **radio**: 'with the measuring rod'. **surgentia sidera dicent**: 'will predict the risings of the stars'.

851–3 These are some of the most famous lines from the *Aeneid*. Having conceded first place in the arts and sciences to the Greeks, Anchises claims for the Romans first place for strong and fair government. Virgil's purpose is twofold: to charge Aeneas with a renewed sense of purpose, now that he knows the greatness of the achievements of his descendants; and to remind his readers, demoralised after protracted civil wars, of their rightful place in the world. **tu . . . memento**: 'you remember' (imperative). **imperio**: 'with your authority'. **Romane**: the meaning is again twofold: Aeneas, because his descendants will be Romans, is virtually a Roman himself; the readers, of course, are also Roman. **hae . . . artes**: as opposed to the ones listed in lines 847–50. **paci imponere morem**: 'to impose custom on peace', i.e. to make peace the norm.

888–9 **per singula**: 'through each individual thing', i.e. through all the sights. Note the slow rhythm of line 888, suggesting that Anchises was prolonging his son's visit. **famae venientis**: 'of the glory to come', i.e. that his descendants will achieve.

890 **bella**: the war that the Trojans would have to fight against the Latins and their allies in order to gain a place to settle in Italy. This war occupies the rest of the *Aeneid*. **deinde**: 'next'. **gerenda**: supply *sunt* or *erunt*.

891 **Laurentes . . . populos**: 'the Laurentine peoples', i.e. the tribes which inhabited the lands around the city of Laurentum, which lay to the south-east of Rome. **urbem Latini**: king Latinus was the king of Laurentum. It was his daughter, Lavinia, that Aeneas would marry.

892 **quo . . . modo**: 'how'. **quemque . . . laborem**: 'each task', i.e. hardship to be faced.

893–6 Virgil took his idea of the two Gates of Sleep, one of horn and one of ivory, from Homer's *Odyssey*. **fertur**: 'is said'; supply *esse*. **qua**: 'by means of which'. **veris . . . umbris**: 'true spirits', i.e. those who had spent their allotted time in the underworld and were ready for a new life. **perfecta**: supply *esse*: 'to have been made'. **candenti . . . elephanto**: ablative of material. **falsa . . . insomnia**: 'false dreams', sent out through the ivory gate by the spirits. There have been many attempts to interpret this image; clearly 'false dreams' are opposed to 'true spirits'; since Aeneas and the Sibyl are not 'true spirits' in the above sense, they are treated as 'false dreams'; perhaps we are meant to see Aeneas' visit to the underworld as being like a dream, false in the sense that he experienced it not as a 'true spirit'.

897–8 **his . . . dictis**: 'with these words', presumably meaning an account of the gates. **porta emittit eburna**: 'he sent them out through the ivory gate', just as was explained in line 896.

899 **ille**: Aeneas. **viam secat**: 'he made his way'.

900–1 **Caietae . . . portum**: Caieta lay a third of the way from Cumae to the mouth of the Tiber, the Trojans' destination. **recto . . . litore**: 'straight along the coast'.

Questions

1 What contrast does Anchises draw between the Greeks and the Romans? Why does he make this contrast?

2 Why do you think lines 851–852 have become so famous?

3 Why do you think Anchises sent Aeneas out through the Gate of Ivory?

Word list

abdo, -ere, -didi, -ditus	I hide
abduco, -ere, -duxi, -ductus	I draw back
abeo, -ire	I go away
abies, -etis f.	pine wood
aboleo, -ere	I remove
abrumpo, -ere	I break off
abscondo, -ere	I hide
absens, -ntis	absent
absisto, -ere	withdraw
abstineo, -ere, -ui, -entus	I refrain, hold back
absumo, -ere	I consume, eat
Acarnan, -anis	Acarnanian
accelero, -are	I hasten
accendo, -ere, -cendi, -census	I inflame, fire
accessus, -us m.	approach, access
accingo, -ere	I make myself ready, arm
accipio -ere	I receive, hear, accept
accurro, -ere	I run up
acer, acris, acre	spirited, fierce, sharp
acerbus, -a, -um	harsh, bitter
Acestes, -ae m. (acc. *-en*)	Acestes
Achates, -ae m.	Achates
Acheron, -ontis m.	river Acheron
Achilles, -ei or *-i* m.	Achilles
Achivi, -orum m.pl.	the Greeks
Acidalius, -a, -um	Acidalian
acies, -ei f.	eyesight, blade
acutus, -a, -um	sharp
adamas, -antis m.	adamant
addo, -ere	I add
adeo	so
adeo, -ire	I face, reach, approach address
adfatus, -us m.	address
adfero, -re	I bring
adfligo, -ere, -flixi, -flictus	I crush
adflo, -are	I breathe . . . upon
adfor, -ari, -fatus sum	I address, speak to
adhibeo, -ere	I invite
adhuc	still
adigo, -ere, -egi, -actus	I drive, hurl
adimo, -ere, -emi, -emptus	I take away
aditus, -us m.	entrance, approach
adiuvo, -are	I help
adloquor, -i, -locutus sum	I address, speak to
admitto, -ere, -misi, -missus	I admit
admoneo, -ere	I advise, warn
admoveo, -ere, -movi, -motus	I move . . . to
adoro, -are	I worship
adquiro, -ere	I gain
adsuetus, -a, -um	accustomed
adsultus, -us m.	assault
adsum, -esse, -fui	I am favourable, present, here
adsurgo, -ere	I rise up
adveho, -ere, -exi, -ectus	I convey (to)
advento, -are	I approach
adventus, -us m.	approach
adversus, -a, -um	opposite
adverto, -ere	I turn . . . to(wards)
advoco, -are	I summon
adytum, -i n.	shrine, sanctuary
Aeacides, -ae m.	Achilles
Aeaeus, -a, -um	of Aea, Colchian
aedes, -is f.	house, room
aedifico, -are	I build
Aegaeus, -a, -um	Aegean
aeger, -gra, -grum	sick, weary, painful, distraught, diseased, heartbroken
aemulus, -a, -um	jealous
Aeneades, -um m.pl.	the family of Aeneas
Aeneas, -ae m.	Aeneas
aënus, -a, -um	(made of) bronze
aequaevus, -a, -um	of similar age
aequo, -are	I make equal
aequo, -are, -avi, -atus	I keep pace with, match, make equal
aequor, -oris n.	level surface, sea, plain
aequus, -a, -um	impartial, equal, fair
aër, aëris m. (acc. *aera*)	air
aeratus, -a, -um	bronze-plated
aes, aeris n.	bronze, oar, cymbal, trumpet
aestas, -atis f.	summer
aestuo, -are	I seethe
aestus, -us m.	tide
aeternus, -a, -um	eternal, everlasting
aether, -eris (acc. *-era*) m.	sky, heaven
aetherius, -a, -um	heavenly
aethra, -ae f.	clear sky
Aetna, -ae f.	Mt Etna

Africus, -i m.	the Southwest Wind	*Amycus, -i* m.	Amycus
age, agite!	come on!	*an*	= *-ne*
Agenor, -oris m.	Agenor	*an*	or
ager, agri m.	field, land	*Anchises, -ae* (acc. *-en*)	Anchises
agger, -is m.	bank, embankment, mound	*Anchisiades, -ae* m.	son of Anchises
aggero, -are	I swell	*ancora, -ae* f.	anchor
agito, -are	I pursue	*anguis, -is* m./f.	snake, serpent
agmen, -inis n.	army, line, course, moving herd, host, band	*anhelitus, -us* m.	panting
		anima, -ae f.	soul, life, breath
		animal, -is n.	animal
agnosco, -ere, -novi, -nitus	I recognise	*animus, -i* m.	mind, heart, spirit, courage
ago, -ere, egi, actus	I drive, treat, chase, hunt, do	*Anius, -i* m.	Anius
		Anna, -ae f.	Anna
agrestis, -e	rustic	*annus, -i* m.	year, season
aio (defective verb)	I say	*annuus, -a, -um*	annual
ala, -ae f.	wing	*ante ... quam*	before
alacris, -e	eager	*ante* + acc.	before, than, in front of
alatus, -a, -um	winged		
Albanus, -a, -um	Alban	*antefero, -ferre*	I put ... before
albus, -a, -um	white	*antiquus, -a, -um*	ancient
Alcides, -ae m. (acc. *-en*)	Hercules	*antrum, -i* n.	cave
aliger, -gera, -gerum	winged	*aper, apri* m.	wild boar
alii ... alii	some ... others	*aperio, ire*	I open
aliqui, -qua, -quod	some	*apertus, -a, -um*	open, clear
aliquis, -quid	some	*apex, -icis* m.	top, point of flame
aliter	otherwise	*Apollo, -inis* m.	Apollo
almus, -a, -um	kindly	*appareo -ere*	I become visible
alo, -ere	I nourish	*appello, -ere, -puli, pulsus*	I drive ... to
alta, -orum n.pl.	the depths	*apricus, -a, -um*	sunny
altaria, -ium n.pl.	altar	*apto, -are*	I make ready
alte	high up	*apud* + acc.	among
alter, -era, -erum	the other, a second	*aqua, -ae* f.	water
alterno, -are	I hesitate	*Aquilo, -onis* m.	North Wind
alternus, -a, -um	by turns	*aquosus, -a, -um*	watery, rainy
altum, -i n.	the deep, sea	*ara, -ae* f.	altar
altus, -a, -um	high	*arbor / arbos, -oris* f.	tree
alvus, -i f.	belly	*Arcadius, -a, -um*	Arcadian
amans, -ntis m./f.	lover	*arcanum, -i* n.	secret, mystery
Amazonius, -a, -um	of the Amazons	*arceo, -ere*	I keep ... from, keep off
ambages, -um f.pl.	a complicated story	*arcus, -us* m.	bow, rainbow
ambedo, -ere, -edi, -esus	I gnaw round	*ardens, -ntis*	keen, furious, blazing, burning
ambiguus, -a, -um	doubtful	*ardeo, -ere*	I blaze, am keen
ambio, -ire	I placate, surround	*ardesco, -ere*	I am inflamed
ambo, -ae, -o	both, two	*arduus, -a, -um*	high, high up
amens, -ntis	out of one's mind, frantic	*areo, -ere*	I am parched
		argentum, -i n.	silver
amictus, -us m.	cloak	*Argolicus, -a, -um*	Argive
amicus, -a, -um	friendly	*arguo, -ere*	I show up, prove
amitto, -ere, -misi, -missus	I lose	*aries, -etis* f.	battering ram
amnis, -is m.	river	*arma, -orum* n.pl.	arms, tackle
amoenus, -a, -um	pleasant	*armatus, -a, -um*	armed
Amor, -oris m.	Cupid	*armentum, -i* n.	herd
amor, -oris m.	love	*armo, -are*	I arm, equip
amplector, -i, -plexus sum	I entwine, embrace, encircle, enclose	*aro, -are*	I plough
		arquitenens, -ntis	carrying a bow
		arrectus, -a, -um	stood on end, raised up
amplexus, -us m.	embrace		
amplius	any more	*arrigo, -ere, -rexi, -rectus*	I raise, lift
amplus, -a, -um	plentiful	*ars, artis* f.	scheme, art, skill

artifex, -icis m.	artist
artus, -a, -um	tight-fitting
artus, us m.	limb
arvum, -i n.	arable field, field
arx, arcis f.	citadel, defence
Ascanius, -i m.	Ascanius (Aeneas' son)
ascendo, -ere	I climb
ascensus, -us m.	climbing
Asia, -ae f.	Asia (i.e. Asia Minor)
aspecto, -are	I look at
aspectus, -us m.	appearance, sight
asper, -era, -erum	resentful, cruel
aspergo, -ere, -si, -sus	I splash, spatter
aspicio, -ere	I look at, see, observe
asporto, -are	I take away
ast	but
asto, -are, -stiti	I stand
astrum, -i n.	star
ater, atra, atrum	black, dark
Atridae, -arum m.pl.	the Atreidae, sons of Atreus
atrium, -i n.	hall
attollo, -ere	I raise, raise up
attonitus, -a, -um	stunned
auctor, -oris m.	ancestor, guarantor
audax, -acis	bold
audeo, -ere, ausus sum	I dare
aufero, -re, abstuli, ablatus	I take away
augur, -uris m.	augur, prophet
augurium, -i n.	augury, omen, foreboding
aula, -ae f.	palace
aura, ae f.	air, breeze, sky, gleam
aureus, -a, -um	golden, made of gold, gilded
auricomus, -a, -um	golden-leaved
auris, -is f.	ear
Aurora, -ae f.	Dawn
aurum, -i n.	gold
Ausonius, -a, -um	Ausonian, Italian
auspex, -icis c.	guide, leader
auspicium, -i n.	auspice
Auster, -tri m.	South Wind
ausum, -i n.	daring attempt
autumnus, -i m.	autumn
auxilium, -i n.	help
avarus, -a, -um	miserly
avehor, -i, -vectus sum	I sail away
avello, -ere, -velli, -vulsus	I pluck off, tear off, tear out
Avernus, -a, -um	of Avernus
Avernus, -i m.	Lake Avernus
averto, -ere, -rti -rsus	I turn away, keep away
avidus, -a, -um	eager
avis, -is f.	bird
avium, -i n.	by-way
axis, -is m.	axle, heavens
bacchor, -ari, -atus sum	I roam frenziedly
Bacchus, -i m.	Bacchus
balteus, -i m.	belt
barba, -ae f.	beard
barbaricus, -a, -um	foreign
beatus, -a, -um	blessed, fortunate, happy
Bebrycia, -ae f.	Bebrycia
bellum, -i n.	war
bigae, -arum f.pl.	a two-horse chariot
bini, -ae, -a	two each
bipennis, -is f.	two-headed axe, two-edged axe
bis	twice
blandus, -a, -um	flattering, charming
bos, bovis m./f.	bull, cow, ox
bracchium, -i n.	arm
brevis, -e	brief
bruma, -ae f.	winter
Butes, -ae m. (acc. *-en*)	Butes
Byrsa, -ae f.	Byrsa (bull's hide)
cado, -ere	I fall, set
caecus, -a, -um	blind, secret, dark, hidden
caedes, -is f.	murder, slaughter
caedo, -ere, cecidi, caesus	I slaughter
caelestis, -e	of the gods
caelicola, -ae m.	god
caelo, -are, -avi, -atus	I engrave
caelum, -i n.	sky, heaven
caenum, -i n.	mud
caeruleus, -a, -um	dark, blue
caesaries, acc. *-em*	hair, locks
caestus, -us m.	boxing glove
Caieta, -ae f.	Caieta
calx, calcis f.	heel
caminus, -i m.	furnace, forge
campus, -i m.	plain, field, battlefield
candens, -ntis	shining, white, white-hot
caneo, -ere	I am white
canis, -is m./f.	dog
canities, -ei f.	greyness
cano, -ere	I sing, prophesy, recount, sing of
canus, -a, -um	ancient
capesso, -ere	I make for, seek, seize
capra, -ae f.	goat
caprigenus, -a, -um	goat-born
captiva, -ae f.	(female) captive
capulus, -i m.	hilt
caput, -itis n.	head
cardo, -inis m.	hinge, crucial moment
careo, -ere + abl.	I am without
carina, -ae f.	keel, ship

carpo, -ere	I wear down, pluck, seize	cirdumdatus, -a, -um	wearing
Carthago, -inis f.	Carthage	Cithaeron, -onis m.	(Mt) Cithaeron
carus, -a, -um	dear	citus, -a, -um	swift
Cassandra, -ae f.	Cassandra	clam	secretly
castellum, -i n.	fortress	clamor, -oris m.	shout, shouting, scream, cry
castigo, -are	I rebuke, punish		
castus, -a, -um	pure, chaste	clangor, -oris m.	flapping noise
casus, -us m.	fall, fate, misfortune, disaster, bad luck	claresco, -ere	I become audible
		clarus, -a, -um	bright
		classis, -is f.	fleet
		claudo, -ere	I bar, shut, enclose
catena, -ae f.	chain	claustrum, -i n.	the bolt of a door
caterva, -ae f.	crowd	clipeus, -i m.	shield
Caucasus, -i m.	Caucasus	Cnosius, -a, -um	of Knossos, Cretan
causa, -ae f.	cause, reason, case	Cocytus, -i m.	Cocytus
cautes, -is f.	rock	coepi, -isse, coeptus	I began
cavatus, -a, -um	hollowed out	coetus, -us m.	assembly
cavea, -ae f.	grandstand	cognomen, -inis n.	cognomen (third name), old name, name
caverna, -ae f.	hollow, cavity		
cavo, -are, -avi, -atus	I pierce		
cavus, -a, -um	hollow	cogo, -ere	I compel, force, assemble, thicken, gather
cedo, -ere, cessi, cessus	I fail, give way, yield, depart		
		colitur	there exists
Celaeno, -us f.	Celaeno	colligo, -ere, -legi, -lectus	I gather together, take in
celebro, -are	I celebrate		
celer, -eris, -ere	swift	collis, -is m.	hill
celero, -are	I hasten	collum, -i n.	neck
celo, -are	I conceal	colo, -ere, colui, cultus	I inhabit, look after, worship
celsus, -a, -um	lofty, high		
centum	a hundred	color, -oris m.	colour
Cerberus, -i m.	Cerberus	coluber, -bri m.	snake
cerebrum, -i n.	brain	columba, -ae f.	dove
Ceres, -eris f.	Ceres	columna, -ae f.	pillar, post, column
cerno, -ere	I see, observe	coma, -ae f.	hair
certamen, -inis n.	contest, race	comes, -itis m.	companion
certe	yet	comitor, -ari	I accompany
certus, -a, -um	sure, reliable, fixed, unwavering, definite	commendo, -are	I entrust
		commisceo, -ere, -ui, -ixtus	I mix, mingle, mix together
cerva, -ae f.	doe, hind		
cervix, -icis f.	neck	committo, -ere	I commit an offence, engage in, perform
cervus, -i m.	deer		
cesso, -are	I am inactive		
ceu	just as	commoveo, -ere, -movi, -motus	I shock, shake, wave
Charon, -ontis m.	Charon		
chlamys, -ydis f.	cloak	communis, -e	shared
chorus, -i m.	band of dancers	compages, -is f.	jointed timber
cieo, -ere	I rouse	compago, -inis f.	fastening
cingo, -ere	I surround, wreathe, enclose	compello, -are	I address
		compello, -ere, -puli, -pulsus	I drive
Circe, -ae f.	Circe	complector, -i, -xus sum	I embrace, hold
circum	around, all round	compleo, -ere	I fill
circum + acc.	across, around	complexus, -us m.	embrace
circumdo, -dare, -dedi, -datus	I surround, put . . . round, enclose	compono, -ere	I settle, allay, build
circumfundo, -ere, -fudi, -fusus	I pour around, envelop	comprendo, -ere, -ndi, -nsus	I grasp, clutch at
		concido, -ere, -cidi	I collapse, fall
circumsto, -are, -steti	I take possession of	conclamo, -are	I shout
		concludo, -ere	I enclose
circumvenio, -ire	I encircle	concretus, -a, -um	matted together
circumvolo, -are	I fly round	concursus, -us m.	gathering
circus, -i m.	race-track, circle	concutio, -ere, -cussi, -cussus	I shake

condo, -ere	I found, hide, establish, bury, store	*Corybantius, -a, -um*	of the Corybantes
confectus, -a, -um	worn out	*Corythus, -i* m.	Corythus
conficio, -ere, -feci, -fectus	I complete	*costa, -ae* f.	rib
confido, -ere + dat.	I trust	*creber, -bra, -brum*	abounding, frequent, abundant
confugio, -ere	I appeal	*credo, -ere*	I believe, entrust
confusus, -a, -um	confused	*crepito, -are*	I rustle, rattle
conicio, -ere, -ieci, -iectus	I throw, shoot	*cresco, -ere, -evi, -etus*	I grow
coniugium, -i n.	marriage	*Cresius, -a, -um*	Cretan
coniunx, -iugis m./f.	husband, wife	*Creta, -ae* f.	Crete
conlabor, -i, -lapsus sum	I collapse, faint	*Cretaeus, -a, -um*	Cretan
conluceo, -ere	I glow	*cretus, -a, -um*	sprung
conor, -ari, -atus sum	I try	*Creusa, -ae* f.	Creusa
conscius, -a, -um	aware, conscious	*crinis, -is* m.	hair
consero, -ere, -erui -ertus	I fasten together	*crudelis, -e*	cruel
consessus, -us m.	assembly, spectators	*crudus, -a, -um*	raw, fresh
		cruentus, -a, -um	blood-stained, gory
consido, -ere, -sedi	I settle	*cruor, -oris* m.	blood, gore
consilium, -i n.	plan	*cubile, -is* n.	bed
consisto, -ere, -stiti, -stitus	I stop, stand	*culmen, -inis* n.	top, summit, roof, peak
conspectus, -us m.	sight		
conspicio, -ere	I catch sight of	*culpa, -ae* f.	fault
constituo, -ere	I place, stand	*cultrix, -icis* f.	female inhabitant
consultum, -i n.	decree, oracle	*cultus, -us* m.	dress
consumo, -ere, -psi, -ptus	I spend	*cumba, -ae* f.	boat
consurgo, -ere	I rise	*cumulus, -i* m.	mass
contactus, -us m.	touch	*cunabula, -orum* n.pl.	cradle
contemno -ere	I despise, defy	*cunctor, -are, -atus sum*	I delay, cling, linger
contendo, -ere	I compete		
contentus, -a, -um	satisfied	*cunctus, -a, -um*	all
conterritus, -a, -um	terrified	*cupido, -inis* f.	lust, desire
conticesco, -ere, -ticui	I fall silent	*Cupido, -inis* m.	Cupid (son of Venus)
contineo, -ere, -ui, -entus	I check		
contingit, -ere, -tigit + dat.	it happens (to)	*cupio, -ere*	I wish
contingo, -ere	I touch, reach	*cura, -ae* f.	trouble, anxiety, sorrow, love, care
continuo	immediately		
contorqueo, -ere, -si, -sus	I hurl	*curo, -are*	I take care of
contra	+ acc.	*currus, -us* m.	chariot
contundo, -ere	I overthrow	*cursus, -us* m.	run, running, course, voyage, speed, race
contus, -i m.	pole		
conubium, -i n.	marriage		
convallis, -is f.	valley	*curvus, -a, -um*	curved
convello, -ere	I tear off	*cuspis, -idis* f.	spear-point, sceptre
convenio, -ire, -veni, -ventus	I come together		
converto, -ere, -verti, -versus	I reverse, turn, change	*custodia, -ae* f.	guardian
		custos, -odis m./f.	sentinel, guard, herdsman
convexa, -orum n.pl.	vault, sky		
convivium, -i n.	banquet	*Cybelus, -i* m.	Mt Cybelus
convolvo, -ere	I roll up, coil up	*Cyclops, -opis* m.	Cyclops
cor, cordis n.	heart, mind	*Cyllenius, -i* m.	Mercury
coram	in person, face to face	*Cynthus, -i* m.	Cynthus
		Cytherea, -ae f.	Venus
coram + abl.	in the presence of	*Danai, -orum* or *-um* m.pl.	the Greeks
corneus, -a, -um	of horn	*daps, dapis* f.	feast, food
cornu, -us n.	horn	*Dardania, -ae* f.	Troy
corona, -ae f.	crown, wreath	*Dardanidae, -arum* m.pl.	Trojans
corpus, -oris n.	body	*Dardanis, -idis* f.	a Trojan woman
corripio, -ere, -ripui, -reptus	I seize, speed over	*Dardanius, -a, -um*	Trojan
corruptus, -a, -um	tainted, infected	*Dardanus, -i* m.	Dardanus
cortina, -ae f.	cauldron	*Dares, -(et)is* (acc. *-n/eta*) m.	Dares
coruscus, -a, -um	gleaming	*debello, -are*	I crush

debeo, -ere, -ui, -itus — I owe
decedo, -ere — I depart
decerpo, -ere, -rpsi, -rptus — I pluck off
decet, -ere — it is proper
decipio, -ere, -cepi, -ceptus — I deceive
declino, -are — I droop
decorus, -a, -um + dat. — fitting, beautiful, appealing
decurro, -ere, -curri, -cursus — I run down
decus, -oris n. — grace
deduco, -ere — I take down, launch
defendo, -ere — I defend
defero, -re, -tuli, -latus — I bring to land, inform, carry (down)
deficio, -ere — I am absent, fail
defigo, -ere, -fixi, -fixus — I fix
defungor, -i, -nctus sum + abl. — I finish (with)
degener, -eris — base, ignoble, disgraceful
dehinc — then
dehisco, -ere — I gape open
deicio, -ere, -ieci, -iectus — I lower, deprive, dislodge, throw down
deinde — then
delabor, -i, -lapsus sum — I swoop down
deligo, -ere, -legi, -lectus — I choose, select
Delius, -a, -um — Delian
delubrum, -i n. — temple, shrine
demens, -ntis — mad, foolish
dementia, -ae f. — madness
demissus, -a, -um — downcast, lowered, hanging
demitto, -ere, -misi, -missus — I hand down, send down, bring to land, let fall
demo, -ere — I take away
demum — at last
denique — at last
dens, dentis m. — tooth
densus, -a, -um — constant
depasco, -ere, -pavi, -pastus — I feed on
depascor, -i, -pastus sum — I devour
dependeo, -ere — I hang down
depono, -ere — I lay down
derigo, -ere — I direct, guide
desaevio, -ire — I rage fully
descendo, -ere — I descend
descensus, -us m. — descent
describo, -ere — I map, plot
desero, -ere — I abandon, desert
desino, -ere — I stop, cease
desisto, -ere + abl. — I give up
despicio, -ere — I look down upon
destruo, -ere — I destroy
desuetus, -a, -um — unaccustomed
desum, -esse, -fui — I am missing
desuper — down, from above
detineo, -ere — I keep back, hold
detorqueo, -ere — I turn aside

deus, -i m. — god
devenio, -ire, -veni, -ventus — I reach, come to
devotus, -a, -um — doomed
dext(e)ra, -ae f. — right hand
dexter, -(e)ra, -(e)rum — on the right, right, suitable
dicio, -onis f. — control
dico, -are, -avi, -atus — I dedicate
dico, -ere, dixi, dictus — I say, speak, call, name
Dictaeus, -a, -um — of Dicte, Cretan
dictum, -i n. — word
Dido, -onis f. — Dido
Didymaon, -onis m. — Didymaon
dies, -ei m. or f. — day, daylight
differo, -erre, distuli, dilatus — I put off
diffugio, -ere — I scatter
diffundo, -ere — I spread
digitus, -i m. — toe
dignor, -ari — I think right
dignus, -a, -um — worthy, proper,
digredior, -i, -gressus sum — I separate, depart
dilectus, -a, -um — beloved
diligo, -ere, -lexi, -lectus — I love
dimitto, -ere — I send forth, send out
dimoveo, -ere, -vi, -tus — I disperse, dispel
dinumero, -are — I count
Diores, -is m. — Diores
dirimo, -ere, -emi, -emptus — I put an end to
diripio, -ere, -ui, -reptus — I plunder, ransack, tear apart
dirus, -a, -um — terrible, dreadful
Dis, Ditis m. — Pluto, Hades
discerno, -ere — I interweave
discessus, -us m. — departure
disco, -ere — I learn
discolor, -oris — of different hue
discrimen, -inis n. — distinction, crisis
dispono, -ere — I distribute, spread
dissimulo, -are — I hide, conceal
disto, -are — I am distant
diva, -ae f. — goddess
divello, -ere — I tear apart
diverbero, -are — I cleave in two
diversus, -a, -um — various, different
dives, divitis or *ditis* — rich, wealthy
divido, -ere — I break through, separate, divide
divinus, -a, -um — divine
divus, -a, -um — divine
divus, -i m. — god
do, dare — I give, allow
doceo, -ere, -ui, -ctus — I teach, tell of
doctus, -a, -um — wise
doleo, -ere, -ui — I grieve, resent
Dolopes, -um m.pl. — Dolopians
dolor, -oris m. — pain, grief
dolus, -i m. — deceit, trick
domina, -ae f. — mistress
dominor, -ari — I hold power
donec — until

dono, -are, -avi, -atus	I reward, present	*ergo*	therefore
donum, -i n.	gift	*erigo, -ere*	I raise up
draco, -onis m.	serpent	*eripio, -ere, -ui, ereptus*	I rescue, remove,
dubito, -are	I doubt		snatch away
dubius, -a, -um	wavering, doubtful	*erro, -are*	I wander, miss
duco, -ere, duxi, ductus	I draw, choose,	*error, -oris* m.	deception
	emit, extend, lead,	*erubesco, -ere, -rubui*	I respect
	think	*eructo, -are*	I belch forth, spew
ductor, -oris m.	leader		out
dulcis, -e	sweet, fond	*eruo, -ere, erui, erutus*	I tear out
duplex, -icis	both, double	*Erymanthus, -i* m.	Erymanthus
durus, -a, -um	hard, difficult,	*Eryx, -ycis* m.	Eryx
	long-suffering,	*Eurotas, -ae* m.	the river Eurotas
	harsh	*Eurus, -i* m.	the East Wind
dux, ducis m.	leader	*Euryalus, -i* m.	Euryalus
ebur, -oris n.	ivory	*evado, -ere, -vasi*	I emerge, escape
eburnus, -a, -um	(of) ivory	*evanesco, -ere, -nui*	I vanish
ecce	see, behold, look	*eveho, -ere, -vexi, -vectus*	I raise up
edico, -ere	I order, proclaim	*evenio, -ire*	I happen
edo, esse	I eat	*everto, -ere, -verti, -versus*	I ruin, overthrow
educo, -ere, -duxi, -ductus	I raise	*evincio, -ire, -nxi, -nctus*	I bind, tie
effero, -re, extuli, elatus	I bring out, raise,	*evinco, -ere, -vici, -victus*	I overwhelm
	carry out	*exaestuo, -are*	I boil up
effetus, -a, -um	worn out	*exanimus, -a, -um*	dead
effigies, -ei f.	image	*exaudio, -ire*	I hear clearly
effodio, -ere	I dig out	*excedo, -ere, -cessi, -cessus*	I depart, withdraw
effor, -fari, -fatus sum	I speak out,	*excido, -ere, -cidi, -cisus*	I cut out, cut
	speak		down, quarry
effugio, -ere, -fugi	I escape (from)	*excido, -ere, -idi*	I fall out, drop
effundo, -ere, -fudi, -fusus	I pour forth, out,	*excipio, -ere, -cepi, -ceptus*	I hear of, rescue,
	stream		take over, catch,
egenus, -a, -um	in want		await, welcome
egeo, -ere	I am in need	*excitus, -a, -um*	excited
egomet	= *ego*	*excudo, -ere*	I hammer out
egredior, -i, -ssus sum	I disembark	*excutio, -ere, -cussi, -cussus*	I beat out,
egregius, -a, -um	eminent,	*exeo, -ire*	I avoid
	outstanding	*exerceo, -ere*	I supervise,
ei! + dat.	alas!		practise, inflict
eicio, -ere, -ieci, -iectus	I cast ashore, cast	*exhalo, -are*	I breathe out
	up	*exhaurio, -ire, -hausi, -haustus*	I wear out, drain,
elabor, -i, elapsus sum	I slip aside, slip		endure
	ahead, escape	*exigo, -ere, -egi, -actus*	I complete
elephantus, -i m.	ivory	*exim*	then
Elissa, -ae f.	Dido	*exitus, -us* m.	death, way out
Elysium, -i n.	Elysium	*exopto, -are, -avi, -atus*	I long for
emico, -are	I dart, dash forth	*exordium, -i* n.	beginning
emitto, -ere	I send forth	*exorior, -iri, -ortus sum*	I arise
emoveo, -ere, -movi, -motus	I pull out	*expedio, -ire*	I explain, relate
en!	see, behold!	*expendo, -ere, -pendi, -pensus*	I pay for
Enceladus, -i m.	Enceladus	*expleo, -ere, -evi, -etus*	I fill up, gorge,
enitor, -i, enixus sum	I give birth to		complete, satisfy
ensis, -is m.	sword	*exposco, -ere*	I demand
Entellus, -i m.	Entellus	*expromo, -ere*	I utter
enumero, -are	I recite, count	*exquiro, -ere*	I seek out
Eous, -i m.	Morning Star	*exsanguis, -e*	bloodless, pale
epulae, -arum f.pl.	banquet	*exscindo, -ere*	I destroy
epulor, -ari	I feast	*exsequor, -i, -secutus sum*	I carry out
eques, -itis m.	horseman	*exsilium, -i* n.	exile
equidem	I for my part,	*exsolvo, -ere*	I release
	truly, indeed	*exsomnis, -e*	sleepless
equus, -i m.	horse	*exspecto, -are, -avi, -atus*	I wait for
Erebus, -i m.	Erebus	*exspiro, -are*	I breathe out

exstinguo, -ere, -nxi, -nctus	I destroy
exstructum, -i n.	platform
exstruo, -ere	I pile up, build
exsulto, -are	I exult, boast, prance, swagger
extemplo	immediately
extendo, -ere, -ndi, -ntus	I stretch out, extend
exterreo, -ere, -ui, -itus	I terrify
exterus, -a, -um	foreign
extrema, -orum n.pl.	furthest parts, death
extremus, -a, -um	extreme, utmost, last, final
exuo, -ere	I put off, drop, take off, bare
exuro, -ere	I burn, scorch
exuviae, -arum f.pl.	spoils, old skin, arms
fabrico, -are, -avi, -atus	I build
facesso, -ere	I do eagerly
facies, -ei f.	appearance, face
facilis, -e	easy
factum, -i n.	deed
fallo, -ere, fefelli, falsus	I deceive, cheat, fail to meet
falsus, -a, -um	deceived, false
fama, -ae f.	rumour, report, fame, reputation, glory
fames, -is f.	hunger
famula, -ae f.	maid-servant
fas n. (indecl.)	right, lawful, allowed
fastigium, -i n.	point, roof-top
fatalis, -e	deadly
fateor, -eri, fassus sum	I confess
fatigo, -are	I harass
fatum, -i n.	fate
fauces, -ium f.pl.	throat, jaws
faveo, -ere	I favour
favilla, -ae f.	ash, cinders
favor, -oris m.	favour, support
fax, facis, f.	torch, fiery trail
felix, -icis	fortunate, happy
femina, -ae f.	woman
femineus, -a, -um	of women
fenestra, -ae f.	window
fere	about, almost
ferio, -ire	I strike
fero, ferre	I bring, take, say
ferox, -ocis	fierce, spirited
ferreus, -a, -um	of iron
ferrugineus, -a, -um	rusty
ferrum, -i n.	iron, sword
ferus, -a, -um	wild
ferus, -i m.	wild beast
fessus, -a, -um	weary, tired
festus, -a, -um	festive, joyful
fetus, -a, -um	pregnant, full
fetus, -us m.	litter, growth
fibula, -ae f.	brooch, clasp

fictus, -a, -um	false
fides, -ei f.	belief, trust, honour, faith
fido, -ere + dat.	I trust (in), dare
fidus, -a, -um	trustworthy, faithful, safe
figo, -ere, fixi, fixus	I fix, wound, plant (a kiss)
fimus, -i m.	mire, muck
findo, -ere	I divide, split
fines, -ium f.pl.	territory, borders
fingo, -ere	I imagine
finis, -is m./f.	end
fio, fieri	I am made
firmo, -are	I confirm, support
firmus, -a, -um	stout, strong
fixus, -a, -um	fixed
flagellum, -i n.	whip
flagro, -are	I blaze
flamma, -ae f.	flame, passion, fire
flammo, -are, -avi, -atus	I set on fire
flavus, -a, -um	yellow
flecto, -ere, -xi, -xus	I bend, turn, influence
fleo, flere	I weep
fletus, -us m.	weeping, tears
fluctus, -us m.	wave, roller
fluentum, -i n.	river
flumen, -inis n.	river
fluo, -ere	I flow
focus, -i m.	hearth, home
foedo, -are	I despoil, smash, befoul, mutilate
foedus, -a, -um	foul
foedus, -eris n.	pact
folium, -i n.	leaf
fons, fontis m.	fountain, water
for, fari, fatus sum	I speak, say
foris, -is f.	door
forma, -ae f.	appearance, shape, figure, beauty
formido, -inis f.	panic
fornix, -icis m.	arch
fors	perhaps
forsan	perhaps
forte	by chance
fortis, -e	brave, strong
fortuna, -ae f.	fortune, prosperity
fortunatus, -a, -um	blessed
foveo, -ere	I favour, hold close, keep warm
fragor, -oris m.	crash, loud noise
frango, -ere, fregi, fractus	I break, smash
frater, -tris m.	brother
fraternus, -a, -um	of a brother
fremitus, -us m.	shouting
fremo, -ere	I shout, roar
frenum, -i n.	bridle, bit
fretus, -a, -um + abl.	relying on
frigeo, -ere	I am cold, stiff
frigidus, -a, -um	cold

frigus, -oris n.	cold, frost
frondesco, -ere	I sprout
frons, -ndis f.	garland, foliage
frons, -ntis f.	forehead, brow
frustra	in vain
frustum, -i n.	piece of food
frux, frugis f.	fruit, grain
fuga, -ae f.	flight, escape
fugio, -ere	I run away from, flee
fugo, -are, -avi -atus	I put to flight
fulgeo, -ere, fulsi	I flash, shine, gleam
fulgor, -oris m.	gleam
fulmen, -inis n.	thunderbolt, lightning
fulvus, -a, -um	golden brown, tawny, yellow
fumo, -are	I smoke, reek
fumus, -i m.	smoke
fundamentum, -i n.	foundation
fundo, -are	I found, build
fundo, -ere, fudi, fusus	I pour, spill, pour out
fundus, -i m.	bottom, depths
funis, -is m.	rope
funus, -eris n.	death
furens, -entis	raving, distraught, frenzied, raging, mad
Furiae, -arum f.pl.	the Furies
furiae, -arum f.pl.	madness
furo, -ere	I rage, am mad
furor, -oris m.	frenzy, madness
furtim	secretly
furtivus, -a, -um	secret
furtum, -i n.	stealth, theft
futurus, -a, -um	future
Gaetulus, -a, -um	Gaetulian
galea, -ae f.	helmet
gaudeo, -ere	I delight, rejoice
gaudium, -i n.	joy
gaza, -ae f.	treasure, wealth
gelidus, -a, -um	cold
geminus, -a, -um	twin
gemitus, -us m.	groan, roar
gemma, -ae f.	jewel
gemo, -ere	I sigh
gena, -ae f.	cheek
genero, -are, -avi, -atus	I beget
genetrix, -icis f.	mother
genitor, -oris m.	father
gens, -ntis f.	race, lineage, stock, people
genu, -us n.	knee
genus, -eris n.	race, offspring, people, descent, origin
germana, -ae f.	sister
germanus, -i m.	brother
gero, -ere	I manage, wage, bear, wear
gesto, -are	I have
gigno, -ere, genui, genitus	I beget
glaeba, -ae f.	soil
globus, -i m.	mass
glomero, -are	I gather round, roll up, mass together, gather
gloria, -ae f.	glory, pride
gradior, -i, gressus sum	I walk
gradus, -us m.	step
Grai, -orum m.pl.	the Greeks
Graius, -a, -um	Greek
gramen, -inis n.	grass
gramineus, -a, -um	grassy
grando, -inis f.	hail
grates f.pl.	thanks
grator, -ari, -atus sum	I congratulate
gratus, -a, -um	pleasing, welcome, dear
gravis, -e	pregnant, heavy, serious, stern
gremium, -i n.	lap
Gryneus, -a, -um	Grynian
gubernator, -oris m.	helmsman
gurges, -itis m.	raging water, sea, whirlpool
guttur, -uris n.	throat
Gyaros, - i f.	Gyaros
gyrus, - i m.	coil
habitus, -us m.	dress
haereo, -ere, haesi, haesus	I concentrate, cling, stick, remain fixed, hesitate
halitus, -us m.	breath, vapour
harena, -ae f.	sand, beach
Harpya, -ae f.	a Harpy
harundo, -inis f.	reed, arrow
hasta, -ae f.	spear
haud	not
haud secus ac	just as
haurio, -ire, hausi, haustus	I drink in, swallow
hebeo, -ere	I am sluggish
Hecate, -es f.	Hecate
Hector, -oris m.	Hector
Hectoreus, -a, -um	of Hector, Trojan
Hecuba, -ae f.	Hecuba
Helenus, -i m.	Helenus
Helymus, -i m.	Helymus
herba, -ae f.	grass, plant
Hercules, -is m.	Hercules
heres, -edis m.	heir
heros, -ois m.	hero
herus, -i m.	master
Hesperia, -ae f.	Hesperia
Hesperius, -a, -um	Western
heu	alas
hiatus, -us m.	gape, mouth
hiberna, -orum n.pl.	winters
hic	at this point, here
hiems, -mis f.	storm, winter
hinc	from here
hinc atque hinc	on each side

hisco, -ere	I gape, stammer	*immanis, -e*	monstrous, cruel,
homo, -inis m.	man		awful, immense
honoro, -are, -avi, -atus	I honour	*immemor, -oris*	forgetful, regardless
honos, -oris m.	grace, beauty,	*immensus, -a, -um*	immense, huge
	honour, glory	*immergo, -ere*	I plunge into
hora, -ae f.	hour	*immineo, -ere*	I tower over
horrendus, -a, -um	dreadful, horrible	*immisceo, -ere*	I mix, mingle
horrens, -ntis	rough	*immissus, -a, -um*	straggly
horreo, -ere	I shudder, bristle	*immitis, -e*	cruel
horresco, -ere	I start to shudder,	*immitto, -ere, -misi, -missus*	I send in
	dread	*immotus, -a, -um*	unchanged,
horridus, -a, -um	dreadful, frightful		immovable,
horrificus, -a, -um	dreadful, terrifying		undisturbed
horrisonus, -a, -um	horrible-sounding	*immundus, -a, -um*	filthy
horror, -oris m.	horror, terror	*impello, -ere, -puli, -pulsus*	I strike, drive,
hortor, -ari	I encourage, urge		compel, stir
hospes, -itis m.	guest	*imperium, -i* n.	power, dominion,
hospitium, -i n.	hospitality,		command
	friendship	*impius, -a, -um*	wicked, impious,
hospitus, -a, -um	strange, foreign		unholy
hostilis, -e	of the enemy	*impleo, -ere, -evi, -etus*	I fill, satisfy
hostis, -is m.	enemy	*implico, -are*	I clasp, embrace,
huc	to this place, here,		instill
	this way	*impono, -ere, -posui, -positus*	I place on, impose
huc illuc	this way and that	*imprimo, -ere, -pressi, pressus*	I press . . . on
humus, -i f.	ground	*improbus, -a, -um*	wicked, vile,
Hydra, -ae f.	Hydra		shameless
hymenaeus, -i m.	marriage	*improvidus, -a, -um*	unprepared
Hyrcanus, -a, -um	Hyrcanian	*impune*	without
iaceo, -ere, -ui	I lie		punishment, safely
iacio, -ere	I throw, cast	*imus, -a, -um*	the depths of, the
iacto, -are, -avi, -atus	I toss, toss about,		base of, the lowest,
	harass, swing,		the bottom of
	buffet	*inanis, -e*	empty
iaculor, -ari, -atus sum	I hurl	*incautus, -a, -um*	off one's guard,
iaculum, -i n.	javelin		unwary
iam pridem	for a long time now	*incedo, -ere, -cessi, cessus*	I proceed, step, go
iamdudum	for a long time,	*incendium, -i* n.	fire
	long since	*incendo, -ere, -di, -sus*	I burn, inflame, set
ianua, -ae f.	door		on fire, set ablaze
Iarbas, -ae (acc. *-an*), m.	Iarbas	*incensus, -a, -um*	inflamed, on fire
Iasius, -i m.	Iasius	*inceptum, -i* n.	purpose
iaspis, -idis f.	jasper	*incertus, -a, um*	badly aimed,
ictus, -us m.	blow, strike	*incesto, -are*	I pollute
Ida, -ae f.	Ida	*incido, -ere*	I fall upon
Idaeus, -a, -um	of Mt Ida	*incipio, -ere, -cepi, -ceptus*	I begin
idem, eadem, idem	the same	*includo, -ere, -si, -sus*	I enclose
ignarus, -a, -um	ignorant	*inclutus, -a, -um*	famous
ignis, -is, m.	fire, flash of	*incubo, -are* + dat.	I lie on, settle upon
	lightning	*incultus, -a, -um*	unkempt
ignotus, -a, -um	unknown	*incumbo, -ere, -cubui* + dat.	I settle upon, lean
ilex, -icis f.	holm-oak		upon, bend to, set
Ilia, -ae f.	Ilia		to work
Iliacus, -a, -um	Trojan, of Troy	*incuso, -are, -avi, -atus*	I accuse
Ilium, -i n.	Ilium, Troy	*inde*	from there, then
Ilius, -a, -um	Trojan	*indignus, -a, -um*	undeserved
illic	there	*induco, -ere, -xi, -ctus*	I lead on, pull on
illuc	that way	*indulgeo, -ere* + dat.	I indulge in
Ilus, -i m.	Ilus	*induo, -ere, -ui, -utus*	I clothe
imago, -inis f.	ghost, image	*iners, -rtis*	timid
imbellis, -e	harmless	*infandus, -a, -um*	unspeakable
imber, -ris m.	rain cloud	*infectus, -a, -um*	not done

infelix, -icis	unfortunate, unhappy, ill-fated, unlucky	*insuper*	above
		insurgo, -ere	I rise up
		intactus, -a, -um	as a virgin
infensus, -a, -um	hostile	*intempestus, -a, -um*	timeless
infernus, -a, -um	of the underworld, infernal	*intendo, -ere*	I stretch (out), bind, stretch taut
infero, -re	I begin (a war)	*intento, -are*	I threaten with
infestus, -a, -um	hostile	*intentus, -a, -um*	eager
inficio, -ere, -feci, -fectus	I stain	*interdum*	at times, sometimes
infixus, -a, -um	fixed		
inflecto, -ere, -xi, -xus	I sway	*interea*	meanwhile
inflexus, -a, -um	bowed, drooping	*interior, -oris*	inner, inside of
informis, -e	shapeless, hideous	*interpres, -etis* m.	messenger
ingemino, -are	I repeat, redouble	*interritus, -a, -um*	unafraid
ingemo, -ere, -ui, -itus	I groan	*interrumpo, -ere, -rupi, -ruptus*	I interrupt
ingens, -tis	huge	*intervallum, -i* n.	interval
ingredior, -i	I move along	*intexo, -ere*	I interweave
ingruo, -ere	I rush towards	*intono, -are, -ui*	I thunder
inhorresco, -ere, -ui	I shiver	*intorqueo, -ere, -si,-tus*	I hurl . . . at
inhumatus, -a, -um	unburied	*intractabilis, -e*	unconquerable
inimicus, -a, -um	hostile	*intremo, -ere*	I tremble
inimicus, -i m.	enemy	*intro, -are*	I enter
iniquus, -a, -um	unfair	*intus*	inside, within
iniuria, -ae f.	injustice, outrage, ill-treatment	*inultus, -a, -um*	unavenged
		invado, -ere	I attack, enter
inlabor, -i + dat.	I glide into, steal into	*invenio, -ire, -veni, -ventus*	I find
		invergo, -ere	I pour on
inlustris, -e	famous	*invidia, -ae* f.	envy, grudge
inluvies, -ei f.	filth	*invito, -are*	I invite
inmitis, -e	pitiless	*invitus, -a, -um*	unwilling
innecto, -ere, -xui, -xus	I bind, weave	*invius, -a, -um*	pathless
inno, innare	I swim in	*ira, -ae* f.	anger
innoxius, -a, -um	harmless	*iste, ista, istud*	that of yours
innuptus, -a, -um	unmarried	*Italia, -ae* f.	Italy
inops, inopis	helpless	*iter, itineris* n.	journey, course, route
inremediabilis, -e	irretraceable		
inritus, -a, -um	unsuccessful	*Ithacus, -i* m.	the Ithacan
inruo, -ere	I rush upon	*iuba, -ae* f.	crest
insania, -ae f.	madness	*iubar, -aris* n.	sunlight
insanus, -a, -um	mad, frantic, insane	*iubeo, -ere*	I order
		iugalis, -e	of marriage
inscius, -a, -um	unaware	*iugo, -are*	I unite
insequor, -i, -secutus sum	I follow	*iugum, -i* n.	mountain ridge
insertus, -a, -um	unshuttered	*Iulius Caesar, -is* m.	Julius Caesar
insido, -ere + dat.	I possess, settle upon	*Iulus, -i* m.	Julus, Ascanius
		iungo, -ere, iunxi, iunctus	I join, yoke, join together, harness
insignis, -e	famous, remarkable, conspicuous	*Iuno, -onis* f.	Juno
		Iunonius, -a, -um	of Juno
		Iuppiter, Iovis m.	Jupiter
insinuo, -are	I steal (into)	*iura, -um* n.pl.	laws
insisto, -ere	I set foot on	*iuro, -are*	I swear
insomnium, -i n.	dream	*ius, iuris* n.	right, law
insono, -ere, -ui, -itus	I resound	*iussus, -us* m.	order, command
insons, -ontis	innocent	*iuvat, -are*	it pleases
inspicio, -ere, -exi, -ectus	I spy on	*iuvencus, -i* m.	ox, bullock
instar + gen.	like, just like	*iuvenis, -is* m.	young man
instituo, -ere, -ui, -utus	I set up	*iuventa, -ae* f.	youth, youthfulness
insto, -are	I press on		
instruo, -ere	I set up	*iuventas, -atis* f.	youth
insula, -ae f.	island	*iuventus, -utis* f.	youth, young men
insulto, -are	I leap upon	*iuvo, -are*	I help, please
insuo, -ere, -ui, -utus	I sew in		

iuxta	nearby
iuxta + acc.	next to
Karthago, -inis f.	Carthage
labefacio, -ere, -feci, -factus	I shake
labo, -are	I totter, waver
labor, -i, lapsus sum	I slip by, pass, sink, slip away, glide, soar, fall, slip
labor, -oris m.	work, hard work, toil, suffering, task, trouble
lacertus, -i m.	upper arm
lacesso, -ere	I provoke
lacrima, -ae f.	tear
lacrimo, -are	I cry
lacus, -us m.	lake
laedo, -ere, laesi, laesus	I offend, damage
laena -ae f.	cloak
laetitia, -ae f.	joy
laetor, -ari, -atus sum	I rejoice
laetus, -a, -um	joyful, happy, glad
laeva, -ae f.	left hand
laevus, -a, -um	unfavourable, on the left
lambo, -ere	I lick
lampas, -adis f.	lamp, torch
laniger, -era, -erum	wool-bearing
Laocoon, -ontis m.	Laocoon
Laomedontiades, -ae m.	Trojan
lapis, -idis m.	stone, marble
lapso, -are	I slip
lapsus, -us m.	gliding, swoop
largus, -a, -um	abundant
lassus, -a, -um	weary
late	far and wide
latebra, -ae f.	hiding place
lateo, -ere	I lie hidden, am hidden
latex, -icis m.	water
Latinus, -a, -um	Latin
Latinus, -i m.	Latinus
Latium, -i n.	Latium
Latona, -ae f.	Latona
latratus, -us m.	barking
latus, -a, -um	broad, widespread, wide
latus, -eris n.	side, flank
Laurens, -ntis	of Laurentum
laurus, -i f.	laurel, laurel tree
laus, laudis f.	achievement, glory, praise
Lavinium, -i n.	Lavinium
Lavinus, -a, -um	of Lavinium
lego, -ere	I pass through
lenio, -ire	I calm, soothe
lenis, -e	smooth, gentle
lento, -are	I bend
lentus, -a, -um	pliant
leo, -onis m.	lion
letalis, -e	deadly
Lethaeus, -a, -um	of the Lethe
letifer, -era, -erum	deadly
letum, -i n.	death
levamen, -inis n.	comforter
levis, -e	light
lēvis, -e	smooth, slippery
levo, -are, -avi, -atus	I polish
libo, -are, -avi, -atus	I taste, lightly kiss
Libya, -ae f.	Libya, Africa
Libycus, -a, -um	Libyan, African
licet, -ere	it is allowed
lignum, -i n.	wood(work)
ligo, -are	I bind
limbus, -i m.	border
limen, -inis n.	threshold, doorway, starting line
limes, -itis m.	track, path
lingua, -ae f.	tongue
linquo, -ere, liqui, lictus	I give up, lose, leave, shrink from
liquefactus, -a, -um	molten
liquidus, -a, -um	clear
lito, -are, -avi, -atus	I perform correctly
litoreus, -a, -um	on the bank
litus, -oris n.	shore, coast
lividus, -a, -um	dark
loco, -are	I lay out, lay, place
locus, -i m.	place
Longa Alba, -ae f.	Alba Longa
longaevus, -a, -um	long-lived, aged
longe	a long way, far, far away, from afar
loquor, -i, locutus sum	I speak
lorum, -i n.	thong
lubricus, -a, -um	smooth, slippery
lucidus, -a, -um	bright, clear, gleaming
luctus, -us m.	grief, sorrow
lucus, -i m.	sacred grove, grove
ludo, -ere, lusi, lusus	I deceive, play
lues, -is f.	pestilence
lumen, -inis n.	light, eye
luna, -ae f.	moon
lupa, -ae f.	female wolf
lustro, -are	I inspect, pass through, survey, illuminate
lustrum, -i n.	forest
lux, lucis f.	light, dawn, daylight
luxus, -us m.	extravagance
Lycia, -ae f.	Lycia
Lycius, -a, -um	Lycian
Lydius, -a, -um	Lydian
machina, -ae f.	engine of war, crane, machine
macies, -ei f.	emaciation
macto, -are	I sacrifice
maculosus, -a, -um	mottled
madefacio, -ere, -feci, -factus	I soak
maereo, -ere	I grieve, lament
maestus, -a, -um	sad, gloomy
magalia, -ium n.pl.	huts

magis	rather, more	miror, -ari, -atus sum	I marvel at, wonder (at)
magister, -tri m.	teacher	mirus, -a, -um	strange
magnanimus, -a, -um	great-hearted	misceo, -ere, -ui, mixtus	I mix, throw into confusion, disturb, mingle
mala, -ae f.	jaw		
male	badly, barely		
malum, -i n.	trouble	Misenus, -i m.	Misenus
malus, -a, -um	wicked	miser, -era, -erum	unfortunate, poor
mandatum, -i n.	command	miserandus, -a, -um	pitiable
mando, -ere	I chew, crush, champ at	misereor, -eri, -itus sum	I pity
		miseret, -ere	it distresses
maneo, -ere, -nsi, -nsus	I remain, endure	miseror, -ari, -atus sum	I pity
manes, -ium m.pl.	spirits, shades	mitesco, -ere	I become civilised
manifestus, -a, -um	plain, clear	mixtus, -a, -um	confused
manus, -us f.	hand, band, skill, craftsmanship	Mnestheus, -ei m. (acc. -ea)	Mnestheus
		mobilitas, -atis f.	swiftness
mare, -is n.	sea	modo	only, if only, just, merely
marmor, -oris n.	marble		
marmoreus, -a, -um	of marble	modus, -i m.	way, method
Marpesius, -a, -um	of Marpesus	moenia, -ium n.pl.	walls, buildings, city, city walls
Mars, -tis m.	Mars		
Massylus, -a, -um	Massylian	moles, -is f.	massive work, task, trouble, mass, bulk, war engine
mater, ris f.	mother		
maternus, -a, -um	a mother's		
Mavortius, -a, -um	of Mars	molior, -iri	I toil at
meatus, -us m.	course	mollis, -e	soft, tender, kind
mecum	with me	moneo, -ere, -ui, -itus	I warn (of)
medico, -are, -avi, -atus	I drug	monimentum, -i n.	tradition
meditor, -ari	I contemplate	monitus, -us m.	warning
medium, -i n.	middle	mons, -ntis m.	mountain
medius, -a, -um	(in) the middle (of)	monstro, -are	I show
medulla, -ae f.	marrow	monstrum, -i n.	monster, portent
mel, mellis n.	honey	montanus, -a, -um	(of a) mountain
melius	better	mora, -ae f.	delay
membrum, -i n.	limb	moribundus, -a, -um	doomed to die, dying
memini, -isse + gen.	I remember		
memor, -oris	mindful, remembering	morior, -i, mortuus sum	I die
		moror, -ari, -atus sum	I delay, detain, take notice of, care for
memoro, -are	I relate, say, recount, celebrate		
mens, mentis f.	mind, intention, heart	mors, mortis f.	death
mensa, -ae f.	table	morsus, -us m.	biting, chewing, bite
mensis, -is m.	month		
mentior, -iri	I lie, say falsely	mortalis, -e	mortal
mentum, -i n.	chin	mortalis, -is m.	human being, mortal
mercor, -are, -atus sum	I buy		
mereo, -ere, -ui, -itus	I earn, deserve	mos, moris f.	character, custom
mereor, -eri, -itus sum	I deserve	motus, -us m.	movement
merum, -i n.	undiluted wine	moveo, -ere	I reveal, move
meta, -ae f.	bound, boundary, goal	mugio, -ire	I bellow, rumble, moo
metallum, -i n.	metal	mugitus, -us m.	bellowing
metuo, -ere, -ui	I fear	mulceo, -ere	I soothe
metus, -us m.	fear	multiplex, -icis	various
mico, -are	I flash	munus, -eris n.	kind action, gift, duty
mille, plur. milia, -ium	thousand		
mina, -ae f.	threat	murex, -icis m.	purple
ministro, -are	I tend	murmur, -uris n.	rumbling, murmuring
minor, -ari	I threaten		
minores, -um m.pl.	younger people	murus, -i m.	wall
minus	less	Musa, -ae f.	Muse
mirabilis, -e	wonderful	muto, -are, -avi, -atus	I change

Myconos, -i f.	Myconos	*numerus, -i* m.	number
Myrmidones, -um m.pl.	Myrmidons	*nuntia, -ae* f.	reporter
namque	for	*nuntius, -i* m.	messenger, report
narro, -are	I relate, tell	*nurus, -us* f.	daughter-in-law
nascor, -i	I am born	*nusquam*	nowhere
nata, -ae f.	daughter	*nutrix, -icis* f.	nurse
nato, -are	I swim, am awash	*ob* + acc.	because of
natus, -i m.	son	*obicio, -ere, -ieci, -iectus*	I throw (to), thrust
navis, -is f.	ship		upon
navita, -ae m.	sailor	*obliquo, -are*	I set aslant
necdum	nor yet	*oblitus, -a, -um* + gen.	forgetful (of)
necto, -ere	I bind	*obliviscor, -i, -litus sum* + gen.	I forget
nefas n. (indecl.)	crime	*oblivium, -i* n.	forgetfulness
nego, -are	I deny, refuse	*obmutesco, -ere, -mutui*	I am struck
nemo -inis m.	no one		dumb
nemus, -oris n.	grove	*obnitor, -i, -nixus sum*	I struggle (against)
Neoptolemus, -i m.	Neoptolemus,	*oborior, -iri, -ortus sum*	I rise, well up
	Pyrrhus	*obscenus, -a, -um*	disgusting
nepos, -otis m.	grandson,	*obscurus, -a, -um*	dark, obscure
	descendant	*observo, -are*	I watch
Neptunus, -i m.	Neptune	*obstipesco, -ere, -stipui*	I am stupefied,
nequeo, -ire	I cannot		amazed
nequiquam	in vain	*obtego, -ere, -exi, -ectus*	I conceal
Nereis, -idis f.	Nereid	*obtunsus, -a, -um*	dull, unfeeling
nescio, -ire	I do not know	*obtutu* (no nom.)	in contemplation
nescius, -a, -um	unaware	*occubo, -are*	I lie buried
ni	unless, if not	*occulto, -are*	I conceal, hide
niger, nigra, nigrum	black	*occumbo, -ere*	I die
nigrans, -ntis	black	*occupo, -are*	I occupy
nimbus, -i m.	cloud, storm-cloud, rain-storm	*occurro, -ere, -ri, -rsus*	I meet, run to meet, come to meet, appear to
nimium	too (much)		
nisi	unless, if not	*Oceanus, -i* m.	Ocean
Nisus, -i m.	Nisus	*ocior, ocius*	swifter
nisus, -us m.	posture, effort	*oculus, -i* m.	eye
nitens, -entis	shining, gleaming	*odi, odisse*	I hate
nitidus, -a, -um	shining, bright	*odium, -i* n.	hatred
noceo, -ere + dat.	I harm	*odor, -oris* m.	smell, stench
nocturnus, -a, -um	nocturnal	*odorus, -a, -um*	keen-scented
nodo, -are	I knot	*Oenotrus, -a, -um*	Oenotrian
nodus, -i m.	knot	*offa, -ae* f.	morsel
Nomas, -adis m./f.	Numidian	*offero, -ferre, obtuli, -latus*	I present, offer
nomen, -inis n.	name	*oleo, -ere*	I smell
nondum	not yet	*olim*	one day
nonus, -a, -um	ninth	*oliva, -ae* f.	olive
nosco, -ere, novi, notus	I learn	*Olympus, -i* m.	Mt Olympus
nota, -ae f.	spot, marking	*omen, -inis* n.	omen, portent, marriage ceremony
notum, -i n.	knowledge		
notus, -a, -um	known, well-known, familiar	*omnino*	entirely
		omnipotens, -ntis	all-powerful
Notus, -i m.	the South Wind	*onero, -are*	I load
novitas, -atis f.	newness	*onerosus, -a, -um*	heavy
novo, -are	I renew, change	*onustus, -a, -um*	laden
novus, -a, -um	new	*opaco, -are*	I shade
nox, noctis f.	night, darkness	*opacus, -a, -um*	shady, dark
nubes, -is f.	cloud, mist	*operor, -ari, -atus sum*	I am busy
nubila, -orum n.pl.	clouds	*operta, -orum* n.pl.	hidden places
nubilum, -i n.	cloud	*opes, -um* f.pl.	wealth
nudo, -are	I reveal	*opimus, -a, -um*	rich, fertile, sumptuous
numen, -inis n.	divinity, divine power, divine will, good will	*opperior, -iri*	I wait for
		oppeto, -ere	I die

oppono, -ere, -posui, -itus	I place in the way, place against	*pasco, -ere*	I feed
oppugno, -are	I attack	*pascor, -i, pastus sum*	I feed upon
ops, opis f. (no nom.)	wealth, help, power	*passim*	everywhere, in all directions
opto, -are, -avi, -atus	I choose, wish for, pray	*passus, -us* m.	step
opus (est)	(there is) need	*pastor, -oris* m.	shepherd
opus, operis n.	work, task, toil	*pateo, -ere*	I lie open, am open
ora, -ae f.	shore	*pater, -ris* m.	father
oraclum, -i n.	oracle	*patera, -ae* f.	bowl
orbis, -is m.	world, coil, circle, cycle	*patesco, -ere*	I am opened up
ordior, -iri, orsus sum	I begin	*patior, -i, passus sum*	I suffer, endure, allow
ordo, -inis m.	order, rank	*patria, -ae* f.	fatherland, homeland
Oreas, -adis f.	Oread (mountain nymph)	*patrius, -a, -um*	of one's country, of a father, ancestral
orgia, -orum n.pl.	orgies	*Patron, -onis* m.	Patron
Oriens, -entis m.	the East, Dawn	*pauci, -ae, -a*	few
origo, -inis f.	lineage	*paulatim*	gradually
Orion, -onis m.	Orion	*paulum*	a little
orior, -iri, ortus sum	I arise, appear, originate	*pavidus, -a, -um*	frightened
		pavor, -oris m.	fear
oro, -are	I beg	*pax, pacis* f.	peace
ortus, -us m.	rising	*pectus, -oris* n.	breast, heart, mind
Ortygia, -ae f.	Ortygia, Delos	*pecus, -oris* n.	herd, cattle, flock
os, oris n.	face, mouth	*pecus, -udis* f.	sheep
os, ossis n.	bone	*pelagus, -i* n.	sea, the open sea
osculum, -i n.	lip, kiss	*Pelides, -ae* m.	son of Peleus
ostendo, -ere, -ndi, -ntus	I show, display, point out	*pello, -ere, pepuli, pulsus*	I drive out, beat, drive, drive away
ostento, -are	I display	*penates, -ium* m.pl.	Penates, household gods
ostrum, -i n.	purple	*pendeo, -ere, pependi*	I hang, am suspended, linger
otium, -i n.	leisure		
ovis -is f.	sheep	*penetralia, -ium* n.pl.	inner rooms
ovo, -are	I triumph, rejoice	*penetralis, -e*	innermost
Palinurus, -i m.	Palinurus	*penitus*	deep within
palla, -ae f.	cloak	*penna, -ae* f.	wing
Pallas, -adis f.	Pallas (Athena)	*perago, -ere, -egi, -actus*	I finish, accomplish, complete
pallens, -ntis	pale		
pallidus, -a, -um	pale		
palma, -ae f.	palm, hand, prize	*peragro, -are*	I wander through
palus, -udis f.	marsh	*percello, -ere, -culi, -culsus*	I knock down
pando, -ere	I open up, expose, reveal	*pereo, -ire*	I die
Panopes, -ae m.	Panopes	*pererro, -are, -avi, -atus*	I wander across, scan, survey
par, paris + dat.	just like, equal (to), similar (to)	*perfero, -ferre, -tuli, -latus*	I bear, endure
Parcae, -arum f.pl.	the Fates	*perficio, -ere*	I complete
parco, -ere, peperci + dat.	I spare	*perfidus, -a, -um*	treacherous
parens, -ntis m/f.	parent, ancestor	*perflo, -are*	I blow across
pareo, -ere + dat.	I obey	*perfundo, -ere, -fudi, -fusus*	I soak, bathe
pario, -ere, peperi, partus	I obtain	*Pergama, -orum* n.pl.	the citadel of Troy, Pergama
Paris, -idis m.	Paris		
pariter	equally, on equal terms, together, side by side	*Pergameus, -a, -um*	of Pergama
		pergo, -ere	I proceed
		periclum, -i n.	danger
Parius, -a, -um	Parian	*permetior, -iri, -nsus sum*	I cross over
paro, -are	I prepare	*perrumpo, -ere*	I break through
pars, partis f.	part, direction, some, share	*persolvo, -ere*	I give (thanks)
		persono, -are	I make resound
partu do, dare	I give birth to	*pertaedet, -ere, -taesum est*	it wearies
parvulus, -a, -um	tiny	*pertempto, -are*	I affect deeply

pes, pedis m.	foot, talon
pestis, -is f.	disaster
peto, -ere, -ii, -itus	I seek, make for
phalerae, -arum f.pl.	trappings
pharetra, -ae f.	quiver
Phlegethon, -ontis	Phlegethon
Phoebeus, -a, -um m.	of Apollo
Phoebus, -i m.	Phoebus Apollo
Phoenices, -um m.pl.	Phoenicians
Phoenissus, -a, -um	Phoenician
Phrygius, -a, -um	Phrygian, Trojan
piaculum, -i n.	atonement
piceus, -a, -um	pitchy, black
pictus, -a, -um	embroidered
pietas, -atis f.	dutifulness, righteousness
piget, -ere, -uit	it disgusts, annoys
pinguis, -e	rich
pinus, -us f.	pine-tree
pius, -a, -um	dutiful, righteous
placide	peacefully
placidus, -a, -um	peaceful
placo, -are, -avi, -atus	I win the favour of, calm
plaga, -ae f.	net
plangor, -oris m.	wailing
planta, -ae f.	sole (of foot)
plausus, -us m.	applause
plenus, -a, -um + abl.	full (of)
pluma, -ae f.	feather
plumbum, -i n.	lead
poculum, -i n.	cup
poena, -ae f.	punishment
poenas do, dare	I am punished
Poeni, -orum m.pl.	Carthaginians
Polites, -ae m.	Polites
polliceor, -eri, pollicitus sum	I promise
polluo, -ere, -ui, -utus	I desecrate, defile
polus, -i m.	pole, sky
Polyphemus, -i m.	Polyphemus
pondus, -eris n.	weight
pone	behind
pono, -ere, -sui, -situs	I place, set up, rest, establish
pontus, -i m.	sea
populus, -i m.	people, race, nation
porta, -ae f.	gate, outlet
porticus, -us f.	colonnade
portitor, -oris m.	ferryman
porto, -are	I carry
portus, -us m.	harbour
posco, -ere	I ask for, beg, demand
posterus, -a, -um	next
postis, -is m.	door, post, pillar
potens, -ntis	powerful
potentia, -ae f.	power
potior, -ius	preferable
poto, -are	I drink
praecelsus, -a, -um	very high
praeceps, -cipitis	headlong
praeceps, -itis n.	steep drop
praeceptum, -i n.	order
praecipio, -ere, -cepi, -ceptus	I order
praecipue	especially
praeclarus, -a, -um	famous
praeda, -ae f.	booty
praedico, -ere, -dixi, -dictus	I foretell
praeficio, -ere, -feci, -fectus	I put in charge
praemium, -i n.	reward, recompense
praesens, -ntis	present, ready, instant
praesentio, -ire, -sensi	I learn first
praestans, -ntis	excellent
praetendo, -ere	I hold out
praeterea	furthermore
praetereo, -ire	I overtake
praetexo, -ere	I hide, cover
praeverto, -ere	I take possession of first
praevideo, -ere, -vidi, -visus	I foresee
pravus -a, -um	crooked, bad
precor, -ari, -atus sum	I pray for, pray to
premo, -ere, pressi, pressus	I press, check, veil, threaten, suppress, tread on
prendo, -ere, -di, -sus	I seize
pretium, -i n.	prize
prex, precis f. (no nom.)	prayer, plea
Priameius, -a, -um	of Priam
Priamus, -i m.	Priam
primum	first
primus, -a, -um	first
princeps, -ipis m.	chief, founder
principium, -i n.	beginning
prior, prius	in front, former, previous, sooner
pristinus, -a, -um	former
prius quam	before, until
pro + abl.	in return for, for, instead of
probo, -are	I approve
procedo, -ere	I come forward, continue
procella, -ae f.	violent gust
procer, -eris m.	chieftain, lord
proclamo, -are	I proclaim
procul	(from) far off, afar, far away
procumbo, -ere, -cubui, -cubitus	I fall forward, down
prodeo, -ire	I advance
proelium, -i n.	battle
profanus, -a, -um	uninitiated
proficiscor, -i, -fectus sum	I set out
profor, -fari, -fatus sum	I speak out
profugus, -a, -um	fleeing
profundus, -a, -um	deep
progredior, -i	I proceed
prohibeo, -ere	I forbid
proicio, -ere, -ieci, -iectus	I throw forward
prolabor, -i, -lapsus sum	I fall in ruin

proles, -is f.	offspring	*quis-, quae-, quid-quam*	anyone
promereor, -eri, -itus sum	I deserve	*quisque, quaeque, quidque*	each, every
promissum, -i n.	promise	*quisquis, quidquid*	whoever, whatever
promitto, -ere, -misi, -missus	I promise	*quo*	whither, to where
pronuba, -ae f.	bride's attendant	*quo* + comparative	so that
pronus, -a, -um	face-down	*quo . . . usque*	for how long
propere	quickly	*quod si*	but if
propinquo, -are + dat.	I approach	*quondam*	once, formerly,
propinquus, -a, -um	near		previously
propono, -ere	I set out, offer	*quoniam*	since
proprius, -a, -um	one's own, proper,	*quoque*	also
	permanent	*quotannis*	annually
propter + acc.	because of	*quotiens*	as often as
propugnaculum, -i n.	battlement	*quove*	or whither
prora, -ae f.	prow	*rabidus, -a, -um*	mad
prorumpo, -ere	I fling out	*radius, -i* m.	rod, compass,
prosequor, -i, -secutus sum	I follow		ray
Proserpina, -ae f.	Proserpina	*radix, -icis* f.	root
protendo, -ere	I stretch out	*ramus, -i* m.	branch, twig,
protinus	immediately, at		bough
	once	*rapidus, -a, -um*	fast, swift, rapid
provehor, -i	I sail forth	*rapio, -ere, -ui, -tus*	I seize, hurry
proximus, -a, -um	nearest, next	*rapto, -are, -avi, -atus*	I drag violently
pubes, -is f.	youth(s), man	*rarus, -a, -um*	infrequent,
pudor, -oris m.	chastity, honour,		disjointed, wide-
	shame		meshed
pugna, -ae f.	war, fight	*ratis, -is* f.	raft, ship, boat
pulcher, -ra, -rum	beautiful	*raucus, -a, -um*	clanging, roaring
pulverulentus, -a, -um	dusty	*recedo, ere, cessi, -cessus*	I depart, recede
pulvis, -eris m.	dust	*recens, -ntis*	fresh
Punicus, -a, -um	Carthaginian	*recenseo, -ere*	I review
puppis, -is f.	stern, ship	*recidivus, -a, -um*	restored
purgo, -are	I disperse	*recipio, -ere, -cepi, -ceptus*	I exact
purpureus, -a, -um	purple, brilliant,	*recludo, -ere, -clusi, -clusus*	I reveal, open
	radiant	*recolo, -ere*	I contemplate
puto, -are	I think, consider	*recondo, -ere, -didi, -ditus*	I hide
Pygmalion, -onis m.	Pygmalion	*recordor, -ari*	I remember
Pyrrhus, -i m.	Pyrrhus	*rectus, -a, -um*	straight
qua	where	*recubo, are*	I lie, recline
quadrigae, -arum f.pl.	chariot	*recurso, -are*	I keep occurring
quaero, -ere	I ask, seek	*recuso, -are*	I refuse
qualis, -e	just like, just like	*recutio, -ere, -cussi, -cussus*	I make to
	when, what sort of		reverberate
quando	since	*reddo, -ere*	I give back
quantus, -a, -um	as much as, how	*redimio, -ire, -ivi, -itus*	I bind round
	much, how great	*reditus, -us* m.	return
quasso, -are, -avi, -atus	I batter	*reduco, -ere, -xi, -ctus*	I bring back
quater	four times	*redux, -ucis*	returning, returned
quatio, -ere	I shake, flap, harry	*refello, -ere*	I refute
queo, -ere, -ivi	I can	*refero, -ferre*	I speak, relate,
querela, -ae f.	complaint		report, recall,
qui, qua, quod (after *si*)	any		answer
qui-, quae-, quod-cumque	whichever	*refigo, -ere, -fixi, -fixus*	I take down
quianam	why?	*reflecto, -ere, -flexi, -flexus*	I turn back
quicquam	anything	*refringo, -ere*	I break off
quidem	however	*refugio, -ere, -fugi*	I flee away, recoil,
quies, -etis f.	rest, quiet		wish to avoid
quiesco, -ere, -evi, -etus	I rest	*refulgeo, -ere, -fulsi*	I shine
quietus, -a, -um	quiet	*regina, -ae* f.	queen
quin	indeed	*regio, -onis* f.	region, district
quinquaginta	fifty	*regius, -a, -um*	royal, princely
Quirinus, -i m.	Quirinus, Romulus	*regnator, -oris* m.	ruler, king

regno, -are	I reign	*rogus, -i* m.	pyre
regnum, -i n.	kingdom, realm, sovereignty	*Romulus, -i* m.	Romulus
rego, -ere	I rule, guide, control	*roseus, -a, -um*	rosy
		rota, -ae f.	wheel
reicio, -ere, -ieci, -iectus	I throw off	*rudens, -entis* m.	rope, rigging
relinquo, -ere, -liqui, -lictus	I abandon, leave, leave behind	*ruina, -ae* f.	shower of ash
reliquiae, -arum f.pl.	remains, relics, remnants, those left behind	*rumpo, -ere*	I force, break down, break, utter, shatter
remetior, -iri, -mensus sum	I calculate back, cross again	*ruo, -ere*	I stir up, rush forth, fall down, rush
remitto, -ere, -misi, -missus	I send back, give up	*rupes, -is* f.	rock, cliff
		rursum	again
remordeo, -ere	I torment	*rursus*	again, back
Remus, -i m.	Remus	*Rutuli, -orum* m.pl.	the Rutulians
remus, -i m.	oar	*sacer, -cra, -crum*	sacred
renarro, -are	I relate	*sacerdos, -otis* m./f.	priest, priestess
renovo, -are	I renew	*sacra, -orum* n.pl.	sacred rites, sacrifice, emblems
reor, -eri, ratus sum	I think	*sacratus, -a, -um*	holy
repello, -ere, -ppuli, -pulsus	I drive back, repel	*sacro, -are, -avi, -atus*	I consecrate
repente	suddenly	*sacrum, -i* n.	sacred object
reperio, -ire, -pperi, -pertus	I find	*saeculum, -i* n.	age, generation
repeto, -ere	I seek again	*saepio, -ire, saepsi, saeptus*	I surround
repleo, -ere, -evi, -etus	I fill	*saevio, -ire, -ii*	I rage, am furious
repono, -ere	I place again	*saevus, -a, -um*	cruel, fierce
requies, -etis f.	rest	*sagitta, -ae* f.	arrow
requiro, -ere	I seek	*sal, salis* m.	salt, sea
reservo, -are	I keep back	*Salius, -i* m.	Salius
reses, -idis	inactive, slumbering	*saltem*	at least
		saltus, -us m.	glade
resideo, -ere, -sedi, -sessus	I stay behind	*salum, -i* n.	sea
resido, -ere, -sedi	I sit down	*salus, -utis* f.	safety
resisto, -ere, -stiti	I stand still, stop	*sanctus, -a, -um*	sacred
resolvo, -ere	I break, relax	*sanguineus, -a, -um*	blood-coloured
respicio, -ere, -spexi, -ctus	I look round, look back (at), consider, look back for	*sanguis, -inis* m.	blood, bloodline
		sanies, -ei f.	gore
		sanus, -a, -um	sane
respondeo, -ere	I respond (to)	*Sarpedon, -onis* m.	Sarpedon
restinguo, -ere	I extinguish	*sat*	enough
resto, -are	I am left	*sata, -orum* n.pl.	crops
resupinus, -a, -um	lying on the back	*sator, -oris* m.	creator
rete, -is n.	net	*Saturnius, -a, -um*	of Saturn
retego, -ere, -texi, -tectus	I reveal	*satus, -a, -um* + abl.	descended from
retro	back	*saucius, -a, -um*	wounded
revertor, -i, -versus sum	I return	*saxum, -i* n.	stone, rock
revincio, -ire, -nxi	I bind fast	*scaena, -ae* f.	stage
reviso, -ere	I visit again, see again, revisit	*scando, -ere*	I climb over
		sceleratus, -a, -um	wicked, impious, criminal
revoco, -are	I restore, retrace		
revolvo, -ere, -volvi, -utus	I roll over	*scelus, -eris* n.	wickedness, crime, sin
rex, -gis m.	king		
Rhadamanthus, -i m.	Rhadamanthus	*scilicet*	to be sure
Rhoeteus, -a, -um	Rhoetean	*scindo, -ere*	I part
rideo, -ere, risi, risus	I laugh	*scio, -ire*	I know
rigeo, -ere	I am stiff	*scopulus, -i* m.	rock
rigo, -are	I moisten, wet	*scrupeus, -a, -um*	stony, rugged
ripa, -ae f.	bank	*scutum, -i* n.	shield
rite	rightly, correctly, duly	*secessus, -us* m.	sheltered area
		secludo, -ere	I banish
robur, -oris n.	oak, timber	*seco, -are, -cui, -ctus*	I cut, saw, cleave

secretus, -a, -um	set apart, isolated, secluded	*similis, -e* + dat.	similar (to)
secundus -a, -um	favourable	*Simois, -entis* m.	Simois
securis, -is f.	axe	*simul*	at the same time
securus, -a, -um	free from anxiety, heedless, free from care	*simul = simulac*	as soon as
		simulacrum, -i n.	image, statue
		simulo, -are	I pretend
sedeo, -ere	I sit, am settled	*sine* + abl.	without
sedes, -is f.	depths, seat, site, sanctuary, home, perch	*singula, -orum* n.pl.	individual details
		singuli, -ae, -a	individual
		sinister, -tra, -trum	on the left
seduco, -ere, -duxi, -ductus	I separate	*sinistra, -ae* f.	left hand
seges, -etis f.	cornfield, corn crop, crop(s)	*sino, -ere*	I allow
		sinuo, -are	I bend
		sinus, -us m.	bosom, fold, bend
semesus, -a, -um	half-eaten	*Sirius, -i* m.	Sirius, the Dog Star
semita, -ae f.	footpath		
semustus, -a, -um	half-burned	*sisto, -ere*	I set, place, stop, bring to rest
senecta, -ae f.	old age		
senectus, -utis f.	old age	*situs, -us* m.	decay, mould
senex, -is	old	*socio, -are*	I ally, unite
senior, -oris	elderly	*socius, -a, -um*	allied, friendly
senior, -oris m.	old man	*socius, -i* m.	companion
sensus, -us m.	feelings	*sol, solis* m.	sun
sententia, -ae f.	opinion, thought	*solacium, -i* n.	consolation
sentus, -a, -um	rough	*solamen, -inis* n.	solace
sepelio, -ire, -ivi, -ultus	I bury	*soleo, -ere, -itus sum*	I am accustomed
septenus, -a, -um	seven	*solidus, -a, -um*	solid, strong
sepulcrum, -i n.	tomb	*solium, -i* n.	throne
sequor, -i, secutus sum	I follow, trace, accompany	*sollemnis, -e*	customary
		sollicito, -are	I trouble
sereno, -are	I calm	*sollicitus, -a, -um*	anxious
serenus, -a, -um	calm	*solor, -ari, -atus sum*	I comfort, console
Serestus, -i m.	Serestus	*solum, -i* n.	ground
Sergestus, -i m.	Sergestus	*solus, -a, -um*	only, alone
sermo, -onis m.	speech, gossip	*solvo, -ere, -i, -utus*	I dispel, set free, dismiss, weaken
sero, -ere, sevi, satus	I sow, bear, beget		
serpens, -ntis m./f.	snake, serpent	*somnus, -i* m.	sleep
serpo, -ere	I creep	*sonipes, -pedis* m.	horse
serus, -a, -um	late	*sonitus, -us* m.	noise, cry
servio, -ire, -ii, -itus	I am a slave	*sono, -are*	I sound, screech, resound
servo, -are, -avi, -atus	I observe, save, keep, maintain, keep safe, watch over		
		sons, sontis	guilty
		soporo, -are, -avi, -atus	I make drowsy
		sordidus, -a, -um	dirty
sese	= *se*	*soror, -oris* f.	sister
seu	or	*sors, sortis* f.	fate, destiny, oracle, lot
si quis	if any		
sibilus, -a, -um	hissing	*sortior, -iri, -titus sum*	I choose by lot, draw lots
Sicani, -orum m.pl.	Sicilians		
Sicanus, -a, -um	Sicilian	*sortitus, -us* m.	drawing of lots
siccus, -a, -um	dry	*spargo, -ere, sparsi, sparsus*	I (be)spatter, scatter, sprinkle
Siculus, -a, -um	Sicilian		
sidereus, -a, -um	starry	*spatium, -i* n.	space, course, track
sido, -ere	I settle		
Sidonius, -a, -um	Sidonian	*species, -ei* f.	appearance
sidus, -eris n.	star	*specula, -ae* f.	look-out position
signo, -are	I mark, indicate, note, observe	*spelunca, -ae* f.	cave
		spero, -are	I hope, expect
signum, -i n.	sign, signal	*spes, spei* f.	hope
silentium, -i n.	silence	*spiculum, -i* n.	arrow-head
silex, -icis f.	flint	*spina, -ae* f.	thorn
silva, -ae f.	wood	*spira, -ae* f.	coil

spirabilis, -e	vital	*suboles, -is* f.	child
spiritus, -us m.	breath, life	*subrideo, -ere*	I smile
spiro, -are	I breathe	*subsisto, -ere, -stiti*	I stop
spissus, -a, -um	thick	*subtexo, -ere*	I veil
spolia, -orum n.pl.	spoils	*subtraho, -ere*	I withdraw
spondeo, -ere	I promise	*subvecto, -are*	I transport
sponte mea	of my own accord	*subvolvo, -ere*	I roll up
spuma, -ae f.	foam, spume	*succedo, -ere, -essi* + dat.	I approach, come
spumeus, -a, -um	foaming		to
spumo, -are	I foam	*succingo, -ere, -inxi, -inctus*	I wrap
squaleo, -ere	I am stiff, rough	*succumbo, ere*	I give way
squalor, -oris m.	squalor, filth	*suesco, -ere, suevi, suetus*	I am accustomed
squama, -ae f.	scale	*suffectus, -a, -um*	tinged
squameus, -a, -um	scaly	*suffero, -ferre*	I withstand
stabulum, -i n.	stall	*sufficio, -ere*	I am able
stagnum, -i n.	pool, marsh	*suffusus, -a, -um*	brimming
statuo, -ere, -ui, -utus	I found, build, establish	*sulcus, -i* m.	furrow, trail
		sulphur, -uris n.	sulphur
stella, -ae f.	star	*summissus, -a, -um*	humble
stellatus, -a, -um	starred	*summoveo, -ere, -ovi, -otus*	I remove
sterilis, -e	barren	*summus, -a, -um*	highest, most
sterno, -ere, stravi, stratus	I fell, flatten		important, top of
stimulo, -are	I rouse, excite	*sumo, -ere*	I take, choose
stipo, -are	I accompany, attend, surround	*super*	in addition, on the surface
stirps, -pis f.	stock, lineage	*super* + abl.	above, on
sto, -are, steti, status	I remain strong, stand, stick, stand out	*super* + acc.	on top of, beyond
		superbus, -a, -um	proud
stratum, -i n.	blanket, couch, paving	*superemineo, -ere*	I rise above, tower over
strepitus, -us m.	din	*superi, -orum* m.pl.	the gods above
strido, -ere	I creak, shriek	*supero, -are*	I defeat, rise above, mount, overpower
stridor, -oris m.	creaking, clanking		
stringo, -ere, strinxi, strictus	I draw	*supersum, -esse*	I am left, remain
struo, -ere, -xi, -ctus	I build, plan	*superus, -a, -um*	above, upper
studium, -i n.	enthusiasm, zeal	*supplex, -icis*	humble, begging
stupeo, -ere	I am spellbound, dazed, amazed	*supplicium, -i* n.	punishment
		supra + acc.	above
stuppeus, -a, -um	made of hemp	*supremus, -a, -um*	last
Stygius, -a, -um	Stygian	*surgo, -ere*	I rise, grow, rise up, raise up
suadeo, -ere, suasi, suasus	I urge, command		
sub + abl.	under (the protection of), close to	*sus, suis* f.	sow
		suscipio, -ere, -cepi, -ceptus	I bear, undertake
sub + acc.	after, close to, under	*suscito, -are*	I rouse
		suspectus, -us m.	view upwards
subduco, -ere, -xi, -ctus	I draw up, beach	*suspensus, -a, -um*	anxious
		suspiro, -are	I sigh
subeo, -ire, -ii, -itus	I go up, come up, approach, enter, submit to	*Sychaeus, -i* m.	Sychaeus
		tabidus, -a, -um	wasting
		tabum, -i n.	gore
		tacitus, -a, -um	silent
subicio, -ere, -ieci, -iectus	I place . . . under, interpose, conquer	*tactus, -us* m.	touch
		taeda, -ae f.	marriage-torch
subigo, -ere, -egi, -actus	I conquer, force, compel, push	*taeter, -tra, -trum*	loathsome
		talis, -e	such (as this, as these)
subito	suddenly		
subitus, -a, -um	sudden	*tam . . . quam*	as much . . . as
sublimis, -e	raised up, exalted	*tango, -ere, tetigi, tactus*	I touch
subnecto, -ere	I fasten, fasten under	*tantum*	only
		tantus, -a, -um	so great
subnixus, -a, -um	propped up	*tardo, -are*	I make slow

tardus, -a, -um	slow	*tigris, -idis* f.	tigress
Tartara, -orum n.pl.	Tartarus	*timeo, -ere*	I fear
Tartareus, -a, -um	of Tartarus	*timidus, -a, -um*	timid
taurinus, -a, -um	of a bull	*timor, -oris* m.	fear
taurus, -i m.	bull	*Tisiphone, -es* f.	Tisiphone
tectum, -i n.	roof, house, building, shelter, dwelling	*Titanius, -a, -um*	of the Titans
		titubo, -are, -avi, -atus	I stagger, totter
		togatus, -a, -um	wearing the toga
Tegeaeus, -a, -um	Tegean	*tollo, -ere, sustuli, sublatus*	I exalt, raise up, raise, remove
tegimen, -inis n.	covering		
tegmen, -inis n.	covering, i.e. hide	*tono, -are*	I thunder
tego, -ere, texi, tectus	I conceal, cover, hide	*torqueo, -ere*	I direct, guide, whirl around
tela, -ae f.	warp	*torrens, -entis* m.	torrent
tellus, -uris f.	earth, ground, land	*torreo, -ere*	I burn, seethe
		torus, -i m.	couch, cushion, bank
Tellus, -uris f.	Earth		
telum, -i n.	spear, weapon, arrow, missile, blow	*torvus, -a, -um*	fierce, grim
		tot	so many
		totus, -a, -um	all, the whole
temno, -ere	I scorn	*trabs, -bis* f.	beam, panel
tempestas, -atis f.	storm	*tractabilis, -e*	manageable
templum, -i n.	temple	*tractus, -us* m.	region
tempto, -are	I try, try to obtain	*traho, -ere*	I draw, drag, spend
tempus, -oris n.	temple	*traicio, -ere, -ieci, -iectus*	I stab, pierce, cross
tenax, -acis	gripping	*tranquillus, -a, -um*	calm
tendo, -ere, tetendi, tensus	I hold up, extend, go, struggle, stretch out, aim	*transeo, -ire*	I overtake
		transmitto, -ere	I cross
		transporto, -are	I transport
tenebrae, -arum f.pl.	darkness	*transversa*	sideways-on
teneo, -ere	I maintain, hold, keep, reach	*tremefacio, -ere, -feci, -factus*	I make to tremble
		tremendus, -a, -um	terrifying
tenuis, -e	insubstantial, fine, thin	*tremo, -ere*	I quiver, quake, shake
tenus + abl.	as far as	*trepido, -are*	I quake, tremble
tepidus, -a, -um	warm	*trepidus, -a, -um*	alarmed
ter	three times	*trietericus, -a, -um*	triennial
terebro, -are	I bore	*trifaux, -aucis*	three-throated
teres, -etis	polished	*triginta*	thirty
tergum, -i n.	back, hide	*Trinacria, -ae* f.	Sicily
termino, -are	I bound, end	*Trinacrius, -a, -um*	Sicilian
terni, -ae, -a (plural)	three	*triplex, -icis*	triple
tero, -ere	I waste, graze	*tristis, -e*	sad, grim
terra, -ae f.	land, world	*trisulcus, -a, -um*	three-forked
terreo, -ere	I frighten	*Tritonis, -idis* f.	Athena
terribilis, -e	terrible	*Troia, -ae* f.	Troy
territo, -are	I terrify	*Troius, -a, -um*	Trojan
tertius, -a, -um	third	*Tros, Trois* m.	Trojan
testor, -ari, -atus sum	I declare	*trucido, -are*	I slaughter
testudo, -inis f.	vault	*truncus, -a, -um*	lopped, cut down
Teucer, -ri m.	Teucer	*truncus, -i* m.	trunk, body
Teucri, -orum m.pl.	the Trojans	*tueor, -eri, -(i)tus sum*	I look (at), protect, watch
Teucrus, -a, -um	Trojan		
Teucrus, -i m.	Teucer	*tumeo, -ere*	I swell
thalamus, -i m.	bed-chamber, bedroom	*tumidus, -a, -um*	swollen
		tumultus, -us m.	uproar, agitation, outburst, tumult
theatrum, -i n.	theatre		
thesaurus, -i m.	treasure	*tumulus, -i* m.	burial mound, tomb
Threicius, -a, -um	Thracian		
Thybris, -is m.	River Tiber	*tunc*	then
Thyias, -adis f.	Bacchante	*turba, -ae* f.	crowd, flock
Thymbracus, -i m.	Apollo	*turbidus, -a, -um*	wild

turbo, -are, -avi, -atus	I trouble, upset, confuse	*vagor, -ari*	I circulate, spread, wander
turbo, -inis m.	tornado, whirlwind	*vale*	farewell
turpis, -e	foul, shameful, filthy	*valeo, -ere*	I am strong enough, I can, I am able
turris, -is f.	tower	*validus, -a, -um*	strong, mighty
tutor, -ari, -atus sum	I defend	*vallis, -is* f.	valley
tutus, -a, -um	safe, protected	*vanus, -a, -um*	pointless, vain, false, empty
Tydides, -ae m.	Diomedes		
Typhoeus, -a, -um	of, against Typhoeus	*varius, -a, -um*	various, different
tyrannus, -i m.	king, ruler, tyrant	*vastus, -a, -um*	huge, immense, enormous
Tyrius, -a, -um	of Tyre, Tyrian, Carthaginian	*vates, -is* f.	prophetess
Tyrrhenus, -a, -um	Tyrrhenian	*vates, -is* m.	prophet
Tyrus, -i f.	Tyre	*-ve*	or
uber, -eris	rich	*veho, -ere, vexi, vectus*	I convey
uber, -eris n.	bosom, richness, teat, udder	*vel*	or
		vel . . . vel	either . . . or
ubique	anywhere, everywhere	*vela do, dare*	I set sail
		velivolus, -a, -um	covered with sails
udus, -a, -um	wet	*vello, -ere*	I tear
ulciscor, -i, ultus sum	I avenge	*velo, -are, -avi, -atus*	I cover, wrap
Ulixes, -is m.	Ulysses	*velox, -ocis*	swift
ullus, -a, -um	any	*velum, -i* n.	sail
ulterior -oris	further	*velut, veluti*	just as if, just like
ultimus, -a, -um	last, final	*vena, -ae* f.	vein
ultrix, -icis	avenging	*venabulum, -i* n.	hunting spear
ultro	voluntarily, spontaneously	*venenum, -i* n.	venom
		veneror, -ari	I pay reverence to, regard reverently
ululo, -are, -avi, -atus	I howl, shriek		
umbo, -onis m.	boss	*venia, -ae* f.	pardon, forgiveness, indulgence
umbra, -ae f.	shadow, darkness, shade, ghost		
umbrifer, -era, -erum	shady	*ventus, -i* m.	wind
umens, -ntis	damp, moist	*Venus, -eris* f.	Venus
umerus, -i m.	shoulder	*verber, -eris* n.	blow
una	together, all together	*verbero, -are*	I strike, punch
		verbum, -i n.	word
unanimus, -a, -um	like-minded	*vereor, -eri*	I fear
uncus, -a, -um	hooked	*vero*	indeed, however
unda, -ae f.	water, wave	*verro, -ere*	I sweep
unde	from where	*verso, -are*	I revolve, spin, turn, consider
undique	from all sides, on all sides		
unguis, -is m.	claw	*vertex, -icis* m.	the highest point, top, summit, peak, head
urbs, -is f.	city		
urgeo, -ere	I crush, confine, press forward, oppress, beset	*verto, -ere, -ti, -sus*	I change, turn
		verum, -i n.	truth
		verus, -a, -um	true
uro, -ere	I burn	*vescor, -i* + abl.	I feed on
ut + indic.	when	*vesper, -eris* m.	the West
ut!	how!	*Vesta, -ae* f.	Vesta
uterque, utraque, utrumque	each, both	*vester, -ra, -rum*	your(s)
uterus, -i m.	womb, belly	*vestibulum, -i* n.	entrance, entrance hall
utinam!	if only!		
uxorius, -a, -um	fond of a wife	*vestigium, -i* n.	footstep, trace, mark, step
vacuus, -a, -um	empty		
vado, -ere	I go	*vestigo, -are*	I search
vadum, -i n.	shallow water	*vestio, -ire*	I clothe
vagina, -ae f.	scabbard	*vestis, -is* f.	clothes

veto, -are	I forbid	*vis*, acc. *vim*, abl. *vi* f.	force, power, violence
vetus, -eris	old	*viscera, -um* n.pl.	insides
vetustus, -a, -um	ancient	*visus, -us* m.	sight
via, -ae f.	journey, street, way	*vita, -ae* f.	life
vibro, -are	I flicker	*vitta, -ae* f.	headband
vicinus, -a, -um	close, nearby	*vivo, -ere*	I live, am alive
vicis f. (defective)	exchange, turn, part	*vivus, -a, -um*	living
		vix	scarcely
vicissim	in turn	*vociferor, -ari, -atus sum*	I shout
victor, -oris	victorious	*voco, -are*	I call
victor, -oris m.	winner	*volans, -ntis* f.	bird
victus, -us m.	sustenance	*volatilis, -e*	flying, winged
video, -ere	I see	*volito, -are*	I flit about
videor, -eri, visus sum	I seem	*volo, -are*	I fly
vigeo, -ere	I thrive	*volo, velle*	I wish, want
vigilans, -antis	watchful	*volucer, -cris, -cre*	winged, fleeting
villus, -i m.	shaggy hair	*volucris, -is* f.	bird
vimen, -inis n.	twig	*volumen, -inis* n.	coil
vincio, -ire, vinxi, vinctus	I bind	*voluptas, -atis* f.	pleasure
vinc(u)lum, -i n.	chain, bond, thong, binding	*voluto, -are*	I hover
		volvo, -ere	I roll, set in motion, consider, writhe
vinco, -ere, vici, victus	I defeat, win		
vinum, -i n.	wine		
violo, -are	I violate	*vorago, -inis* f.	whirlpool
virectum, -i n.	meadow	*votum, -i* n.	vow, prayer, offering
virens, ntis	green		
vires, -ium f.pl.	strength	*vox, vocis* f.	voice, shout, word
virga, -ae f.	twig, rod	*vulgo, -are*	I make widely known
virgo, -inis f.	maiden		
viridans, -antis	green	*vulnus, -eris* n.	wound, heavy blow
viridis, -e	vigorous, green, fresh	*vultus, -us* m.	face, expression
virtus, -utis f.	courage, virtue	*Zephyrus, -i* m.	West Wind

INDEX

Printed in the USA
CPSIA information can be obtained
at www.ICGtesting.com
LVHW060845010823
754026LV00003B/129